Readers respond to
the word on the street

"The Bible is something I have lived with all my life . . . but this is the first bible that has had me truly gripped. Through Rob's gift God has breathed a new life into his word."

"I couldn't put *the word on the street* down . . . [I] read all the way through in one day. I'll go back and read it again and again too. Well known text suddenly becomes new. It jumps out of the page in fresh ways. I found it exciting and refreshing, funny and challenging. It's a brave book and it's great."

"This is a wonderful bible edition for people (young or old) who are just starting out. It helps to demystify and clarify some of the more confusing books of the Bible. *the word on the street* will show them that God's Word is FAR from boring."

"I gave one to a mate from college who's not really into religion. He tells me he came back from a club at two in the morning, picked up *the word on the street* and didn't sleep the rest of the night [because] he was so gripped. Thank you for writing it."

"*the word on the street* was hugely impressive. I'm using it regularly, and it is so refreshing to hear familiar passages speak so clearly again. I'm more impressed that I've had to manage without it for a couple of days whilst my 16-year-old son read it from cover to cover."

More commendation for the word on the street

"The Bible with street cred: Lacey has a refreshingly down-to-earth attitude to the Bible and a wry sense of humour."

Publishing News

"Very different! It makes the Bible as easy to read as a tabloid newspaper. It's great fun if you know the Bible fairly well. But it's also, of course, aimed at people who've never ever opened it. And maybe we do underestimate just how difficult that is if you don't know where to start. I could read it all morning actually!"

BBC National Radio 2

"Aims to be a page turner and succeeds."

Christianity and Renewal

"I read some of *the word on the street* to the 250 people I was speaking to on Sunday morning. It got gasps and laughs and a spontaneous round of applause! Someone described it as *The Message* with attitude. I had a long queue at the end wanting to know how to get hold of a copy. It really is a brilliant piece of work."

Duncan Banks, author, Breakfast with God

"On scholarly grounds . . . I found little to correct and much to praise. Rob helped me discover angry and sad voices in passages of the Bible that had left me indifferent before, and he made me laugh at other passages that were so familiar to me that I had never seen the healthy irreverence, humour and irony they expressed."

Dr. David Trobisch, Professor, Bangor Theological Seminary

rob lacey

the word on the street ™

ZONDERVAN™

GRAND RAPIDS, MICHIGAN 49530 USA

ZONDERVAN™

the word on the street
Copyright © 2003, 2004 by Rob Lacey
formerly titled *the street bible*

This title is also available as a Zondervan ebook product.
Visit www.zondervan.com/ebooks for more information.

Requests for information should be addressed to:

Zondervan, *Grand Rapids, Michigan 49530*

www.zondervan.com

ISBN 0-310-93225-4

Interior design by Beth Shagene

Printed in the United States of America

09 10 11 12 • 16 15 14 13 12 11 10 9

Contents

Old Testament

History of a Nation

The Pentateuch / www.instruction-manual.com.ot

History Section / www.new-nation.com.ot

The Wisdom Books / www.peoples-poetry.com.ot

The Prophets / www.couriershotline.com.ot

The Major Prophets / The Famous Four

The Minor Prophets / The Dangerous Dozen

N e W T e S T A m e N T

New Promise

The Liberator

The Jesus Liberation Movement

Paul's Work "Sent Items" Box

Paul's Private "Sent Items" Box

Other Email Writers

Foreword

In antiquity, literature was almost always read aloud to an audience. And the Christian Bible is no exception. Readers experienced the text by watching and listening to a performer. Authors designed their works as records of sound bytes with stage instructions. And even in the unfortunate case that there was no one available to perform, people would read the text aloud to themselves, experiencing it through the ears and not as we often do today, in silence and through our eyes.

Long before the time of Jesus, when passages of the Hebrew Bible were read aloud during worship, interpreters would immediately translate it into Aramaic, the language of the common people. The so-called Targum was done in an effort to make the text accessible to everyone. Interpreters would sometimes paraphrase and elaborate as they put the sacred reading into the words of the living language, relating the message to the current situation of their audience and to contemporary problems. Later, when Paul writes to the Thessalonians, he insists that his letter be read aloud to everyone (1 Thessalonians 5:27). And when early Christians collect the stories of Jesus, they edit them so they can be used as the text base for public performance during worship. Paul prepares Timothy for his leadership role in Ephesus by reminding him of the three qualities of a good pastor: to teach, to exhort and to be able to read the Scriptures aloud (1 Timothy 4:13).

For a couple of years Rob Lacey would send me installments of his *the word on the street*, and I would go over it and try to make sure that his interpretation was acceptable on scholarly grounds as well. I found little to correct but much to praise. Rob helped me discover angry and sad voices in passages of the Bible that had left me indifferent before, and he made me laugh at other passages that were so familiar to me that I had never seen the healthy irreverence, humour and irony they expressed. I looked forward to Rob Lacey's mail and dreaded when the project came to an end. And invariably I had to commend his creative energy and lively style and make the biggest compliment of all: "Rob, I can hear your voice!"

The Christian movement has bought heavily into the concept that the Word of God cannot come alive if no one listens. And how can they listen if they do not understand? The first edition of the Christian Bible surfaced in the second century CE and was published in Greek. The publishers knew well that most of the Old Testament was written in Hebrew and that Jesus spoke Aramaic when he addressed the peasants and fishermen of rural Galilee. But still, they published the Christian Bible in Greek. What use is the Word of God if no one understands? The English Bible arguably is the most heavily edited English book of our time. How many revisions have you experienced during your lifetime? How many modern translations do you know? How many are on the bookshelves of your local bookstore?

Rob Lacey not only encourages us with his good example to continue this old Judeo-Christian tradition of translating the words of the Bible into our own language, he admonishes us: "Go, and do thou likewise," or as Rob Lacey translates Luke 10:37, "Go, do the same!"

Dr David Trobisch
Throckmorton-Hayes Professor of New Testament Language
and Literature, Bangor Theological Seminary

FAQs

What is it?

I've created an overview, paraphrasing the basic story of God and "his people" as told by a twenty-first-century storyteller / performance poet. I see it as a bridge to the "proper Bible," and introduction to it, an advertisement for it, a trailer! And this is just one part of Zondervan's goal of getting "more people engaging the Bible more."

Who's it for?

Those who've never read the Bible and those who've read it too much. Probably in that order! And, no, this isn't only "for the yoof." It's proved immensely popular from 7 to 70 plus.

Special features?

A website structure, Psalms as song lyrics, the Gospels interwoven as one story with four narrators, Epistles as emails and Revelation seen through a virtual-reality headset.

Style?

I guarantee – an absolute minimum of religious words (so "Bless your heart" for reading it).

Why?

To make the Bible a page-turner again. To try to turn the "most published book" into the "most read book" by intriguing people enough to check out the proper Bible, capital *B*.

What's it not?

It's not The Bible; rather, it's a bible with a lowercase b. It's not meant to replace the real thing or steal royalties from the thousand and one publishers since Luther dropped the Latin for the people's language of German.

So what's changed?

Most rural images are replaced with urban ones. Our population structure is changing – more people live in cities than ever before. But who today in inner city Manchester has the first clue what a shepherd does? And words change! My mum used the word *gay* the other week (meaning "jolly"); then corrected herself by saying, "That's got a different meaning these days, hasn't it?" My wife, who's German but fluent in English, has been in Britain for ten years, so she had to ask, "Why, what did it used to mean?" Words change!

Precedents?

Plenty. Some Asian Bible translations have spoken of Jesus as being "the rice of life" since bread means little to people in the Far East. African translations have changed "snake" to "scorpion" in cultures where snakes are a luxury food. So Jesus' question "Would you give your child a snake?" would be completely misunderstood and the answer would come back, "'Course I would, given half the chance!" Which misses the point slightly!

Experience?

Twenty-five years' (seventeen years' professional) experience "translating" the Bible into theatrical stories / performance poems for a broad range of audiences.

Qualifications?

Passed an eighteen-year course in the Brethren School of Bible Facts. A degree in economics. (Helpful to manage huge financial wealth from being a touring actor / storyteller . . . not!) And possibly the only author to have a diploma in mime!

Fav bits?

Probably Job – as I've been seriously ill through the writing process. (See page 490 for more back-story on my journey through terminal cancer while writing this book.) I also love the honesty of the Psalms, the logical progression of Romans and the wild, almost drug-induced (heresy alert!) images of Revelation.

Problems?

Too many good bits that had to be left out. I already pushed my publishers up from their initial word request to a book double the size. But it still leaves some juicy bits scattered on the cutting-room floor!

Left bits out! How dare you?

I fast-forward through the bits we generally ignore anyway. So you could argue that it's not sooo different from most complete Bibles with the pages in Leviticus and the Minor Prophets still stuck together after five years' (non) usage. Discuss! I fast-forward through these detail sections with some summary stuff which gets us to the next chunk of Scripture paraphrase. These sections always end with "Rob" so you can tell which bits are proper Bible and which bits are me skimming through.

And all this on your own?

Hardly. There've been a lot of people who've come in to advise me at different stages of this three year project. It all kicked off with a solid grounding in the Bible from my parents' church in Cardiff – thanks to all those people who inspired me to dig into it. The original idea of *the word on the street* itself was inspired by the innovative drive of Duncan Banks at Spring Harvest. Then I approached Amy Boucher Pye at Zondervan who adapted my ideas to a more workable structure, gave the project the green light and then stuck with me during a year off with serious ill health. Early edits were done by Bill and Rachel Taylor-Beales and the Rev. Phil Jump. Bill and Rachel also stuck close while *the word on the street* (and life!) were on hold. But most of all I must thank my incredible wife, Sandra, for looking after me while also bringing up our three-year-old boy, Lukas, virtually as a single mum. Crucial supporting roles in holding us together were played by my family and the

Harnisch family in Germany, Paul and Jane Francis, Phil and Julie Stokes, Tim and Joy Watson and James and Kath Fathers. Richard Swan used his songwriting skills to suggest music styles for the Psalms / Song Lyrics. Mike Bernardin cut loads of waffle from this very introduction. Other friends – too many to mention – fed back detail stuff at different times. My ultimate safety nets in style and content have come from the Zondervan editors Amy Boucher Pye, Colin Duriez and Eldo Barkhuizen, and our theological expert Dr David Trobisch of Bangor Theological Seminary, Maine. Of course, ultimately it's all my fault! But I'm hopeful that it'll bring the whole thing alive in a fresh and slightly quirky way. May you see yourself in the story as it gets under your skin.

For more information, visit www.roblacey.com

Upgrades

In order to get the word out onto the street, I've changed the language from the sort of thing you'd hear in a formal lecture setting to more what you'd hear in a coffeehouse just chatting with a mate. I've also made up a series of words/phrases as alternatives to religious terms, which may have become stale through overuse or association with dry religion. I have to say, the standard "religious" word is often better than my version . . . but then I've been brought up speaking the lingo!

Call it nerve, call it passion to connect, call it poetic licence,* whatever. The main question is, Do the words get in the way of the story? If so, either change 'em or insist everyone goes to evening classes on Religious Speak.

Rob's Term \ *Religious Term* \ *Definition*

Absolutely \ Amen \ From the root "sure, steady". Used at the end of a prayer almost like an exclamation point, bold print or underlining — you could say, "I endorse those sentiments", but you'd sound pompous, or "Not 'alf", but you'd sound stupid.

Acquit \ Justify \ A judicial term meaning "declare righteous", "found innocent" or "vindicated". See "Sorted" below.

Anti-God stuff \ Ungodliness \ Not showing reverence/respect toward God.

Awesome God \ God almighty \ Term for God meaning "all-sufficient", "unlimited". Technical term = "omnipotent", lit. "all round potent"!

Be convinced \ Believe \ You get the point.

* And yes, I've got one framed and hanging on my office wall. I've got permission not only to use language creatively but also to make some words up!

**Rob's Term \ *Religious Term* \ *Definition*

The Big Ten \ The Ten Commandments \ People have tried to rebrand these as "God's Ten Suggestions", but like it or not they're the moral fabric of our society, even if they're tricky to keep. Having said that, they needn't be read with pointed finger and angry brow. Think of them as promises as well as commands, along the lines of "if God's Holy Spirit's changing you, you won't steal, you won't murder, etc."

Boss \ Lord \ In this context, "the no. 1 person in your life".

Celebrate \ Praise \ In the Old Testament it often refers to a combination of words meaning "noise", gestures" and "music" — sounds like a night club to me! In the New Testament it's more "to give thanks", "be grateful".

Chat/discuss/thrash out with God \ Prayer \ A word for ways in which the human spirit approaches God. If I knew any more about it I'd not be in this state!

City council \ Sanhedrin \ Title for the highest tribunal of Jewish decision-making set up by their Roman governors; 71 men with the High Priest as Chairman of the Board.

Coach \ Teacher \ Just don't think of the bully with elbow patches at your old school. Think more your most inspiring tutor in whatever you love doing.

Coaching \ Teaching \ Not just telling or informing; but inspiring, suggesting, hinting, showing.

Coming back from the dead \ Resurrection \ "To rouse from sleep" — where sleep is poetic-speak for death. Nothing to do with reincarnation, in case you were wondering.

Communicator \ Evangelist \ Greek for "one who announces good news", but TV journalist wouldn't quite do it — nice idea though.

The Contract \ The Law \ The Jewish Torah, an order from a higher authority on their expected standards of behaviour/lifestyle.

Conviction \ Belief \ Ditto with "Be convinced" above.

Councillors \ Elders \ General term for Big Wigs who make decisions based on the law.

Crew \ Saints/Church \ In the New Testament the term mostly designates a local congregation/gathering of Christian people, not the physical building.

The dark side \ Sinful nature \ Some translations (which shall remain nameless) render this "the flesh", which would almost be funny if it weren't such an insult to God's beautiful creation — not that I feel strongly about the false Greek dualism that's created this spiritual/secular divide! De-Greece the church — NOW!

Rob's Term \ *Religious Term* \ *Definition*

Deep places \ Heart \ The term is used of "the centre of things" and not so much the muscular blood pump in your chest.

Doing the right thing \ Righteousness \ Possibly from the Arabic root "straightness" – which none of us are, without connection with Jesus.

Evicted \ Exiled \ Posh word for "kicked out", from the Hebrew verb "to uncover" or "to remove" into captivity.

Flyby Festival \ Passover \ A major Jewish religious festival, like our Easter/Christmas, to celebrate God liberating their ancestors from the sweatshops of Egypt. The name derives from when the angel of death passed over/flew by Jewish homes.

Giving some slack \ Mercy \ Traceable back to words like, "kindness", "favour".

The God in charge \ Sovereign Lord \ Like I say . . .

God's Chief Rep \ High Priest \ See below "God's Reps" but higher!

God's Couriers \ Prophets \ Whether "foretelling" or "forth telling"; whether "predictive" or "prescriptive" – it's about a spokesperson getting messages from God through to the people.

God's HQ \ Temple \ Literally, a house for God.

God's New World \ Kingdom \ Same as with monarchies, but with God in charge.

God's over-the-top generosity/Good stuff/Freebies \ Grace \ Too big a word to define, "favour", "forgiveness", "salvation", "regeneration", "love of God" – all these don't quite make it. Hence my struggles to redefine it – don't blame me!

God's Reps \ Priests \ The "go-between" for God and his people . . . not to be mistaken for the "get-in-between".

God's Voice \ The Word \ John's poetic term for Jesus, but a word can be just ink on paper, a "voice" has to be embodied . . . mmm!

The Good Book/The Instruction Manual \ The Scriptures \ Refers to different bits depending on when it's used and how much they'd got together by then. Basically, a document of writings on/by God.

Good news story \ The Gospel \ Like I say, good news.

Heaven on earth \ Kingdom of heaven \ God's realm, the extent of his reign. But not just defined geographically – anywhere where what God says goes.

Rob's Term \ *Religious Term* \ *Definition*

The Jesus Liberation Movement \ Church \ What Jesus started. Like it or loathe it, it's God's chosen community of expressing/representing himself . . . don't ask me why.

Kept out of the pollution \ Sanctified \ A process, literally "to make holy".

Liberation \ Salvation \ Basic meaning is "to bring into a spacious place", metaphorically, it's about "freedom from limitation". I'll have some of that!

Liberator \ Christ/Messiah/Saviour \ The Jewish term for the "central figure of expectation", the one "appointed/anointed" to bring deliverance. 'Course, some people assumed deliverance was defined politically and couldn't handle it being more, much more.

Limitless life \ Eternal life \ Not just in the sense of time, but also capacity for life, quality of life.

Loyal \ Faithful \ Get a thesaurus for some other great words. I was always taught the acronym, "Forgetting All, I'm Trusting Him", but it's about "Remembering" everything – all the mess, pain, hassles – and still "trusting him". I guess there's no word "RAITH"!

Made happy/laughing \ Blessed \ Mostly an Old Testament word, generally denotes a state of happiness: "to endue with power for success, prosperity, fecundity, longevity, abundance, etc." – enough to make anyone happy.

Maker's instructions \ Commands \ The Big Ten Rules and others. Director's tip: Try reading them as promises as well as threats.

Mess \ Sin \ Anything that gets in the way of us and God, generally "missing the goal", "rebellion against God", "twisting".

The messed up \ Sinners \ From above, those "missing the goal", "rebelling against God", "getting twisted up"!

Picked out \ Called/Chosen \ Tricky theological concept, which better minds than me can't agree on; some sense of God picking us out to be his.

Polluted \ Impure \ Whatever isn't "a state of heart with complete devotion to God" – which is a definition of "pure".

Prospects \ Hope \ The Bible word doesn't mean "fingers crossed, it should happen", it's way stronger, more like, "I know it's going to happen".

Religious law enforcers \ Scribes/teachers of the law \ Experts in Moses' law; academics, who sadly often became "academic" in the sense of "irrelevant".

Rob's Term \ *Religious Term* \ *Definition*

Religious leaders \ Pharisees \ A faction calling themselves literally , "The separated ones" – "The Exclusives" perhaps.

Respect \ Honour \ Like I say . . .

Serenity \ Peace/shalom \ Shalom means, "soundness", "wholeness", "well-being" – so much more than a lack of noise.

Sorted \ Righteous \ In the sense of "cleared", "acquitted", not just trying to do the right thing.

Standing out as outstanding \ Holy \ From old words like "to cut out or separate", not just defined by what people don't do: don't swear, don't smoke, don't be "holier than thou" . . . (whatever).

Story \ Parable \ Derived from the Greek, "putting things side by side". Same root as "parallel". A longer version of a simile – a simile with the imagination set free to grow into a story.

Straightened out and sorted \ Saved \ Less "sitting in church" more "being dragged from the freezing arctic ocean". Much more vivid.

Stubborn \ Stiff necked \ Not telling you . . . not . . . not . . . not . . . etc.

The survivors \ Remnant \ Technical term for the Jews that didn't die in several takeovers by world super powers.

The system \ The world \ Not the planet called "Earth", more the prevailing attitude of our culture; the systematic expression of human sin in human cultures, which transforms the saying, "buck the system".

Taking God at his word \ Faith \ OK, so it's five words to explain one, but it's a big concept. See "loyal" above.

Traditionalists \ Sadducees \ A party of strict traditional Judaic religious leaders.

Turn back round 180 degrees to God \ Repent \ Even my three year old knows this. Lukas: "Sorry, Papa." Me: "And what does sorry mean?" Lukas: "It means we don't do it again."

Victimization \ Persecution \ Religious intolerance. In our PC world you can't be racist, sexist, ageist or any other "–ist", except Christian-ist – only it's not called that, it's called "freedom of speech".

Wipe the slate clean \ Forgive \ Carries the idea of "atonement", "to atone for", to make "at one" again . . . all that, and more.

The Big Picture

To work, to grab the attention, you need a story that impacts the audience. What about a film to launch the movement? Clearly, you'd need a genuine hero. Someone everyone will empathize with. Someone noble but common. Safe but dangerous. Pure but streetwise. Gentle but confrontational. Someone with supernatural powers used only for the benefit of the community.

Then you'd need a "baddie". An enemy force. Something all-enveloping, ruthless, sinister. Ideally this battle should have a back-story centuries old, only now coming to a climax. Maybe you'd kick off with an exciting opening sequence of genuine horror. Why not open the film with shocking scenes of babies being murdered and one family, babe in arms, racing from the infanticide?

Having established the scale and intent of the opposition, you'd show the hero growing to confront this evil and discover his mission, to save the planet from this insidious, all-consuming power. A small group of followers would supply different viewpoints through which you'd see him begin to fulfil this mission. They'd work well to draw out the principles of his radical thinking. They'd also provide humour and light relief with their mess-ups.

The danger facing the hero would gradually build as he confronts the authorities, who are the prime suspects in a conspiracy theory of the control of the masses through a dominating worldview and an elaborate political system ensuring the subservience of the people. Time-honoured blockbuster stuff.

Eventually, inevitably, it'd build towards confrontation and the tragic betrayal of the hero by one of his own crew. Rifle-fire scenes propelling you through his false trial and execution at the hands of the corrupt authorities. Slow up to show his heroism prevailing right to the end with his harrowing call for his executioners to be forgiven for what they're doing. The crowds would turn against him and the hero would die an unheroic death. Long pause. The shell-shocked cinema audience would rustle their bags and make to move – but the credits would refuse to run.

It can't stop there. There has to be a reversal, a twist. Something that changes the worst thing that could happen into the best thing possible. You'd need to have a visual mechanism, maybe 3D film footage, to give an insight into the supernatural side of events as they unfold below the surface. You'd see the dead hero travel into the underground head-quarters of the enemy and wrestle Death himself into submission. Bloodstained and scarred the hero would walk away with the power over life and death. He'd come back to his crew with a package that would change their lives for ever.

Then the credits could roll with God right at the top so no one misses it while groping for their bag.

Read on.

Old Testament

History of a Nation

The Pentateuch
www.instruction-manual.com.ot

Genesis / Stuff Starts Up

Something out of nothing (Genesis 1:1-2:3)

1-2

First off, nothing . . . but God. No light, no time, no substance, no matter. Second off, God says the word and WHAP! Stuff everywhere! The cosmos in chaos: no shape, no form, no function – just darkness . . . total. And floating above it all, God's Holy Spirit, ready to play.

3-5

Day one: Then God's voice booms out, "Lights!" and, from nowhere, light floods the skies and "night" is swept off the scene. God gives it the big thumbs up, calls it "day".

6-8

Day two: God says, "I want a dome – call it 'sky' – right there between the waters above and below." And it happens.

9-13

Day three: God says, "Too much water! We need something to walk on, a huge lump of it – call it 'land'. Let the 'sea' lick its edges." God smiles, says, "Now we've got us some definition. But it's too plain! It needs colour! Vegetation! Loads of it. A million shades. Now!" And the earth goes wild with trees, bushes, plants, flowers and fungi. "Now give it a growth permit." Seeds appear in every one. "Yesss!" says God.

14-19

Day four: "We need a schedule: let's have a 'sun' for the day, a 'moon' for the night; I want 'seasons', 'years'; and give us 'stars', masses of stars – think of a number, add a trillion, then times it by the number of trees and we're getting there: we're talking huge!"

20-23

Day five: "OK, animals: amoeba, crustaceans, insects, fish, amphibians, reptiles, birds, mammals . . . I want the whole caboodle teeming with *a million* varieties of each – and let's have some fun with the shapes, sizes, colours, textures!" God tells them all, "You've got a growth permit – use it!" He sits back and smiles, says, "Result!"

24-31

Day six: Then God says, "Let's make people – like us, but human, with flesh and blood, skin and bone. Give them the job of caretakers of the vegetation, game wardens of all the animals." So God makes people, like him, but human. He makes male and female (for the "how", see later). He smiles at them and gives them their job description: "Make babies! Be parents, grandparents, great-grandparents – fill the earth with your families and run the planet well. You've got all the plants to eat from, so have all the animals – plenty for all. Enjoy." God looks at everything he's made, and says, "Fantastic. I love it!"

2:1-3

Day seven: Job done – the cosmos and the earth complete. God takes a bit of well-earned R&R and just enjoys. He makes an announcement: "Let's keep this day of the week special, a day off – a battery-recharge day: Rest Day."

> Then we rewind a bit for the detail on people's arrival on the scene.   –Rob

First of billions (Genesis 2:7-9)

7

God takes some mud from the ground, and moulds the essential chemicals into the shape of a man. Then he breathes his life into the body and the man starts living.

8-9

God places the guy in the special garden he's planted, called "Eden". God's planted loads of types of trees in the garden – they look great and their fruit tastes great. Smack bang in the middle of the garden are two one-of-a-kind trees: "the tree of life" and "the tree of knowing right from wrong".

We get some detail on the local rivers making the area fertile, and then . . . –Rob

Adam needs a partner (Genesis 2:15-25)

15-17

God gives the man a job: warden in the Eden Garden. Job spec – to protect and till it. In God's Contract he clearly states the man has free pickings of anything that grows in the garden, except the tree that tells you the difference between right and wrong. If you eat from *that* tree, the rules are pretty direct – you'll die.

18

Then God says, "He's doing all this solo and it's wrong. Adam needs a partner."

19-20

God parades all the animals in front of Adam to see what names he'll give them. God doesn't dispute any of his names, no limits on the wacky scale: whatever he calls it, that's its name. Adam gets through the lot – the cattle, the birds, the beasts – but none is anything near partner potential.

21-22

So God puts the man under some sort of divine general anaesthetic, carries out a ribectomy, then closes up the gap in his side. God works on the rib until he's sculpted it into woman-shape, and then he presents her to Adam.

23-24

"Whoa! Now we're talking!" says Adam. "She's like me . . . only not. Same bones, same skin, same shape . . . only not. She's . . . uh . . . sexy. If I'm 'man', she's . . . uh . . . 'woman'." (Which is why when people get

married, they leave their parents behind and set up their own family
unit. Sex makes them one person: you can't tell where one stops and the
other starts.)

25

They're both stark naked, not that they've noticed — they've got no
hang-ups about nudity.

Enter "Mess" stage right (Genesis 3:1-24)

1

Now the snake was top of the Animal Cunning League. Undisputed
King of Sly among all God's creative work. He sees the woman, slith-
ers up to her and asks, "Are the rumours true? Did God really slap a
ban on eating the fruit off these trees?"

2-3

"We can eat what we like," answers the woman, "apart from the fruit
off the tree right in the middle. If we eat off that, we'll die."

4-5

"Die?! Unlikely!" sneers the snake. "God well knows that if you eat off
that tree, it'll open your eyes to a few things. You'll know the difference
between good and evil, just like God does — so you'll be like God!"

6-7

The woman eyes up the fruit and thinks, *It does look pretty tasty — especially
if it's instant wisdom in a couple of bites.* So she grabs herself a juicy one,
and takes a large chomp out of it. Then she hands it to Adam, and he
takes a mouthful too. Straight off, their eyes are opened and they realize they're stark naked. A new feeling — embarrassment. They stitch
together some fig leaves and cover the necessaries.

8-9

Later in the day, the heat has eased off a bit and they hear God's footsteps in the garden. Seconds later they're hiding from him behind some
bushes. God calls out, "Adam, where've you got to?"

10

Adam calls out, "I heard your footsteps, and I wobbled, 'cos I was starkers. So I went under cover."

11

"Who told you that you were starkers? It never bothered you before," says God. "You've eaten from the tree I slapped a ban on, haven't you?"

12

"The woman you brought in gave me some, and I ate it."

13

So God calls out to the woman, "What've you done?!"

She says, "The snake lied to me."

14-15

So God says to the snake, "You'll pay for this, big time. People will shudder when they even think of you. You'll scrape along the floor. You made them eat – so you eat dust! And I'll make you and the woman enemies down the centuries. And one of her descendants will stomp on your head and bruise it. You'll damage his heel, but he'll crush your skull!"

16

Then God turns to the woman, "For this, I'm going to turn up the pain dial on childbirth. You'll scream with agony as you have your children. The mess you've made also means you'll have to put up with men running the place."

17-19

To Adam God says, "You listened to her – you ate when I told you not to. So your sentence is this: You'll have to break up the soil to get anything worth eating. It'll fight against you. It'll grow thorns, thistles, nettles and other nasties – you'll have to break sweat if you want any food on the table. And at the end of it all, you'll be buried in the same soil. I made you out of mud, so that's where you'll end up. Full circle."

20

Adam gives his wife a name. Calls her "Eve" (pun on the word *life* in their lingo) 'cos she's the ultimate mother figure.

21-24

God sorts out some clothes for them both from his own designer-leather label. Then he says, "Now they are like us – sort of – they know the difference between good and evil. But this rebellion is way too huge for them to be able just to reach out and grab from the tree of life and live for ever. Way too huge." So God kicks them out of the Garden of Eden, to start digging the earth and growing the food. Straight after, he orders an angel from the cherubim corps to stand at the east side with his flame-throwing weapon loaded and ready to stop anyone from just strolling in and eating off the tree of life.

Generations come and go. Then, yonks later ... Noah Lamechson ...   –Rob

Wipe out! (Genesis 6:1-7:5)

1, 5-7

As world population increases, so does the mess. The evil-good ratio goes through the roof and turns God's stomach. He has to watch as people spend every waking moment thinking, planning and doing evil. He starts regretting day six of his creation project, wishing he'd never made people. Heartbroken, he says, "Enough! I've got to stop this. Wipe them out, the whole thing: people, animals, everything! The whole thing totally depresses me – Waterworld!"

8-10

But there is Noah, a genuinely good guy. Even his enemies would have struggled to make any charges stick. He hangs out with God and brings a smile to his face. He's a father of three: Shem, Ham and Japheth.

11-13

But the rest of the earth? Corrupt, depraved, rotten to the core. God won't block out their violence any more and tells Noah, "I'm going to wipe them all out, the whole population. They've packed the planet with everything vicious and vulgar, and I've no choice but to take them out of the equation. Here's the plan . . ."

God outlines the design of a 140 x 23 x 13 metre (or 460 x 75 x 43 foot) ship, purposely built as a floating zoo to preserve every species from extinction when the global flood comes. God carries on . . .   —Rob

18-22

"But I'm making a contract with you, Noah. You, your wife, your boys and their wives get to survive by doing the zookeeper job. You'll be taking male and female of every animal, so stock up with food for you and the animals." Noah follows the plan to the letter.

7:1-3

Later, God tells Noah, "Get in, you and your family, because you do the right thing."

More detail on livestock breakdown, and then God announces the timing. —Rob

4-5

"One week from today, rain will absolutely tip down – a forty-day deluge. It'll wipe out every living thing from the planet." Noah does exactly as he's told.

And God does exactly as he warned: once Noah's family and the livestock are inside the boat, God seals the door. Then millions of tons of water course up through cracks in the earth, millions more pour down from the sky. After a forty-day downpour, the whole planet's one big ocean. Everything dies. Total wipe-out. The flood waters last 150 days. But God doesn't forget Noah and his cargo – he arranges a strong wind and the floods start receding. Noah checks the state of play by sending out first a raven and then a dove. The dove eventually comes back with a fresh olive leaf in its beak – proof positive that the waters are going down. Eventually, God says to Noah . . .   —Rob

Exit (Genesis 8:15-22)

15-19

God says, "Time to leave your floating zoo. Bring the livestock out, release them and let them make babies!" Noah and Co. let them all out.

20-22

Noah builds a sacred altar to God. He goes through the religious ceremony of dedication – sacrificing some of the spare animals and birds as a gesture of loyalty and gratitude to God for saving them. God is pleased: the smell of the roasted animals is like sweet perfume in his nostrils, and he says, "Never again! No way am I going to repeat this, ever. However far they push me with their evil, I'm not doing this again:

As long as there's a planet called Earth,

Day and night will play tag, cold and heat will take turns;

The seasons will run and hand over the baton to each other,

And nothing's going to stop them again."

Start again (Genesis 9:1-17)

1-11

Then God says to Noah and his family, in bold print, "You're in my good books. Go make babies. Fill the place!"

Some instructions on eating and accountability. Then he says . . .   —Rob

12-17

"Plus, I'll give you a visual aid, a symbol of the contract I'm laying out in front of you. See that rainbow? It's not just some fancy physics trick — it's symbolic. A visual image of my contract with the planet. Whenever a rainbow appears in the clouds, it'll jog the memory of the deal I've made with you and all the animals — that I'll never flood the place and wipe out all life forms."

Population grows again. People go it alone without God again. Then, generations later . . .   —Rob

The first "Jew" (Genesis 12:1-3)

1

God says to Abram, "Emigrate! Pack up and take off. I'll tell you where . . . *en route.*"

2-3

"I'm going to make you the father-figure of a great nation. Your name's going to be a legend. You're going to be a vehicle bringing in good stuff for millions of people. If someone does you good, I'll reward them. If someone slaps you down, they'll pay for it. Every nation is going to benefit, because of the nation I'm kicking off through you."

Adventures of Abram, his wife (Sarai) and his nephew (Lot) in Egypt and elsewhere. Abram's bank balance starts to make good reading.   —Rob

Abram's future (Genesis 15:1-6)

1

God projects an image in Abram's imagination. The scene shows God saying, "Don't bottle out, Abram: I'm your minder. The long-term payoff for all this is going to be massive!"

2-3

But Abram moans, "God, I know you know what you're doing, but what's the point in you giving me all this dosh when I've got no kids to leave it to? Right now my butler, Eliezer Damascuston, is sole beneficiary in my will! You've not given us kids, so some senior staff member's going to be drooling and rubbing his hands at my funeral."

4-5

God comes back at him, "Eliezer's not going to be visiting any investment advisors after you die. You're going to have your own son." God takes him outside to look at the night sky. "Look up. Count the stars, if you can!" Then God gives him the equation: "Total number of stars equals the total number of your descendants – i.e. *millions!*"

6

Abram believes him and so God marks him down as straight and sorted.

Some time later Sarai decides God's well behind schedule on the kids front and organizes a few things for him. She persuades Abram to impregnate her servant girl, Hagar Egyptianson. The girl gets pregnant but also gets her own ideas about whose baby this is. Major friction between the two women. God says that the boy (Ishmael) will start a nation himself (the Arabs), but that Jews and Arabs will almost constantly be at war.

God does a subtle spelling change on their names: Abram becomes Abraham ("Father of Many"), and Sarai becomes Sarah ("Princess"). God launches the practice of circumcision (ritualistic lopping off a newborn baby boy's foreskin). Then he confirms his promise that Abraham will have a son with Sarah (to be called "Isaac") – Abraham believes it, but Sarah laughs – the last time in a long while.

God's fuming again, not just at Sarah, but at the capital cities of sleaze – Sodom and Gomorrah. He's at boiling point, about to blast the cities off the planet 'cos of the filth going on there. Abraham panics – his nephew Lot's still living there. He's down on his knees, negotiating with God to give the cities a break if there's fifty good people living there. God agrees. Abraham realizes he's probably over-estimated on the "decent people count" and knocks God down to forty-five, then to forty, then thirty, then twenty, then ten. Each time God agrees to back off with the lightning bolts if there's x number of good people on the electoral role. It turns out that even ten is way over the odds and two angels give Lot, his wife and his two daughters their marching orders before the burning sulphur fries the place. Lot's wife goes against direct angelic orders and looks back longingly at the cities. As warned, she turns into a statue of salt. Eventually . . .   –Rob

Sarah's pregnant! (Genesis 21:1-7)

1-5

God's good to Sarah – she gets a baby boy with Abraham. They're both well past it, but God sticks by his promise and gives them a son. Abraham calls the boy "Isaac" ("Laughing Boy") and on day eight, as instructed, has him circumcised. Abraham's just hit the hundred mark. Big party!

6-7

Sarah's giggling: "God's reinstalled my laugh! Everyone who gets word will join in. Who'd have thought, breastfeeding in my *nineties!* I can't get my head round it: I've given my man a son when they all thought he was past it."

More fighting between Sarah and Hagar. Abraham sends Hagar and Ishmael into the desert, but God puts his arm round Hagar and vows that Ishmael will also father a great nation. He survives the desert and grows up to do a degree in archery and marry an Egyptian girl.

Back in Philistine territory, Abraham's making business deals to stick around long-term.   –Rob

Abraham's dilemma (Genesis 22:1-18)

1-2

Some years on, God sets up a test. "Abraham!" he calls.

"I'm here," says Abraham.

God drops the bombshell: "Isaac, your one and only, the one you love, totally – take him up Moriah Mountain and sacrifice him to me: I want a burnt offering. I'll tell you where on the way."

3-5

Abraham sets off with Isaac, first thing next morning. He takes a couple of staff with him, a donkey and enough wood for a fair old fire. After a three-day trek, Abraham looks up and sees the mountain ahead of them. He tells his staff, "Hang around here with the donkey. Isaac and I need to go off, spend some quality time with God, and then we'll come back."

6-7

Abraham loads up Isaac with the wood and takes the knife and the lighter. The two of them are walking up the mountain when Isaac susses something's missing. "Dad," he says, "the wood and the fire are sorted, but where's the lamb? Surely we need a lamb if we're going to sacrifice to God?"

8

Abraham answers, "God'll give us a lamb for the offering." And they carry on up.

9-11

They arrive at the location God has described to Abraham. The old man constructs a stone altar and arranges the wood. Then he takes hold of Isaac, ties him up and straps him on top of the wood. He pulls out his knife, raises it above his head and is just about to plunge it into his precious son's chest when an angel shouts down from heaven, "Abraham!! Abraham!! Whoa!"

12

"What?!" Abraham reacts to the voice.

"Don't touch him," the angel says. "Now there's no dispute – you respect God, big time. You take him seriously enough to give up your only son."

13-14

Abraham looks round and spots a ram with its horns caught in some brambles. He goes over, yanks it out and sacrifices the ram instead of his son to God. Abraham names the place "God Comes Up with the Goods" – and the name sticks: people still use it.

15-18

The angel has another message on the direct line from God: "I swear, on my life, 'cos you've done this, 'cos you've not held back your only son from me, I'm going to make you so whole, so happy. And your descendants? We're talking the number of stars in the cosmos. We're talking the total sum of sand grains on a beach. We're talking success and asset-overload for them. And we're talking every nation on earth benefiting, big time, through them – all because you did what I told you to do."

(One of many subtle hints at the future Liberator.)

Sarah dies, having clocked up 127 years. Isaac, now 40, marries Rebekah. Abraham dies, having reached 175. Isaac inherits the works. After years of watching all the other women having kids and coping with all the snide comments, eventually Rebekah gets pregnant with twins – two more nations in the making. Big-brother-by-a-bit Esau (all-round action hero – Dad's favourite) and kid-brother-by-a-bit Jacob (quiet type – Mum's boy). They don't get on, especially after Jacob lives up to his name ("Deceiver") and swindles Esau out of his inheritance as the oldest. Jacob legs it. Esau's tamping mad.

On the run, Jacob sleeps rough and has a dream – huge ladder, extendable model going right up to heaven. In the dream God pledges the region to Jacob, does a similar speech to the one for Abraham; this time it's the "number of grains of dust" metaphor, but the idea's the same – millions of descendants.   –Rob

Jacob's deal (Genesis 28:13-22)

13-15

God says from the top of the ladder, "I'm God, your father's God, your grandfather's God! Know what I'm doing, right now? I'm drawing a thick red line around this land on my map and I'm scribbling in 'Jacob and Family' right across it. Check out the ground. Count the dust grains, if you can!" Then God tells him, "Total number of grains equals the total number of your descendants – i.e. *millions.* You'll spread out, every point of the compass – there'll be some of your family everywhere. And they'll do people good. Every day, the top of my to-do list says, 'Look out for Jacob.' You'll come back here, and I'll be your minder – I'm not quitting on you."

16-22

Jacob wakes up and thinks, *Whoa! God's here. I had no idea! Awesome. Totally. This is God's place, or at least the gate to God's place. Whatever!* He takes the stone he used as a pillow, pours oil on to dedicate it to God, and then changes the place name from Luz to Bethel ("God's place"). Then he swears, "If God's going to be my minder, my sponsor, and if he's going to manage the trip and get me back to Dad's place in one piece, then I'm in! My old man's God will be my God. This stone's the first of a huge cathedral. And, tell you what: from now on, 10 percent of my total turnover's God's commission!"

> Jacob works for his uncle Laban partly 'cos he fancies his cousin Rachel (which was legal then!). But he's tricked into marrying Rachel's big sister, Leah, and has six boys with her. He's still in love with Rachel and marries her as well. But same story: Rachel can't have kids. Jacob's continually in trouble, ducking and diving his way through life. Making money, but struggling to make friends. Eventually God gives Rachel a baby boy by Jacob, called "Joseph". Jacob's on the run from Rachel's old man and from Esau (who's still livid with him). It's only when Jacob decides to face the music with his big brother that God finally sorts him out during an all-night wrestling bout. He sends his family and stuff on ahead, so . . .   – Rob

God changes Jacob's name (Genesis 32:24-28)

24-26

Jacob's on his own and this angel turns up and starts wrestling with him. The bout goes through around 150 rounds till sun up. Exhausted with Jacob's wriggling and writhing, the angel's got him in a full nelson, but the guy's not screaming "Surrender!" So he turns the screw and bores into Jacob's hip socket, dislocating it and crippling him, permanently. The angel says, "Leave me go, will you? It's morning already!"

"No way," groans Jacob. "You're not going anywhere till you get God to do me good!"

27-28

The guy asks, "What's your name?"

"Jacob. Why?"

"'Jacob'? As in 'Deceiver'?" the angel asks. "No. Doesn't work any more! The name-change documents are all sorted. From now on you're 'Israel' ('Wrestles with God') 'cos you've wrestled with God, with men and with me, and you've won through."

> Which is why the place is now called "Peniel" ("Face of God") – 'cos Jacob, sorry, Israel, did some name changing too. He limps off a different guy. He gets some sort of relationship back with Esau, takes the Israel family back to Bethel. Rachel dies giving birth to her second and Israel's twelfth – Benjamin. Isaac dies aged 180. Israel and Esau both go to the funeral.   –Rob

"Dream Boy" (Genesis 37:1-11)

1-2

Back in Canaan, Joseph's now seventeen and working on the same "sheep security team" as his brothers. He goes back to his dad and grasses his brothers out: claims they've been slacking.

3-4

Joseph was born when Israel (formerly Jacob, remember) was well past it, so he's the blue-eyed boy. Jacob has an outrageous designer jacket made to measure for the boy. 'Course, his brothers see the favouritism in full colour and we're looking at brotherly hatred squared. Even polite conversation just sticks in their throats.

5-7

Joseph rubs it in further by making them listen to a dream he's had: "We're out in the fields tying up bundles of wheat; then my bundle stands up all proud, and your bundles form a circle and bow down to mine."

8

They come back at him, "You reckon? We pay dues to you? No way!" The mood shifts to hatred cubed.

9-11

Another dream, another rusty old nail in the coffin of family relations. Joseph tells his brothers, "This dream had the sun, moon and eleven stars all kowtowing to me." Later he tells his dad, who's not best pleased: "What? Your own mother and father? Your own brothers? Tugging our forelocks and twiddling our caps nervously in front of *you?* I don't think so." The brothers' hatred is off the graph by now. But his dad mulls it all over in his grey matter.

Joseph mugged (Genesis 37:18-36)

Israel sends Joseph to check his brothers are OK.   —Rob

18-20

They see him about a mile off and brainstorm plans to silence him, permanently. "Look who's coming – 'Dream Boy'! Who says we kill him? Chuck him in the cesspool and make out he came off second best to some lion? Might just lengthen the odds on us lot licking his boots!"

21-22

But Reuben, the oldest, sticks up for his kid brother: "We can't kill him!" Frowns all round. "But we can stick him in the cesspool." Faces brighten up. (He's got plans to sneak the kid back to Dad on the QT.)

23-24

Joseph struts over and is jumped by his brothers. They whip off his outrageous designer jacket and muscle him into the cesspool, the *empty* cesspool – "Some consolation!" groans Joseph.

25

As they sit down for their barbecue, they spot a convoy of foreign traders coming down Gilead Road, probably heading for Egypt. Their camels are stacked high with spices and stuff – not far off "last-straw" level by the look of them.

26-27

Judah gets an idea: "What's the point in killing 'Dream Boy'? Once the fun's over we'll be covering our tracks, rehearsing our alibi stories late into the night. Who says we sell him to these guys? Make a quick profit on him. He *is* our brother!" They like the idea. So Judah saves his brother's life.

28

The Midianite travellers lope past, Joseph's dragged out and they start haggling. They settle on twenty silver coins and Joseph gets his ticket to Egypt, third-class travel.

29-30

Reuben's been off somewhere. He comes back to the cesspool, sees it empty — and is absolutely gutted. He says to his brothers, really twitchy, "The kid's gone! What's plan B? I've got no plan B!"

31-32

But the others have: they cover Joseph's jacket in goat's blood, take it back to their dad and say, "We found this. Is it his?"

33

Israel, of course, doesn't need a second look. "It's his," he mumbles. "He's been torn to bits by a lion or something."

34-35

The old man's grief closes him down. He's in mourning 24/7. His kids try to lift him out of it, but he's inconsolable: "I'll not stop. Not till I die." He cries enough tears to irrigate a desert.

36

By this time Joseph's already in Egypt, sold as slave labour to a guy called Potiphar, captain of Pharaoh's guard.

Beware: bored housewife! (Genesis 39:2-23)

2-6a

So Joseph's alone in Egypt. Apart from God, who's working every situation, networking every meeting, so that whatever Joseph goes for, succeeds! He lives-in at Potiphar's house, and the boss soon spots that this guy's "lucky" – he gets results. He rates him, likes him being around, so he promotes him to personal assistant (still a slave, but loads more clout). Joseph's now top man in the house: he's got the keys and the codes to all the boss's stuff. The second he's promoted, God ups a gear on working things to Potiphar's advantage – everything flourishes, internal, external, business, leisure, receding hairline, everything. He just lets Joseph get on with it. He doesn't even bother checking, delegates the lot to Joseph. All he's interested in is what they're having for dinner.

6b-7

Thing is, Joseph's a bit of a looker and it doesn't take Potiphar's wife long to spot it. She coos, "Boy, have I got the hots for you. The silk sheets are freshly washed. Let's go to bed!"

8-10

Joseph turns her down flat. "I run the place. The boss doesn't even bother checking, 'cos he trusts me 100 percent. I'm No. 1. He'd let me have anything I wanted . . . except you. You're his wife! No way am I going to bed with you. God would hate it." But she doesn't give up; she wears the low-cut dresses, she slinks along the corridors, but Joseph keeps his mind on the job and avoids her like she's contagious.

11-12

One day, he's getting on with some project and the rest of the servants are off duty, or out, or sent away. She sidles up to him, grips his lapels and starts seducing him, panting, "Let's get it on, eh, big boy?" Joseph manages to wriggle out of his jacket and legs it, leaving her holding his coat.

13-15

Frustrated, jilted and totally humiliated, she screams the house down. Off-duty servants race in to see her with Joseph's jacket in her lap.

"Look!" she cries. "That Jew abused me, attacked me, tried to rape me! I screamed and he panicked. He was so freaked, he dropped his jacket."

16-20

She keeps the jacket ready till Potiphar gets back, and then she rolls off the same story: The tabloid headline read, "Jew raped me – by Mrs Potiphar". She screams at her husband, "Your slave abused me!" Potiphar's taken in, hook, line and sinker, and is furious. He has Joseph thrown straight in jail (the same one the king's prisoners are locked up in).

21-23

Joseph's chained to the dungeon walls but he soon realizes God's still around, working behind the scenes, influencing the warden. The guy begins to like Joseph and he puts him in charge of the other inmates, gives him responsibility for the whole place. Again, the warden doesn't bother checking up on Joseph, 'cos God's working overtime, making sure everything Joseph touches, works.

> While he's inside, Joseph gets to know Pharaoh's baker (ex) and his drinks tester (ex). God tunes him in to interpret their dreams and Joseph makes them swear they'll put in a good word for him once they get out. And do they? No. Freedom wipes him clean off their memory banks.   —Rob

Pharaoh's dream life (Genesis 41:1-8)

1-4

Some years after Joseph was unfairly locked up, Pharaoh gets a dream: he's standing by the Nile River and seven fat cows come up out of the water. Then seven more cows come out; this time you can play xylophone on their ribs! The anorexic-looking cows start eating up the stocky cows, but they're just as gaunt as before. Then he wakes up and realizes it was all a dream!

5-7

He drops off again and has another weird dream: seven heads of grain growing on one stalk. Then seven more heads sprout; this lot are thin, scorched and worse for wear from the easterly winds. Then, same thing:

the seven ill-looking heads swallow down the healthy heads. Again, he wakes up and realizes it was all a dream.

8

He's really freaked – these dreams are doing his head in. He calls an emergency meeting of all his magicians and mystics; he goes through the dreams and waits for someone to come up with a logical explanation. No one's even close!

> Then Pharaoh's reinstated drinks tester gets a flashback of Joseph interpreting *his* dream in prison. He tells Pharaoh, and Joseph's hauled out of jail, tidied up a bit and within hours he's standing in front of Pharaoh.   –Rob

Joseph gets it right (Genesis 41:15-46)

15

Pharaoh tells Joseph, "I had a dream, but no one has the first clue what it's getting at. You're supposed to be a pro at all that stuff. No?"

16

"No," Joseph answers. "But my God is. He'll clue you into what the dream means."

> Pharaoh tells Joseph both dreams.   –Rob

25-27

Joseph tells Pharaoh, "They're the same dream. God's speaking to you in stereo. Getting you ahead of the game. The seven fat cows and the seven good heads of grain symbolize seven boom years of bumper harvests. The seven skinny cows and the seven sad-looking grains are metaphors for seven years of recession and food shortages."

28-32

"Like I say, God's getting you ahead of things. Your farmers will have seven fantastic years, then seven catastrophic years. People will forget Egypt was ever wealthy, it'll be that severe. You got the dream twice because God's absolutely not shifting on this."

33-36

"The timing's tight, so I suggest you headhunt a really sharp cookie and make him Minister of Agriculture pretty quick. Set up a whole network of bureaucrats who'll keep back 20 percent of the foodstuffs in purpose-built barns in specified cities. Hold these supplies back for the seven years that'll be hot on the heels of the seven great years. Then Egypt will scrape through, just about avoiding absolute bankruptcy."

37-38

Pharaoh likes what he's hearing. So do his top civil servants. He quizzes them, "Have we got anyone on a par with this guy? Who've we got on our books who's got this God's Spirit in them?"

39-43

So he tells Joseph, "Your God told you all this; you're the man. You get the job! You'll run the palace; my people will do whatever you tell them. I'm the only one you answer to." Pharaoh backs up his word by sticking his signet ring on Joseph's finger, power-dressing him in a snazzy suit and presenting him with a ceremonial chain. He provides him with a top-of-the-range chariot and a driver. As Joseph travels around, people shout, "Get out the way!"

44-46

So Joseph gets the job one down from the top – Executive Director. Pharaoh tells him straight, "I'm the No. 1, but no one lifts a hand, foot or finger without your say so." The salary package includes a wife thrown in, Asenath (daughter of the Priest Potiphera). All this and he's just turned thirty!

> Everything goes swimmingly: Egypt rides out the boom and the bust. Every other country has to come begging to Joseph for rations – including the Jews back in Canaan.
> —Rob

What goes around ... (Genesis 42:1-16)

1-2

Jacob (aka "Israel") hears the rumour that Egypt's got grain supplies, and says to his sons, "Don't just sit round gawking at each other's sunken cheeks. Word is, there's food in Egypt. Get down there and get us some of it, so we've got some chance of survival."

3-5

Ten of them set off (Jacob reckons Benjamin's too young, and the trip's too dangerous). They file in with all the other gaunt-looking Canaanites, hoping to queue for some grain in Egypt.

6-7

Joseph's job, being the governor, was selling grain to people. His brothers get to the front of the line and hit the ground, flat out, faces in the dust. 'Course, straight off Joseph knows who they are, but decides to milk it. He goes all stern, "Where you from?"

"Canaan, sir," they answer. "We're here to buy food."

8-9

They had no clue who this guy was. It smacks Joseph between the eyes: this is his dream – they're bowing! He says, "You're spies! You're casing the joint. Working out the weak point."

10-11

"No, sir! Really." Totally flustered: "We're just here to buy food. We're brothers, honest men. No way are we spies!"

12

Joseph keeps pushing it: "No, you're out to rip us off."

13

"Sir, we're a family of twelve brothers from Canaan! One brother's at home with our old man; the other's dead."

14-16

"Don't talk back at me. You're spies and I'll prove it! One of you goes off and gets this 'brother'; the rest of you – prison! We'll see if you're lying. If you are, then sure as Pharaoh's the boss round here, you're spies."

After three days of prison Joseph lets nine of them go back with food, but keeps Simeon hostage till they bring in Benjamin. They're all riddled with guilt and reckon it's Fate's payback time for the Joseph mess. They find the silver that Joseph had planted in their grain bags and they're convinced it's a set-up. Israel (formerly Jacob) hears what happened and how the guy in the flash suit wants Benjamin brought down. He's convinced it's all going pear-shaped. Reuben promises Benjamin will be OK, but Israel isn't into letting his youngest out of his sight. It's only when the famine really kicks in, and they're starving, that Israel finally lets his favourite son go with them. He's convinced he'll never see him again.

The brothers make the trip with gifts to sweet-talk the main guy, and with double the silver, in case. Benjamin goes with them. Joseph sees they've brought in his kid brother, and his staff prepare a lavish lunch for them all. The brothers are escorted over to Joseph's place, totally bottling, convinced this is about the theft of the silver. Simeon's released, and they eat lunch together. Joseph asks about their father and gets "introduced" to Benjamin whose plate's piled five times higher than anyone else's. The brothers haven't a clue what's going on.

They're sent off with more food. Again Joseph plants stuff: this time, a silver goblet in Benjamin's bag. They're caught red-handed, and get dragged in to grovel in front of Joseph again. Benjamin's looking at years in an Egyptian jail and the brothers know this'll finish their dad off. Things can't get much worse!   – Rob

Joseph comes clean (Genesis 45:1-11)

1-2

Joseph's just about bursting. He tells his staff, "Everyone out! Leave me with them." Once they're alone, he spills the beans. He's crying so loud, the staff hear him and pass word on to Pharaoh's workers.

3

He says, "It's me, Joseph! Is Dad still alive?" The brothers are gob-smacked, totally frozen. Petrified at what he's about to do to them.

4-7

He says, "Come here!" They move in, nervously. "It's me, Joseph, the one you sold off as a slave" (as if they'd forgotten!). "Chill, guys! Don't beat yourselves up for selling me down the Nile. God sent me ahead of you to save lives. The famine's only two years in; there's five more to go. But God's worked it so you'll survive."

8-11

"You think *you* sent me down here? No! God did. He catapulted me to Governor, answering only to Pharaoh himself. So get back to Dad and tell him Joseph says, 'God's put me in charge of Egypt. Come on down! Get a move on! I'll sort out accommodation in Goshen (East Egypt) – you'll be just down the road! And you'll have food – there's still five years of famine to get through. But you'll make it.'"

Major emotional outburst! Brothers breaking each other's ribcages with bear hugs. Years of suppressed tears fall on estranged brothers' shoulders. Things calm and brothers catch up. Lots to talk through. Pharaoh gets to hear what's happened and commits to getting them and their dad the best Egypt has to offer. They return in style and tell their dad.   –Rob

Israel comes back to life (Genesis 45:25-46:4)

25-28

"Joseph's alive!!! He's not just alive; he's running Egypt. He's the main man!"

Israel's so stunned, he can't take it in. They tell him the whole thing. He sees the flashy transport Joseph's laid on for the return journey and he starts to dare to believe it. He's a different man: animated, wild, alive again. "I believe it; it's true. Joseph, my boy, is alive and I'm going to see him before I die!"

46:1

So Israel sets off. His stuff loaded high. He gets to Beersheba and offers sacrifices to God in gratitude.

2-4

That night, God downloads a dream into Israel's sleep. In it God says, "I'm God, your father's God. Don't panic; enjoy the journey down to Egypt. I'm going to turn you into a great nation there. I'm coming with you! I'll bring you back, and Joseph's own hand will close your eyes when you finally die."

They arrive in Egypt and settle in Goshen. The brothers start jobs lined up by Joseph. They have kids. Elsewhere the famine is taking its toll. Around twenty years later, Israel's limped his last – he's on his deathbed surrounded by all twelve of his sons. He gives each of them his final words of advice and outlines their future as the twelve family lines of Israel – big stuff. Israel dies, Joseph heads the funeral cortège and they bury him back home in Canaan, as he requested. The brothers return, in virtual silence, to Egypt.   —Rob

Still guilty? (Genesis 50:15-21)

15-17

When Joseph's brothers recover from the funeral, they worry, "What if Joseph's just waiting his moment? He's all charm now, but what if he's bluffing?" So they send a note to him: "Dear Joseph, Your father's last request was that you lay off your brothers for treating you so bad. Don't let it all fester. Forgive and forget, eh? Sincerely, Your brothers." Joseph reads the note and breaks down.

18

His brothers arrive and do the grovelling routine again: "Treat us like slaves. We deserve it. Well, we deserve *less*. But please, treat us like slaves!"

19-21

Joseph wipes his tears, and says, "Don't panic. Chill. Am I God? Do I get to play judge and jury? OK, *your* plan was to do me in. But *God's* plan was to do me good and have me do good for millions. I've saved millions of lives and I'm going to keep on saving your lives and your kids' lives." His kind words eventually convince them.

Before Joseph dies, he reminds his brothers that God's contracted to bring them back to Canaan. He says, "Bury me here, but swear you'll carry my coffin with you when we move on out." He's 110 when he dies.   —Rob

Exodus / Shift Yourselves!

The twelve family lines of Israel's (Jacob's) sons stay in Egypt for over four centuries and make babies like there's no tomorrow. The Nineteenth Dynasty pharaoh realizes this "army" of working men is a major threat to national security and makes the Israelis slaves. After an unofficial birth-control scheme fails, Pharaoh loses it, and orders every Israeli boy to be drowned in the Nile. One survives – Moses. He's discovered by Pharaoh's daughter floating on the Nile in the very first Moses Basket! He gets brought up like a prince but grows to hate the oppression of his people. In a rash moment he murders an Egyptian guard for beating a Jewish slave, and then escapes to Midian, where he marries Zipporah, the daughter of the local priest. He ends up as sheep-minder for her old man. He leads the flock to the west end of the desert – Sinai Mountain ("God's Mountain").   –Rob

Wot, no ashes?! (Exodus 3:2-14)

2-3

God sets a desert bush on fire. Nothing unusual there, but Moses does a double take when he realizes it's been going a good while but not burning into a pile of ash. He goes over and thinks, *Weird! This needs some checking out!*

4-6

God sees him coming closer and calls out, "Moses! Hold it right there. This is sacred sand. I want your shoes off and I want your head straight. I'm God – Abraham's God, Isaac's God, Jacob's God." Moses covers his face, scared witless at the prospect of looking God in the face.

7-10

God says, "I've got miles of footage of my people's rough time in Egypt. I've got weeks' worth of audio, groans of desperation through long sleepless nights. It's echoing round my head and it's gutting me. So I'm going to do something. I'm going to liberate them. Move them out, all of them, into a land with lush fields, milk and honey virtually on tap. Right now it's being rented to Canaanites, Hittites, Amorites, Perizzites, Hivites and Jebusites. But my people have got through to me; I've got hard evidence – their oppression is well documented. You're off to Pharaoh; tell him to release them. Tell him they're leaving Egypt, as of now!"

Moses isn't convinced. —Rob

13-14

"Who shall I s . . . s . . . say s . . . sent me?" he stutters.

God replies, "I am who I am and I will be who I will be. Tell them the 'I AM' sent you."

Moses makes more excuses, plays on his stutter, but God works on him, promising spectacular special effects. Moses eventually agrees to go if someone else will speak for him. God suggests Moses' brother, Aaron. So . . . —Rob

"God who?" (Exodus 5:1-2)

1

Moses and Aaron get an appointment with Pharaoh and tell him God says, "My people – let 'em go. They've got tickets to a Godfest in the desert."

2

Pharaoh says, "God who? Which God? Who's he think he is, expecting me to drop everything and lose my workforce? You're having a laugh!"

Out of spite, Pharaoh cuts straw supplies and Jewish labourers have to make bricks without straw, the same target rates of productivity as before, but with no straw – virtually impossible. Pharaoh gets off on their exhaustion: "Lazy dogs! The lot of them." The people are well angry with Moses and Aaron. Moses tells God, "It's only made it worse!" —Rob

I said, "Let 'em go!" (Exodus 6:1-10)

1

God says to Moses, "OK, watch this! Pharaoh is history! I'll clench my fist and he'll let them go. In fact, he'll be so scared of me, he'll escort them to the border personally!"

2-5

He carries on, "I'm God. Abraham saw me, Isaac saw me, Jacob saw me – they all saw me as Awesome God. You're about to see the real me, the God who supernaturally buys back his own stolen people. I made a contract with them, that they'd live in Canaan (they lived there, but only paying rent to foreigners). I've heard their complaints and I'm about to get on with my side of the bargain."

6-8

"So tell the Israelis this: 'I'm God and you're leaving your *Made in Egypt* chains behind you. You're not slaves any more; I'm buying you out. It'll be spectacular! You're mine; I'm yours. And you'll know it! You'll know who's God around here when I give you the land deeds I promised Abraham, Isaac and Jacob. You'll own it. I'm God!'"

9-10

Moses tells them. But they're so frazzled, they can't hear all this liberation hype. God tells Moses to go back to Pharaoh: "Tell him I said, 'They've got to come and celebrate me in the desert. Let 'em go!'"

So Moses delivers the memo but Pharaoh's not budging. God turns up the pressure: the river Nile turns into blood – it stinks of dead fish curdled with stale blood. Court magicians try to reverse the "spell" but fail. Pharaoh takes it in his stride.

A week later, God threatens Pharaoh with a plague of frogs. He won't let God's people go. So frogs everywhere. Everywhere! Pharaoh starts making the right noises, God calls off the frogs but Pharaoh does a U-turn.

Next up, God infests the place with gnats. Like before, Pharaoh's still adamant – he's not losing his workforce.

Again God warns him, threatens swarms of flies, and, in case he's in any doubt who's sending this stuff, he announces Goshen (the Israeli enclave) will be a Fly-Free Zone. Pharaoh starts to twitch: "Worship God here. I'll allow it." Moses doesn't shift: "No. It's in the desert or nowhere!" Pharaoh agrees, on the condition it's not far outside Egypt. God calls off the flies, but again Pharaoh does a U-turn on the deal.

It carries on: God sends some sort of killer livestock disease, festering boils, ginormous hailstones, swarming locusts, three days of pitch-black darkness. Each plague chips away at Pharaoh's resolve. Moses keeps pushing, but Pharaoh keeps hanging in there. Then God says to Moses, "One more – the big one! After this Pharaoh will kick you out willingly."

–Rob

The big one! (Exodus 11:4-6)

Moses tells the people what God says: "Around midnight I'll work my way through all Egypt and every firstborn son of Egyptian parents will die – from Pharaoh's eldest to a slave girl's eldest to a cow's eldest. Egypt will never hear wailing like it again. This is the big one!"

Moses tells the Israelis, "Today's the start of a brand-new calendar. Do the prep: sacrifice a perfect animal and daub its blood on the doorframe of your houses. Eat a sacred meal; eat it with your shoes on, and eat it quick: God's passing over your heads, and you're out of here."

–Rob

Blood insurance (Exodus 12:12-14)

God's instructions continue: "Tonight I'm flying past your houses. I'll wipe out every firstborn – man or beast – and I'll sort the dud gods of Egypt, permanent: I'm God! But the blood on your doorframes will be your insurance. I'll fly by your house, but no one's going to die – not if there's blood smeared around your door. So make today a permanent public holiday. For thousands of years to come, your ancestors will take time off on National Flyby Festivals to retell the stories of what's about to go down."

At midnight God carries out the carnage. All Egypt suffers for Pharaoh's stubbornness. The Egyptians (who actually liked the Israelis) send them off with expensive freebies. It's been a long 430 years, but they're finally out. Moses takes Joseph's bones with them. On the journey God directs their route to avoid confrontation with the ruthless Philistines and lays out some basic instructions on lifestyle both for now and once they get to Canaan. Moses and Co. camp for the night at the Red Sea.

Meanwhile Pharaoh realizes he's lost his "workforce" and sends the army (many of them grieving dads) after them. They corner the Israelis at the sea

and panic sets in. Moses tries to calm things, telling them God'll fight for his
people.   —Rob

Toll-free crossing ... for some (Exodus 14:15-16)

God tells Moses, "Why you whining on at me? Tell them to march! Lift
your stick up and stretch out your other hand to split the water right
and left, so they can go through without getting their feet wet."

He did, and it worked! Not a puddle!
    'Course Pharaoh's horsemen and chariots pile in as well, but God tells Moses to
do the arm thing again and the waves crash down on them and sweep them off
down river. The people start realizing how awesome God is. They also give Moses
a lot more respect.
    God becomes their tour guide using a huge pillar of cloud (in the day) and fire
(in the night). God does daily deliveries (except Rest Days) of heaven harvest
bread, but they're not that grateful. Three months after leaving, they get to the
Sinai Desert (old stomping ground for Moses). God calls Moses up the mountain
and gives him ten basic rules.   —Rob

The Big Ten (Exodus 20:1-17)

1-3

God dictates to Moses:

"No. 1: I'm your God, your God who liberated you from slave labour
in the sweatshops of Egypt. I get total priority. You won't have any other
gods taking your attention away from me. I'm it, the only God! No
other god's worth squat."

4-6

"No. 2: You won't idolize anything else of any shape. Nothing that *is*
something, or *represents* something — you'll waste no time polishing
them or showing them off to your mates or looking to them for the big
answers of life. 'Cos I get jealous! And when I'm jealous, I'm ruthless.
I punish families even three or four generations after those who hated
me have rotted in their graves. But those who live by my rules, I show
them incredible love for thousands of generations of their family line."

7

"No. 3: You won't use my name lightly, as some sort of magic word, supposed to blackmail me into action. You won't use it as a swear word. If you do, you won't go unpunished. Handle my handle with care!"

8–11

"No. 4: You'll keep my Rest Day different, distinct, special. You'll do what the word means – 'stop'. You'll work six days, do all you've got to do, then the seventh day is my day. You won't work, your family won't work, your staff won't work, your equipment won't work, your guests won't work. 'Cos I made everything you see in six days. Then I took a break on the seventh. So will you."

12–17

"No. 5: You'll treat your parents with respect. Then you'll live long and prosper in this new land I'm moving you into.

"No. 6: You won't snuff out a life, stop someone's clock, blow anyone away, bump anyone off, dole out the big chill, erase, drop, hit, top, waste anyone.

"No. 7: You won't sleep with someone else's wife or husband, put it about, cheapen yourselves.

"No. 8: You won't thieve, nick, lift, blag, fleece, half-inch, swipe or get sticky-fingered.

"No. 9: You won't deceive, lie, fib, fudge about someone, in or out of the witness box. You won't!

"No. 10: You won't drool over your mate's wife/husband . . . depending. You won't drool over their house, garden, staff, equipment, gadgets or anything they have and you don't."

> Moses treks back down the mountain and delivers The Big Ten freshly chiselled out on two stone slabs, but the plonkers have already blown Rule No. 1 – they've constructed a grotesque statue shaped like a calf, all in gold. God's so livid he wants to wipe them out and start again with Moses, but Moses puts his own neck on the line and talks God round by begging him to stick to his contract with Abraham and Co. God agrees.

Moses hands out loads more small-print stuff – crucial detail for setting up a new nation and running things God's way: laws on employment, personal injury claims, property, social responsibility and social security. General justice, Rest Day instructions and three annual Godfests. God rubber-stamps the previous contract. Moses takes on Joshua ("God Liberates") Nunson as his No. 2. They go up Sinai Mountain together and get specific instructions on the construction of God's tent, God's sacred chest, God's sacred altar – all meant to symbolize his presence ahead of settling and building a permanent HQ. Loads more details on rep outfits and orders of service. God commissions Bezalel to run the artistic design of all the religious artefacts – he's brim full of God's Spirit.

God guides them round the desert for forty years, but they're a stroppy lot – moaning and mumbling against both God and Moses.   –Rob

Leviticus /
God-Reps' Orders of Service

Moses writes out God's Instruction Manual on just about everything: rituals, national festivals, offerings, service outlines for God's tent and piles of stuff on personal and spiritual hygiene. Other countries have their laws on sacrifices etc. but God's plans are in a different league – spanking new stuff like levelling social greed via wealth redistribution with sabbatical years (every seven) and Jubilee years (every fifty). God's got a threat and a promise for most of what he reckons the Israelis are likely to get up to. The detail on sacrifices (both "can do" and "must do" varieties) shows how God's going to deal with the mess that blocks his people off from him – blood! It's that serious. Messing up God's order makes him mad. He's got a long fuse, but he still hates it. It screws his people up and it screws his world up. So he sets up a sacrifice system that wipes the history-menu clean and reboots the system, virus free. The whole manual redefines the meaning of the word "pure". —Rob

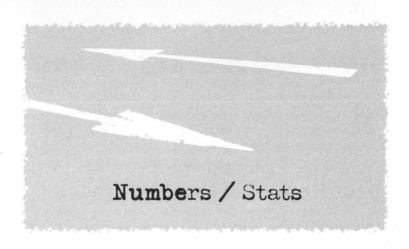

Numbers / Stats

Still in the desert, they take two national censuses, thirty-eight years apart. Stats are always dodgy, but the total columns are looking good – moving nicely towards Abraham's "number of stars in the sky" target. But desert conditions get the Israelis ratty: they gripe about just about everything and God has to come down heavy. A dozen spies go on a forty-day reconnaissance trip into Canaan. The good news – the place is lush. The bad news – the locals look like action-hero bad guys. Only two of them reckon they can take the land God's allocated them – Joshua and Caleb. The others reckon they should go crawling back to Egypt, tail between their legs.   –Rob

"Yes" / "No" (Numbers 14:6-11)

6-9

Joshua Nunson and Caleb Jephunnehson are distraught and tell the people, "You've never seen anything like it: lush fields, beautiful streams – it's perfect! If God's happy with us, he'll stride in ahead of us and we'll have milk and honey on tap! But don't wind him up. And don't bottle out just 'cos the locals flex their pecs. They're no problem, not with God on the team. Don't bottle out!"

10-11

The people are about to pelt them with stones when God turns up. He says to Moses, "How much more do I have to take from these people? How long are they going to write me off? What more do I have to do? How many more special effects? Haven't I been spectacular enough?!"

God wants to wipe them out again. Moses talks him round again. But God says only their kids will make footmarks in Canaan. For forty years God leads them mumbling and grumbling round the desert till a whole generation's pegged it – except Joshua and Caleb, who're still going strong. Moses is stressed out trying to keep them all in line. One time they're too much for him and he loses his cool. God's standards for statesmen are much higher and Moses pays for it – he's told he won't get into Canaan either. Aaron dies and the people go into free-flow complaint mode, reminiscing about the "good ol' days" in Egypt. God sends in poisonous snakes; loads die, but then he comes up with an antidote – a bronze snake on a pole. (Another symbol of the Liberator who'll come later.) God says if you look at it, you'll live. Some do, but many don't. The Israelis start making some progress against the locals who're getting twitchy about these new kids on the block. God tells Moses that Joshua is the next number one. By the time the second national census is totted up, none who came out of Egypt are alive to tell the tale, except Joshua and Caleb. Having jaywalked around the south end of the Dead Sea, they set up camp on the flatlands of Moab, east of Canaan, with just the river Jordan blocking their way to milk and honey on draft.

–Rob

Deuteronomy /
Maker's Instructions

In Moab, Moses pushes home the Terms and Conditions of enjoying the land in three last, chunky speeches.   —Rob

The Big Ten, one more time
(Deuteronomy 5:1-2, 32-33)

1-2

Moses calls a meeting. All Israel arrives and Moses begins, "Listen up! The rules I'm laying out in front of you today, memorize them; make them a lifestyle choice. God made a binding Contract with us at Sinai Mountain."

He goes over the Big Ten and prints No. 1 large, bold and double underlined – "God's it, the only God! No other god's worth squat." Later he sums it all up by saying, "Love God with everything you've got – your emotions, your will, your power."
                                                                        —Rob

32-33

"Make sure you check yourself, regular. Do what God's contracted you to do. Don't add in riders, reinterpretations or get-out clauses. Just do it! If you do all God's contracted you to do, you'll own this land, and you'll live long, and you'll prosper."

Then Moses works through some more detailed stuff they'll need to know on the other side, juicy stuff – full of God's threats, promises, battle instructions, peace plans. His buzzwords and catchphrases are "Remember when God . . .", "Make sure you check yourself, regular" and "It's life or death – your choice!" The people agree to "choose life" and re-sign the Contract. Moses swears Joshua in as the next main man, gives him a pep talk and rounds off with an epic poem stashed full of images of all the things on God's to-do list – those already checked and those still pending. Moses climbs up Nebo Mountain. God blows the clouds off and shows him the land he promised his people. It's here Moses is reminded he's not going in (punishment for losing his cool earlier).   –Rob

Moses dies (Deuteronomy 34:5-12)

5-8

Moses, God's main man, dies on the mountain. God buries the body himself and, even now, no one's ever found the grave. He was 120 years young – his eyesight still fully functional, his stamina still impressive. The Israelis cancel everything for thirty days – black armbands, the works – out of respect.

9

Joshua Nunson is full of God's ideas and God's ways, especially after Moses publicly backs him and swears him in. No dispute – God's onside. The Israelis don't dispute his appointment and they keep to the Contract, like Moses told them to.

10-12

Moses was one-of-a-kind. No one like him. He was God's mate. They chatted face-to-face, and Moses lived to dole out the news, direct from source. No one will even get *close* to the spectacular stuff he and God pulled off in Egypt.

History Section
www.new_nation.com.ot

Joshua / Good from Evil

<u>Joshua's job spec (Joshua 1:1-11)</u>

1-5

Once Moses is dead, God has a chat with Joshua Nunson. God says, "Moses, my man of the moment, has seen his *last* moment. You're the new number one. So get up, tell the people to pack their stuff, and cross the river Jordan. The whole territory is going to have an Israeli flag over it. Every sandalprint will mark out the real estate I'm giving you, just like I told Moses I would. The territory you're inheriting will stretch from the Sinai Desert in the south, to Lebanon in the north, from the Euphrates River in the east to the Mediterranean Sea in the west. No army will have the mind or the muscle to stop your progress, not while you're still breathing. You know how I was with Moses – well, ditto with you. I don't mess up. I don't let people down. I'll be there for you, guaranteed."

6-9

"So I want you gutsy and going for it, 'cos I'm going to give you the land deeds I promised your grandparents. No room for getting the frighteners on. You've got to have guts to stick to the Big Ten I dictated to Moses. Don't add provisos or conditions, subclauses or cop-outs. Stick to them and you'll see success – big time. Chew over Moses' Rule Book like it's gum (it won't lose its flavour). Mull it over all day, dream about it all night – marinate your brain in it. It should be a reflex, a natural-born instinct to live right, like the book says. 'Cos then you'll all do well, you'll succeed, you'll live long and prosper. This isn't a suggestion; it's an instruction, an order, a Head Office Directive – go for it, full on, large. Now's not the time for wimps, losers or lard-hearts, 'cos the big-guy-in-the-sky goes with you wherever you go. Got it? Then DO it!"

10-11

So Joshua gives the order to the officer ranks: "Tell the people to pack some grub; in three days they'll be on the other side of the river, picking up the keys for the new homes God's giving them. Go!"

And they go! Joshua does Moses' Red Sea "Who-needs-a-bridge?" thing on the river Jordan and they pile through. No seminar notes on preconditions justifying Holy Wars. No ethical debates about the role of violence in the late Bronze Age. Just loads of blood and gore. God gets on with his long-term goal – proving to everyone who's interested that he's the only God. He gets his people strategically into place and checks off the next stage of his plan to liberate the planet through them. And yes, you guessed it – the Israelis mess up!   —Rob

Judges /
New Line in Leaders

Joshua's follow-up acts (Judges 2:6-22)

6-7

Joshua sends the people out to take ownership of their allocation of land. While Joshua and his leaders are alive – while people can still reminisce about the phenomenal stuff God did for them – the Israelis do things God's way.

8-9

But having notched up 110 years, Joshua "God Liberates" Nunson, God's right-hand man, dies. They bury him in his allocation of land at Timnath Heres (hill country of Ephraim, up the map a bit from Gaash Mountain).

10-15

So Joshua and his whole generation are gone. And the kids grow up with not the first clue about their theology or their history. Basically they have no clue who God is. So God cringes as he has to watch the Israelis do stuff that shatters their Contract into a million pieces: They get heavily into the Baal religion where you pick 'n' mix your "gods" as suits your mood. They chuck out all their God-stuff – their heritage, their history – and they merge in with the locals, going after whichever god's flavour-of-the-month. 'Course, all this nodding and kneeling, saluting and kissing of these home-made gods makes God livid. God's so angry he gets local raiders to fleece them every time they attack. God lets them sell Jewish people as slave labour in local markets. Whenever the Israeli army goes out to fight, God changes sides and fights against them, just as he warned he would. They've had it.

16-19

So God installs new leaders who put a stop to the foreign thugs' sport. But these new guys still can't get through to the Israelis. They go on about loyalty to God, but people glaze over; they draw a complete blank – the people are like the service end of the sex trade, going after anything that flashes the right money. You'd never believe they were related to the previous lot. Joshua's crowd kept to the Contract agreed with God. This bunch does whatever feels good at the time. And it's not just once – it's every time. Like a rerun of some depressing soap, they're ripped apart by the locals, God takes pity on them, God appoints a new leader, God backs him/her to the hilt; the local gangs back off, the leader dies and the people go back to their old habits – only worse – sucking up to man-made gods and getting stuck in, head first, to so much dark stuff. Then, 'course, the local gangs kick-start more trouble and we're back to the old plot. Square one.

20-22

So God's well angry with Israel. He rants, "They've trashed the Contract, burnt their history books, treated me like I don't exist. Why should I keep their rivals on a lead? Maybe these vulgar pagans will teach my people a lesson. Who knows, maybe they'll wake up and smell the filth. Maybe they'll remember the stories their granddads told them. Maybe they'll remember who I am and what I've done for them. Maybe."

> Maybe not! After a dozen or so of these leaders, the cycle continues. The commentator sums up the whole era with ... —Rob

No king (Judges 21:25)

These days, with no king to call the shots, everyone does their own thing: if it feels good, just do it.

Ruth /
Foreign Girl Gets God

Same time, same place, different scale: focus in on one Jewish family. Central character a girl from Moab – Ruth, Great Grandma of King David and therefore "great" to the power of . . . (you work it out) . . . ancestor of the Liberator. Backtracking a bit: Naomi and family have abandoned the land God gave them and are living in Moab. Naomi's son's in a mixed-race marriage with Ruth. When Ruth's hubby dies she goes way beyond the call of duty, escorting her depressed Jewish mother-in-law, Naomi (also a widow), back to her home in Bethlehem, southern Israel . . .

—Rob

Naomi's shadow (Ruth 1:16-17)

Ruth responds, "Don't force me to leave you. I'm going where you go. I'm staying where you stay. For 'your people' read 'my people'. For 'your God' read 'my God'. I'll die where you die, and they'll bury me there. May God rip into me if I ever let anything separate us."

Going back to Israel blows her slim chances of remarriage, since she'll be a foreigner and most Israelis aren't overkeen on "Moabite scum". Enter Boaz, distant relative of Ruth's mother-in-law and therefore a sort of (stretching it) technical relative of Ruth. Boaz knows straight off that she's a foreigner but he likes what she's done for Naomi, so authorizes special privileges for Ruth as she works on his farm. After a party Ruth and Boaz start getting closer (rumours say "very close" as in "sex"), and eventually Boaz sorts out the legal blockages so he can marry her. Not long after, Ruth's pregnant and Naomi's to get a grandchild. Baby Obed arrives and grows up to become Jesse's dad and King David's granddad.

—Rob

1 Samuel /
Kingmaker, Book 1

Scene change: up in the hills of Ephraim. Another woman can't have kids – Hannah Zuphson. She makes a deal with God: if he gives her a son, she'll hand him over to Eli, God's rep, as a live-in help. God does a miracle in the gynaecology department and Hannah calls the baby Samuel ("God listens") Zuphson. It's a rough time for Israel; communication with God has almost dried up and the Philistine thugs are pretty much running the place. One time, they carry off God's sacred chest, but soon hand it back, totally freaked by the "weird stuff" going on. As a boy, Samuel has sharp ears when God has something to say – rare these days. He grows up to become God's rep. He makes it his life's work to get the Israelis to jack in "gods" like Baal. When they do, God turns up and they're singing victory songs. Samuel grows old.

—Rob

"We want a king" (1 Samuel 8:1-22)

1-3

Samuel knows he's not getting any younger, so he installs his two sons, Joel and Abijah (in that order), as national leaders based in Beersheba. But the boys are nothing like their old man: they're easily influenced, especially when there's a backhander greasing the decision.

4-5

So other leaders approach Samuel on the quiet in Ramah, saying, "You've not got that long left, and your boys aren't anything like the same calibre. We need a proper king, a monarchy, like the other countries."

6-9

Samuel's disturbed that they're so sold on having a king. He talks it through with God, who says, "Listen to them! It's not you they're kicking into touch; it's me! I'm their King, but they're blocking me out, like they've done since I dragged them out of the sweatshops of Egypt. They go off after whichever monstrosity is that particular god-of-the-month, whichever god is top-of-the-gods chart. Now you know how I feel! Go with what they want, but only after you give them a wake-up call. Give them a rundown on what it's like living in a monarchy."

10-18

So Samuel passes on what God said: "You want a king? D'you know what a king'll do? He'll conscript your sons into his army, or his fields, or his munitions factories. He'll confiscate your best land and properties, move his sharp-dressing yes-men into the best houses. You'll object, but you'll have no leg to stand on. Plus, who pays these yes-men's salaries? You do, with your taxes! He'll headhunt your best staff, he'll co-opt your best equipment, he'll take over your best products. You'll wake up and realize you're not working for yourself any more, but for him. You'll kick the cat, you'll punch the walls, you'll diss the king, and I'll just frown, 'Told you so.' You'll be stuck with him. Your choice!"

19-20

But the people won't budge. "We want a king!" they tell Samuel. "It's non-negotiable. Then we'll be a proper country, like the others, with someone to fight our corner for us."

21-22

Samuel discusses this with God, who says, "Let them have their king."

Samuel tells the people, "You got it. Give me some time."

Samuel does some prep on finding someone suitable.   —Rob

Saul gets the job (1 Samuel 10:17-25)

17-19

Samuel calls a national conference at Mizpah. Everyone's there, on the edge of their seats to hear Samuel's update on God's king proposal —

which goes, "I'm God, the one who liberated you from Egypt and all the other countries that were picking you off at will. But now, apparently, I'm not good enough for you, despite my sorting out the mess you got yourselves into. Now you start the chanting, 'We want a king – can't wait. Won't wait.' So file past, by name, in alphabetical order, and you'll get your king."

20-22

Samuel whittles down the crowd by tribe, then clan, then family. At the end, Samuel gives the nod to a guy called Saul Kishson. Only problem is, he's not there! Samuel checks with God, who's got him on his monitors: "He's lying low, holed up with the baggage."

23-24

They run and get him. He stands there looking down on even the tallest. Samuel says, "This is the guy God's selected for your king. He's one-of-a-kind."

The crowds start up, "God save our gracious king", etc.

25

Samuel goes through the constitution with them and puts a written copy in the HQ. Then he sends the people home.

> Saul has his coronation. Then starts the saga "How to be a naff king". Faced with the threat of the Philistines, he compromises on the important stuff and goes all ruthless on the trivial. Pretty soon into his reign, God rejects him.   —Rob

God gives Saul notice (1 Samuel 15:10-11)

Then God says to Samuel, "I'm gutted that I made Saul king. He's done his own thing, on his own terms, in his own time. He's treated my instructions like they were suggestions or discussion points." Samuel doesn't take the news too well, and argues with God through the small hours.

> Samuel breaks the bad news to Saul, who disputes the decision. But Samuel lost the argument with God, so Saul loses this one with Samuel.   —Rob

Headhunted (1 Samuel 16:1-13)

1

God asks Samuel, "How long are you going to reminisce about the good ol' times, wearing out old stories of when Saul was the people's hero? Saul's a reject! I've as good as sacked him. Pick up the necessaries and get yourself to Bethlehem sharpish. Track down a guy called Jesse Boazson – I've earmarked one of his boys as replacement king."

2-3

"Yeah, likely!" Samuel gripes. "If Saul gets to hear, I'm dead meat!"

God sighs, "OK. Take a calf with you. Make out that you've come to sacrifice the calf to me, but make sure Jesse turns up with his boys. There'll be no interview panel – I'll tell you which one to pick."

4-5

When Samuel gets to Bethlehem, the city bureaucrats come out, "Are you in a good mood, or are you looking for trouble?" they wobble.

"Don't panic!" says Samuel. "I've come to sacrifice this calf to God. Sort yourselves out. Make sure you're in sync with God and come join me." Then Samuel takes Jesse and his boys through the purifying service and invites them to the ceremony.

6-7

When Jesse and the boys arrive, Samuel takes one look at Eliab, the oldest, and says to himself, "Job done! He's the biz, for sure."

But God said, "Whoa. Hold on. OK, so he's a pin-up; he'll look great in publicity shots and interviews. But he's not getting the crown. Good job I don't look at the same stuff you do – the image, the voice, the perfect teeth. I look at inside stuff, and I'm not talking the lining of his designer jacket: I'm talking character."

8-11

So Jesse calls the next one, Abinadab, who stands for inspection. But Samuel says, "Nope! God's not picked this one either." Then he calls Shammah, but says, "Nor this one." Altogether seven stand for inspection, but Samuel says the same: "None of these." Then he asks, "Any more? Or is that it?"

Jesse says, "Well, there's the kid, my youngest, but he's out with the sheep."

"Go get him," says Samuel. "We don't start anything till he shows."

12-13

When David strolls in, Samuel sees straight off that he's a stunner: well-toned, strong features, and obviously sharp as a flick knife. God says in Samuel's ear, "This is the one! Do the prep." So Samuel goes through the official ceremony, and earmarks David as future king in front of all his brothers and dad. From then on God's Holy Spirit hangs around David day and night. Meanwhile Samuel goes off to Ramah.

> David's the king-elect, but he has to wait years to feel the weight of the crown on his head.   —Rob

David trounces the Big Guy (1 Samuel 17:1-51)

1-3

Location: the Philistine army pitch camp at Ephes Dammim, near Socoh, in southern Israel. Saul and the Israeli army set up camp the other side of the Elah Valley. It's a stand-off: two armies on two hills facing each other, neither side liking what they see.

4-7

The Philistines' top fighter, Goliath from Gath, strides down the hill. He's a giant, over 3 metres (9 feet) tall. He's wearing some serious combat gear, weighing over 57 kilos (125 pounds / around 8 stone), and he's carrying a huge javelin – its iron point alone weighs 7 kilos (15 pounds / more or less a stone)! And his shield! Let's just say the guy carrying it must have pumped some iron in his time.

8-11

Goliath stands there and bellows over to the Israeli army, "Why've you turned up? I'm a Philistine; you're Saul's army. This is how it works: you send someone out; we fight. If your guy does me over, fair cop – we're *your* slaves. If your guy dies, tough – you're *our* slaves. Deal, or what?"

Goliath goes through this little routine twice a day for weeks and everyone in the Israeli camp, including Saul, is totally bottling.

12-19

Back in Bethlehem, Jesse Boazson is getting on by now. His three eldest sons, Eliab, Abinadab and Shammah, are in Saul's army, but David,
the youngest, is still on sheep duty. Jesse says to David, "Take some
bread and grain to your brothers at the camp. And these cheeses, for
their officer. Find out how they're doing."

20-24

So early dawn, David loads up and sets off. He arrives at the camp just
as the troops are doing their battle chant, face-to-face across the valley
like two sets of heavily armed football fans. David leaves the food boxes
with the quartermaster general and legs it to the front to check on his
brothers. They're busy catching up when Goliath comes out to do his
regular slot of frightening the tripe out of the Israelis. David checks out
the giant and the reaction he's getting.

25-27

The troops are muttering about him saying, "He's having a laugh!
What's Saul got stashed away for the guy who takes him out? He'll get
a lottery jackpot. He'll get to marry the princess. He'll never pay tax
again. Nor his family. Nor his mates."

David quizzes the soldiers next to him, "What d'you reckon you get if
you terminate this plonker?" They churn out the rumours – the cash,
the princess, the tax exemptions.

28

But his oldest brother, Eliab, catches the end of the conversation and
loses his cool with his kid brother: "What you doing here? Who'd you
leave the sheep with? You're an arrogant little tyke – manipulative too –
you're only here to get a grandstand view of the action."

29-31

"Oh, right; I can't even *talk* now!" snaps David. He goes off, asks the
same question elsewhere, gets the same answer. All this speeds down
the grapevine back to Saul, and he sends for David.

32-33

David's in front of the king spouting, "We shouldn't be losing sleep over this overgrown teddy bear. I'll take him out."

Saul says, "No way! You're a kid. This guy's been a gladiator since he started shaving – probably around twelve!"

34-37

But David comes back, "I've looked after my dad's sheep. Some lion or bear comes after one of them and I go for it, smack it one and take back the stolen goods. It turns on me, roaring its head off, and I grab it by the hair, whack it again and kill the thing. I've killed a lion and a bear, no problem. This pagan Philistine is going to get the same treatment. He's insulting the army of the Vibrant God. No one does that and lives to mouth off about it. God's protected me from the lion's paw and the bear's paw; now he'll protect me from *this* animal's paw!"

Saul shrugs, "OK, go! And God better go with you."

38-39

Saul sticks his combat gear on David. The full works: boots, jacket, helmet. All size triple X. 'Course David's rattling around in it, trying to learn to walk again.

40

Pretty soon he gasps, "I can't wear this stuff! I'm not used to all this army gear." He takes the body armour off, picks up his sheep patrol stick, selects five pebbles from the stream, puts them in his pack and, with his sling in hand, goes off to pick a scrap with Goliath.

41-44

The Philistine and his muscle-man shield carrier close in on David. He soon sees that David's just a kid, a good-looking kid, but just a kid. He starts giving him some verbal: "What! I'm some dog, am I? You come at me with sticks and stones?" He starts calling down filthy curses, invoking every "god" he's ever heard of to give vent to his temper. "Get here!!" he booms. "I'll tear out your liver and let the birds and dogs loose on it!"

45-47

David shouts straight back, "You come at me with your fancy sword and spear, but I come at you with something far more dangerous – the backing of Israel's God, who you've spent the last month ripping into with your mocking and taunting routine. Time's up, Goliath! Enough provocation. Today God's going to hand you over to me. I'll take you down and slice off your ugly head. The birds and the dogs will get a bigger meal than you planned. Then the world will wise up to the fact that Israel's God's not to be messed with, that he doesn't need state-of-the-art weapons to look after his people. Today's God's day – you guys lose!"

48-49

The Philistine giant lunges at David, who reaches into his bag as he runs forward. He grabs a pebble, sticks it in his sling, whips it round his head and lets fly. The stone flies like a bullet, smacks Goliath full on the head and carries on through – it breaks through the forehead and lodges in his skull. Goliath's huge bulk collapses and lands face down in the dust.

50-51

So David wins – with a sling and a stone! No sword. No spear. Just *one pebble* and God. He runs over, pulls out the giant's humongous sword and lops the lanky loser's head off. The Philistine army stands there, for a split second too stunned to move. Seconds later, they're legging it.

> God's people rout the Philistines in retreat, while Saul does some background research on David's origins.   —Rob

Saul jealous of David (1 Samuel 18:1-9)

1-4

David finishes debriefing Saul. Saul's son, Prince Jonathan, bonds with David big time – he loves him like his own life. King Saul seconds David on to his army payroll and won't let him out of his sight – he doesn't even let him return home. Jonathan and David virtually become blood brothers, with Jonathan sealing the contract by handing over his jacket and throwing in his best fighting gear on top.

5

David can't fail: whatever job Saul lands him with, David comes out on top. Saul promotes him up the ranks, which keeps both the public and the officers happy.

6-7

They come back from David's fracas with the Philistines, and local women line the streets to party. They're bopping away to the rhythms and music, singing, "Saul takes out a thousand, David ten thousand" and "There's only one David Jesseson, one David Jesseson!"

8-9

Saul's well annoyed by these chants: "How come he takes out ten times my tally? He's got everything a guy could want." Then it hits him: "Everything except my crown!" Saul's jealous gland goes into overactive mode.

> More success for David only stokes the jealousy, until ...   —Rob

Watching David's back (1 Samuel 19:1-3)

Saul gives Jonathan and his officers the order to eliminate David. 'Course Jonathan's not about to jack in his contract with David and warns him, "My dad's after your blood – all eight pints of it. Be on the ball tomorrow morning; make yourself scarce and stay like it. I'll take a walk with him, suss him out and get the news to you."

> Jonathan works on his dad and brings him round. David's back at the royal court. Safe – for a while.   —Rob

Target practice (1 Samuel 19:9-10)

David's playing some easy listening on his harp, but Saul's not picking up the mood. What he does pick up is his spear, tries to pin David to the plaster! David moves out of the way, just in time. The spear drills into the wall and David's out of there before Saul can stop him.

> Saul's on the chase, but David's always one step ahead. Saul's going schizo. One day he's calm about the David thing, the next he's foaming at the mouth. Jonathan keeps on at his dad to give David a break, but Saul starts flinging spears at *him*.

David hides for a while in Gath; then the caves of Adullam; then in Hereth Forest; on to Horesh; then the Maon Desert; then the En Gedi Desert ... always on the run, adding men to his posse as he goes (around six hundred last count).   —Rob

God's timing (1 Samuel 24:1-7)

1-2

Saul's coming back from giving the Philistines a hard time, and he gets the message, "David's in the En Gedi Desert". Saul hand-picks 3,000 of Israel's best fighting men and moves in on the Wild Goat Crag, where his informers tell him David's been spotted.

3-4

Saul's just passing some sheep pens when he's busting for the loo. He sees a cave and goes in to do the business. David and posse are hiding right at the back end of the cave. The men whisper, "This is it! God told you he'd hand Saul over to you and that you could do what you like! Go for it!" So David creeps up on Saul and, while Saul's focused on the job at hand, David takes out his knife and ... well ... just slices the corner off Saul's jacket.

5-7

Seconds later David's conscience is giving him a hard time. He says to his men, "God slap me down if I lift a finger against the one he's selected. He's still the king! No one even thinks about taking him out, got it?" Saul, totally oblivious of all this, strolls out of the cave and moves on a little lighter.

Once he's gone David stands at the cave mouth and waves the corner of Saul's jacket. Saul realizes David could've killed him. He goes all matey, saying stuff about David being God's future king. But the mood doesn't last long and within months he's stomping round the country again, after David's blood.

Bizarrely, David faces the same scenario a second time: Saul sleeping in a cave and at his mercy. The fugitive's chomping at the bit, but David again lets Saul live, reckoning God'll sort out the timing without his help. On hearing, Saul goes all friendly again and backs off for a while. David's not dense, though: he stays scarce. He launches numerous forays into enemy territory. God backs him and his track record looks increasingly awesome.

Saul's facing serious threats from the Philistine forces. He's desperate for God's backing, but God's so angry with Saul, he's fighting for the enemy. Saul catches an arrow and knows it's terminal. He falls on his sword and commits suicide.

(During this time David wrote some of his best songs – haunting tunes with angst-ridden, autobiographical lyrics that resonate with anyone who's ever wrestled with God and got to know him in the process. See later for song lyrics from some of his "greatest hits" in www.peoples-poetry.com.ot/songlyrics.)

—Rob

2 Samuel /
Kingmaker, the Sequel

"Disk full!" The first scroll is packed full and Samuel carries the story on with a new one. At age thirty, David gets crowned king, initially just of southern Israel, then of the whole country. David starts his forty-year reign by taking Jerusalem off the Jebusite army. The Philistines are still at it – but so is God – and David routs them. He gets on with his manifesto promise to bring the sacred chest of God (the national symbol of God being around) back to its proper place – the religious HQ of the country. As they bring it into the City, David's dancing like he's on something illegal. He's not bothered by what people think, only what God thinks.   – Rob

God's long-term plans (2 Samuel 7:1-19)

1-3

David's nicely settled in his palace, his enemies are sorted, and he says to Nathan (God's new courier, after Samuel), "What am I doing, living in luxury when God's sacred chest is stashed under canvas?"

Nathan comes back, "Go for it; God'll back you."

4-5

But that night God tells Nathan to inform David, "Whoa! Hold on. You're not the guy who's going to build me my HQ."

God doesn't give much explanation, but tells him . . .   – Rob

9

"I've backed you all the way, and it's not going to stop, even once you die. You're going to be one of the top guys: worldwide respect."

Other stuff about Israel getting their own place, then ...   —Rob

12-16

"Once you're gone, I'll inspire one of your direct descendants to build me an HQ. I'll be a dad to him, loving and firm. But I won't disown him, like I did Saul. I wrote him off to bring you in. No, your family line, your reputation, your influence is not going to fade, ever."

David's blown away.   —Rob

18-19

David comes back, "Why me, God? How come you do all this for me? Already you've been incredible and now you're talking permanent – long after I'm worm-feed. Is this how you normally treat people?! You're over the top, God; you really are!"

David's a success. He runs things fair, right and good, until ...   —Rob

David's wandering eye (2 Samuel 11:1-27)

1

It's spring – normally Battle Season. But David stays at home and sends Joab to look after the army.

2

It's evening. David's had a lazy day. He gets up from his bed and wanders round the palace roof. By design, it's got great views. Then he checks out this naked woman in the bath – an absolute stunner! David starts to dribble.

He finds out who she is – Bathsheba, wife of Officer Uriah – who, conveniently, is off with the army. He sends for her and they have a night of passion. Then she realizes she's pregnant and tells David the news. He tries to cover his back by calling her husband away from the front, hoping he'll sleep with her. But the guy's a pro and sleeps at the gate of the palace with the staff. David calls him in.   —Rob

11

Uriah says to David, "It's war time! Everyone's sleeping rough. Even God's sacred chest lives in a tent. How could I go to my house? How could I have a romantic meal with my wife and end up in bed together? I couldn't. Not while my men are sleeping in open fields."

12-13

David says, "Hang around another day. Relax! Go back tomorrow." So he does. David invites him for a meal, gets him well plastered. But still he doesn't go home. Again he sleeps outside with the staff.

14-15

Next morning, David writes to Joab and sends the sealed note with Uriah. The orders: "Stick Uriah on the front line, and when the action hots up, pull back and leave him stranded."

> David's the king; so Joab follows his orders and Uriah dies in action.   —Rob

26-27

When Uriah's wife hears her husband's dead, she's devastated. In good time David marries her and she has his son. But God's going ballistic.

Nathan: storyteller (2 Samuel 12:1-14)

1-3

God sends Nathan to David. Nathan tells a story, making out it's real: "Two guys. One's loaded. The other's just about keeping his head above water. The rich guy has too many sheep and cattle to count. The poor guy has nothing except one lamb. He's looked after it so carefully, it's almost a family pet. No. It's like a daughter to him!"

4-6

"One evening the rich guy gets a visitor and instead of killing one of his flock, he steals the *poor guy's* sheep and his guest tucks into lamb casserole, courtesy of the poor guy."

David's fuming; he says to Nathan, "This guy's got to pay for this — with his life. That's unforgivable. Get the lawyers in here, draw up the papers, sue him for at least four lambs. Who'd be that ruthless?"

7-10

Nathan gulps and says, "You would! You're the guy. This is what the God of Israel says: 'I make you king of Israel, I keep Saul off your back, I give you his palace, I give you wives, I give you the whole country. And if you wanted more, I'd give you more. So why d'you throw it all back in my face and go grabbing what's not yours? Why d'you do this? It's evil, having Uriah killed so you can take his wife! You'll pay! Swords are going to be a running theme in your family.'"

11-12

Nathan passes on God's sentence: "Your family is going to give you grief. I'll take your wives from under your nose and put them in the bed of a close friend. They'll get off on sex fests in broad daylight. You had your romp behind thick curtains, but they'll be exhibitionists and all Israel will watch their porn."

13-14

David, totally broken, admits, "I've broken the Contract. I've gone against everything God wants for me. I'm gutted, totally gutted."

Nathan says, "God wipes it off your track record. He's not going to waste you here and now. But because you've given his enemies so much ammunition, because they're laughing in his face, he'll punish you more by having your son die."

The child is born and quickly gets ill. But despite David not eating, sleeping on the stone floor and begging God with every breath — despite all this, the child still dies.

David adjusts quickly: he begins eating again. He celebrates his God. He comforts Bathsheba. In time, she's pregnant again . . . with another son . . . Solomon Davidson.

(This whole chapter in David's life was the inspiration for one of his top songs, No. 51.) And they all lived happily ever after? Do they heck! The rest of David's rule is a Royal Family soap opera full of personal and political upheaval: deceit, incestuous rapes, hatred, revenge murders, alienation, family rifts, self-promotion, conspiracy, revolt. David ends up being chased out of his palace by his own son's *coup d'état,* being cursed by Saul's old posse, living on the run and then seeing his own son die before him.

David moves back in at the palace and faces another revolt from one of the twelve tribes, a three-year famine, plagues, more wars with the Philistines and many other major hassles. But as David notches up the years, hindsight shows him how God's pulled him through all these personal and political crises. He's not slow in writing songs where God gets the credit full on and strong in the chorus (go to www.peoples-poetry.com.ot / songlyrics). His last recordings are about God's contract with him — on which there's no shifting. His last project is to build a place to offer sacrifices to God. He sees God pull the plague-dial back down to "off". —Rob

1 Kings / Carry on Monarchy

King David's past it. He's tucked up in bed, a dozen duvets, but still dying of hypothermia. Rumblings of "who's next" echo round the palace. Nathan, God's courier, doesn't need to be a detective to work out that Adonijah, the oldest prince, is throne-grabbing. He updates David in his bedroom. The king calls in Zadok, God's rep, and they make it official – Solomon's going to be the next king of Israel. The public love it. Adonijah doesn't – he's scared witless of his half-brother.   —Rob

"If the crown fits ..." (1 Kings 2:1-12)

1

David's time's up. He calls Solomon in to give him some last-minute tips.

2-4

"Not long now, son," he whispers. "Show some spine, some muscle. Prove you're a good man. Keep both eyes on God's target. Live God's way. Keep the Moses Contract and you'll be successful, whatever you do, wherever you go. Do it, and God'll keep his side of the bargain – he told me, if my descendants keep themselves in line with God's lifestyle, if they're passionate about living God's way, then I'll always have a son with a crown on his head!"

He points out the unfinished business with some dodgy characters, but leaves Solomon's "wise head" to finalize policy.   —Rob

10-12

King David dies. Big funeral in Jerusalem, "City of David". He's been king of Israel forty years – seven in Hebron, the rest in Jerusalem. Solomon sits on his dad's throne and wears his dad's crown. No one's about to dispute it.

Wise up! (1 Kings 3:4-15)

4-5

King Solomon goes to spend some quality time with God in Gibeon (top location, pre-HQ). He went for it big time, sacrificing a thousand animals to God. That night God tunes into Solomon's dream patterns, and says, "What d'you want? What d'you really, really want? Just say!"

6-9

Solomon dreams himself saying, "God, you've redefined 'kind'. My dad lived your way and, ever since, you've stuck by us, looked out for us, gone over the top in doing us good. You've made me king, but I'm just a kid! I've no idea where to start. How am I supposed to manage your people? So many of them! I'll tell you what I want . . . what I *need* – a probing mind . . . and a wise heart. I need to wise up! I want to be able to tell white from black when everything's grey. Otherwise, the odds are against me running this lot with any success."

10-15

God's well pleased with this: "Good answer! You could've milked me for long life; you could've submitted outrageous personal wealth targets; you could've requested some particularly gruesome death for your rivals – but you didn't. You asked for wisdom to do the job justice and to do justice in the job. Done! You've got it! I'll give you the sharpest mind, the most instinctive, intuitive, discerning heart in history – past, present or future. Plus, I'll also throw in the stuff you've not gone for: huge personal wealth, total respect, worldwide, so you'll be the main man around. There's more! If you live life my way, if you keep the Contract (like your dad did), I'll also throw in long life – you'll go well past your sell-by date." Then Solomon wakes up and realizes it's all been a dream.

Wise (1 Kings 3:16-28)

Back in Jerusalem two prostitutes are in Solomon's courtroom – fierce dispute over a baby and who's the real mum. Solomon's got to decide who gets to keep the boy. Tricky! He calls for a sword and makes as if he's about to slice the baby in half, so they both get some of it! 'Course the *real* mum goes bananas and screams, "Don't kill him! She can have him! Please don't kill him!" Solomon gives the baby, alive and kicking, to the woman who screamed. Her reaction was a giveaway. The whole courtroom knows it's a stroke of genius, and soon the whole country realizes Solomon has God's wisdom, in major helpings. The whole region gets to hear about Israel's wise king.

Solomon publishes 3,000 proverbs and over a thousand songs. Check them at www.peoples-poetry.com.ot/wiseup.   –Rob

Fame and fortune (1 Kings 6:1-11:40)

Solomon kicks off his HQ Building Project. Seven years later it's finished. Awesome! They start on the elaborate fittings inside, precision craftsmanship that even the artist Bezalel would've been proud of. It's a big day when God's sacred chest is brought in – a permanent home at last for the chest and its contents. Solomon also finishes his palace – every interior decor mag wants exclusive photo rights. His profile's huge. His name's synonymous with the two W's – wisdom and wealth. Foreign dignitaries come crawling with their presents, checking out the rumours, asking tricky questions and ensuring future name-dropping opportunities. Even the Queen of Sheba is blown away by his two W's, and the God who doled them out to him. Surprise! It all goes to his head. Thing is, King Solomon has a soft spot for foreign women – his bed! God warns him, "They'll bring their gods with them, and you'll forget Rule No. 1." But does he listen? Does he heck! As Solomon grows older he becomes less like his dad; his thousand wives slowly erode his 100 percent loyalty to God. He starts constructing hill shrines for their pagan religious festivals (which, at times, include child sacrifice), and God is Furious, capital F! He announces the future split of the country into two – northern and southern kingdoms.

Catch up with Solomon's romantic side by going to www.peoples-poetry .com.ot/youaregorgeous. Check out his reflective side by looking up www.peoples -poetry.com.ot/whatsthepoint.   –Rob

Split loyalties (1 Kings 11:41-16:34)

After forty years as king, Solomon dies. His son Rehoboam carries on with the family business. He gets a bit cocky and the Israelis revolt against his policies but, out of loyalty to David, God leaves him with just the southern kingdom of Judah to run. Jeroboam moves in as king of Israel in the north and sets up competing hill shrines so his subjects don't hike down to Jerusalem and drift back to Rehoboam. He funds an extensive shrine-building programme, despite God's couriers, who shout down the plans as blatant Contract-breaking. All this on top of being at war with Rehoboam, king of Judah, who's also busy winding God up down south.

As if in competition with Israel, Rehoboam spends his seventeen-year reign building hill shrines: disgusting rituals involving male prostitution – exactly the stuff God had just got rid of. Five years in, King Shishak of Egypt raids Solomon's temple in Jerusalem and cleans up. He lifts the lot. Abijah is the next king of Judah after Rehoboam. Three years of similar stuff. Then Asa moves into the palace: good and bad – he kicks out the idols and male prostitutes, but doesn't smash up the hill shrines.

Meanwhile, back up in Israel, a whole list of naff kings who wind God up big time: Jeroboam's son Nadab runs things for two years before being killed in a coup led by Baasha. Baasha exterminates the rest of Nadab's family and is king for twenty-four years. Elah's next up. Two years in, he's drunk one night and Officer Zimri picks his moment to assassinate him. Zimri lasts only seven days as king before he tops himself to avoid dying, courtesy of Omri. Omri lasts twelve years, and winds God up more than most. After he dies, his son Ahab Omrison moves into the king's palace in Samaria. He marries Princess Jezebel of Tyre and Sidon and she manipulates him into permitting equal rights for foreign "gods". The downward spiral continues and foreign "gods" push God down the people's priority list. Ahab's the worst king yet, easy. Then God's courier, Elijah, turns up ...   –Rob

God stops the rain (1 Kings 17:1-24)

1

Elijah Tishbiteton says to Ahab, "Sure as the God I work for is alive and well, there's not going to be any rain, or even dew, for the next few years. Nothing, till my say so."

The drought bites. Elijah parks himself by a stream and is kept alive by God-piloted ravens bringing him bread and meat twice a day. When the stream dries up, God arranges a widow landlady to look after him. She's got no food, but agrees anyway.

God fixes her utensils so they just keep pouring out food on demand. Then her son dies, but Elijah gets God to bring the guy back. The widow's totally sold on the fact that Elijah's a courier of God.

After three years of drought, catastrophic famine and Jezebel's systematic and ruthless elimination of God's reps, God sends Elijah to tell King Ahab the weather forecast . . .   —Rob

God vs "gods" (1 Kings 18:17–39)

17

Ahab sees Elijah, and says, "Look who it is: Top Troublemaker in Israel!"

18-19

"Me, a troublemaker? Hilarious!" Elijah laughs. "You and your old man make all the trouble. You trash the Contract and go after the foreign 'gods' of Baal. Right. Listen up. Get the people to Carmel Mountain. I want the Baal cronies there too. All 450 of the guys who vote Baal every time and the 400 who drool over the goddess Asherah – basically all those who are on Jezebel's dinner-party list."

20-21

Ahab arranges it. The Jewish people and the Baal couriers arrive at Carmel Mountain. Elijah goes to the people: "How long are you going to 'um' and 'ah'? How long are you going to hobble round on two crutches? It's make-your-mind-up time! If God is God, do things *his* way. If Baal is god, then do things *his* way. Who you going to lean on?" The people stay schtum.

22-24

He carries on: "I'm an endangered species, a courier of God. I'm the only live specimen left. Me against 450! This is how it works: two bulls, here and now. Baal's guys can pick one. Let them butcher it and stick it on the altar. But hold the fire. I'll do the prep on the other bull, stick it on my altar. But, again, no fire. Then, the moment of truth: you guys get Baal to provide the matches, and I'll ask God. The God who provides the matches for the sacrifice – he's the genuine article." The people agree.

25-26

Elijah counts the Baal reps in: "Pick your bull. Get it ready; there's enough of you! Then contact your 'god'. But no cheating: no hidden matches! Baal's got to do the business."

They get it all ready and launch into their routines, "Ohhhhh Baal! You there? It's us! Answer. Ooooohhhh. Got a light?" They go on from morning to noon. Not a spark. Nothing. They strut their stuff, do their best fire dances but nothing's happening. "Oooohhh!"

27-29

Elijah starts milking it: "From the diaphragm, boys! Pump up the volume! He's a god, he's probably busy; he's thinking or travelling or . . . just busy! Loads to do if you're a god! Maybe he's having a power nap. Probably a heavy sleeper. Put some energy into it! Wake him up! Check the toilet door for the 'engaged' sign." They go up a gear, working themselves into a frenzy. They start cutting themselves with knives and swords till they're getting faint from loss of blood. By late afternoon, they're danced- and tranced-out – exhausted, but still no response. No one home, no one listening, no one there . . .

30-35

So Elijah tells the audience, "Get over here." They move and watch him repairing the altar of God, which Jezebel had demolished. He takes twelve boulders, one for each of the tribes of Jacob (who God relaunched as Israel) and he rebuilds the altar. He digs a trench around it capable of holding about 15 litres (26 pints) of water. He lays out the wood, slices up the bull, puts the meat on top of the wood and says, "Get me four big pitchers full of water – soak the thing." They do it. "And again," he says. They do it. "And three times for an Israeli! Do it again." They do it again. The water saturates the meat, the wood, the whole altar and pours down the side, filling the trench. We're talking WET!

36-37

Right on the dot of evening sacrifice time, Elijah steps out and shouts to God, "Oh God! Abraham's God, Isaac's God, Israel's God. Show them! Prove it! Don't leave anyone in two minds. Let them see that you're God and that I'm your courier and that I'm just following orders.

React, God. React! So they'll know you're God and that you're winning them back round to you."

38

Huge lightning bolt! Perfect shot, zaps into the meat on the altar. Flames licking around the bull till it's just steam and ash. When the smoke clears, there's no water left, even in the trench – it's boiled away.

39

The people hit the deck. Scared of the lightning and the God who might have more to throw: "God is God. He's our God, the only God – the only God worth squat."

> Elijah has the Baal reps killed. He tells Ahab the forecast is for rain. Black clouds gather. King Ahab tells Jezebel the whole story and she swears she'll kill Elijah within twenty-four hours. Elijah wobbles and runs for his life. He gets to the desert and collapses under a juniper tree, exhausted and, adrenaline on empty, he's totally depressed. He begs God, "Take me now; I'm useless," until he drops off to sleep. An angel turns up with hot bread and fresh water. Elijah wakes, eats and then sleeps some more. The angel makes a second visit, gets him to eat more before he makes the journey. Elijah eats and then walks the forty-day trip to Sinai Mountain. He spends the night in a cave. –Rob

God's quiet side (1 Kings 19:9-18)

9

God says to Elijah, "Why you here?"

10

Elijah moans, "I've worked my butt off for you, God! The Israelis have thrown out your Contract, trashed your altars, assassinated your couriers. I'm the last one standing, and now they're after me!"

11-13

God says, "Go outside and stand on the mountain. I'm about to show."

Then something like a hurricane hits the place. It rips the rocks out of the mountain and smashes them into tiny pieces. But God's not in the storm. Then *more* special effects: this time an earthquake – "pretty scary" on the Richter scale. But God's not in the earthquake either. Next up, a raging fire. But again, no God in it. After all this, God turns up and speaks quietly and calmly. Elijah hears the voice, catches on sharpish, pulls his jacket over his face and goes out from the cave.

The voice whispers, "Why you here, Elijah?"

14

He comes back with the same patter: "I've worked my butt off for you, God! The Israelis have thrown out your Contract, trashed your altars, assassinated your couriers. I'm the last one standing, and now they're after me!"

15-18

God says, "Retrace your steps. Go to the Damascus Desert."

God tells him to make three new appointments: Hazael as king of Aram, Jehu as king of Israel and Elisha Shaphatson as God's courier elect, i.e. Elijah's apprentice. He also drops in the fact that there are actually still 7,000 other people in Israel who've been just as loyal as Elijah.

Elijah sorts out the trainee first off. Elisha has a mentor.   —Rob

More kings (1 Kings 20:1-22:53)

After twenty-two years in charge, Ahab comes to a gory end in battle. He's buried in the northern capital, Samaria. His son Ahaziah takes the crown. Quick check on the scene in Judah: Asa dies and his son Jehoshaphat's now king. Like his dad, he does some good stuff, but again, like his dad, he leaves the hill shrines standing. So people in Judah still ignore Rule No. 1. For most of his twenty-five years they're at peace with their northern neighbour Israel. Back up to King Ahaziah of Israel: like father (and mother), like son. Two years of tying people up and winding God up.   —Rob

2 Kings / Carry on Monarchy Continued

"Disk full!" The writer inserts a new disk and presses "OK" to continue.   —Rob

Who you gonna call? (2 Kings 1:1-18)

Ahab's son, King Ahaziah, has just fallen off the balcony of his palace. He's stuck in bed worrying about Moab's troop mobilization against Israel. Does he go to God? No. He sends his errand boys to get Baal's take on the situation. Elijah intercepts them with God's message that Ahaziah's not going to recover from his fall. Ahaziah wants words with Elijah and eventually Elijah gets the green light from God and he tells him, "Is there no God in Israel? Is that why you send errand boys to Baal?" Sure enough, Ahaziah snuffs it.   —Rob

New courier, new king (2 Kings 2:1-7:2)

Elisha completes his apprenticeship; so God takes Elijah to heaven in a chariot of fire with a whirlwind providing the uplift. Elisha literally picks up his old mentor's mantle (old German word for "coat"). Elisha purifies a poisonous well with a handful of salt, and it's obvious that God's new courier is even more imposing than the last one. A mob of teenagers find out first-hand. Elisha's on his way to Bethel and they start having a go at him: "Get out of here, baldy!" Elisha mutters something and two bears leap out of the forest and maul forty-two of them. Don't mess with this guy!

King Joram pulls things round a bit in Israel (the northern Jewish kingdom). He smashes up Ahab's stone statue of Baal, but still leads the people off line in plenty of other ways. He puts his army on alert and teams up with Jehoshaphat, king of Judah (the southern Jewish kingdom) and Edom against Moab's muscle flexing. Elisha prophesies they'll win, giving them some tactics direct from God, involving ditches, water and a fluky sunrise reflection effect that makes the fields look as if they're soaked in blood. The Moabite army fill in the spaces and race back home, freaked.

Elisha's reputation as God's courier is rocketing. He brings one guy back from the dead, neutralizes a poisoned stew with flour and feeds a hundred people with twenty rolls of bread! He also heals Naaman, a foreign army commander, who's got a severe skin condition. Elisha gets him to wash in the Jordan River seven times. The officer is won round to God being God and offers Elisha a huge reward. Elisha won't take it. But Elisha's assistant Gehazi fancies some of the readies and goes after Naaman saying Elisha's changed his mind. He gets the goodies, but when Elisha rumbles him, the guy comes out in the same sores Naaman had. Fair cop!

Elisha's hotline to God proves handy in Israel's war with Syria. But Syria regroups and lays siege to Samaria, the capital. The people are starving. Grotesque situation of eating all sorts of disgusting stuff, *including their own kids.* King Joram catches on this is God's punishment and so he's keen to separate Elisha's head from his shoulders. Elisha tells the king's runner that the siege and the starvation will be done and dusted by the next day. The king's right-hand man is sceptical and Elisha tells him he'll see it but won't get to eat any of the new grub coming in.   —Rob

Spread it around (2 Kings 7:3-9)

3-4

Four guys with contagious skin conditions, locked out of the city on health grounds. They're arguing, "So we just sit here till we die, do we? We break into the city – there's no food, we die! We stay here – no food, we die! But who says we go out to the Syrian army and surrender? If it works, we live; if not, we die anyway! What d'you say?" They say, "Yes."

5-7

Late evening, they walk out to the army and find the whole camp deserted. Not a soldier in sight. (Backtrack a bit.) God had created sound effects of a whole army of chariots and horses. The Syrians were convinced the Jews had hired a whole army of mercenaries from Egypt to take them out; so they panicked and legged it, leaving horses and donkeys tied to the tents.

8

The four guys are delirious. They get stuck into the food and the wine. They loot the best gold, silver and clothes, burying them to collect later. Then they come back and lift some more stuff.

9

Then they catch themselves: "Hold up. This is bad. We've got good news here — major league, and we're keeping it a best-kept secret. If we've not spread it by morning, something dodgy'll happen to us. Let's go. The palace *has* to know."

> When the king hears, he suspects the Syrians have laid an ambush, but his scouts come back with evidence of Syrian armour just strewn along the roadside — the whole scene screams "panic"! King Joram realizes Elisha's prophecy was spot on — the siege is over.
>
> —Rob

Fast-forward – naff kings (2 Kings 8:16–17:5)

Quick jaunt down to Judah: Jehoshaphat dies and his son Jehoram takes over. Married to one of Ahab's daughters, he's a naff king. God fumes but, out of loyalty to David, bites his lip for the eight-year reign. The son, Ahaziah, is just as bad as his dad.

Back up in Israel, Elisha picks up on God's brief to his former mentor Elijah and headhunts Jehu as future king. God's so furious with the late King Ahab and his sons (not to mention the old witch Jezebel) he gets Jehu to wipe out the whole family. The coup starts with the two sons, then moves on to Samaria where he persuades some palace eunuchs to throw Jezebel out the window. She hits the street and is trampled by horses. Ahab's family gone; next up Baal's couriers. Jehu's hot on the bloodshed stuff, but not so keen on keeping God's Contract. In his twenty-eight years as king of Israel he is as much use to God as Jeroboam — not a lot. His son Jehoahaz follows him and is just as bad. Same story with Jehoash — sixteen years of Israel being led into more and more mess. Jeroboam II also distracts the people from their God. Around this time God's courier Jonah gets the brief to go the capital city of Assyria, Nineveh. He's got to tell them to wise up and turn to God, or else! (Long story — see www.couriershotline.com.ot/courieron-adetour.) Jonah eventually delivers the message and they get their act together. God doesn't need to implement the "or else" bit.

Meantime in Judah, Athaliah's seven dire years are followed by forty years under King Joash, who first sits on the throne as a boy of seven. He starts repairing God's HQ but doesn't trash the hill shrines to foreign "gods". After Joash comes

Amaziah, who does some good stuff, but doesn't go all the way – the hill shrines still lure people away from God. Azariah's next in line – similar mixed results. While Jehoash is king of Israel, Elisha takes ill and dies. God soon starts sending messages through a new courier, Amos (go to www.couriershotline.com.ot/god hatesyourreligion). The next bunch of kings – Zechariah, Shallum, Menahem, Pekahiah and Pekah – all ignore Amos's warnings direct from God. Soon after, God has Hosea tell Israel that being their God is like marrying a prostitute (go to www.couriershotline.com.ot/yourwifesatart). God gives them options: "Turn things round and I'll do you good; otherwise . . ." Again they blank him out, carrying on with their filthy paganism.

Down south, more mixed obituaries: King Jotham gets a mixed review, but King Ahaz tilts things back in Baal's direction by sacrificing his own son in a pagan ritual. Isaiah warns them that God's planning their impending deportation. He also prophesies that someone – with an incredible list of names (www.couriers hotline.com.ot/nopainnogain) – is going to liberate them from the captivity of a major world power. Meanwhile the courier Micah is also sounding downbeat about prospects for Judah (www.couriershotline.com.ot/justicesdownside). He lays into the politicians, bureaucrats and courier wannabes for leading the people up a blind alley. Ahaz hands the crown down to Hezekiah.

But God's patience with Israel finally runs out. Since Solomon there's been 200 years of kings screwing up the people and entangling them with foreign "gods". Hoshea has the dubious honour of being the last king of Israel. Shalmaneser, king of Assyria, sweeps in from the north-east and sets up siege around Samaria . . .

–Rob

Last straws (2 Kings 17:6-19)

6

Year nine of Hoshea's rule: the king of Assyria takes Samaria and deports its residents to Assyria. He allocates them to the cities of Halah and Habor.

7-13

Why'd this happen? The Israelis messed up! They systematically broke the Contract agreed with God: same God who dragged them moaning and mumbling away from the tyranny of Egypt's pharaoh and into liberty land. No sooner do they get their own place, and they're sucking up to foreign "gods"; you can't tell them apart from the pagans round them with the rituals their kings introduce. Behind closed doors they get up to some vile stuff, which God clearly labelled "wrong". In public places, from isolated outposts to crowded cities, they build hill shrines to foreign "gods" and break Rule No. 1 every time they go through the rituals – pushing and taunting God to the point of no return. God told them "You won't . . .' ten times, but they do – a million times. God sends couriers with the command "Do a three-point turn away from the evil that's sucking you in. Check out the Contract again and keep to it – it's your heritage. Your national heroes set it up on your national holidays."

14-15

But they have a severe case of selective deafness. Like it's a long-running family tradition, they're stubborn and pig headed, sticking their heels in and flatly refusing to take God at his word. They make snide remarks about the Maker's Instruction Manual passed down from their predecessors – not that they've read them. They block out the warnings that come attached. They take on the values of the "gods" they waste their time on. They cheapen themselves. God told them, "Don't be like them," but they set up "Best Pagan Impression" nights; for-eigners enter, but rarely get through the first round, the Jewish com-petition's so stiff.

16-17

They break the Contract and get creative with things to bow down to: cows, poles, stars, whatever – as long as it's not God. They sacrifice their *own children* in pagan rituals, contact demons, cast spells, sell out to evil! God has to watch this filth and somehow channel his anger.

18-19

God evicts them because they're into evil. Only the Judah tribe are still around, and they're pushing it!

> God did as the couriers warned he would – he evicted them . . . to Assyria. Assyria's king relocated loads of Babylonians into the recently vacated property of Samaria. 'Course they have no concept of what God requires, so they are stalked (and some killed) by lions with a hotline to God's anger. The king of Assyria catches on and sends an Israeli God-rep back to teach them how to live in this God's land. They give it lip service, singing the hymns and sitting through the sermons, but they've still got their religious baggage with them and can't handle Rule No. 1 of Moses' Manual.   –Rob

At last!! (2 Kings 18:1-20:20)

You sitting down? King Hezekiah not only does good stuff; he undoes the bad stuff, bulldozing the hill shrines, taking God at his word, keeping to Moses' Contract with God. And God works things out for him. Six years into his twenty-nine Judah gets the sober-up call as the northern Jews from Israel are packed off to Assyria for their punishment. A while later the new king of Assyria, Sennacherib, is also after some action. His army pulls up outside Jerusalem and threatens King Hezekiah with their usual flexible terms, "Surrender or die!" Hezekiah goes into HQ for a long session with God. The new courier, Isaiah, gets the news hot from heaven that Sennacherib's insults of God aren't going to work. Sure enough, Sennacherib gets a visit from an angel with attitude, loses almost two hundred thousand men, and limps back to Nineveh. God says, "That's for David."

Hezekiah falls critically ill but God has Isaiah literally stop the sun in its tracks to prove to the king that he's going to survive. He does. He gets a second inning of fifteen extra years. God says again, "For David." Later, Isaiah talks of bad news for Hezekiah's descendants — they'll get carted off even farther than Israel: to Babylon.

–Rob

Didn't last long (2 Kings 21:1-26)

After Hezekiah, we're back to the norm — two naff kings: Manasseh for fifty-five years, and then Amon for two. Manasseh models himself on Ahab and actually rebuilds the hill shrines his dad wrecked! He drags Judah into worse stuff than the pagan countries around them. His son Amon is a chip off the old block. Even his own officials hate him and assassinate him in his own palace. Another courier, Zephaniah, chips in with a really heavy message — more doom and gloom for Judah (and other countries) 'cos they won't turn round from the mess they're entangled in (go to www.couriershotline.com.ot/judgementdayandbeyond).

–Rob

Change? (2 Kings 22:1-23:30)

Amon's eight-year-old son, Josiah, swings his short legs from his dad's throne. He's a breath of fresh air. When he's twenty-six he starts repairing the HQ, and the repairers find a dusty old Moses Instruction Manual. When he hears it read he realizes Judah's in big trouble: they've been slack on all this stuff and he knows God's frustrated with them. Huldah, a woman courier, tells Hezekiah that God is going to discipline Judah, but that as Josiah's listened to God, he'll be gone by the time it kicks in. Not interested in any "I'm all right, Jack" attitude, Josiah reads the whole Manual out loud to a huge crowd. He renews the Contract between the people and God. The people go with it. He implements the policies by grinding the altar at Bethel into dust, tearing down the digs of the HQ prostitutes and ripping into the shrines of the sun "gods". Totally ruthless.   —Rob

Wot, no Jerusalem? (2 Kings 23:31-25:30)

But Josiah's the exception. His son Jehoahaz's evil; his grandson Jehoiakim's evil; his great-grandson Jehoiachin's evil; his great-great grandson Zedekiah's evil. The twenty-odd years they run things, King Nebuchadnezzar's flexing his pecs, and future prospects for Judah are looking decidedly Babylonian. The couriers Habakkuk and Jeremiah keep the warnings coming (same website: www.courier shotline.com.ot/sortitoutgod and /warningswithtears). But no one's listening. Jerusalem gets taken out.

Three stages: First, the Babylonians take off the cream of the bunch — Judah's noble and educated (including Daniel) are "found jobs" in Babylon. Then, nine years into Zedekiah's reign, Nebuchadnezzar sets up a siege around the city of Jerusalem. The Jews hold out for three years, but eventually crack, their army legs it and the Babylonian army moves in to export their new slave labour back to Babylon. The last thing King Zedekiah sees, before his eyes are gouged out by a Babylonian blade, is his two sons being killed. He's handcuffed and taken off with his people to Babylon, head down, for more reasons than he can remember.

The people of Judah are now refugees. Third stage of the rout, the Babylonians loot and then torch every building. They tear down the HQ, the palace, the city walls — the city of David is unrecognizable, trashed! Many senior figures, such as the courier Zephaniah, are executed on the spot. Other rebels hibernate and work as an underground resistance movement to the Babylonian occupation. Eventually they assassinate the ruler Gedaliah Ahikamson. Thirty-seven years later Babylon gets a new king — Evil-Merodach (unfortunate name!) — who gives amnesty to Judah's imprisoned king, Jehoiachin. Maybe there is hope! The last line of the file shows God still has prospects for David's family line.   —Rob

1 Chronicles /
Events, Part 1

Press "Pause". Rewind right back to day one. Different guy telling the Jew-story, wider-angle lens. With the benefit of hindsight he scans through their history, covering similar stuff as Carry on Monarchy, plus some "exclusives" worked in.
—Rob

"ID, please" (1 Chronicles 1:1-9:44)

Family tree of the national heroes: kicking off with Adam; moving through to Noah; then to Abraham, Isaac, Jacob/Israel, Joseph and his brother Judah. From Judah through to Caleb; down a bit further to Boaz; then to Jesse, to David and to Solomon. Back up again and we race through from Benjamin to Saul — first king of Israel. More genealogies of kings and royal lines (when kings have no throne to park themselves on). Family trees of the twelve tribes of Israel. Loads of lists: surnames are important these days.
—Rob

David (1 Chronicles 10:1-22:16)

After Saul's suicide, David takes over as main man and takes Jerusalem as his capital. He builds up a loyal army and his palace is full of victory parties. He brings God's sacred chest to a plush tent in Jerusalem with ideas flying round his head for a rocking central HQ. But God says his hands are too bloody and that his son will do the building honours. God promises David's family line will always have a king in it! David's incredibly grateful.

God works things for David, who throws more victory parties. It goes to his head: he thinks it's his numbers, his muscle, his strategy, his equipment that's pulling it all off. God sets him straight – David cuts himself a large slice of humble pie and still has the crumbs around his mouth when he buys a plot of land to make sacrifices to God. God turns up and David announces this is the site where the HQ should be built. Just 'cos David's not got God's planning permission doesn't mean he can't get the materials sorted. He collects safes full of gold, vaults full of silver and bronze, builders' merchant quantities of iron, wood and stone.

But Solomon knows that he'll be the one actually to build the HQ once he's king, which isn't far off.

–Rob

"Over to you, son!" (1 Chronicles 22:17-19)

David calls in all the movers and shakers of Israel and gives them the royal directive to cooperate with his son, Solomon. He says, "Is God on your side or what? Has he, or has he not given you peace on every border? He's handed the locals over to me and God's country is being run God's way. Now, your bit: keep your loyalty to God up at 100 percent. Work at it, keep communication lines open, stay online to heaven and bring in the builders. Get the HQ started – God's sacred chest and the priceless stuff inside needs a decent home!"

They sort the reps, the staff, the singers, the admin people, the finance people, the managers. David hands over the plans God's given him for the structure and the décor. He covers the cost of materials and organizes a collection from the people to sort the labour costs. People are elbowing into positions to hand in their family jewels – they're well up for it.

Solomon's given the crown. He's God's choice and the polls show he's in landslide territory with the people. After forty years as king, David dies at a good old age.

–Rob

2 Chronicles / Events, Part 2

"Disk full! Please insert new disk to continue writing." The writer starts his second scroll. —Rob

God views his HQ (2 Chronicles 1:1–6:13)

Solomon asks God for the mental software to run the country wisely. God's happy to oblige, throwing in serious assets on top. He starts on the HQ: none of your cheap gold-leaf rubbish – the furnishings are *solid gold* and the place is incredible! When it's all ready, they bring in God's sacred chest. Big Day! The symbol of God being around finally gets a permanent home. Then a wall-to-wall cloud fills the place – they know God's in the house. Nobody can do anything. God's just too awesome, too stunning, too staggering, too breathtaking, too mind-blowing, too overwhelming, too massive, too . . . too . . . just too . . . too much!

Once God turns the dials down, Solomon pulls the chord to open the place and dedicates it to God. —Rob

"I declare God's HQ . . . OPEN!" (2 Chronicles 6:14–21)

14–15

Solomon says, "Israel's God: you're it, the only God! No other god's worth squat. Heaven or earth – no contest. You keep your side of the Love Contract with us. You've kept your side of your Contract with my dad, David; you said it – you've done it. Today!"

16-17

"Now, God, please keep your side of the Contract you made with my dad, David, when you swore, 'There'll always be one of your family on the throne, provided you do things my way, like he did.' Do it, God, please."

18-21

"But whoa! Hold on! Is God really going to hang out with us rabble? How come? The cosmos can't squeeze you in. How's it work with you living in this HQ I've built? But I'm begging you, please: don't drift off on us; don't turn your back, please; listen to me; listen to us as we come crawling for acquittal from the mess we're entangled in. Please straighten us out and sort us."

After all the official stuff...   —Rob

"If you talk, I'll listen" (2 Chronicles 7:12-22)

12

God turns up in the middle of the night and says to Solomon, "I heard what you said. The HQ's great; it'll do nicely."

13-16

"Say I put the clouds on a 'non-drop' policy; say I send a swarm of locusts and they binge on your crops; say I send some epidemic. This is how it works: if my people, who use my name on their letterheads, if they'll stop being cocky, approach me with respect, hunt me down if I'm making myself scarce, if they'll do a permanent U-turn from their mess — then I'll be all ears. I'll acquit them, liberate them. I'll repair the damage to the land too. I'll keep both eyes open, both ears on alert for what you ask for in this new HQ. It's my pad, my home — it's special. I'm not going to take my eyes off it for a moment."

17-18

"Your dad, David, obeyed my orders; you must too. Run things in line with the Maker's Instructions. I'll protect your crown, right down the generations, longer than you can get your head round."

19-22

"But! If you go jaywalking away from me, following someone else's directions or some self-drawn map, if you let my Instruction Manual get dusty on the shelf, if you go off and flirt with other 'gods', give *them* your attention instead of *me,* then I'll pull you up by the roots; I'll kick you out of the land I allocated you; I'll walk out of my HQ and not turn round. I'll drop jokes into the minds of the locals and they'll bust a gut laughing at the place. Yeah, it's all very impressive now. But people will stand by the ruins and shudder, 'Why's God sent the bulldozers in? Why's he ruined such an awesome HQ?' The guy next to them'll say, ''Cos they walked out on their God, that's why! They were virtually on personal terms with the God who liberated them from Pharaoh's clutches and then they start bowing and scraping to other fourth-rate gods — now it's a junkyard!'"

Solomon takes good notes. His wealth and wisdom become legendary. Visits and presents from world leaders including the Queen of Sheba. He writes loads (go to www.peoples-poetry.com.ot/wiseup/whatsthepoint and /youaregorgeous). And he dies an old man.   —Rob

Jaywalking away (2 Chronicles 10:1-20:19)

After Solomon's gone, 300 years of different kings with different ideas on how important God's ideas are on running things. (See www.new-nation.com.ot/carryonmonarchycontinued.) It's obviously too simple for people to work out: breaking the Contract = disaster; turning round and doing what God says = good news. Quick-fire obituaries of king after king prove it time and again.

One exception: King Jehoshaphat is facing the army of Moab, Ammon and the Meunites. He has a serious chat with God and begs for protection. The courier Jahaziel gives him the battle plans. Bit weird, but he gives it a go . . .   —Rob

"Sing it like it is" (2 Chronicles 20:20-24)

20-21

First thing, they leave for the Tekoa desert. Jehoshaphat booms out, "Listen guys, whether you're from Judah or Jerusalem — listen up! Take God at his word and we'll get the protection we need. Give respect to his couriers and we'll do great." He holds a series of meetings with people and then appoints a choir. They're to sing up-beat songs with lyrics on God's qualities, like purity. And they're to sing them on the front line. He tells them, "Thank God! His love keeps pouring out. It just keeps on coming: perpetual motion."

22-23

They're still on the first verse when God triggers off a series of ambushes in the enemy ranks: the troops from Ammon and Moab wipe out the Meunites! Once they've massacred them, they turn and destroy each other! Total confusion. Total home win for Judah.

24

They get to the ridge and look down into the huge desert expecting to see the reflection of enemy weapons. But whoa! The place is covered with corpses. Number of escapees: zero!

> They spend three days loading up all the goodies left behind and go back to Jerusalem on a high. Party time for Judah. Big-gulp time for their enemies. Judah's God is not to be messed with. Nobody goes looking for a scrap with Judah. After twenty-five years in charge, Jehoshaphat renews trading relations with Israel's dodgy king, Ahaziah. They sign a joint contract for the construction of a fleet of cargo ships, but the courier Eliezer doesn't like the alliance and announces God's verdict – "they won't float". Sure enough, they never do.   —Rob

Couriers vs kings (2 Chronicles 21:1-36:10)

But kings like Jehoshaphat are in the minority. The kings who take God seriously are portrayed as prototypes of the Liberator to come. The kings who go it alone set up the need to be liberated. Jerusalem has a close shave with King Sennacherib of Assyria besieging the city, but Isaiah and a heavy-duty angel send him flying back to Nineveh seething. Josiah virtually trips over the old Maker's Instruction Manual and brings people back round to their God-stuff heritage. The courier Ezekiel gets the rumours confirmed straight from God that Jerusalem's countdown clock has been started. But the kings who listen to God and his couriers are rare exceptions in a depressing list. The last king of Judah's obituary is typical.   —Rob

Jerusalem ruined (2 Chronicles 36:11-20)

11-14

Zedekiah's twenty-one years old when he takes the throne of Judah. He lasts eleven years. He lays out loads of evil for God to wince at and shows God's courier Jeremiah zero respect, even though Jeremiah's God-hearing is spot on – virtually digital quality contact. King Neb-uchadnezzar makes him swear an oath in God's name – not such a big deal to Zedekiah – but he double-crosses the Babylonian king. Zedekiah has a "heart transplant", exchanging emotions for a small, rough rock. He sticks his heels in so he can't turn back to God, and it's contagious: the leaders and the people break God's Contract in increasingly inventive ways; they get into the disgusting lifestyles that the locals have paraded; they bring it all into God's HQ and pollute the pure aroma of God with their filth.

15-19

The God who'd accompanied their forefathers sends them messages through his couriers 'cos he pities them and doesn't want his HQ wasted. But they recite their best courier gags, carry on as if God hasn't even spoken. They make a mockery of the couriers till God's so furious, there's no way back. He manoeuvres Nebuchadnezzar into place and hands them over to him. The Babylonian king is Mr Ruthless: he kills young men in sacred places. He's not fussy: men/women, young/old – all killed. The treasures of the king (and his yes-men), the treasures of the HQ, all packed off to Babylon. Then the palaces and the HQ are torched – nothing worth anything is left.

20

Anyone who's escaped death gets dragged off to Babylon as slave labour for the royal family till Persia take over as biggest noise on the planet.

(Back to where we pressed "Pause". Different place, slight change of angle, same ending. Jerusalem gets trashed.) Jeremiah writes a lament that'd move the hardest man to tears. He captures the grief of a people at the sight of their sacred city flattened (go to www.couriershotline.com.ot/atozofgrief). While they're slaves in

Babylon he comes out with loads more incredible stuff on God's discipline and that God's sticking to his side of the deal – so they've still got prospects.

Ezekiel's up to strange antics, trying to get the message through that God's not turning a blind eye just 'cos they're David's relatives. He gives them their only short-term option: "Sort things out with God while you're away." They go retro and check out the old writings of Isaiah – the bit about God sending a Liberator and doing his people good again (go to www.couriershotline.com.ot/nopainnogain). They start to realize, maybe the Contract and the couriers are more important for their links with God than whether or not they've got a king.

We also get the account of Daniel and Co. in Babylon and loads of picture messages from God about the long-term future (go to www.couriershotline.com.ot/godsrunningtheshow). During Daniel's lifetime the world powers shift and Cyrus's Persian Empire takes over from the Babylonians as top dogs.)   –Rob

Fallow land and building plans
(2 Chronicles 36:21-23)

21

The fields of Judah take their rest days. It's desolate. Nobody farms anything. It's rest time till the seventy-year sentence God announced through Jeremiah is worked off, long day by long day.

22-23

Like Jeremiah promised, God works on the new king of Persia, Cyrus, and he distributes the press release: "God, heaven's God, has made me the world superpower, and he's also earmarked me to build a new HQ for him in Judah. Any Jews reading this and up for construction work back home – ring the palace info line. God be with the workers!"

Ezra / We Can Rebuild It

Ezra starts where "Events, Part 2" left off. Cyrus's full announcement was recorded as . . . —Rob

HQ mark two (Ezra 1:2-4)

King Cyrus says, "God in heaven has made me the new world superpower and has handed me all the nations on earth on a plate. He's also appointed me to construct a new HQ for him. It'll be in Jerusalem, Judah. If any of his people want to go back and join the workers – fine. Your God go with you. Go back to Jerusalem in Judah and build the HQ. Your neighbours are to donate some heavy-duty leaving presents – gold, silver, equipment and whatever else they want to throw in on top for the construction work."

> Prince Sheshbazzar of Judah leads around 50,000 of the tribes of Judah and Benjamin plus God's reps back to Jerusalem, loaded up with 5,400 items of gold and silver. Morale: great. Priorities: sorted. First job – build the altar. Second job – use it. *Then* start on the HQ building, with Zerubbabel Shealtielson as foreman. –Rob

Rock the foundations! (Ezra 3:10-13)

10-11

The builders lay the last bit of the HQ foundations and God's reps throw a party! They're dressed in their full regalia, blasting away on their trumpets and thrashing the life out of their cymbals – all strictly in line with the order of service King David set out. They give the credit totally to God and it's obvious they're genuinely grateful as they sing, "He's good. He loves us through the long haul." The crowds holler and whoop up to God – HQ foundation's in place!!

12-13

Most of the older reps and heads of family start weeping – they saw HQ version one. Now a new one's under construction. The others connect with it by shouting and laughing simultaneously. The noises crash around and you can't tell the difference between the weeping and the shouting. They're making such a racket, everyone knows something incredible's going on – from miles off.

Which brings the hassle-merchants out of the woodwork. They chip away at morale, set the workers on edge, hire professional demotivators to make sure whatever *can* go wrong *does* go wrong. Change of king in Persia: Cyrus replaced by Artaxerxes. They lobby Artaxerxes, basically threatening to stop paying their taxes if the building carries on. He stops the building work – by force. It's a building site for about ten years.

Another new king, Darius.

Second wind (Ezra 5:1-5)

1-4

God's couriers Haggai and Zechariah pass messages with God's name on to the Jews in Judah and Jerusalem. Zerubbabel Shealtielson and Jeshua Jozadakson restart the "build-God's-HQ-in-Jerusalem" programme.

They get more opposition from local jobsworth bureaucrats.

5

But God keeps his eye on the Jewish leaders' project – they don't stop working till crucial correspondence to King Darius gets through and gets a response.

> They ask Darius to check back through the records to Cyrus's reign. Basically, are the Jewish leaders speaking the truth? Did he or did he not give them planning permission? Darius's civil servants dig out the relevant document and the king writes back, "Yes, he sure did." Darius writes . . .   —Rob

Backing from the top (Ezra 6:6-12)

6-7

"So, Governor Tattenai (Trans-Euphrates Region) and Shethar-Bozenai and all your cronies, stay off the patch. Don't stick your noses into the building of God's HQ. Let the Jewish governor and leaders rebuild God's home on its proper site."

8-10

"Plus, here's what you're to do for the Jewish leaders in the construction work: to make sure work isn't slowed up for lack of funds, put these guys on the royal payroll, from the Trans-Euphrates Region budget; whatever they need for sacrifices to God in heaven – young bulls, rams, male lambs, whatever – they get daily deliveries without fail. I want them in God's good books so they'll put in good words for me and my sons."

11-12

"If anyone tampers with this announcement, tear a beam from his house and impale him on it. Then trash his house. God picked out Jerusalem as a prime meeting point in earth-heaven relations, and I hope he does serious damage to any king or nation who overturns this announcement. No one messes with God's HQ in Jerusalem. That's my decision – do it, to the letter."

So the HQ has its grand re-opening day. Major party. Around sixty years later Ezra comes back from Babylon. –Rob

Refugees? No, citizens (Ezra 7:6)

Ezra Seraiahson, a scholar specializing in Moses' Instruction Manual got straight from God, arrives from Babylon. The king OK's Ezra's rider list and God's working things for him.

Ezra arrives in Jerusalem with around 5,000 Jews. He's got a letter giving the king's backing and stacks of gold and silverware to prove it. He arrives to hear from the God-reps in Jerusalem that the returned Jews are *again* polluted by local customs! He thrashes it out with God at the building site. –Rob

Not again, surely?! (Ezra 9:6-10:3)

6-7

"Oh God, I don't know where to put myself. Sooo embarrassed!! I can't even look in your direction. Our mess piles up over our heads and chokes me. Our guilt wafts up to heaven and stinks the place out. From our ancestors' time till now, our reputation has been pitiful. We've broken the Contract, deliberately, systematically, repeatedly. Our people, our kings, our God-reps – ripped into by enemy weapons, survivors, humiliated then as now, marched off into foreign countries under the whim of ruthless dictators."

8-9

"Then you give us a break – you do what we don't deserve; you leave us some survivors and give us a firm footing on the ladder back up to self-respect; you give us the chance to live safe, sorted and sound in this special place. You've given us back our freedom, a sparkle in our eyes. We were slaves, but you didn't leave us to rot in our chains: you worked on the kings of Persia and have given us a new lease of life to work on your HQ, to repair its ruined shell – you've even made sure we can work in safety."

10-12

"But now, God, what can we say after this? We've done it again – we've broken the Contract your couriers gave us! It clearly says, 'The country you're being allocated is full of corrupt people. They've filled the place with the disgusting pollution of their evil rituals. So back off! You're absolutely banned from marrying them. Don't become partners with them in any context, so that you can live long and prosper in the land. So you can leave it in your wills to your children as a flourishing, vibrant inheritance.'"

13-15

"All the stuff that's come flying at us – we've soaked up the punishment 'cos we knew we had it coming. But, God, you've not slapped us down like you could have: you've left us with survivors. So what? Are we now going to give your Contract the finger again and settle down with these people who carry out such filth – as our wives?! If we do, you'll be so angry you'll destroy us, totally. It really *will* be genocide this time. God, you're totally in the right. We're only here 'cos you left us some survivors. We're here, totally ashamed, not even risking to stand up in front of you."

10:1-3

Ezra's thrashing it out with God, admitting it all, crying bitterly, throwing himself around in front of the foundations. While he's doing this, a crowd builds up – men, women, kids – and they start crying too. Shecaniah Jehielson (Elam's descendant) says to Ezra, "You're right. We *have* broken the Contract by marrying local women but it's not too late! Let's make a contract with God to divorce these women, to send them off with their children."

> Ezra gets up and makes the leaders of Israel swear under oath that they agree to do this. Three days later all the returning refugees and those who'd been back awhile meet up in Jerusalem. It's tipping down with rain, but they sit there shivering in front of God's HQ.   —Rob

Stop merging in (Ezra 10:10-12)

Then Ezra, God's rep, gets up and says to them all, "You've broken the Contract! You've married foreign women and piled more and more shame on to Israel. Admit it! Admit it in front of God and do what he says: divorce yourselves from the locals and their women."

Then the huge crowd answers as one man, "You're spot on! You've said it – we'll do it!"

> Ezra lists those guilty of intermarrying. The courier Malachi also spots that their priorities need disentangling. (See www.couriershotline.com.ot/halveyour doublestandards.)   —Rob

Nehemiah /
Another Brick in the Wall

Nehemiah is the king's butler. His job's more than just looking good: he has to taste the king's food and wine (could be worse!) ... in case it's poisoned (ah!), which takes some commitment! Some reckon he's a eunuch (castrated so as not to mess about with the king's harem), which also loses him major spiritual points with his fellow Jews.

—Rob

What d'you mean, "It's just bricks"?
(Nehemiah 1:1-11)

1-2

The story of Nehemiah Hacaliahson, in his own words:

It's round late November, year twenty of King Artaxerxes of Persia. I'm in his fortress city of Susa and one of my brothers, Hanani, gets back from Judah with a whole crowd. I'm quizzing them about the Jewish survivors (some in Mesopotamia, others in Jerusalem), but what's really bugging me is how Jerusalem's looking.

3

They tell me, "The survivors are back but having a rough time of it. It's almost embarrassing to be a Jew: the place is a tip. To call them 'defensive walls' is really stretching it – 'wild-look rock garden' is closer. The gates are still as we remember them, burnt down."

4-7

I hear all this and I'm sitting there weeping, for days. It's like a bereavement. I can't eat; all I can do is beg God, something like, "God in heaven, you're totally awesome. You keep the Contract with those who love you and do what you say. Please listen up. Please focus on me. I'm begging you, 24/7, for the Jews of Israel. I'll hold my hands up: we've screwed up big time, me, my family, the whole nation. We've been evil, and you've felt it. We've ripped up the Contract Moses gave us and we've chucked it up in your face."

8-9

"D'you remember the bit where you told Moses, 'If you go off with other gods, I'll scatter you around foreign nations you can't even pronounce. You'll have nowhere to call home. But if you come round and come back to me and start living by the Maker's Instructions, then you could be almost off the map, you could be in "here be dragons" territory, but I'll bring you together and I'll bring you back to the place I've picked to be my earth HQ.' That bit? Remember?"

10-11

"Well, they're your people! You've bought them back from temporary owners with incredible stories of irresistible power. They're yours! God, I'm begging you: listen up. I'm yours. You say, 'Jump!' and I'll say, 'Where?' in midair. I buzz when I connect with how awesome you are. You have my total respect. Please work things for me as I bring the king his wine, 'cos I'm going to ask him this favour."

When you've got to go ...
(Nehemiah 2:1-20)

1-2

Four months later, around March, I'm bringing the king his wine and I can't help it – a bit unprofessional – but I'm down and it's showing through my normal butler poker face. The king asks me, "What's up? You're not ill, but you look like someone just broke your heart." I'm physically shaking with fear.

3

I manage to put a sentence together: "King, live forever! I'm down because the city where my ancestors are buried looks like a bomb's hit it. The gates are melted, stuck and rusting away."

4-5

Then the king says, "What d'you want *me* to do about it?"

I shoot a quickie up to God, and say to the king, "If it fits with your plans, and if it's not too much trouble, and if I've been an OK member of staff . . . uh . . . I'd like you to send me back to my home so I can rebuild the city."

6

The king's sitting there, with the queen right next to him, and he asks me, "How long's the trip? When d'you expect to be back?"

7-9

I was on a roll, so I pushed it a bit further, "If it fits with your plans, and it's not too much trouble, I'd really appreciate having a travel-pass letter for the governors of Trans-Euphrates, so they'll let me travel through without any border hassles. And, could I possibly have a letter for Asaph, head warden of the king's forests, so he'll let me have the timber I'll need for beams for the gates of God's HQ and for the city wall and for the house I'll live in? Please?"

'Cos God was working things out for me, the king says yes to the whole list! So I go to the governors of Trans-Euphrates and let them read the king's letter. The king also comes up with a convoy of army officers and cavalry, to travel with me.

10

Sanballat from Horon and Tobiah from Ammon – both officials – were well put out at the news that some guy was arriving with plans to do good to the Jews.

11-12

I go to Jerusalem. After about three days, I gather a small posse and we wait till it's dark before we go out. I'd kept mum about the ideas God'd downloaded into my heart for Jerusalem. I was on a donkey; the rest were on foot.

13-16

With night as our camouflage, we skulked around. Through the Valley Gate, round to the Jackal Well and the Dung Gate. We check out the walls of Jerusalem – rubble. We check out the Gates – burnt and melted. I'm heading for the King's Pool, via the Fountain Gate, but there's too much rubble for my donkey to get through, so I go up the valley, still checking the walls. Eventually, I turn back and come through the Valley Gate. The officials haven't spotted me; they have no idea what I'm doing or what I'm planning – I'd said nothing to anyone.

17-18

I say to the guys with me, "You see the mess we've got ourselves into? Jerusalem is more like a stone quarry than a city. Its gates are fried. Come on! Let's rebuild the walls. Let's get some pride back!" I tell them how God's been working things for me and the stuff the king has said. They're well up for it: "When do we start?!" And they launch into it with everything.

19

'Course, Sanballat from Horon and Tobiah from Ammon, plus Geshem the Arab get to hear along the grapevine and they start ripping into us with their sarcastic guff, giving it, "What you doing? You're not rebelling against the king, are you?"

20

I just tell them straight, "God in heaven will make it successful. We're his workers: we'll do the work. You guys have nothing to do with this place. You've no history here."

> Different groups get allocated different bits to break sweat on. They get more mocking from the Sanballat and Tobiah double act. Nehemiah delegates it to God to sort out and commandeers half the workers as armed guards. The labourers have bricks in one hand and a knife in the other. They work every hour that isn't pitch-black darkness. They take fifty-two days to complete the walls. Their neighbours realize God's on the job and lose sleep. But S and T's intimidation keeps coming. Nehemiah finds a record of the kids of those who came back from eviction first and calls them together.   —Rob

Listen up! (Nehemiah 8:1-3)

1

The square in front of the Water Gate is jam packed with people. Ezra, God's rep, is told to bring out Moses' Instruction Manual that God laid down for the Jews.

2-3

It's mid-September and Ezra's standing there reading the Rules to everyone with the brain capacity to take it in. He's going from sunrise to midday, reading the Rules out, live and loud so the whole square can hear. No one's nodding off. The atmosphere's electric.

> This carries on for a week. Reading from the Rule Book and partying – big time. Ezra runs a review of their history – depressing stuff; things sober down. It's pretty clear that they've messed up (to the power of a thousand) and God's been incredible (to the power of ten thousand).
> —Rob

"We're not worthy!" (Nehemiah 9:5-38)

5-6

God, it's your reputation that gets the boost. You're the one who gets the credit: it's your fame that should balloon from this. You're the only God. You made the cosmos, the furthest nether-regions of the solar system, the stars in their trillions, the earth and all its microcosmic detail, the seas teeming with weird and wonderful life forms. You're the ultimate source of life. The powers of the cosmos bow low before you in respect.

7-8

God, you headhunt Abram. You direct him out of Ur in Chaldea. You change his name to Abraham. You prove his heart to be true to you and make a contract with him to give his descendants the land deeds to the area where the Canaanites, Hittites, Amorites, Perizzites, Jebusites and Girgashites are. You keep your side of the deal – 'cos you do the right thing.

9-12

You clock the agony of our ancestors in Egypt. You don't block out their desperation as they scream up at you by the Red Sea. You launch the most spectacular miracle-show against Pharaoh, his cronies and his people – you're up to speed with how cocky they are in their Jewish policy. You pick up an awesome reputation, and it's not faded even now. You split the sea in half in front of your people. They walk through on dry ground, but the chasing Egyptians don't, 'cos you sweep them away a split second later – as much chance as a frog in a whirlpool! Daytime, you direct the Israelis by a huge pillar of cloud; night-time, a pillar of fire does the job.

13-15

You put in a personal appearance at Sinai Mountain and speak direct. You give them your Maker's Instructions – rules for lifestyle that ring true, sound right, make sense. You kick off your Rest Day ruling. You give them the whole caboodle through your main man Moses. When they're chomping hungry, you give them bread, delivered direct from heaven's bakeries. When they're spitting feathers, you produce spring water from a rock. You give them clear instructions: "Go in and take up your allocation of land," the land you promised them.

16-18

But wait for it – our forefathers get cocky, they indulge their stubborn streak and they stomp on your Contract with its Rules for lifestyle choices. They put their hands over their ears and even manage to forget the spectacular miracle-show you put on around them. They turn their backs on you and stick their heels in, appointing some guy as the new number one to take them back into slave labour. But you've got a long fuse, God. You know how to hold in your anger with dignity. You love us with a passion that bubbles up and gushes over everything. So you don't leave them in the desert with no map and no supplies – even when they spend days creating a gold monstrosity to bow down to, even when they start spouting, "This is the god that did the business and brought us out of Egypt." How come they insult you like that?

19-21

You love them too passionately to leave them stranded in the desert. You keep the pillar of cloud well supplied in the day and the pillar of fire well stoked at night. You put your own Holy Spirit on the job as Guide. You don't cut back on the heavenly bread supplies; you don't ration the water. For forty years you keep them going in the desert. Do they need anything? Nothing. Their clothes don't wear or tear or rot. Their feet don't flare up with swellings or blisters or boils.

22-25

You hand over whole kingdoms to them. They're given control over the most remote border points. They walk into the territory of Sihon, king of Heshbon, and of Og, king of Bashan. You make their child-count more like a star-count. You escort them into the land you told their fathers to take. Their children walk in like they own the place. You tame the locals. Their kings and people are like putty in their hands. They virtually waltz into fortified cities; they take over the farming rights of fertile fields; they move into houses with ready-made luxury facilities: wells, vineyards, olive groves and orchards. They fill their faces and get nicely rounded in the belly areas – they lap up your benefits package.

26-27

But they don't keep the Contract: they turn their backs on you; they do away with your couriers who have the guts to go against the grain and try to drag people back to you; they insult you, big time. So you take the reigns off their enemies' necks and let them apply the tricks they'd learned at Oppression School. 'Course as soon as the good times stop and the oppression starts affecting their standard of living, they start crying out for you to rescue them. You choose to tune in from heaven and, 'cos of your passionate love for them, you commission liberators who break the ties they've been stitched up with.

28-31

You give it to them in straight, easy-to-understand warnings, words of one syllable – get back to the Rules! But they start strutting around again and flout your instructions. They stomp on your Instruction Manual, which is designed to bring life when read and applied. Like stroppy kids, they give you the cold shoulder. They get all sulky and just won't listen to a word you say. Year after year after year you stick it out, patiently waiting for them to wake up and listen to the Holy Spirit of God coming through your couriers. And did they? Did they heck! They stonewall you completely, so you hand them over to the local thugs again. But you go easy on them, you don't let them get wiped out completely 'cos you're over the top in your tolerance, God.

32-35

So, God, with all this history flying round our brains, with vivid images of a God who does the spectacular without breaking sweat, with sobering memories of how you keep your love Contract with us, God, don't minimize our struggles, the hassles we've all wrestled with from the king of Assyria's time till now. The struggle's affected everyone: our kings, our leaders, our God-reps, our couriers, our ancestors and all our people. Everything we've had crash down on us we don't deny – it's just payback time. We've earned every bit of hassle we've had. You've been well within your rights and kept your side of the deal. They chucked out the Contract, ignored the Maker's warnings. Even when they're in the land, enjoying the good times, piling on the second helpings, opening the next bottle of wine – even then they don't work with you or walk away from their evil.

36-37

Which is why we're in this mess! Slave labour again, but this time in the land you allocated to our ancestors, the land with the high-life on tap. We've messed up and the good stuff gets siphoned off for the foreign kings to pig out on. They run us and our equipment as they like. We're beside ourselves with anxiety.

38

So, our action plan is this: we're making a binding agreement. We're putting it in writing. Our leaders and our God-reps are giving it their formal approval.

> They make their agreement to keep to the Contract from now on. They dedicate the new walls with more loud partying, singing, bands, two huge gospel choirs shaking their stuff and moving in opposite directions along the tops of the walls. Some sound! Nehemiah returns to the city of Susa and the winter palace of King Artaxerxes of Persia – his butlering skills not at all rusty after the twelve-year gap.
>
> – Rob

Esther / Total Holocaust of the Jews?

Talking of Susa, rewind back to before Nehemiah's King Artaxerxes to his predecessor King Xerxes — powerful guy, top banana from India through to Ethiopia. Three years in, he throws a seven-day banquet. A week-long binge and he thinks he'll show off his beautiful queen, Vashti, to the guys. He calls her in, but she refuses to come! Panic among the nobility — women having a mind of their own?! Serious threat to the status quo! They get him to issue an irrevocable decree to keep women in their place — i.e. wherever their men want them to be! He does; it's duplicated, translated and mailed out across the 127 provinces. Then they start the search for a new queen to replace Vashti.   —Rob

Babewatch (Esther 2:5-11)

5-7

In the fortress city of Susa there's a Jew from Benjamin's tribe called Mordecai Jairson (granddad, Shimei; great-granddad, Kish). Mordecai's one of those carted off with King Jehoiachin of Judah by Nebuchadnezzar, king of Babylon, when he blew the Jerusalem defences away and strolled in. Mordecai's got a cousin called Hadassah, aka Esther. She's an orphan and he's brought her up like a daughter. The girl's an absolute stonker, a babe among babes!

8-9

When the king's edict to find the new queen gets round, loads of girls are sent off to Susa, and Esther's one of them. They all have to answer to a guy called Hegai, who runs the harem. But Esther catches his eye, and he makes sure she gets the pick of beauty treatments and the best food. He allocates seven of the king's maids to her and gives her top place in the harem.

10-11

But Esther doesn't give any clues away as to her Jewish blood – Mordecai warned her not to. He does his daily stroll to the courtyard to check she's doing OK.

> Cut to the chase.   –Rob

A Jewish queen of Persia! (Esther 2:17-18)

The king is infatuated with Esther more than the other girls – she's top of his list by a long way. So he makes her queen instead of Vashti. He throws a huge banquet, with her name at the head of the invites in large flowing letters. Everyone who's anyone is there. He announces a national holiday across his empire and hands out presents like there's no tomorrow.

> Mordecai's still keeping his eye on Esther, making sure she doesn't let on about her history. He overhears a plot to kill King Xerxes and tells Esther to tell the king. She does and credits Mordecai with the detective work. The would-be assassins are caught and hanged. Later an Amalakite guy called Haman Hammedathason is promoted to second in charge next to the king. Trouble is, the Amalakites are long-term sworn enemies of the Jews, and Mordecai can't just kneel and bow to the guy like you were expected to.   –Rob

Sign here for genocide (Esther 3:5-11)

5-6

Haman spots that Mordecai's the only guy standing upright as he struts past. He's Mr Angry. He does his homework on Mordecai's nationality and decides it's not enough to snuff the one guy out. No, he gropes around for a way of getting all the Jews wiped out – across the whole empire.

7-9

Year twelve of King Xerxes' reign, around mid-March. Haman and crowd are throwing dice to set the best time for their plans – it lands on 13 February. So Haman goes to Xerxes, "There's a group of people spread right through the empire who have weird customs that stop them from keeping within the king's legal system. It's going to damage the king's position to let them get away with this. If you like, let's pass a ruling to wipe them out. Tell you what, I'll personally add over 300 tons of silver to the royal coffers to cover the extra work hours it'll take."

10-11

The king gives the anti-Semitic Haman his signet ring. "Keep the money," he says, "and do what you like with these . . . uh . . . Jews? Right, Jews."

So the royal secretaries set the law and send it through the whole empire: "Annihilate all Jews, men, women and children. Date of execution: 13 February."

Mordecai hears and in desperation tells Esther to beg the king to save the nation. Problem is, no one, but absolutely no one, gets to go to the king unless he invites them. Anyone flouting this rule dies, unless the king's in a good mood and sticks out his royal sceptre and spares the idiot. Second problem is, it's already a month since Esther's seen the king. She figures she's going to die anyway, once they rumble her nationality; so she bites the bullet and goes for it.   —Rob

Esther risks it (Esther 5:1-3)

Three days later Esther's psyched herself up and she's in her best queen costume and standing in the inner court of the palace, just outside the throne room. The king, on his throne, is facing the inner court. He looks up and sees her standing there. He smiles and holds out his royal sceptre. She moves up to him and touches the tip of the sceptre. The king's intrigued. "What's happening, Esther? What d'you want? Up to half the empire — yours for the asking!"

But she doesn't let on straight off. She invites the king and Haman to a banquet she's prepared. They get there and the king repeats his up-to-half-the-empire offer. Again, she keeps him in suspense, says, "Come to another banquet tomorrow, both of you, and I'll tell you."

Haman's enjoying this special treatment — just him and the king! He loves it. It's only spoilt by the sight of Mordecai — still not in kneeling mood. So before the next night's banquet, Haman has a gallows built — over 20 metres tall — with Mordecai's neck in mind. The thought of the old Jew swinging in the wind cheers him up no end.   —Rob

Set up for life (Esther 6:1-10)

1-2

That night the king's got insomnia and has the history books read to him. They're reading away and they get to the bit where a guy called Mordecai alerts the king to an assassination attempt and saves the king's neck.

3

"Has this Mordecai had any sort of bonus for this?" asks the king, sitting up.

"Nope, nothing!" they tell him.

4-5

"Who's outside?" asks the king.

Haman has just arrived to talk to the king about his gallows for Mordecai. The king's servants say, "Haman's standing in the court."

"Bring him in," commands the king.

6-9

Haman strides in and the king hits him with the question: "What sort of honour should the king give to someone he wants to thank?"

Haman's thinking, *Who could the king want to honour more than me?* So he answers, "The man the king wants to honour should be dressed in a royal robe worn by none other than the king himself, sat on a horse the king has ridden, with a royal crest on his head. Then the robe and horse should be handed over to one of the most dignified princes who would lead the man the king wants to honour through the streets of the city with shouts going out for everyone to hear, 'This is the man the king wants to honour!'"

10

"Go," says the king to Haman. "Get the robe and the horse and do all this for Mordecai the Jew. He's at the king's gate right now. Don't skimp on any of the details you laid out."

Furious, Haman does the job and has to lead Mordecai through the streets, shouting out, "This is the man the king wants to honour!" Just as he realizes his plans against Mordecai can't possibly work, he's whisked off to Esther's banquet, where she's about to come back on the king's offer. —Rob

Who needs half an empire? (Esther 7:3-10)

3-4

Queen Esther answers the king's question, "If I've brought you any pleasure, please give me the one thing I ask for – that you don't kill my people. Please don't kill my people. We've been set up for annihilation. If we'd been sold off into slavery, I wouldn't have risked being so cheeky: I'd have kept quiet and wouldn't have disturbed the king for that. But total annihilation!"

5-6

King Xerxes asks her, "Who's set you up for total annihilation? Who'd dare kill my queen?"

"Sitting right next to you, sir!" she answers. "This excuse for a man, Haman, is the guilty one." Haman is dribbling uncontrollably.

7-10

The king gets up furious and strides out into the palace garden. Haman knows the king's already decided his fate, stays back and begs the queen on his knees for his life. The king comes back in and sees him lying across the couch where Esther is and roars, "Now he's trying to rape my queen in my own palace!!!"

Before the words finish echoing round the room, the servants cover Haman's head with a bag. Harbona, one of the servants, yells, "There's a huge gallows erected outside Haman's own house. He's planned it for Mordecai who's loyal to the king."

"Hang him on his own gallows!" barks the king. They do and the king calms down . . . eventually.

Queen Esther gets to own Haman's whole estate. Mordecai, instead of Haman, gets to be the king's number two and is given the royal signet ring. King Xerxes allows a new edict overruling the previous one and grants the Jews the right to defend themselves. The letter, which kicks in on 13 February, is dispatched first class around the whole empire. The next two days are party time – same time every year the Jews celebrate their national survival.

In the whole book God doesn't even get a mention – not by name. But the sheer number of "coincidences" make it obvious that he's around, working things behind the scenes, protecting his people and David's family line through which the Liberator is lined up to come.

After the refugees come back to Jerusalem, there's around 400 years of silence from God – no couriers. The Greek Empire takes over from Persia as top world power, followed by the domination of Europe and the Middle East (including the land of Israel) by the Romans – the Liberator arrives in occupied territory.   – Rob

The Wisdom Books
www.peoples-poetry.com.ot

Job / Mess Happens

Possibly some of the oldest poems known. The poetry of Job and "mates" come out of the following story.   —Rob

Job the patient (Job 1:1–2:13)

1–3

Scene: northwest Saudi Arabia way back when it was called Uz. Central character: Job, a spiritual, moral, good-living guy who gives God the respect he deserves and does all he can to avoid evil. He's got seven sons and three daughters and is rolling in it: 7,000 sheep, 3,000 camels, 1,000 oxen, 500 donkeys, a huge payroll of staff. With all these major assets, his accountants tell him he's the wealthiest man in the East.

4–5

The kids are party animals, taking it in turns to outdo the previous do. Each time after the big clear-up, Job lobbies God for each of them, offering up ceremonial sacrifices to God, thinking, *Partying's fine, but maybe, just maybe, at the height of frenzy one of them thought, or said, or did something to cuss God out. Who knows?* So Job lobbies God regularly for them.

6–7

Cross-fade into new scene: heaven. Central character: God. The angels turn up for inspection and Satan's there with them. God turns to Satan and asks where he's been.

"Oh, strutting round the planet; bit of this and that," Satan sneers.

8

"What d'you make of my man Job?" asks God. "He's out on his own: spiritual, moral, good living, giving me total respect and slapping down anything evil that tries to trip him up."

9-11

"Yeah," concedes Satan, "but he knows which side his bread's buttered. He's not about to bite the hand that feeds him, that houses him, that does just about everything for him 'cept blow his nose for him! He's spoilt rotten. You've seen to it, and he knows it. The acid test is – what's he like if you take all the stuff away? What if you slap the guy down? He'd soon change his tune. He'd be the first to cuss you out."

12

God answers, "OK, you're on! You control the board on everything he has, but you don't lay a finger on him. Understand?" Satan leaves, grinning.

13-15

Back in Uz. Job's house. An exhausted worker runs in and tells Job, "The Sabeans attacked, massacred your staff, made off with all the oxen and donkeys. I'm the only one who got away to tell you."

16

Before he's finished, another worker runs in and pants, "Lightning struck the sheep and the rest of the duty team – they're fried to the bone. I'm the only one who got away to . . ."

17

A third guy runs in: "The Bedouins attacked in three groups, killed all the workers, rounded up the camels and made off with them all. I'm the only one who . . ."

18-19

Another guy: "Your children were partying over at the eldest's place, when this whirlwind blew in from the desert, flattened the house. They're all dead! I'm the only one who got away to tell you."

20-21

Job stands up. His heart's ripped to pieces, so he does what any dad of the day would do — rips his coat, so it looks like his heart feels: torn to shreds. His life's been stripped from him; so he shaves his hair to prove it. He falls flat on his face in front of God and whispers, "I was born with nothing; I'll die with nothing. God gives; God takes back. God is God and God is good, always."

22

In all this carnage Job doesn't go against God or bad-mouth him for what had happened — not once.

2:1-2

Back in heaven: same scenario — the angels on inspection and Satan waltzes in. "Where've you been?" asks God.

"Oh, strutting round the planet; bit of this and that," Satan answers with attitude.

3

"So what do you make of my man Job, then?" asks God. "Still spiritual, moral, good living. Still giving me total respect. Still steering clear of evil. He passed the acid test and his integrity's intact, even though, for no good reason, you were bent on winding me up to destroy him."

4-5

"Yeah, but he's not actually felt anything himself, has he?" Satan hisses. "Hit him with something really nasty, something that hurts him physically, and he'll spend his last breath cussing you out."

6

"You think so?" says God. "He's yours. Do what you want; only, I draw the line at murder."

7-9

Satan leaves and hits Job with festering sores. His skin's covered in them, from his scalp to the soles of his feet. He's in agony, toe-curling, gut-wrenching, fist-clenching, lip-biting agony. He's smashing the nearest pot and scraping his skin with the sharp side to try to relieve the pain for a split second. His wife comes in and says, "You still holding on to all that God stuff? Cuss God out, then die!"

10

"You're talking like an idiot, woman," Job screams. "What? Do we only take the good stuff God offers? We just fair-weather fans? Or do we stick it out when results don't go our way?" In all the mess, Job doesn't say one thing God wouldn't be proud of him for.

11-13

The second Job's mates hear the news, they call a meeting and agree to visit. When Eliphaz, Bildad and Zophar arrive, they hardly recognize him. They've got the best intentions, great ideas on what to do, but it all goes out the window when they see the state of him – all they can do is cry like babies. For seven days no one offers any clever ideas or wise words – they're so stunned by his pain, all they do is cry.

> Then the poetry starts to come . . . —Rob

Why wasn't I stillborn? (Job 3:1-13)

1-3

Eventually, Job curses the day he was born. He says, "Someone go back and delete the day the midwife shouted, 'It's a boy!'"

> And it all pours out, an open sewer of regret. —Rob

11-13

"Why didn't I die at birth? Why wasn't I stillborn? Why did my mother survive to breastfeed me? Why didn't I die? Then I'd be oblivious and blissfully unaware. I'd be blank. I'd be a million miles from all this agony."

> Several death wishes later, Eliphaz starts saying that God's putting Job straight, sorting him out, and that everything'll be all right in the end. Really helpful stuff – not! —Rob

Heavy stuff (Job 6:1-3)

Job answers Eliphaz back, "Go get the bathroom scales; weigh all this grief. Or stick me on a weighbridge – I must weigh at least a ton with all this agony on board. I'm so dragged down, so done for. Heavier than all the sand on the ocean floor . . ."

And more grief. This time it's Godward . . .   –Rob

Why me? (Job 7:17-21)

"How come you're so focused on people? Haven't you got better things to do? I, for one, need a break! Just ten minutes free of this torture – is that too much to ask from you? OK, maybe I messed up, but was it really so bad that you staple me on to your target and pummel bullets into my soul? Am I really that much of a pain, that you need to do this? Can't you cut me some slack? Don't I get some sort of break? 'Cos I'm on my way out – I'll be dead before you know it. You'll send search parties out, but they'll blow it. I'll be gone. Then who'll you pick on?"

Bildad chips in with more encouraging stuff like, "Your kids had it coming to them", and "If you're innocent, then God'll step in . . . if"! Thanks, Bildad!   –Rob

No one argues God down (Job 9:1-3)

Job comes back at Bildad, "All I know is that no one's innocent in front of God, no one. Even if I want to have it out with God, I wouldn't win one in a thousand arguments . . . Not one. His wisdom's profound. His power – all round. You don't take him on and win."

Other lines like "His fury folds mountains", "His word pulls the plug on the sun", "His miracle checklist fills hard drive after hard drive" and "He would wipe me out like a hurricane".   –Rob

Get me a lawyer (Job 9:32-35)

"He's not like some bloke you can shout down. You can't take him to court and twist a jury against him. This is God we're talking about! What I need is someone to negotiate, someone to broker some sort of peace deal. I can't talk to him direct; I'm way too petrified. If I had a diplomat I'd chosen, he'd talk for me, 'cos on my own I'm fear-frozen."

What've I done? (Job 10:1-3)

Then Job thinks, *Oh stuff it! I hate myself, everything about me. Why not? Can't lose much more,* and calls out skyward, "God! Don't demolish me like this. What've I done, huh? You enjoying this? D'you get some sort of sick kick out of blasting me out like this? And how come you kiss the corrupter's cause? How come you open their doors?"

The "how comes" keep coming: "How come you design me, then malign me? How come you shape me, then rape me? How come I was clay and you sucked me dry to dust? How come you made me walk, then stalked me? How come you midwived me to mature, then manured me? How come I wish I'd never come? How come I long for the deep shadow and disorder where even the light is dark? How come?"

Then Zophar sticks his oar in and goes on about not talking back at God. He tells Job to try harder and it'll all work out wonderfully! Job gets sarcastic... —Rob

I'm not worthy! (Job 12:1-3)

"Oh yes, you guys are the wise ones! You've cornered the market on 'smart'. You've bought up all the rights on the cleverest of ideas, and no one else has a clue, have they?!"

Then he goes for the throat... —Rob

Just shut it! (Job 13:2-5)

"All this guff coming out of your mouths – I know! Enough already! I know! Do I really look that stupid? All I'm after is to argue my case with God. All you guys do is diss me. You're quack doctors, the lot of you. As much help as a tanning bed in a desert. Just shut up, will you?! Give it a try – zip your lip and see if you don't sound cleverer than when you're spouting all your top tips..."

He begs them to listen to him: "What if God was pushing your limits? You'd crack under the pressure too!" —Rob

Talk back at God? (Job 13:13-15)

"Shut it. It's my turn to talk, if I dare. (I don't know, am I insane? Talking back to God? What if he kills me? Even if he kills me, he's still God and I'll still lean on him. What else have I got?) I've got to stand up for myself."

The argument hots up. Eliphaz hits back, swears they're right and Job's wrong. Job loses patience with them.   —Rob

Clichés (Job 16:1-7)

"So many clichés! You're sad; you really are sad. You drone on and on – if I wasn't in such agony you'd have sent me off to sleep ages ago! What's got into you? Why won't you drop it? Swap places: I could rabbit on, enjoying the sound of my own voice, laughing at my own jokes, milking the audience. But I'd not kick a man when he's down: I'd lift him up. I'd use words to lift him up or, at least, lift his head up. Not you guys! No, you stick the boot in! But what difference does it make if I mouth off or not? God, you've knackered me and my whole family and I'm done in."

> Poetic splurge with lines like: "God, you rip me up. You chew me through." "Men mouth off at me, loathe me, lynch me, pinch me. But has God turned me over to the mob, to rob?" "Am I suddenly target practice for his lightning bolts of hate? Am I his sparring partner who's past his sell-by date?" "The countdown to death is below ten. What then? Do I die? And if so, why, when?" "When did people start cursing, 'I've been Jobed!'?" "Will my desires go down to the place of the departed with me? Yes, but only to hunt me, haunt me."
>
> More bad advice from his "mates". More silence from God. More blind conviction from Job ...   —Rob

Somewhere over the rainbow (Job 19:25-27)

"I know, my Liberator's out there, somewhere. I know it. Some day he'll turn up. I don't know what state I'll be in by then, but I know I'll see God. I will; I know. Till then I'll lie low. But he'll show."

> He still wants to argue with God, but God's nowhere. So Job argues with Zophar who's spouting off about gangsters getting what's coming to them. Job can't see the gangsters getting anything but gout from their full-fat lifestyle. He says God's above our simple rules: some die happy; others die sour. God controls life's lottery balls. Eliphaz starts knocking on again about God punishing Job for living a mess. He lists the charges against him and rounds it off with an altar call, with "Just As I Am" playing cheesily in the background: "If you eat humble pie, God'll give you plenty more goodies to chomp and you'll skip and frolic through sunny days with high and happy-clappy hands and woodgy words of wonder."
> Job's not buying it ...   —Rob

Search party (Job 23:1-17)

1-2

Job says, "Right now I'm bitter, OK? I'm groaning but God's hand is still grinding me down."

3-5

"If only I had a map, saying, 'God is here,' and a big arrow pointing. If only I knew where he lived, I'd break in, I'd argue my case, reason with him ..."

8-10

"But if I go into the city, he's not there. If I go out to the suburbs, he's not there. Rumours of him out in the country, but I miss him. Up, down, over, across he's not for finding – I've looked and I don't need reminding. But he's satellite-tracking me, fast-tracking me through fire to be the golden boy we both desire."

11-17

"I've followed his feet. I've not sidestepped away. I've not gone against orders. Forget food: his words are all I need today. He's out on his own. Who stares him out? He does what he likes and likes what he does, which is pulverize me, which is frightening me, and yet nothing in me says, 'Be as quiet in remark as the night is still dark.'"

> Job knows that "ruthless moneyed men cause poverty, misery and death". He knows that "dark is the dung that grows dodgy deeds". But he also knows that "evil men are forgotten again; no one remembers when they were with us, as all their work withers".
>
> But Bildad rubs it in that people are like maggots compared to God's purity – filthy and puny. Job comes back with, "So are your actions to rescue the poor," and refocuses his lens on God's running of the cosmos and how this is just the edge of his power: "We just get a whisper, but it blows our eardrums away."   —Rob

Not guilty (Job 27:1-6)

Job goes public on where he stands: "As sure as God lives (even though he's denied me all my rights), and as long as I've got breath in my lungs, I'm not going to lose it and loose words without use. I won't suddenly spew words with no view. Bitterness won't get through. Nor am I going to admit to you that you're right – I'll die before I plead guilty. Watch me!"

A long poem about evil men mining for minerals but having no sense to "drill for Wisdom – the treasure of real depth". But God knows Wisdom. He knows where she is and what she looks like. One line goes, "Respect for me is the key to unlock the block that'll be hiding She." Job reminisces about "the good ol' days" when "a warm haze gave the world a soft-focus feel, when contentment was real". But now no one hears him out; the sons of low-calibre men just diss him down to nothing. And God gives him "a rodeo ride on the raw hide of hell". He's a dog being kicked when it's down. His skin is burnt and black and peeling. His guitar's superglued in a minor key. His harmonica wails like a wolf. But why? He's not "indulged his wandering eye even in summer months when girls go by". Why? He's not run a sweatshop, or been mean with his wealth, or picked on the poor, or flashed his Rolex too often, or opened the bubbly when his enemy crashed. So why? Why? He calls out for justice, and then says no more. Nothing. He just waits for God to say something.

Then, at just the wrong time, a younger guy, Elihu, starts up. Shows Job respect initially, but soon picks up the same tune as the others: "It's all your fault: you're getting what you deserve. It's your fault, and oh, you've got a nerve." He goes on and on till, eventually, God speaks directly to Job ...   –Rob

God's answer (Job 38:1-33)

1-5

Then God answers Job from the centre of a whirlwind, "Who d'you think you are? How come you talk so much when you know so little? Brace yourself; I've got some questions of my own. Where were you when I created all this? If you're so clever, tell me about it! Were you the guy who drew up all the plans, who totted up all the costings? Was it you, or someone else? Huh?"

6-7

"Tell me about the foundations. Who laid down the million tonnes of rock? It was you, wasn't it? Or was it someone else? Don't you remember when the stars formed a chorus and the angels screamed like popstar groupies?"

God goes on ...   –Rob

12

"Have you ever told the sun, 'OK, you can rise now'?"

    And on ...   –Rob

19

"Have you a map to get you to the place where light lives? And where does darkness hang out?"

    And on ...   –Rob

32–33

"Can you tell the stars where to go? Can you drag the Bear by its lead and tie it to the Plough? Do you know the rules that run all this?"

    And on, until ...   –Rob

Job's turn (Job 40:1–9)

1–2

God says to Job, "You asked me some tough questions. Well, what's your answer to my questions?"

3–5

Job answers, "I'm an idiot – how can I answer back to God? I'm nothing and I know nothing. I'll shut my stupid mouth."

6–9

God carries on from inside the whirlwind, "Brace yourself. I'll ask, and you answer – if you can. D'you really have the nerve to slag off my sense of justice? Could you arm-wrestle me and win? Could you beat me in a shouting match?"

    And more impossible questions, so many more unanswerable questions ... until he rounds off.   –Rob

How dare you? (Job 41:1, 26–27)

"You wouldn't dream of disturbing a crocodile, who treats clubs and swords like grass, who snaps iron like it's straw. So how come you dare talk back at me, the one who made the crocodile and all the other wild beasts on the planet?"

I take it all back (Job 42:1-6)

Job speaks, "I know you can do anything and everything you like, when you like, how you like. And when you do, nobody dares get in your way. You asked me, 'Who is this that questions me?' I had no idea what I was talking about – it was all way too big for me to get my head round. I can't believe I had the nerve to say to you, 'Listen to me when I'm talking. I ask the questions, and you give the answers.' I'd heard rumours of your reputation. Now I've seen you with my own eyes, and I'm dying of embarrassment at my attitude. I take it all back, every question, every accusation. Sorry. Won't happen again."

Then we find out how the story ends.   —Rob

End twist (Job 42:7-17)

7-9

Once God's sorted Job out, he moves on to Eliphaz: "I'm livid with you and your cronies; I'm suing for misrepresentation. If only you'd been more like my man Job. So I want a seven-bull, seven-ram ceremonial sacrifice off you. Take it to Job: he'll represent you in my court and I'll agree to his request. I'll not deal with you as your stupidity deserves. Total misrepresentation! Not like my man Job." So Eliphaz, Bildad and Zophar do as they're told, and God listens to Job's defence argument.

10-11

Job finishes defending his mates, and God kicks off the new era. He makes Job twice as prosperous as before. His brothers and sisters and all who'd made themselves scarce come back and party with him. They sympathize with him for the whole episode. Each one donates a pile of cash and top-of-the-range jewellery.

12-15

God makes Job wealthy again, makes his previous stash seem like small change. Now he owns 14,000 sheep, 6,000 camels, 2,000 oxen, and 1,000 female donkeys – double what he had before! He also has seven more sons and three more daughters.

16-17

After all this, Job lives to 140, and sees his grandchildren have their children. In good time he dies, old and full of memories.

Psalms / Song Lyrics

An incredible anthology of 150 songs. A compilation of the songs a nation sings to connect with their God. List your top five singer/songwriters: if David Jesseson's not up there, your musical education's sadly lacking. We're talking depth, insight, connection and huge scope — from intimate one-on-one love songs to God, to storming stadium anthems; from vulnerable songs of failure to protest songs hitting out at corrupt corporate fat cats. The material's timeless: centuries later his songs still capture the mood of people from all cultures and musical tastes. He's the ultimate crossover artist, a prolific writer who becomes the grandfather of Jewish spirituals. These are just a few excerpts from the best of his greatest hits (with a few from Asaph, Korah's Boyz and Anon chucked in for fun).   —Rob

Who's laughing? (hip hop)
©Anon (Psalm 1:1-3)

1

(backing)   Who's laughing?
(lead)   The guy that don't take no tips from the godless,
            Who takes no trips on strip-poker picnics.
(backing)   Who's laughing?
(lead)   The guy that don't tune into Filth FM,
            And talks tough with the cynics and sceptics.

2-3

(verse)   He's laughing 'cos he knows the good book;
             God's website gets a good long look.
             He's growing 'cos he's the evergreen
             By the picture postcard mountain stream.
(chorus)   He may lean; oh yeah, he may lean,
             But the wind won't make him crack. (x 2)

Drowning man (rock anthem)
©David (Psalm 3:1-3)

David's kingdom's cracking up, and he's on the run from his own son – who wants
his throne.   –Rob

1-2

(verse)   Oh God, those with a down on me are building up;
             Those with an opinion on me are coming out,
             Saying, "God's not bailing him out this time, not this
                 time.
             No, this time he's going under: he's a drowning man!"
(verse)   Those with a thing against me are about to start:
             They watch the breakers for my waves to stop,
             Saying, "God's not bailing him out this time, not this
                 time.
             No, this time he's going under: he's a drowning man!"
(instrumental break)

3

(chorus)   But you, God, are my state-of-the-art amphibious
                 armoured car:
             From way out of reach you drive me back onto the beach;
             You parade my heart, straighten my back. Results.
                 Results.
             You lift my chin, put a groove back in my pulse. Results.
(coda)   You lift my chin, lift me from the hole I'm in; you lift
                 my chin,
             You make me sure one day we'll win; you lift my chin.
                 Results!

Kids sing you songs (garage)
©David (Psalm 8:1-4)

Imagine David staring into a starry sky: his mind starts to muse.   −Rob

1
(intro)   Oh God, you're ace and you blow me away;
             Your fame explodes, sets the tone on everything you say.
             Stars burst beyond scientists' prying eyes −
             So much we don't realize!

2
(chorus)   And you get kids to sing you songs:
             Unqualified praise from the amazed
             Blows the curse from your enemies' twisted lips,
             When the kids sing you songs! (x 2)

3-4
(bridge)   I peer up through the smog,
             Try to wrap my head round the size of it all:
(verse)   Just how big *are* you, God? How big are your hands?
             The moon, the stars, placed just the right place,
             The planets pushed just the right pace.
(chorus)
(verse)   Just how big *are* you, God? How big is your heart?
             How come you notice me, care for this lowlife,
             This lonely life, the other end of space?
(chorus)

How long? (blues/rock) ©David (Psalm 13:1-6)

David's ill − big time. Could die. He knows some would throw a party if he
does.   −Rob

1-2
(chorus)   How long, God? How long you gonna forget me?
             How long, God? How long since you last met me?
             How long this confused? How long to play mind games
                 and lose?

How long will my enemies sneer? How long with all this
fear?

3-4

(verse)   Look at me, God; look at the state of me, God.
Get some light in here or I fear I'm gonna die,
And that whole crowd can start their victory chant:
They'll gloat 'cos they kept saying, "I can't."

(chorus)

5-6

(bridge)   I'm depending on you, God, deep ending;
Diving into your river of love for me:
A river of love that knows no seasons,
A river of love, always full to catch a diving life.
I'll celebrate my escape into your white waters, God;
The record shows, you'll be with me for the ride.

(chorus x 4)

Ain't no one doing good (new-wave punk)
©David (Psalm 14:1-3)

It seems some "don't-need-God guy" has just got up David's nose...   —Rob

1

(intro)   Who says, "There ain't no God"? Johnny No-Brain!
Who says, "There ain't no God"? The dumb, the insane!
Who says, "There ain't no God"? The corrupt, the vile!
Who says, "There ain't no God"? Those keeping evil in
style!

(chorus)   Ain't no one doing good; no, no one doing good;
Not one, no! (x 2)

2-3

(verse)   Meanwhile God's looking over, looking down, looking
round
See if understanding can be found,
See if there are any looking up to catch his eye,
See if there are any asking, "Why?"

(chorus)
(verse)   But everybody's eyes are looking down, on the ground,
                See if there's any more suckers around,
                See if there's any girls looking up to catch his eye,
                See if there are any worth a try.

(chorus)

Cover me (rock love ballad) ©David (Psalm 16:1-2, 5-6)

David's got no time for anything except the real thing ...   —Rob

1
(chorus)   Cover me, when it all crashes in;
                Lover me, when my love life's thin.
                I run to you and, when I hit your heart,
                You guard me, guide me, hide me. (x 2)

2
(verse)   You're my best, my top, my number one;
                I'm just earth but I orbit round your sun.
                You're my first, my thirst, my once, my only:
                All I've got is from what you've done!
(chorus)
(verse)   All the buzz, the vibe, the good, the fine,
                The more, the most, the rest;
                All the rhythm, the tone, from you, all the time —
                All I've got from you is the best.
(chorus)

5-6
(coda)   You've dealt me a good hand;
                You've sat me in a good seat;
                You've put me in the right land;
                You've set me on the right street. (x 4)

Stars (hip hop) ©David (Psalm 19:1, 7-14)

Nature blows him away, Godward ...   —Rob

1
(chorus)   The stars, like satellites, send songs through space,
           Saying, "Hand-made by God!" (x 2)
           The skies carry radio waves, frequenting every frequency,
           Playing, "Hand-made by God!" (x 2)

7-8
(verse)   God's ways are perfection; the soul gets resurrection.
           God's rules are reliable; wise hearts become viable.
           God's drill salutes good things done; sad hearts march
               t'ward the sun.
           God's laws are so right, dull eyes become bright!

9-11
(verse)   Respect for God is purity, lasts through eternity.
           God's orders are secure, make the right thing sure.
           The price is more than gold; the taste, fresh honey sold.
           They keep the warning strong, their bonus lasts long.

12-13
(bridge)   Who knows who I've stepped on in my all-day rush-hour
               life?
           Acquit me, though I'm guilty.
           I know how I've stretched my stride and added to their
               strife.
           May their ghosts not torment me.
           If you acquit me, I'll quit: you'll see;
           Acquit me, and I'll be free.

14
(coda)   May the views in this Muse
           And my heart's response
           Bring a smile to your face, my God,
           My security, my sponsor. (x 4 to fade)

Stay (grunge) ©David (Psalm 22:1-11)

Utterly alone. Attacked by people he's done nothing against. Picked up on and
recited in agony by the Liberator at his execution . . .   —Rob

1-2
(intro)

God, my God, why d'you clear off like that?
Why d'you turn your army round and march 'em off like
    that?
You walked out of earshot of my groans, my agony.
Why d'you leave me? (x 2)
God, I scream like a madman all day long – no reaction.
Night-time: I'm still calling, crawling along – still no
    interaction.

3-5
(verse)

But you're the big noise, bigger than the big boys;
You're the one on the big throne,
Known by your people as the one who must be shown
To be better than the best, better than the rest.
They relied on you and you came up with the goods;
They cried to you and you sorted trees out from the
    woods.
They leant heavy on you and you always turned up . . .
    then.
Come again. (x 2)

6-8
(chorus)

But me? I'm a slug: don't qualify as humankind;
They step on me, poison me, put me through the grind.
The second I'm spotted, it's down to the ground,
'Cos they throw them hard, all those rumours they've
    found:
"He says he leans on God, so why's he crawling down the
    road?
If he's such mates with God, let *him* take off his load."

9-11
(coda)

You're my midwife: you delivered me to the world;
You put this instinct in me, as my mother fed me:
"Lean heavy, lean hard, lean long on God."
From the womb you've always been my God,
So don't go scarce on me; don't go away;
Don't go distant – demons here to keep at bay;

Stay. (x 4) There's no one else who can sort today:
Please stay, stay. (x 8 to fade)

You comfort me
(rock opera à la "Bohemian Rhapsody")
©David (Psalm 23:1–6)

1–3
(verse)   You're my guide and my guard, my minder,
                    my mentor.
                What more do I need? What's better at the centre?
                You sit me down, put my best CD on,
                And my soul remembers who I am again.

4
(chorus) (backing) You're with me; you comfort me. (x 2)
(lead)   And you hold my swaying heart – so soft, so strong.
(backing)   You're with me; you comfort me. (x 2)
(lead)   You stop them tearing me apart – I fear no wrong.
                You show me where to go, without telling me;
                You set a value on my life, without selling me.
(backing and lead) You're with me; you comfort me. (x 2)

3
(verse)   You call me to the streets; you show me such good
                    things,
                Right things with no hidden strings –
                Just your name on, and its game on.
                Your great repute, like a distant flute it comforts me.
(chorus)

4
(verse)   I crawl through the alley of the shadow of cancer;
                I know you know the answer, and the battle won't rattle me.
                You're around, and I've found there's something about
                    your empathy,
                Your symphony of sympathy, that comforts me.
(chorus)

5

(bridge)   You lay out a table; you sit me down;
            My rivals arrive from the greatest to the least,
            But my cup's kept full, and my head's held high
            As you boast about me, your least priest,
            And make them toast me right through the feast.
            Boy, does it comfort me!

(chorus)

6

(end song) I know that your good, your best, your love and passion
            Will stalk me, steer me, stand alongside me,
            Outlast every fad and fashion, through all eternity.
            For I'm going to live with you,
            See heaven's great views from my own cosmic mews;
            No lease to renew, no terms to review, no one else
                to view —
            Just me and you, me and you, me and you,
            Right through, to the end of time.

Satisfy (Motown) ©David (Psalm 24:1-6)

Used in public procession. Could've been when David brought the sacred chest up
to Jerusalem, or to celebrate it on some public holiday . . .   —Rob

1-2

(chant)   God owns the planet: the title deeds, the plants, the
                seeds;
            God owns the planet: the animals, the land, the seas;
            God owns the planet. (x 2)
            And everything in it.
            He laid the foundations of the oceans, the rivers running
                down;
            He owns the life, the love, you and me: God owns the
                planet. (x 2)

3-4

(verse)   Who gets to walk into God's personal space?
            Who gets to stand there in his white-hot holy place?

The clean-handed, the pure-hearted,
Who don't waste their soul on would-be, wannabe gods;
Who don't make flash promises, then ride roughshod
When something lengthens the odds.

5-6

(chorus)   Some people God'll make so content, he'll satisfy;
Some people will get his consent, he'll ratify:
Those who seek out God and it shows.
To those the God of Jacob knows, he goes,
"I'll make you so content, I'll satisfy;
I'll give you my consent, I'll ratify;
You seek me out, and it's clear, it shows,
You are those the God of Jacob knows."

Your way (up-beat indie)
©David (Psalm 25:1-7)

Under pressure: ruthless enemies champing at the bit to get at him, he turns to
the only safe place he knows...   —Rob

1-3

(verse)   To you, I'm giving my soul to you: I trust you with it,
        God.
        You won't let them put me down. Block off my enemies,
        God.
        No one who trusts in you gets the runaround;
        Those who lean on you don't fall flat on the ground;
        But the two-timers, the cheats, the promise erasers,
        They get put down, go flat on their faces!

4-5

(chorus)   I need a map and a torch if I'm gonna to go your way;
        I need good shoes and a guide, if I'm gonna go your way.
        Where else would I go? You're my God;
        I really want to go your way.
        Who else is worth relying on? You get the nod,
        'Cos I really want to go your way.

6

(verse)   Don't go low on the mercy front;
Don't run down the love supplies —
They're your trademark, what we recognize.
No, don't go low on the mercy front,

7

(bridge)   'Cos my track record from youth needs some editing out.
Wipe off the tapes, clear up my past, give my future a
   shout;
Remember me as a lover would; remember what I'm
   really about.
Remember me as a lover would; remember you're only
   good.

You turn the lights on (trance)
© David (Psalm 27:1)

David knows God's made a contract with him, and he's holding on to it in the face of more gangs after his blood . . .   —Rob

1

(chorus)   You turn the lights on, you liberate, you captivate, you
   fortify.
Don't know about anxiety, when you turn the lights on;
You fortify me. (x 2)
Don't know about anxiety.

(verse)   God's a streetlight in a dark alley on the wrong side of
   town.
He's my bodyguard — so who's about to mug me?
He's my protection — what's about to worry me?
Don't know about anxiety, since you've been around.

(chorus)

Elevate you (rock anthem)
©David (Psalm 30:1-5,11-12)

David writes a song for general release, probably to celebrate his recovery from a life-threatening illness . . .   —Rob

1-3

(intro)   All I want to do is look at you,
              Elevate you. (x 2)
              You lifted up my head: I was staring at graves;
              You saved me.
              You stopped the gloat in the throat of my enemies,
              You made their mockery cease; I begged for help:
              You healed me, arranged my early release;
              You gave me a hand up and out from the grave with my
                  name on,
              And now, it's game on.

4-5

(chorus)   So let it rip: sing it strong!
              Let his crew take the roof off with this celebration song;
              His fury don't last so long; his favour lasts a lifetime.
              We cry through the night, but the morning sun begins
                  its climb,
              And it's celebration time.

11-12

(verse)   You turned my tears to cheers,
              My moping through coping and on into dancing.
              You made me take off my funeral gear,
              And suddenly vibrant colours appear.
              My heart's gonna sing: it's not gonna stop.
              God, I'm going to thank you till I drop – you're top!
                  (x 4 to fade)

You got nothing on me (R&B)
©David (Psalm 32:1-5)

David wants God's HQ to get a glimpse of his stubbornness being melted by God's
patience, and his slate being wiped clean by God . . .   –Rob

1-2

(chorus)   Wanna be the guy whose mess is sorted out,
              Who'll die with no regrets,

Who's OK with his past, walks past everyone he knows, goes,
"You got nothing on me"? (x 2)
Wanna be the guy who sits down with God and knows,
"You sorted me"? (x 2)
The guy who's no fraud, whose tongue's no double-edged sword,
The guy who's free? Want him to be me.

3-4
(verse)   Before I came clean, my groans eroded my bones;
You held me back, dried me out, as I kept you at arm's length.
So low, so low: solo sailing saps your strength. Didn't feed me;
It blew me where my mess would lead me. Free me!
(instrumental break)

5
(verse)   Then I faced the music; then I took the rap,
Laid it all out, admitted it all, held my hands up, bared my back.
You know; you know, but you didn't put me away, didn't bleed me,
Didn't send me where my mess would lead me. You freed me!
(chorus)   Now I'm the guy . . . (etc.)

Rave on (hi-NRG dance track)
©David (Psalm 34:1-9)

David acted insane (at least in bad taste) in front of a foreign king. Bad times for David, well before he's king . . .   —Rob

1-3
(chorus)   Gonna go on about you, 24/7;
Applaud, go overboard, drown out heaven.
Gonna name-drop that I know you;
My soul's gonna show off about you,

So, come on (x 4), let's amplify, let's turn it right up!
Rave on! (x 4) Let's give it up for God; let's give it up.

4-7

(intro)   I sought you out: you were already calling, sorting my
           anxiety;
        Look him in the face – you'll glisten with God.
        You'll gleam, your face'll scream, "GOD!"

(bridge)   Joe next door cries out to God – gets his voice heard,
        Situation sorted, agony aborted;
        God's angel sets up base camp where "respect" is the
           word;
        Give God respect: you can fully expect safe
        passage to the top.

8-9

(verse)   Go on, taste how good God is, feel how strong;
        Look how stunning; smell how pure; listen to the
           overture
        And sing along, as he sets your senses soaring!
        So hide, deep down inside; confide in him –
        You'll always know what content meant;
        You give God respect,
        You'll miss out on nothing you need – we're talking
           contentment!

Trophies of the sly
(acoustic folk-protest song remix)
©David (Psalm 37:1-9)

David's eaten up by the big question: Who wins – the good guys or the bad guys?
        –Rob

1-2

(intro)   Don't lose sleep at them getting away with it;
        Don't go green at the trophies of the sly.
        They get mowed down like a field with grass in it;
        Plants come and go – they too are going to die.

3-4
(chorus)   Lean on God: do the right thing
And live safe, strong and long;
Let God be the one who excites you.
He says, list your deep longings,
'Cos soon they'll be your belongings.

5-6
(verse)   Commit 100 percent to him,
Rely on him – this is what he'll do:
He'll make right the stuff you do
Eclipse the morning sun from view;
He'll make the justice of your fight
Be warm as midday sunlight.

(chorus)

7
(verse)   Slow the pace: take some space with God;
Wait for him till you're sure he's shown;
Don't hassle when the wicked win;
Don't freak when the winners cheat. (last two lines x 2)

(chorus)

8-9
(bridge)   Channel the anger; tune the fury; don't panic – don't lose
the jury,
For the evil ones, they'll get mowed down;
When you're picking up the deeds, they won't be
around:
They went on ahead;
You waited for God, and God owns the ground.

(chorus)   'Cos you lean on God . . . (etc.)

Many will hear (rock ballad)
© David (Psalm 40:1-3)

David feels like he's sinking in quicksand . . .   –Rob

1-2a
(verse)   I waited, waited quiet, quite calm;
             He turned towards me, grabbed my arm,
             Pulled me up from the cesspool's hold,
             Away from the filth, the mud, the cold.

2b-3a
(verse)   He stood me firm on solid rock,
             A place no one dare knock.
             He taught me a brand-new song to sing,
             Spot on for the only true King.

3b
(chorus)   Many will hear; many will see and fear
             And rely on Awesome God making it here. (x 2)

Gagging (gangsta rap)
©Korah's Boyz (Psalm 42:1-5)

Send depression packing: talk yourself back into getting together with God and
his people . . .   —Rob

1-2
(chorus)   I'm desperate for you, gagging for you to be around;
             I'm lost without you, desperate to be found.
             I need you like the athlete needs air, like a twin needs its
                 pair;
             I need you like life needs to be "fair", like a mother has
                 to care.
             Vibrant God, got the cravings for you;
             I'd brave the worst to quench this thirst,
             But where do I go to get to know you?
             Where do we rendezvous?

3-4
(rap)   All I've eaten is tears; all I've seen is through smears,
             So blurred. Been up all night, my talk's so slurred;
             Then I heard these words: "Where's God? Where's he
                 gone?

Is he dead? What's wrong? Is it really so absurd?
Has it never occurred to you, it could be true: God's
    through?"
But memories freeze the lie right there,
Thoughts dredged up by my churning soul: I'm where?
At God's HQ, in a leading role,
How we'd sing full blast; how the bells would ring!
And now at last, the thoughts bring back such memories
That I'm down on my knees,
And my soul feels whole again. (x 2)

5

(verse)   So why so sullen, soul? Why so moody, me?
Why so down, so depressed, so incapable of breaking
    free?
Don't give up – let God lift your life up;
Stack that weight on God, all of it, complete;
See if he can't juggle it, smuggle it away at last,
And set you back on Celebration Street.

(chorus)
(verse)   So why so sullen, soul? Why so moody, me?
Why so down, so depressed, so incapable of breaking
    free?
Don't give up – let God lift your life up;
Pour all that pain on him and crawl back out alive;
See if he can't handle it, file it under "P" for "Past",
And set you back on Celebration Drive.

(chorus)

Connect (DJ over trance tracks)
©Korah's Boyz (Psalm 46:10)

Busy lives aren't just a twenty-first-century phenomenon . . .   –Rob

10

Shut up . . . Shut off . . . Shut out . . . and
In the silence . . . (x 3) sense God: connect!

He says, "For I'll be profiled and praised, the world will
    be amazed;
I'll be known and named, shown and famed.
My name will be large, lifted, enflamed!
So shut up . . . Shut off . . . Shut out . . . and
In the silence . . . connect!" (x 4 to fade)

Mercy me (alternative angst) ©David (Psalm 51:1-19)

God's courier Nathan's just got David to admit his guilt with the Bathsheba
fling . . .   —Rob

1-2
(chorus)   Mercy me; God, mercy me, in line with your limitless
                   love,
               In line with your passion for me, wipe out my mess;
               Wash off my filth; clean up my life. Mercy me; yeah,
                   mercy me.

3-4
(verse)   I know what I've done: I replay it time and again;
               It's you I've offended; it's them, but it's you all the same.
               I've done evil right in front of you;
               When you judge me you're right; when you sentence it's
                   true.

5-6
(verse)   Been a mess all my life, been an instinct since birth,
               But you demand integrity: you're into values and worth.
               Teach me to accept your correction;
               Your standards are total, your model perfection.

7-9
(verse)   Use those disinfecting leaves – and I'll get clean;
               Wash me whiter than a winter snow scene.
               I want to learn about laughter again:
               Block your eyes from my guilt; black out my blame.

10-13
(bridge)   But my heart needs a transplant –
            A fresh, clean heart, never used before today,
            A gleaming, pure heart and a boost of resolve to keep it
                that way.
            Don't banish me: I need to be right next to you;
            Don't punish me; don't take away your Spirit too!
            Give me back the buzz at being yours,
            Then I'll take them all around on tours;
            I'll say, "Stick everything else on pause;
            Put everything you've got behind this cause."

14-15
(verse)   Protect me from the guilt of murder, liberating God,
            And if you let my tongue go, my mouth won't stop:
            I'll sing to you at the top of my voice –
            With all you've done for me, is there any other choice?

16-17
(verse)   You're not into sacrifice: I'd give up everything I could,
            But it'd get up your nose, make you weep it would.
            The offering you want is me flat on my face,
            A smashed-up heart and a vulnerable soul: much more
                your taste.

18-19
(verse)   Do my people good, despite all I've done;
            Protect their protective walls from every enemy gun;
            Then we'll sacrifice to you and you'll love it;
            We'll give it up for you, the world – we'll rise above it.

Fat cats (metal)
©David (Psalm 58:1-11)

Justice is a God-thing. David wants it now!   –Rob

1-2
(intro)   Can you politicians talk true?
            Can you judges let the good come through?

Can you trust the bureaucrats, take cream from the fat cats?
No way: not today; not yesterday; not tomorrow!
Their hearts scheme with injustice, violence, sorrow.

3-5
(bridge)   Day one on, their first words – lies;
             Like snakes that won't be charmed,
             Stand back, get armed . . .

6-7
(verse)   Remove their teeth, God. Take the claws from their
                 cause:
             Reduce them to harmless ex-predators.
             Wipe them from the memories; make their weapons
                 freeze!

8-9
             Like the slugs they are, they leave behind such slime,
             Like a stillborn, dying before his time and buried in the
                 soil;
             They'll be swept off the face of the planet
             Before you and your anger boil.

10-11
(chorus)   Good people party when their prospects dive,
             Laugh at their desperate last propaganda drive.
             People will say, "It's worth it, keep your hands clean:
             God sorting out the bad guys ain't no dream."

Persuade them (industrial)
©David (Psalm 59:1-5)

Written when David was surrounded by Saul's cronies. Probably re-released when
Jerusalem was under siege . . .   –Rob

1-2
(chorus)   Whisk me out of the danger zone when the rioters arrive;
             Pull your minders around me when the damage
                 merchants show.

Keep me well away from evil-makers, dignity takers,
From those who only know how to get things to go
By making blood flow.

3-5
(verse)

They're lurking in doorways trying not to be seen:
The psychos plan their ruthless scheme
Of me paying over the odds – and why?
For nothing I've done, for nothing I've not;
Still they're going to take me for all I've got,
Unless you step out and stand in the lamplight;
Move into action-mode: wipe them from sight;
Persuade them in the language they best understand;
Convince them with the fist of your powerful hand!

(instrumental break)

No other time (Britpop)
©David (Psalm 62:1-8)

Could've been written when David's getting on a bit and Saul's family are planning a coup ...   –Rob

1-2
(chorus)

My soul's serene when I rest in your arms,
Like no other time. (x 2)
Peacetime arrives when I switch off my drives
And float in your ocean sublime.
You're where I run to when there's war at my door;
You're where I come to when I just need more –
My security force, my passport to peace.
How come so calm? You're why.

3-4
(verse)

How long will they assault me?
How long drag me down?
I'm a condemned house, a wasted wall;
How long till they make me fall?

(verse)

How long will lies take precedence?
How long for this grand old residence?

When will the bulldozers get their call?
How long till they make me fall?
(instrumental break)

5

(bridge)   What do I do? I wait for God.
My future's with him, that's all I know.
So stop your soul stress; calm your mind mess;
    wait for hope to grow.

6

(verse)   For so long he's been my foundation,
For so long my only salvation;
Reinforced steel that cannot be shaken,
Defences that'll never be taken.

7

(verse)   My liberty and dignity are totally up to him:
Not my own efforts, or Fate's daily whim;
He's my top-grade concrete, my underground den,
My basis for life again and again!
(chorus)

8

(coda)   I tell you: lean on him 24/7; rely on him this side of
    heaven;
Pour it all out and he'll take it all in.
Hide yourself in him!
(instrumental break)

Nearly lost it (hip hop)
©Asaph (Psalm 73:1-28)

Choir leader Asaph wrestles with the same question as David: Who wins – the good guys or the bad guys?
                                                                    –Rob

1

(intro)   God is good to his people: his whole-hearted get the
    best! (x 2)

2-3
(chorus)   Me? I'd nearly lost it, hanging off some ledge;
It was you, the cocky ones, who pushed me to the edge.
I was eyeing up your homes, your stuff; I was ogling your
   kit,
And it looked so good, so very good – I wanted a piece
   of it!

4-11
(rap)   You stroll through life with your health, your wealth,
Your gorgeous wife in tow: worry-free days,
And the stress don't show.
With your cheap parking permits in vandal-free bays,
Your peacock furs check nothing occurs
To threaten your privileged ways;
You keep violence near as your hard hearts hone
Each malicious idea. You sneer,
You slander, you mock, you meander,
Claiming front-row views from heaven's veranda,
While you make big deals on the earth;
So people don't see the size of your soul:
They see what you're worth and the cash signs roll,
Saying, "What does God know? These guys got it
   sussed –
How can God say what he thinks is a 'must'?"

(chorus)

12-13
(verse)   This is what they're like: the wicked suck you in;
They're calm and cool – their money says, "We win!"
So what's the point? Don't make no sense.
Why've I washed my hands in innocence?

14-17
(verse)   Every day's been a struggle; every morning's like a war;
I try to make some sense of it; it drags me down some
   more –

Till I step into your territory, and see things more
   clearly:
I see his heavenly view; I see their final destiny.

(chorus)

18-20
(verse)

I saw him make them slip; I saw him send them down;
All happened so quick, the time I saw them drown!
It's real world versus dream life and when reality wakes
   up too,
These people are like fantasies who try opposing you.

21-24
(verse)

I realized my jealousy was totally absurd,
My bitterness so stupid, I couldn't say a word;
For I'm always with him: he'll never lose his grip;
He'll advise me with his wisdom as we stand here hip
   to hip.

25-26
(verse)

I've got heaven coming, got relationship with him:
Nothing here on earth's worth a second view!
Me? Maybe I'm weak. Me? Maybe I'm dumb,
But he's my energy source, and he'll long outshine the
   sun.

27-28
(verse)

Those who wander off from him will soon run out of air:
He'll wipe out all who betray him, and they'll all know
   it's fair.
But me? It's so good to be close to the one who decides,
To be totally in with him on whom the future rides.

(verse)

So I've made him my safe place, my security, my den
And I'll be coming back to him again and again;
I'll be going public with everything he's done —
The people within earshot will know he's the only One!

Your place (R&B)
©Korah's Boyz (Psalm 84:1-4,12)

Something's stopping them getting to God's HQ, and it's driving them crazy...
—Rob

1-2
(chorus)
Your place is best, God;
I'm gasping for it, almost collapsing for it, God;
My skin, my soul, the whole of me screams
For more of you, vibrant one.

3-4
(bridge)
A thousand-day break, top luxury hotel –
I'd trade it in for one perfect day at yours;
A tax-fraud-millionaire lifestyle –
I'd trade it in for the lowest-paid job at yours.

(chorus)
(verse)
God's the sun, the shield that keeps us warm and whole:
Dignity beams out from him, benefits the soul;
He don't hold back on nothing good,
For those who walk with him as they should.

12
(coda)
Awesome God, we're well content
When we rely 100 percent on you.

(last two lines x 4 to fade)

We're God's (hip hop) ©David (Psalm 100:1-5)

David connects with his emotions and with his God...
—Rob

1-2
(verse)
Let it rip! Let it out! Shout!
Let the planet pulse with songs that elevate, celebrate
him:
Party songs, get-up-and-dance songs
'Bout the one who rights those wrongs!

3
(verse)   Let it rip! Let it out! Shout,
               "We know God makes us grow!"
               Let there be no doubt, God is God; so elevate, celebrate
                   him.
               We belong, belong to him, sing along;
               With him we'll sing those strong songs.

4
(chorus)   So, come on in, party on up, give it on out;
               Let the celebration in your soul shout out!
               Let him know, let it show, throw your thanks about;
               Spread his name around, bang the drum:
               Make a solid sound with what you've found!

5
(rap)   For God is top, large, in charge and pouring out
               A barrage of good things! His love rings true,
               Bringing in love when the new's not new;
               Bringing in love from the future right through.
               Bringing down love on everything you do.
               So, everybody sing, strong and true:
               "He's top, till you drop – but he still don't stop!" (x 2)
(chorus)

How fine (soul classic)
©David (Psalm 103:1-22)

Again, David's just blown away by God and his pen manages to capture it . . .
                                                                    –Rob

1-2
(chorus)   Soul of mine, let it out, how fine he is;
               Everything inside of me, profile his purity.
               Soul of mine, get it out, how fine he is;
               Keep the memories alive of all he's given me.

3-4
(intro)
He wipes my slate clean, heals me from every ailment;
He bails me out of this wreck I built,
Untangles my derailment;
He decorates me with medals of passionate love,
Fits me out from above – soul of mine, feel his love!

5
(verse)
He knows what I really long for, satisfies me with good
    things,
And I'm young again, riding up high on eagle's wings!

6-7
(verse)
God works things out the right way, gets justice for the
    oppressed;
Moses saw him right the wrongs: the people saw it, yes!

(chorus)

8
(verse)
He's got passion, patience, natural grace:
To wind him up takes many tries;
But he'll always look you straight in the face
And embrace you with his eyes.

9-10
(verse)
He's not always going to be this stern,
Or accuse us time and again;
He won't punish even though we don't learn,
Or charge us our part of the blame.

(chorus)

11-12
(verse)
How far off is heaven from earth?
The respectful get this scale of love;
How far apart is east from west?
As far as he's removed our mess.

13-14
(verse)   As a dad loves his kids with a passion,
            So God loves those giving respect.
            We're fragile, our lifetime's on ration:
            We're dust! What else d'you expect?

(chorus)

15-16
(verse)   We flower and that's our finest hour:
            We've got the lifespan of some lawn;
            Then the winds of time just blow us away –
            No one even remembers we're born!

17-18
(verse)   But from eternity past to eternity to come
            God's love lingers with those who respect;
            And it's a generation thing for the select "some"
            Who keep the Contract, and hope for perfection to come.

(chorus)

19
(verse)   God's position of strength is absolute:
            His empire runs everything, everywhere;
            Who would stand up and risk a dispute,
            Rebel against God? Who's going to dare?

20-22
(end)   Celebrate him, you angels, you powerful warriors,
            Who wait on his command – obey with consummate
                    ease;
            Celebrate him, you angels, you hierarchies of heaven,
            Who wait at his right hand, you staff who live to please.
            Celebrate him, everything he made, with whatever
                    you've got,
            Wherever you've got to. Celebrate him, oh soul of mine,
            You too!

Applaud the Lord (gospel)
©Anon (Psalm 112:1-10)

The prospects of godly people . . .   —Rob

1
(chorus)   Applaud the Lord. Celebrate him! Venerate him!
               Time taken talking him up? Well spent.
               Those who respect him? Well happy.
               Those who love his laws? Well content.
               So applaud the Lord some more.

2-3
(verse)   Their kids will be figures in society:
               The family of the good you'll be able to tell;
               They'll have more than enough stuff to see;
               Their family name will be remembered well.

4-5
(verse)   OK, so it's dark, but they won't need to sweat:
               Light's around the corner of the darkest time;
               Good things gravitate to the generous guy,
               For the one who runs things straight down the line.

(chorus)

6-7
(verse)   They don't panic when things go wrong;
               Good people last, long into history!
               They don't go paranoid when it all falls in:
               They trust God, so the future's no mystery.

8
(verse)   The hearts of these guys are in great shape:
               They don't know the meaning of fear;
               They'll win, and look into their enemy's gape
               From up close – dangerously near!

(chorus)

9
(bridge)   They've been over the top with cash for the poor:
           They were generous and everyone saw;
           Their dignity will stand like a statue ever more.

10
(coda)   But the wicked will be eaten by worms of jealousy:
           They'll curse and crawl off, hoping no one'll see;
           Their schemes and plans will just cease to be.

He got my call (reggae)
©Anon (Psalm 116:1-7)

Probably written by a king, but sung by the people. Brings back memories of
Egyptian and Babylonian slavery eras . . .   —Rob

1-2
(chorus)   I love him 'cos he took my call: he knew I was in a state,
           But he didn't screen me out: he picked it up
                immediately;
           So, I know, he's proved he's got time for me:
           I'll call him. When? Again and again!

3-4
(verse)   Mortality almost strangled me,
           Looked up from my very own grave;
           Wrestling to get free from terror and grief,
           I screamed, "Save me, God! Save me!"

5-6
(verse)   God is generous and good to the core;
           His passionate love bubbles over and out;
           He protects the naïve, the innocent ones –
           When I was desperate he heard my shout.
(chorus)

7

(da coda)   Relax! Calm down, my stressed-out soul;
Let peace pour through:
You've got proof that God's been good to you.

Who's laughing? (west coast)
©Anon (Psalm 119:1-11)

Probably written once they'd come back from being slaves ...   —Rob

1-2

(intro)   Who's laughing? The innocent ones;
Who's playing the way it's meant to be played?
Keeping to the rules?
Who's staying on the road long enough
To prove God's Contract right?
Who's laughing? The obedient ones;
Who's staying on the search till they find him,
Keeping to the rules?
Who's keeping on keeping on with their heart full on,
Finding him to be infinite?

3-6

(chorus)   They do nothing wrong, but keep singing your song;
You've set out a Contract to be kept at all costs.
I want to be strong, my stride to be long,
But I'm so inept, my account's so in debt:
So ashamed, every time you come along.

7-8

(verse)   I wanna give all the credit to you
With a heart strong in integrity!
I wanna run things as laid out by you:
Please, don't get rid of me!

9

(verse)   The chances of a young guy staying pure?
The odds on a girl not getting hurt?

Way higher when we live within the Contract,
Way higher when the Instruction Manual's still intact.

10-11
(verse)   I'm after you, like a police dog on a trail:
Don't let me stray from the Way you lay down;
I've memorized, internalized your words in my heart
As my guarantee not to make you frown.

Step sure (gospel) ©Anon (Psalm 121:1-8)

Sung by the crowds on a pilgrimage to Jerusalem …   —Rob

1-2
(verse)   I'm straining my eyes, scouring the scene:
Where can I get me some help?
Direct from God the unseen,
Who made the place, who created space!

3-4
(chorus)   He'll keep my step sure, keep my foot steady.
He don't doze off – he's always there, ready!
He's on watch for his people, don't need no sleep,
Don't need no doze. When they're in danger he shows.

5-6
(verse)   God's watching every step you take,
Sorting out shade for your unprotected side:
Sunstroke won't touch you as you stroll about today,
Moonlight won't freak you at night.

7-8
(verse)   God'll protect you, won't let harm near you;
He'll keep his eye on you, check you're OK.
God's into your life, as you hit the sofa or the town.
Right now and every single day.

Riddled with joy (dance/Ibiza)
©Anon (Psalm 126:1-6)

Probably written for the return trip from exile, celebrating new community . . .

—Rob

1-3

(chorus)

Were we dreaming? Was it for real
When God brought us all back home?
Laughter filled everything; songs filled the rest!
The rumours flew round, "God works things for the
    best."
It's true: you've done so much for us!
It's true: we're riddled with joy!

4

(verse)

Bring us back to where we were:
Give us back our winning ways;
Let us flow again like the southern streams,
Bubble like the old days!

5-6

(verse)

Those who invest with tears in their eyes
Will see the pay-off – they'll dance and sing out loud!
Those who go to work with broken hearts
Will stride back with results, humbled yet proud.

Never forget you (solo acoustic)
©Anon (Psalm 137:1-6)

Memories captured of the torment of the "imprisonment" in Babylon . . .   —Rob

1-3

(verse)

The Babylon rivers flowed along,
But our tears nearly broke their banks;
Our hearts were wading in the rivers back home,
Our instruments dumb in this depression zone;
And what? They expected us to sing our songs?
These slave drivers request our party songs!

4-5

(bridge)   Just how? No way, impossible to do;
              Sing of home when we're stuck in prison with you?
              They're not just songs – they're our memories too;
              And may my right hand forget how to strum if I ever
                  forget you.

6

(chorus)   May my tongue get stuck to the top of my mouth if I
                  ever forget you.
              Jerusalem, I'll never forget you!
              (last two lines x 4)

Known (rap) ©David (Psalm 139:1-24)

David takes the plunge – asks God to examine and test him . . .   —Rob

1-6

(intro)   God, you've picked me over and you know me,
                  intricately;
              You've sussed me out: you know me, intimately;
              You forecast my every move: my body, brain, my big, big
                  mouth!
              You know all my tendencies, my habits, my times:
              Before I've even said it, you've worked out if it rhymes;
              Your armed guard stands round me, above me, below
                  me;
              You've put your arm around me: you know me;
              My head doesn't have the capacity –
              It's Overload City, this "YOU and me"!

7-13

(rap)   But whoa! Hey, what if I fall, go AWOL, try to lose it
                  all?
              What do I do to hide from you? How do I outrun
              The one who's faster than sunshine?
              Shuttle me to Saturn? Fine! You're waiting for me there!
              Use the cover of dawn as camouflage? You're there!
              Get reborn, other side of the world, even off the map?

Your arm's around me: you've found me, surround me.
Hit the lights! The darkness bites and I hide from you:
No difference – God's vision don't dim;
Your arm's around me: you've found me, surround me,
For you made me: I ain't no whim;
You double-stitched my DNA, hand-picked my brain
the very next day,
Made some room in my mother's womb, and hey! I'm
away!

14
(chorus)   God, I'm amazing! The credit's down to you;
I'm incredible: nothing to edit or review!
Everything you do fills up our wonder-tanks,
And I know I'm wonder full. So thanks!

15-16
(verse)   On the production line I'm not kept back from you;
In the secret places I develop as you view.
My design's on the drawing board; you come and take a
look,
And the work that I'm to do's already written in your
book!

17-18
(verse)   Your ideas, your plans – beyond priceless to me;
The scale's so huge, so awesome, like dew-drops in the
sea.
Try and list them – it's easier to count the sand grains on
a beach;
I wake up and enormous God is there, within my reach!

19-20
(verse)   But, God! Don't let the evil ones live to gloat and
drool –
Get away from me, you bloodsucking leeches!
They spend their nights calling you a fool,
Their days mouthing off with their anti-God
speeches.

21-22
(verse)

Don't I hate the ones who hate you?
Don't I long for their decline?
Don't I detest the ones who test you?
Your enemies are enemies of mine.

23-24
(verse)

Cross-question me, God:
Suss out my subconscious;
Check me over thoroughly:
See if there's any fear in me.
Root out any tumour that'll hurt or harm;
Lead me by the arm – take me there, your way.

110 percent (jazz/funk)
©Anon (Psalm 146:1-10)

Probably written once they've all come back from eviction – loads to thank God
for...   –Rob

1-2
(chorus)

God gets the credit – 110 percent!
Slow soul of mine, open up your value vent;
I'll talk God up all my life: as long as I've got breath
I'll raise his ratings by singing my songs, full out, full
     on, till death.

3-4
(verse)

Don't bank on men with titles, letters behind
     their name:
They may be powerful now, but they'll die just the same;
A contract dies, a cheque comes back, a scandal, a heart
     attack:
Their ambitious plans are shot, they're looking pretty
     lame.

5-6

(verse)　　　But well content are those who bank on Jacob's God,
Who rest, rely, apply their hope on him making the
grade;
He made the earth, the sky, the stars, the sea,
Everything you can and cannot see, he made!

7

(verse)　　　He fights for the rights of the left out, the down and out;
He feeds the needs of the beggar in the doorway:
The ones without a shout find a new voice on their case;
The inmates go free and get to stay that way.

8-9

(verse)　　　He brings light to dark eyes, lifts lowlifes to
their proper size,
And he loves, just loves, the guys who do the same!
He sets special surveillance to protect the outsiders,
Watches out for those who used to lose the game.

(bridge)　　But the wicked – he gets in their way:
He messes their plans and blows them away!

10

(coda)　　　God says what goes, and this goes on for good;
This is your God – you people he sent;
Generation after generation give him total veneration.
He gets the credit, 110 percent!

Proverbs / Wise Up

Solomon wrote piles of this material. This is just some of his stuff. Scroll through the wisdom God gave the guy. Download it; print it out large; paper your walls with it. —Rob

What for? (Proverbs 1:1-7)

1

The sayings of Solomon Davidson, Israel's king:

2-6

For getting wise and for getting trained. For knowing what's what. For getting to grips with the deeper things. For a life kept in control and going somewhere. For doing the right thing, fairly and squarely. For giving common sense to the uneducated. For helping the young know what's right and helping them buy into it. Let the wise guys listen and learn some more, let the enlightened watch the lights come on – as sayings, illustrations, allegories and riddles do the rounds.

7

Wisdom? She kicks off with respect for God. Only idiots write off Wisdom and training.

> Father-son chats. How to pick your mates; how to pick your partner; what happens when you live Wisdom-free. God's the one doling her out – so get in the queue for Wisdom. —Rob

Wise words (Proverbs 3:5-12)

5-6

Base your confidence on God. Build your life on the girders God sets in place, not the flimsy scaffolding of your own good ideas. In everything you take on, put God top of the list of credits and he'll direct you.

7-8

Don't talk to a mirror and expect to lip-read the answers to life. Giving God respect and giving evil the cold shoulder is better than double the daily dose of vitamins and minerals.

9-10

Recognize that God sorts your assets. Prove you've got the idea by giving away the best of what comes in. And guess what? You'll get more. The sums don't work, but God does: you'll come out better off, having put his chunk at the top of your budget.

11-12

Son, don't gripe about the exercise regime God sets you. Don't mouth off when he lays into you 'cos you're slacking. Given that God loves you, he's going to train you hard – like a dad empowers his favourite son, like a coach trains his team.

> More on the pricelessness of wisdom. Listen to your dad: sieve out the Wisdom and treat her like gold. —Rob

Gorgeous, but ... (Proverbs 5:3-6)

A woman with no morals may have chocolate-flavoured lipstick. She may have a voice that pulls you in like a magnet. But after it all, what've you got? A bad taste in your mouth from the rusty razor blade she slipped you mid-snog. She'll mince her way down to death, lead you to your very own grave on the way. She's got no idea where the road to life is – she missed it miles back and she's too dumb to turn around.

Don't look back and regret your lifelong service to your hormones. Learn from others' mistakes, not your own. Get up close and personal with your husband or wife. Full stop.

Don't tie yourself up (Proverbs 5:21-23)

For everything you get up to, public or private – God's watching on his widescreen TV. The red "record" light is on: your every step, stumble and stop is digitally stored. The evil stuff the wicked do entangles them. The ropes of rebellion will be tightly knotted and they'll be trapped. They'll die 'cos they couldn't be bothered to train themselves, dragged around by every whim of their greedy guts.

Oy! Couch potato (Proverbs 6:6-8)

Go take a close-up look at an ant, you couch potato. Spend some time thinking how hard it works and wise up. Does it have anyone shouting orders at it? Nope. Does it have a boss or a chief? Nope. But it works up a sweat all summer to get enough in to last it through the hungry months.

Stuff God hates (Proverbs 6:16-19)

Six things God hates, seven things he absolutely can't stand: eyes wide with conceit, mouths full of lies, hands shedding innocent blood, hearts plotting rip-off schemes, feet racing into doing evil, witnesses telling bare-faced lies, anyone stirring up trouble and splitting up families.

More on escaping the claws of the danger-babe. More on Wisdom demanding attention . . .   —Rob

Choose life (Proverbs 8:10-11)

You've got choices! So choose well between the silver that needs polishing and my advice, which just keeps on shining. Choose to be someone who *knows* stuff, rather than someone who *has* stuff. The exchange rate is far off what people think – a million diamonds don't come to an ounce of Wisdom. There's nothing you think you want that you could part-exchange for Wisdom.

How God lined up Wisdom before he set about creating the world. Then long lists of cracking one-liners. Easy-to-remember gems that keep life on line. Some examples . . .   —Rob

Integrity (Proverbs 11:3)

The integrity of a good guy guides him through life. But crooks get double-crossed by their own lies.

Generosity (Proverbs 11:24)

One guy doles out the dosh like there's no tomorrow and his wallet's never empty. But the tight-fisted hide their cash and end up broke.

Insults (Proverbs 12:16)

An idiot's quick to fly off the handle, but the sorted bite their lip at some cheap jibe.

Envy (Proverbs 14:30)

When a heart's not at civil war with itself, the body gets energy. But jealousy's a real bone eroder.

Billy "No cash" (Proverbs 15:16)

It's better to have debts outstanding and respect for God than to be loaded but worried stiff about looking after it all.

Plans (Proverbs 16:9)

In their hearts, they've got it all mapped out, but it's God who's in the driving seat.

Instinct (Proverbs 16:25)

Sometimes your gut knows which way to go. But it only takes you down Death Drive.

Schtum (Proverbs 17:28)

If an idiot keeps his mouth shut, some might think he knows something. They might guess he's weighing it all up to spout something profound.

Dosh (Proverbs 18:11)

The money of the rich is just a protection zone: they imagine it's a wall no one's going to get over or through.

Pride (Proverbs 18:12)

Before they fell flat on their face, they were strutting along quite cool. But those who know their place get promotions.

Kind (Proverbs 19:17)

Those who help out the poor, lend to God. And he'll host the Reward Ceremony for them.

Depth (Proverbs 20:5)

Intentions are deep as the Atlantic: only someone with depth can bring them out.

Traders! (Proverbs 20:14)

The buyer complains, "It's trash, a total waste!" Then they go off and boast about the bargain they've bought.

Fraud (Proverbs 20:17)

A meal paid for with a stolen credit card tastes great, but the next morning the gut-ache kicks in.

Heart test (Proverbs 21:2)

Everyone thinks they're doing the right thing at the time, but God tests your motivation.

Plans (Proverbs 21:30)

You can plan and scheme all you like, but nothing succeeds if God's got other ideas.

Kids (Proverbs 22:6)

Train children to click on what's right when they're young – they'll be downloading it long after you're gone!

Sharpeners (Proverbs 27:17)

As iron sharpens up iron, so people can sharpen each other.

Ecclesiastes / What's the Point?

A disillusioned old king trying to make sense of it all. Some cuttings . . .   —Rob

And the point is? (Ecclesiastes 1:1-14)

1

The words of the wise one, Solomon Davidson, king in Jerusalem:

2

What's the point?! What IS the point?! asks The Wise One. It's all utterly worthless: everything's a total waste of space.

3-4

What's the pay-off from all the hours we work? What's the point in even breaking sweat? One generation dies; another takes its place: the world keeps turning.

Even nature is repetitive: the wind, the water cycle – it's all so predictable. —Rob

8-9

Everything's so totally boring, mind-numbingly dull. But you keep looking, listening as if something new's going to happen. What's gone down will go down again; what's been done will be done again: there's nothing new, original – it's all repeats.

10-11

It's all been done before. Claims at originality are clichés already. But no one remembers their history.

12-14

Me, "The Wise One", I'm king of Israel in the Big-Smog Jerusalem. I set myself strict study regimes. Desperate to understand what goes on and why? I tell you, God's slapped a heavy-duty job on us! I've studied what goes on, who does what and what it all means – and it means zilch, zero, nothing, a big fat 0. Trying to wrestle with it is like trying to catch the wind in a fishing net!

Pointless (Ecclesiastes 2:1-26)

1-3

I thought (and my gut agreed), *Right, let's take this pleasure thing all the way, see if it works.* But it was pointless, totally pointless. "Laughter's a waste of energy," I said. "What good does it do?" I tried wine, see if that could lighten the mood. I tried messing around – all deliberate experimentation, desperate to work out if anything was worth squat in the few years we've got on this backwater of a planet.

4-6

I buried myself in work, took on worthy projects. Built houses, set up businesses, made gardens and parks, planted every fruit tree you can think of.

> He goes on with his checked-off to-do list, which pushed him into the major league of wealth.
> —Rob

10-11

Whatever I fancied, I bought. Whatever caught my eye, I went for it and sucked the life out of it. There was some job satisfaction in making things, some sort of pay-off for my hard work. But when I sat back and assessed it all, when I did a stocktake of all I'd made happen, I still thought, *What's the point? Why chase wind? Am I really any better off than I was?*

12-14

Then I mulled over the word *wisdom* for a while, grappled with *insanity* and *stupidity,* trying to make some sense of it all. What's the next king going to do that I've not already done? I made *some* progress: wisdom outguns stupidity, like light overpowers darkness. Wise people use the eyes in their heads, while the stupid grope around in the dark. *Some* progress. But then — they both die in the end, so what's the point?

> He faces the fact that he'll go the same way and soon be forgotten, how all his work will land in the lap of someone who's done nothing to earn it. And if the next guy's an idiot — even more depressing! He grasps at another possible conclusion.
>
> —Rob

24-26

What more can a guy do than eat, drink and get some sort of satisfaction from his work? But even this is subject to God handing it over, for without God around, who can eat and enjoy? If, somehow, we please God — he doles out wisdom, understanding, contentment. But if we wind him up — he makes us work our socks off just to hand it over to the ones he's taken a liking to. Pointless wind-chasing.

Right timing (Ecclesiastes 3:1-14)

1

Everything's got its time; everything has a season:

2-8

Birth times, death times. Planting times, harvest times. Killing times, healing times. Times to tear things down, times to build things up. Times to cry, times to laugh. Times to grieve, times to party. Times to throw stones, times to collect them up. Times to hold someone close, times to hold back. There's a right time to turn the whole place upside down till you find something, a right time to write it off as lost. There's a time to hoard, there's a time to chuck things out; a time to tear things up, a time to repair things. Sometimes it's best to shut your mouth; other times it's crucial you speak up. There's a right time to love, a right time to hate; a right time for war, a right time for peace.

9-11

Where's the pay-off? What's the point? All this backbreaking, brain-aching work that people do day in day out – why? God's set seasons for everything – at the right time everything can work. But he's also pro-grammed us with the huge questions of 'life, the universe and every-thing' echoing round our brains. But we can't know! How can we? It's way too deep, like trying to get to the bottom of the ocean when all we've been given is a plastic snorkel and flippers.

12-14

Where's all this got me? What am I sure of? I know the best thing is for people to be content and do good things while they're alive. For someone to be able to eat, drink and enjoy their job is a gift from God. What God does lasts long after we've snuffed it. What he does can't be talked up or down – it stays, permanent. And he does all this to win our respect.

> He's still groping for answers; he knows wisdom's good, but he also knows life's a bit of a lottery and even the wise die. He hangs on to some of his famous say-ings, but he knows they're just jigsaw pieces and God's hidden the lid with the picture on.
> —Rob

Conclusion (Ecclesiastes 12:1, 13-14)

1

Remember the God who made you, while you're still young, before the hassles of adult life kick in and you too end up saying, "Where's the fun gone?"

13-14

Now it's out in the open; now I've had my moan. Here's my conclusion: respect God and live his way – this is our role, our responsibility. For God'll judge everything we do, secret or known, good or evil.

Song of Songs / You Are Gorgeous!

Back when he was a young romantic, Solomon writes love letters to his lady and she writes back. Some people read it from a different angle – that they're love letters between the Liberator and his people ... whichever, it's hot stuff ...   —Rob

Kiss me (Song of Songs 1:1-3)

She says, "Kiss me. Kiss me full on, till my lips tingle. Our mouths say it better than words. Your love tastes better than vintage wine."

Come out with me (Song of Songs 2:8-13)

"Who's that?! It's my lover. Look, he's on his way, pounding his long muscular legs down the mountainside, leaping the streams on the adrenaline of coming to me! He's graceful as a gazelle, smooth as a stag, sheer poetry in motion! Now he's behind my back wall, seeing if I'm in. He's calling, 'Come out with me, my beauty! Come on! It's a beautiful spring day: no rain, no winter chill – they've escaped north leaving the summer to us. Come on out! Spring flowers are beginning to show, the blossoms in exhibition mode, the birds are back to give the soundtrack to our day. Get up, my lover, my beauty – come out with me.'"

She joins him and when they're out on the hills, he recites a love poem ...   —Rob

Gorgeous (Song of Songs 4:1-7)

"My love, you are beautiful! Stunning! Gorgeous. Totally edible. Your eyes are like spring-water mountain pools, and I'm a waterfall, diving in, diving in, diving in. Your hair flows, so full and thick. Your teeth, so perfect, shine like pearls on your presentation basket of lips made from strips of scarlet satin. And when you talk, your mouth moves like a thousand variations on a melody, a thousand and one different moods all intriguing and warm and . . . your voice! Your voice carries your ideas like a chauffeur-driven Merc purring out from between your two crafted cheekbones, clothed in perfect skin. All this displayed with such style by the sleek lines of your neck carrying my eyes up and down, up and down . . . to your shoulders and drawing my eyes down, down to your perfect breasts – which rise above their million silicon cousins in shape and size and texture and tone. I'll adore you till the streetlights go off and the day drags me away. My love, you're completely beautiful. Devastating. Nothing to be improved. You're totally 'ten out of ten'."

By chapter 7 he's still going strong . . .   —Rob

Kiss (Song of Songs 7:1-13)

1-9a

"You're so beautiful, everything about you totally desirable. You stand like an exotic palm tree, your breasts clusters of succulent fruit. I'll climb your tree, hold your branches tight, taste your sweetness; I'll breathe your fruit-fresh breath and kiss your sweet wine lips."

She responds . . .   —Rob

9b-13

"Let the wine flow! Let it pour over lips and teeth and tongues. I'm yours; you're mine. Come on, let's get out of here: let's go to the country, spend the night together in a romantic cottage, get up with the birds and walk through vineyards, check if the vines have buds, see if the trees are blossoming. I'll make love to you there. You'll taste the aphrodisiacs I've got in – all kinds of exploding tastes for you, only you, to enjoy."

Later, she says . . .   —Rob

Priceless (Song of Songs 8:6-14)

6-7

"I'll be the password to your heart. For love is stronger than death; and a lover's passion is as jealous as the grave. It bursts into flame and roars like a searing hot blaze – oceans of water can't put it out; whole rivers can't quench its light. Love can't be bought – the world's richest man can't afford a takeover bid on love: it's priceless."

It ends with her calling...   –Rob

14

"Let's get out of here, my lover. Won't you make like a gazelle and be as virile, as strong, as agile as a young stag on the aromatic hills above?"

The Prophets
www.couriershotline.com.ot

The Major Prophets / The Famous Four

A quartet of guys with a hotline to God. Isaiah, Jeremiah, Ezekiel and Daniel were the big noises of God for his people. These four produced more than three times the amount written by the twelve minor couriers. They were prolific, and their stuff was crucial for the Jews before, during and after their evictions. They were a lifeline to God.

Isaiah / No Pain, No Gain

Back before all the Poetry we had over three hundred years of www.new-nation.com.ot. God tried to get through to his people using hand-picked couriers. Scroll down Jewish history till you get to King Jotham of Judah and you'll soon figure out that Isaiah Amozson is the first major voice trying to pull the Jews kicking and screaming back to God. God's "cruel-to-be-kind" discipline programme has allowed the superpower Assyria to steamroller the northern state of Israel. Isaiah's first splurge of material tells their "southern cousins" in Judah not to be suckered into thinking, *It'll never happen to us!* Isaiah's pretty blunt – they've broken the Contract with God and he's going to kick them out as well. This time it'll be the superpower waiting in the wings – the Babylonians. Isaiah's second splurge has him projecting into the future when the people are already evicted and living (or "existing") in Babylon. It's stuffed full of God's assurances that he's going to liberate them, this time by using the Persian Empire. It also points forward 700-odd years to the Liberator who'll bring permanent freedom to the people through his sacrifice. –Rob

Discipline

God's case (Isaiah 1:2-4)

2-3

Listen up, stars! Hear me out, planet Earth! This is what God says: "I raised children, I brought them up – now they give me the cold shoulder and stride off to do their own thing. The ox knows who's boss; the donkey knows where the carrots come from and who holds the stick. But Israel just don't get it: they can't get their brains round how it works."

4

"Talk about a messed-up people: guilt-ridden, evil corrupters! They walked out on me, blocked out purity and turned their backs on anything good."

> More regret about the tragic fall of Israel. But God's still got Jerusalem, although right now a time traveller could mistake the place for Sodom or Gomorrah! He gives it to them straight ...   —Rob

Your choice! (Isaiah 1:15-20)

15-17

"You do the praying pose — I can't watch. You rattle through the prayer book — I can't listen. The blood on your hands is drowning you out. Wash off the grime: stand in the shower for a day or nine. Get your evil schemes out of my sight. Quit doing wrong. Kick-start good stuff like tracking down justice, backing the oppressed, blocking the oppressors, defending the vulnerable and giving the poverty-stricken a voice."

18-20

"Let's thrash this out together," says God. "OK, so your mess stands out like a bloodstain on a cream carpet: it will be white as fresh snow. And OK, so the evil you've done is as in-yer-face as crimson graffiti on a whitewashed wall: it will be as white as pure new wool. IF you do as I say, you'll have feasts full of food you've grown on your own land. But if you stick your heels in and go against me, your enemy's weapons will have the last laugh. These are your options. Your call."

> God paints both pictures — the devastation of Jerusalem and the city of peace. Parallel futures are laid out before them. God changes the metaphor to his people being a vineyard.   —Rob

Sour grapes (Isaiah 5:4-6)

"What more could I have done for my vineyard? Haven't I done everything I could? But I come looking for juicy grapes and the few I find are mouldy and flea-ridden! So this is my action plan: I'll tear down the protective hedge and the wind'll rip it all out of the ground. I'll demolish the walls and it'll be trampled into the ground; it'll become a wasteground. There won't be a pruning knife within miles of the place and the weeds and thorns will move in and take over – I'll even block off the clouds so no rain will irrigate it."

God lays out the bad news through Isaiah, but even in the middle of a good telling off, God can't leave them without hope. They may be looking down the barrel of a dark time, but at the end of it is light and space.   —Rob

The Liberator (Isaiah 9:6-7)

It's a boy! And he's ours! He'll grow up to carry the government on his shoulders. His titles will include Wonderful Wise One, Awesome God, Father Who Stays, Peace Prince. His tranquil rule will just keep on spreading. He'll sit on David's throne and run a kingdom full of justice and goodness right into eternity. God's burning enthusiasm will see this is done.

But before that ... the only things burning are God's anger and the ruins of Jerusalem. Again God counters the despair with hope – a remnant will come back home and live in peace.   —Rob

Liberation

Imagine it's happened. Picture Jerusalem as a ruin and the Jews as Babylonian slaves. Then someone remembers the stuff Isaiah wrote before they left. They dig it out, dust it off and flick through ... there is hope.   —Rob

Comfort my people (Isaiah 40:1-10)

1-2

"Comfort my people; hug them. Speak gently to the Jews. Tell them they've had all their punishment. They've had double discipline. It's over!"

3-5

What's that voice? Drifting in from the wasteland, "Give us a motorway. A straight line of lanes. A Route 1 for God to travel on. Flatten those dips; penetrate those mountains. Make it flat all the way for God's cavalcade to come."

6-8

A voice from off shouts, "Holler!!"

Isaiah calls back, "Just tell me what and I'll shout the house down."

The voice says, "Holler, 'People are like blades of grass. Their best years, like the short flowering season, don't last – they're gone. Grass gets mown down, flowers droop and drop off, but the Boss's message stands strong and long.'"

9-10

The voice again, "You! You want to spread the good news? Shift yourself! Get up that mountain. You! You want Jerusalem to know? Project from the diaphragm; give it all you've got and holler. Don't choke on it; free your mouth up and yell, 'Ladies and gentlemen, it gives me great pleasure to introduce to you – your God! Arriving centre stage, totally in control, power pouring from every pore – your God! With his diamond-studded trailer behind, holding rewards for you, prizes for you.'"

> The MC goes on describing the scene, groping for superlatives to do this God justice. He's like a minder, a mentor carrying the vulnerable close to his heart, holding hands with the young mums. Same hands that scooped up the sea. Same hands that spanned out the stars. Same hands that carried the basket from which he'd make the earth. Shift to the question of things people never say, like "Here, God; let me tell you something you don't know"! Shift to the question of how small the nations are, compared to God – a water droplet? No, smaller. A grain of dust? No, smaller. Nothing? That's more like it! The question "What other 'god' gets close" doesn't even deserve an answer. The compere can't believe we don't know that God views us like grasshoppers, views the cosmos like a tent, views the world leaders as nothing – blades of grass on the compost heap of power. Then God opens his mouth to speak, the compere mutes his own mic . . . —Rob

Comparison?! (Isaiah 40:25-31)

25-26

God says, "Compare me to what? Is there anything that even comes close? Look up; see the stars. Who made them? Who switches them on at night? Who knows their real names? Who has the sheer power to keep any of them from imploding?"

So how come you moan, "God's got a blind spot with me. He's ignoring me"? Aren't you up to speed? He's the infinite one. Designer. Creator. He doesn't get tired. No one can scratch the surface of his understanding. And he lets the weary ones plug into his strength reserves. He recharges the weak with his power. Even teenagers need him to fill their energy tanks. Even they trip up. Even they land flat on their face. But those whose prospects are tied up with God will get a second wind, third wind, fourth, fifth, sixth. They'll fly, magnificent, like eagles on the Nature Channels. They'll run marathons back to back. They'll walk mountains at midday, midsummer and not even break sweat.

> Isaiah gets first-hand images of God in charge of world politics. He mocks the media-made gods of today. He jogs the Jewish memories of being picked out by him, of being with him. He prints out copies of promises of protection, of God holding their hands, of giving them a grip on making a living, of providing them with clean drinking water. All so they're sold on the fact that God's on their case. More satire at the expense of idols. Then a preview of a king on God's payroll (could be Cyrus) who'll make things happen for them despite their selective deafness towards God.
>
> —Rob

The Liberator (Isaiah 42:1-7)

"Take a good long look at the servant I'm backing. I'm so proud of the one I've picked out. I'll saturate him with my Spirit so he'll teach the nations the meaning of the word *justice*. He's not the loudmouth type; he won't step on a slug, or leave a helpless turtle on its back to die. He's totally focused on his 'Justice for All' campaign. Nothing will put the brakes on him achieving it. Countries you've never heard of will pass laws based on his ideas."

The God who constructed the cosmos, who sculpted the earth and everything that grows on it, the God who breathes life into people says, "I'm in charge and I've picked you out to do the right thing. I'll walk hand-in-hand with you, protect you, make you the proof of the Contract with my people. You'll be a lighthouse for other nations. Why? To open blind eyes and to liberate prisoners from the hellholes they've been chained up in."

"I'm God. That's my name. No one else's getting the credit for what I do. Water's gone under the bridge. Water's about to fall – and I'll tell you when; I'll turn the tap. Before the weather forecasters get a sniff, I'll tell you the whole deal."

Then a celebration song to the Warrior-One. God talks of not biting his lip any longer but letting the screams of birth pain out. He talks of flattening mountain ranges, of drinking dry the irrigation pools, of leading the blind and turning the lights on for them along smooth, disabled-friendly paths. Turns out it's the Jews who are disabled: blind and deaf to God and looted and uprooted by their enemies at God's say so. They went through war without thinking to ask why! —Rob

It won't touch you (Isaiah 43:1-3)

Your creator says this: "Don't panic! I've bought you back. I've picked you out by your first name – you belong to me. When life's floods threaten to sweep you away, I'll be holding you: you're not shifting! When forest fires sweep through your campsite, I'll be directing it round your tent: you won't even get singed, 'cos I'm God, your Liberator."

God restates his love for them. Underlines his plans to be with them through the rough times. Prints out and frames his promise to bring them back home. He broadcasts his new policy – his desert Motorway Programme for his entrance . . .
—Rob

New life, just up the road (Isaiah 43:18-21)

"Wipe your memory banks; quit living in the past. Look, I'm into new stuff; it's just coming to the boil. Can't you sense it? I'm building a road through the wasteland, and I'm redirecting rivers alongside it. The wild dogs and foxes give me respect because I'm rejuvenating their deserted land. My people will drink fresh water on their way back home – they're mine and I made them to celebrate me."

All this despite the fact that they're not exactly suffering with Priest's Knee from their begging. But he wipes their slate clean and then forgets where he put it. They've not got a leg to stand on, but God has the blueprints for a designer garden (with water features) where the wasteland was. And they'll all reconnect with their heritage; names from the Instruction Manual era will be trendy again. God reminds them he's the only God worth squat, and rips into idols again . . . —Rob

DIY Devotion (Isaiah 44:16-18)

He saws the tree trunk in half. One half gets chopped up: some on the open fire; some for the wood-burning stove. He cooks his meal and eats it in front of the fire. He nods off mumbling, 'Don't you love a real fire?' The other half he chisels away at and sculpts into an idol. When it's done he kneels in front of it and asks it to look after him in rough times. How dumb is that?! They're denser than the wood; their closed minds are looking at a blind spot and they just don't see it.

But no one catches on to the absurdity of what they're doing. Despite this, God "blows their mess away like a cloud on a windy day". He wants them back with him, now he's bought them out of slavery. "The hills are alive with singing; the trees move their boughs to the beat" because Cyrus is shaping up to release the Jews to go home. Not because they've begged God enough, but just out of loyalty to Jacob.

—Rob

Just clay (Isaiah 45:9)

Big trouble building up for the guy picking word wars with his Maker. You're just one of many clay pots on his workshop floor. Does the pot say to the potter, "Let me just check your plans, see if they'll work"? Does the pot start rumours with the other pots that the potter's got no hands? Er . . . don't think so!

God lays it out, "So don't question me. Cyrus is ready, on his toes, to facilitate the building work on Jerusalem and to send back the evicted with a mission. Your enemies will bow reciting their new mantra 'Your God's God. The only God. He's way out there, way in here; he's way out on his own.' Israel's liberation's not far off. Get into your skull, I'm God. The only God. I'm on my own. Babylon's got it coming to them." God used them to discipline his people, but they're cocky in their superiority and they'll come crashing down from their penthouse suites; their life coaches and fortune-tellers will dive with them. The Jews are so stubborn! He told them the result; the game went as he'd read it, against the form book. So listen up to what he says is next: "You've been road-tested, you've been hardened up by life and I've done it so you don't give me a bad press anymore. I've done it so I get the credit." If they kept the Contract they'd be as serene as an Alpine lake, their right way of life would be a tidal wave of change. The Liberator's ready, on call. Equipped to bring them home. To do what he does – to liberate."

—Rob

<u>Unforgettable (Isaiah 49:14-16)</u>

"You Jews say, 'God's forgotten us, written us off as a bad job. We're scrubbed off his agenda.' Can a mother forget she's got a baby smack-bang in the middle of breastfeeding? Can she not care for the child she pushed out? Maybe! But I won't forget you. Your name's tattooed on my palms. The 'reconstructed you' is always in my eye line."

And there'll be loads of reconstructed people. A nation. A rich nation. God asks them, "When did I sign any divorce papers?" He didn't. They're still his bride. And the groom, the Liberator, will go through ridicule and agony to get them living back together again. Connect again with your heritage, your Rules, your gut feelings of what's right. God'll bring you back and you'll be singing upbeat celebration songs. Stop your quivering. Wake up. You've been mugged by God's anger, doped by God's tragedy. But he's detoxing you. Waking you up, cleaning you up. Open the windows; listen to the gossip – God's spreading the good news, the grapevine's passing on the juicy news that God's setting up his band and you'll be singing freedom songs, gospel songs. You'll be singing along with God, "The main man has come through with the goods. He's got scars on his scars. He's got authority. He's got the king stuck for words. He's got respect."   –Rob

The Liberator predicted (Isaiah 53:1-12)

1-3

Who would credit it? Who'd have foreseen this plot line in God's liberation story? He grew up vulnerable as a sapling in a concrete yard. Not especially attractive; nothing particularly regal about him: he didn't stand out in a crowd, your Mr Average. He was dissed by most, given the cold shoulder by many. There was a sadness about him. You could see in his face he was on personal terms with grief. People blocked him out, verbally abused him, didn't rate him.

4-6

But whoa! Step back a sec! Weren't those our weaknesses he took on? Wasn't that our sadness he carried? But we were convinced he'd been rubbed out of God's good books, punished by him, held down by him. How wrong can you be?! He was messed up for our mess. He was knocked down for our slip-ups. The slapping we should've got – he got. And we got serenity instead. His punishment beating left him half-human and us whole and fully human. We've all wandered off like lost boys, all followed our own directions. And God's punished him for everything we've done.

7-9

Victimized and tortured, but did he rant against this injustice? No, he shut his mouth, like a lamb entering an abattoir – eerily silent. Terminated by the oppression of a corrupt legal system. Leaving no kids – cut down in his prime. Silenced for the foul-ups of my people who'd been pushing God's patience for years. Killed like a common criminal (but buried by a rich man) even though he was totally in the clear. No blood on his hands. No hint of a half truth in his mouth.

10-12

But God had planned all this way before. God knew he'd be ripped apart and killed as a sacrifice, a ceremonial offering to cancel our guilt. And he'll see the final score, how he won generations of "children". And God will give him his life back because the plans were completed to the letter. He'll remember his agony, look at the results and be completely satisfied. Knowing him, being connected with him will lead to the acquittal of many in God's court – he's already been punished for their mess. So God will reward him big time! A king-size jackpot of a reward, 'cos he poured out his life till he was empty. In his death he's associated with the lowest of the low. He takes on the blame for the mess of so many: he stands up for our failures.

> So those of you who thought you were nothing – sing! Build extensions, ready for God to fill them. Why worry? God's your husband. OK, so he was livid with you; but now feel his heart, his passion for you. "It's like way back with Noah – I swore no more world-wipe-out floods. Now I'm swearing – no more anger; my love's on the line and limitless. So ... "
>
> —Rob

Gasping for it (Isaiah 55:1-3, 6-9)

1-3

If you're gasping, if your mouth's like the Sahara in summer, get yourself to the reservoir. If you've got no cash – come buy good wine and full-fat milk without spending your last bit of cash. Where's the logic in spending money on plastic bread? What's the point in working your socks off for stuff that can't satisfy? Listen up! Fill your mouths with something worth chewing: food with 100 percent of daily vitamins for your soul. Clean out your ears, listen up and do your soul a favour: I'll make a permanent Contract with you in line with my loving vows to David.

God says, "I'll make you trendsetters, leaders, movers and shakers. I'll clothe you out in charisma."   —Rob

6-9

Search for God while he's around. Evil people, quit your dark stuff; cancel your evil schemes. Turn round and face God: he won't treat you as you deserve. He'll throw out every charge against you, 'cos God makes it clear as clean glass, "My thoughts are totally 'other' compared to your thoughts. My methods aren't in any of your manuals. My ideas and your ideas, my methods and your methods are light years apart."

God carries on, "Rain and snow don't drain and melt without watering the ground. Neither does a word leave my lips without it having the impact I want. You'll breathe in peace and breathe out joy. Nature will sing along with your song: for 'nettles' read 'trees'. For 'thorns' read 'more trees'. You won't need a plaque on the trunk; it'll be clear it's me that takes the awards." God's got more: "I want justice and right and rest on the Rest Day." But the Jewish leaders just work on their beer bellies while the good people go under. They tune in to the filth of their surroundings and get no peace.   —Rob

True religion = doing something about it (Isaiah 58:1-9)

1

"Turn up the PA: blast it out. Get up close to the mic and let it rip! Tell my people that they've done the dirty on me and broken the Contract."

God slams into them about the hypocrisy of their religious abstinence from food, which just ends in fights. 'Course they still expect God to come up with the goods on their bulging request lists! He puts them straight.   —Rob

6-9

"This is the type of fasting I've asked for: getting the heavy-duty cutters on the chains of injustice. Chainsawing through the ropes holding down the oppressed. Isn't religion about spreading the food out to include the starving? Isn't it about putting a roof over the heads of refugees? About putting clothes on the naked? About not turning a blind eye on your own family? You do this and you'll be like the sun after a long dark night. It'll do you good too! Your catchphrase will be 'just doing the right thing'. Your back-up will be my aura. Do this and I'll answer your questions. You'll cry out and I'll be there for you instantly!"

> God holds his sword hand back as they rip off their workers, grimacing as he goes, "Trample on oppression; waste yourself for the wasted. Then you'll get the handle 'ruin rebuilder' from the ruined people, 'street remaker' from the slum dwellers. And you'll rest on the Rest Day knowing that God's your joy dealer and he's giving out freebies for you."
> Then more promises stuffed full of hope for their future, not least . . .   —Rob

The Liberator's job spec (Isaiah 61:1-3)

The Spirit of God is coursing through every part of me. He's commissioned me to announce the breaking news — fantastic news for the poor! He's sent me to mend broken hearts, to liberate those slammed up in dark prisons, to announce the news that this is the era of God going gentle on his people. It's payback time for our enemies! My manifesto is to get alongside the grieving — to swap their burnt-out hopes for beautiful crowns, to exchange their regrets for delight, to trade in their despair for celebration songs. They'll be like towering sculptures — chiselled out by God to be a constant reminder of his brilliance.

> Plus loads on the consequences for those refusing God's offers of life and the perfect world he's going to create for those who don't.   —Rob

Jeremiah / Warnings with Tears

Scroll down from Isaiah through loads of naff kings to the exceptional Josiah; i.e. just before Jerusalem gets totalled by the Babylonians. God sends an insecure twenty-year-old, Jeremiah, with a message of disaster for a nation in serious denial. His life morphs into a visual memo to Judah: as symbolic proof of his belief in God's threats, he doesn't marry or have kids. Like Ezekiel (click on www.couriers hotline/wotnohq) he acts out many of the messages in street-theatre spectaculars. He delivers his warnings weeping for his people, but they still lock him up. The messages square with Isaiah's material: discipline; then liberation. But now the Babylonians have become a serious world power, it's even more scary. Many of his writings kick in in his lifetime, but some point well past the survivors' return from Babylon and fill us in on the arrival of the Liberator.   —Rob

"After all I did!" (Jeremiah 2:6-17)

6-9

God says, "Your ancestors stonewalled me, cold-shouldered me, went solo on me. Even though I rescued them from slavery in Egypt and led them through the wild desert – where no one dares live or travel. I brought you into a great place – fields full of great food – and you messed it! You made my special place an eyesore. God's reps are supposed to teach my Contract, but they've no clue who I am. Your kings make it up as they go along. Your so-called couriers tune in to worthless gods for their predictions. So I'm charging you with this ..."

He accuses them of trading him in for gods that aren't even gods.   —Rob

13

"My people have messed up double:

1. They've emigrated from my Spa Town of life-giving water.

2. They've dug their own cracked reservoirs that can't even *hold* water!"

And he's pretty blunt about whose fault it is.   —Rob

17

"You've only got yourselves to blame. You deserted your God who gave you your direction — no wonder you're lost!"

So Jeremiah paints the future: Jerusalem razed to the ground by the Babylonians. He offers the escape route of renewing the Contract with God, but they're not interested. It's "Carry on, corruption". They reckon Jeremiah's off his trolley: "God won't let Jerusalem crash out, will he?"   —Rob

Follow your heart? (Jeremiah 17:5-10)

5-8

God says this: "People who trust in their contacts, their networks, their mates but ignore me are heading for very bad news. They're like shrubs in an abandoned yard — no chance of growing to their potential. No one's around to water or replant them. But well happy are the people who base their confidence on me. They're like a fruit tree planted in a park by a stream, with no concrete around to block its roots. No worries in the summer: its leaves stay green. No worries when they ban the use of garden hoses: it's still dripping with fruit!"

9-10

Don't let your heart pull a fast one on you: its specialism is deception. There's no operation that'll stop it cheating on you; no way to understand it. "But I'm your God and I operate on hearts — I open them up and see exactly what they're made of. I X-ray into the brain and read minds. Then I dish out the rewards for what people have done."

Crucial to all this is the Rest Day being what it's meant to be. God then gives Jeremiah the same image as Isaiah got – the potter and the clay. They've got to know who's the boss. So God's making plans for their wake-up call using the usual suspects: famine and death. —Rob

Street theatre (Jeremiah 19:1-15)

1-6

God tells Jeremiah, "Go buy an earthenware jar; get the leaders of the people and some of my middlemen to follow you out to the Ben Hinnom Valley. Tell them, 'Listen to the message of the Awesome God: spine-tingling catastrophe. Here, I'll see to it. My people have abandoned me and imported the newest, trendiest foreign gods their parents had never imagined. They've stunk the place out with the innocent blood of their own children in sacrifices to these non-gods. There's no law against it – it's so disgusting I hadn't even thought of making one! So watch out. Soon people won't call this place the Ben Hinnom Valley but Genocide Vale!'"

God goes into gory detail on the desperation coming – so extreme, people will resort to eating their own children. He instructs Jeremiah... —Rob

10-11

"Then smash the jar to smithereens right in front of them; tell them, 'This is what God's saying: I'll smash this nation and this city like I've smashed this pot – no amount of superglue'll sort it. They'll even run out of cemetery space!'"

Jeremiah does quite a job on the jar and no one misses the pun – the Hebrew word *jar* sounds like "ruin". He leads them back to God's HQ and lets the people in on the messages he's downloading from God. —Rob

15

"This is what Awesome God says, 'Listen up! You've all heard the prospects of catastrophe for this city and the surrounding villages – I'm going to make sure they all happen. Why? 'Cos you were stubborn and drowned out my words with other noise.'"

More splurges against corrupt kings, the "everything's fine" couriers and spineless God-reps. We get the image of seventy years of captivity for the Jews. Jeremiah's almost lynched but carries on giving out the bad news. Then it starts. First off, the Babylonians round up the movers and shakers and take them off to work for them in Babylon (Daniel and Co. and the Queen Mum are in this first lot evicted). Jeremiah writes them a letter.   −Rob

He's got plans (Jeremiah 29:10-14)

"This is what God's saying: 'When the seventy-year sentence is served, when Babylon's had its time of giving the orders, I'll turn up and keep my promise to bring you back to Judah. What?! D'you think I've lost the plans I drew up for your lives?' asks God. 'That they've fallen down the back of my desk, or got snarled up in heaven's red tape? No, they're open, on my desk, permanent. They're plans to do you good, not to pull you down. Plans that'll be worth waiting to see in 3D. You'll call out for me and I'll be all ears. You'll look for me and you'll find me if you *really* look. I'll bring you back from slavery. I'll draw you back like a magnet pulls in iron filings. I'll welcome you back from your time in exile.'"

More talk of the Great Return. They'll know it's God bringing them back, they'll have got their attitude to him sorted and they'll rebuild Jerusalem under his protection. But back to the NOW: Babylonian troops have the city surrounded; people are so starved, they're turning to cannibalism. Jeremiah knows it's been decided: God's told him. Then, bizarre! God tells him to buy the deeds to a local field! Jeremiah spots the symbolism and does as he's told. He tells the people they'll be carted off, but they'll come back: "This is proof. Would God tell me to buy a field if he wasn't bringing us back?" There are more promises of rebuilding projects that'll be state of the art; of new levels of purity as God acquits the people of their dysfunctional mess; of peace (both absence of war and the deeper kind) and prosperity. All this will hit its peak when the Liberator arrives. But before that we have the account of how the city of Jerusalem was ruined, like a shattered jar.   −Rob

Lamentations / A to Z of Grief

Jeremiah (and others?) gush out their pain at the destruction of Jerusalem (586 BC). It's classic Jewish poetry – some Jews still recite this weekly at the Wailing Wall in Jerusalem; many Roman Catholics read it on the last three days of Lent. Five separate poems, each line starting with consecutive letters of the Jewish alphabet, making an "A to Z of Grief". (Actually "A to Th" in their alphabet.) But this is no pity-party: they know it's punishment for their slackness. The book shifts from grief to hope, and then on to a change of attitude towards God.   —Rob

Ghost Town (Lamentations 1:1-3)

1

A City deserted, a ghost town turned more tragic by the memories of the bustling crowd. She's a widow with no visible means of support. She was queen of all cities. Now? A slave, on report.

2

Bitter tears pour down her cheeks all night. Old mates legged it way back: no one's left to put an arm round her. They've turned traitor on her; now they're enemies. Please!

3

Gone, every one of them. Dragged away, mere units of labour for the Babylonians to say, "Do this; do that!" No rest from their grief, no escape from their trap; they're wasted.

Jeremiah pours out his grief on to the end of the alphabet . . .   —Rob

Seeds of hope? (Lamentations 3:19-24)

19-21

Thrown down on my grief, my homelessness poisons me, pulls me down into the jaws of depression. But hope hovers above me when I make myself remember . . .

22-24

His love. His incredible love has protected us — we're still alive, aren't we? His passion for us doesn't go hot and cold. It's pumped in daily; with every sunrise we get a brand-new dose of your loyalty and love, God. I tell myself, "God's all I've got: I'll wait for him to show."

> God's love's bigger than his anger. His love outlasts his loathe. His fury will flag and his pain will peter out.   —Rob

Help!!! (Lamentations 5:1-3, 15-22)

1-3

Awesome God, don't wipe us from your memory banks! We're begging you, look down at the mess we've got ourselves into: stand-up comics milking our national shame dry!

Bloodthirsty, godless foreigners striding into our homes demanding to know our alarm codes and passwords!

Grieving is all we're good at — they've killed our dads: our mums are widows.

> And more grief, until . . .   —Rob

15-18

Smiling's impossible; dancing's right out. All we do is groan. Impaled pride looks down as they loot everything our nation ever had.

Drowning in our own mess; powerless and sick in body and soul: we can't even see straight.

Cleaned out, totally. Our capital city's a ghost town; looted, trashed and overrun by foxes and rats.

19-22

Quit the negatives! Nobody cheats God; nobody kicks him out. Heaven will never display an "Under New Management" sign.

Have you abandoned us? Any plans to contact us again? Are we deleted from your address book? Show us the sequel, God, please; give us another chance.

Make it like the old days, only better – that is, if you haven't completely written us off as a bad job. Are you still so violently mad with us?

Ezekiel / Wot, No HQ?

Scroll down a tad and change the backdrop to Babylon. Ezekiel Buzison was one of the earlier Jewish prisoners whisked off to Babylon – i.e. one of the elite. So it's on foreign turf that he gets his socks blown off by a gobsmacking vision of the God 110 percent in control. From then on this courier's electric; his memos come hot from the top. Before and after the demolition job on Jerusalem, he delivers clear images of God as both punisher and comforter – God's HQ in Jerusalem is going to fall, but rebuilding sketches are already drawn up in heaven. Ezekiel has his own unique style. He's a visual guy with a razor-sharp mind and he's able to grasp huge issues and relay them as pictures, which he word-paints for the Jews. Like Jeremiah, he doesn't just spout; he also acts out symbolic messages in the street. Being both a courier and from a rep family, he's well focused on God's HQ building . . . or lack of it . . . and where God hangs out when his HQ is only good for a garden rock feature.   –Rob

It's over! (Ezekiel 7:1–4)

God says to Ezekiel, "Mortal boy! The God who says what's what, says this: It's over! You've had it. I'll let rip with my anger. I'll assess your case and look at all the evidence of your repulsive carryings on, and I'll sentence you. No, I won't go soft on you. I don't have a blind eye – you're going to get what's coming to you for your disgusting actions. Then you'll know who's God round here!"

The sentence is announced: disaster! Jerusalem's going to be gutted by the Babylonian army. Sword or famine will see to most of them; the rest'll get hauled off to Babylon. Then Ezekiel gets a vision of "why" – a guided tour of God's HQ with a first-hand view of the filth going on inside. He sees God leave in disgust; then God tells him to act out the plan . . .

—Rob

Watch this (Ezekiel 12:1-16)

1-2

God says to me, "Mortal boy! You're surrounded by a bunch of rebels. They've got eyes in their heads, but they don't see. They've got ears under their caps, but they don't hear. Like I say, a bunch of rebels!"

3-6

"So, mortal boy, pack a bag for your eviction. Do it in the day, so they don't miss it. Then, as your audience watches, leave. Go off somewhere else. Maybe they'll get the point."

When they ask, he's to say it's symbolic – they'll be packed up and carted off as captives. Why?

—Rob

15-16

"So they'll know who's God round here, when I roll them round the Middle East like dice! But I'll work it that some of them escape the sword, famine and deadly epidemic, so they'll eventually come clean and face up to all the disgusting things they've done. Then they'll know who's God round here!"

Strong competition from wannabe couriers who're making it up as they go along and putting out the more user-friendly message: "Relax, nothing bad's going to happen!" God's livid with these cop-out couriers, and they'll get the sharp end of a Babylonian sword for lying to his people: "Then they'll know who's God round here!"

—Rob

"Pretty Lady" – Rating: C for Caution (Ezekiel 16:1-63)

1-5

Another time, God says to me, "Mortal man, they've got to know how much they repulse me. Tell them, 'The story of Jerusalem: you're born and bred Canaanites; on your dad's side, Ammorites; on your mother's, Hittites. You arrive and no one cuts your umbilical chord, no one washes the gunk off you, no one puts any blankets around you or does any of the normal baby stuff. Worse, they chuck you over a hedge and into a field.' Rejection or what!?"

6-7

"I walk past and see this blood-caked baby, kicking and screaming, and I shout, 'No, this baby's got to live!'"

> So he takes responsibility for her. She grows up into a beautiful woman and he protects her from men who fancy her but only want to use her. He's totally committed, buying her dresses and jewellery – treating her with dignity, like she's a queen. Then he says . . .   –Rob

15

"You had it, so you flaunted it! You knew men would queue up to have you, so you became a prostitute."

> From queen to whore – out of choice! Unbelievable! But there's more: she had the jewels and gold chains he'd given her reworked into phallic idols, and then committed acts of gross indecency with them . . . for money! Then he says . . .   –Rob

20

"The children we had together, you had them sacrificially killed to appease these non-gods you were into. Wasn't being a whore enough?!"

> By now she's completely forgotten her childhood, when he was her lifeline. She's a sex-slave and she loves it, can't get enough. She's had most of the Jewish men; so she starts putting it about with the Assyrians; then the Babylonians. And she doesn't even want their money – she pays them! Grossed out, God's got to punish her, but he lets her lovers do it for him; in a vicious gang rape they take everything she's got – dignity, possessions, self-esteem – and they leave her naked, bruised up and totally humiliated. She's worse than her sister Samaria! Worse than her other sister Sodom! But . . .   –Rob

59-63

"This is what God says, 'Yes, I'm going to punish you. You can't make out you don't deserve it! You've broken our commitment, ripped up our Contract. But I'll remember my side of the deal we made years back: I'm still totally committed to you ("till death us do part!"). Maybe then you'll replay your lifestyle and be shamed into facing up to it in front of all your sisters. In fact, I'll bring them back to you and they'll be like daughters to you, even though this is above and beyond our agreement. I'll make our commitment solid – then you'll know who's God round here! Then you'll be speechless, knowing all you've done and being eaten up by embarrassment about it, but knowing that I've forgiven you completely. This is what the Awesome God says.'"

But it's not just the Jews who are in for God's judgement; Ezekiel sounds the alarm bells for surrounding nations who oppress Judah and lead them up the garden path looking for non-gods. Ezekiel gives it to them straight: God is God – no one tells him what to do. He can come down like a truckload full of concrete or he can be a gentle, loving parent. It's his call.

Then God allows Jerusalem to fall. From the eviction onwards, the images get more hopeful. But just 'cos they're "God's people" doesn't mean they get off lightly. There'll be no instant return home, no parole for good behaviour: the memos are clear – just sit tight, get right with yourselves and with God; eventually he'll bring you back home, but only 'cos he's a God of his word. —Rob

Grilled lamb (Ezekiel 34:1-30)

1-5

God speaks to Ezekiel, "Mortal boy, get this message out to the leaders of my people; tell them, 'This is what Awesome God says: you're in big trouble! You're supposed to look after my people, be like a shepherd to them. But you're too busy looking after number one. You're happy wearing the woolly sweaters, filling your faces with lamb stew. But what d'you do to protect them? A big fat nothing! You've not bothered to single out the weak or ill ones for special treatment. You've not gone out looking for the strays. You've whacked them and battered them, so now they're all over the place (in every sense) and picked off by predators wanting an easy lunch!'"

So God gives them the sack. From now on he'll look after them, bring them back and . . . —Rob

16

"I'll be the search party for the lost ones. I'll be the vet for the weak and the injured. It'll be the overweight ones I'll slaughter – I'll do what's fair for my flock."

God'll take sides with the weak sheep against the bully boys.   —Rob

25

"I'll make a Peace Contract with them. I'll clear the countryside of predators so they can live and sleep safely."

God vows to do them good, give them security.   —Rob

30

"Then they'll know that the Awesome God is on their case and that they're my people," says God.

Ezekiel pronounces God's sentence on Edom. But better news for the hills of home – they'll be ready to be harvested when the Jews come back.   —Rob

God's image issue (Ezekiel 36:23-38)

So why's God so ruthless with the overweight ones who've butted the wimpy sheep away from the best grazing? 'Cos God's reputation is taking a battering with next-door nations. Most places the sheep have wandered off to, you mention God's name and you get anything from a snigger to a belly laugh.   —Rob

23

"I'll have the nations do a rethink on their first impressions of me. I've been totally misrepresented by my people: I'm a trigger for bad-god jokes right across the Middle East. No more. The nations are about to find out who's God round here! I'm about to show my true colours. How? By the way I treat you."

God outlines how he's going to bring them back, clean them up and give them a heart transplant.   —Rob

26-29

"I'm going to operate on you; lose your stone heart and replace it with one with feeling, one with a new attitude. I'll infuse you with my Holy Spirit and motivate you to want to choose life by keeping the Contract. You'll live in the land I handed to your ancestors. You'll be my people. I'll be your God."

God will overload them with goodies and they'll turn their backs on their mess. He'll clean them up, turn wasteland back to Eden's "Heaven on Earth" garden.   —Rob

37-38

God says, "Not for the first time I'll go with what my people are begging me for; I'll help them. I'll make them as numerous as sheep around sacrifice time in Jerusalem. The trashed cities will be jam-packed with flocks of my people. Then they'll know who's God round here!"

Dem bones (Ezekiel 37:1-14)

1-3

I'm there, totally there. So absorbed with God being in the place that I'm totally oblivious to anything else. Then he whisks me away and suddenly I'm standing in the middle of a "Killing Fields" valley – the place is covered with dismembered human remains. He leads me round. I'm picking my way through the skeletons. It's some sort of mass grave after genocide, and it's all I can do not to step on them; they're so old and dry, they'd snap like twigs. God turns to me and asks, "Mortal boy! Can these bones come back to life?"

"Beyond me, God! That's your territory," I answer.

4-6

So he says to me, "Speak to these bones for me. Tell them, 'Dry bones! Listen up, this is God talking: I'm going to give you new breath and you'll come back to life. You'll get tendons again, fresh flesh, new skin and breath – you'll come to life! Then you'll know who's God round here!'"

7-8

I follow orders. I've not got through the message when there's this rattling sound, bones trembling and shaking and finding their previous dance partners. Then, from nowhere, tendons and ligaments, muscles and skin arrive and know exactly where to go – it's like a high-tech biology lesson, in 3D! But where's the breath? The bodies are still dead.

9-10

Then he says to me, "Call it in, mortal boy! Say, 'Breath! I've got your orders from the Awesome God: come with the wind. Blow like never before, cover every angle, breathe into these murdered bodies and bring them back to life.'" I do, and the wind blows. It enters the bodies and they start breathing, moving, getting up, walking around – a huge army of the no-longer-dead!

11-14

Then he spells it out: "Mortal boy, these bones are the Jews. They admit, 'We're dried up. Hope's long gone. We're like scattered skeletons.' So tell them, 'This is Awesome God's message: my people, I'm going to exhume you from your graves, bring your rotting bones back to Israel. If I've opened your graves and brought your bones back, you'll know I'm in charge. My Spirit in you will pump breath into your lungs. You'll come to life and live in your own homeland. Then you'll be sure that I'm running things round here, and what I say goes, says God.'"

Ezekiel rounds off his contribution with God's plans beyond resurrecting his people: firstly, national reunification (no more north/south divide; no more Judah vs Israel) – one king from David's family line running the place. Then a final battle, which, against all odds, God wins for Israel. And following up behind, the rebuilding of his HQ and God turning up to blast the place into life. No dates given, but Ezekiel knows the hotline's cooking. In case you're wondering, the total for the line "Then they'll know who's God round here!" is sixty-five times. Could be God's making a point?

–Rob

Daniel /
God's Running the Show

The first lot ousted from Judah were the talented ones – the ones the Babylonians could use; e.g. Daniel and Ezekiel. Getting to grips with this book is a game of two halves: the first half is downhill and with the wind – i.e. dead-simple stories of Daniel and Co. proving God's in charge. Progress through the second half is trickier: uphill and into a stiff breeze with wild symbolic images hitting you at every turn. Kick-off . . .   –Rob

"I'll skip the bacon, thanks" (Daniel 1:1-21)

King Nebuchadnezzar of Babylon gets the pick of the young men from foreign nobility to train as his servants. Among them four Jews: Daniel, Shadrach, Meshach and Abednego. They're just getting used to their new Babylonian names when they realize they've got to eat the king's food – dodgy, since some's been offered to Babylonian gods.   –Rob

8-10

Daniel decides there's no way the royal food and wine are going to pollute his Jewish taste buds. He goes to the guy in charge of all the trainees to get the OK not to have to eat the stuff. Even though God's been warming the guy to Daniel, he still says, "The king wants you to eat it; they'll carry me off in a body bag if he sees you looking rough when the others are sharp-eyed and fit-looking."

11-14

So Daniel goes down a level of command to the guard in charge of him and his three mates Shadrach, Meshach and Abednego. "Give us a ten-day trial," he bargains. "We'll have nothing but veggies and water; then compare us to the guys eating off the royal menu card. Make your decision on what you see. Deal?" Deal. The ten-day trial is on.

15-16

They pass! Ten days later they look the pick of the bunch. So the guard goes along with swapping the royal food for veggies on a long-term basis.

17-21

God sharpens the minds of these four Jews. They pick up the language and literature like they'd been born there. Daniel also develops an incredible knack for telling people what their dreams and visions mean. The three-year apprenticeship is up and the guy in charge presents "his lads" to King Nebuchadnezzar. After the interviews, the king is blown away by the four Jews – no one gets close – so the king employs them himself. Whatever comes up, the king soon realizes they're ten times as sharp as any of his advisors. Daniel keeps the job until the first year of King Cyrus.

Year two: Nebuchadnezzar has a dream. All his astrologers and magicians grovel round him making out they can interpret it. The king knows they'll just bluff some ambiguous, new-age tripe, so he raises the stakes: they have to tell him what he dreamt *and* what it meant. If not, they die – Daniel and Co. included. The Jews lobby God like crazy. That night God gives Daniel a dream that gives him all the info he needs. He tells the king his dream: a humongous statue with different bits made of four different materials representing his kingdom and the three world powers to follow. All four are then smashed to pieces by a demolishing rock that's clearly not man-made. The final image of the dream is focused on this rock, the only permanent thing left: God's kingdom. The king is majorly impressed with Daniel and with his God who prompted him. He's promoted and spoilt rotten with expensive gifts. Daniel also manages to negotiate top jobs for his Jewish mates.

Another huge statue; this time it's real, made of gold and standing almost 30 metres (100 feet) high and 3 metres (9 feet) wide – just about big enough to represent the king's ego! The idea is that whenever the band plays everyone has two options: bow down to the king's image or step into the blazing ovens. Not great options! 'Course, Shadrach, Meshach and Abednego don't have an option – out of loyalty to God they stay standing. The king hears and gives them another chance; they don't take it. The king's furious, but they tell him . . .   –Rob

"No can do" (Daniel 3:17-18)

"If we're chucked into this blazing oven, the God we work for could pull us out alive. He'll rescue us from your cruelty, King. Even if he doesn't and we fry, you should still know, there'd be no regrets – no way are we bowing down to your gods or your overgrown gold Action Man."

The king turns up the heat on the oven dial from one to seven and has them thrown in. It's so hot it kills the soldiers doing the throwing! The king's looking in to gloat and he sees *four* guys strolling round, chatting – the fourth one looks like the son of a god. He calls them out and the three step out not even singed. They don't even smell like they've been to a barbecue! The king's so impressed with them and their God that he bans any bad press on the Jewish God, on pain of death. The three Jews get a well-earned promotion.   –Rob

The writing's on the wall (Daniel 5:1-5)

1-4

Nebuchadnezzar's son takes over as king of Babylon. They're having one of their poseur parties: thousands of guests drooling over King Belshazzar's financial muscle. He calls for the servants to bring extra goblets – the ones brought back from God's HQ in Jerusalem! So they're drinking from the sacred cups while they're celebrating the gods of wood and stone (among others). Then . . .

5

From nowhere, the dismembered fingers of a man's hand starts writing on the palace wall next to the lampstand. The king's eyes are hanging out, his red-wine cheeks turn rosé, then white; his knees literally knock with fear (before giving way completely!).

The astrologers and enchanters can't make head or tail of the words. Then the queen remembers Daniel's track record with these things and he's called in. He's not interested in the lavish rewards offered; he just launches into the king for his rejection of the God his father admitted was running the show. End result? God sends this hand to tell him his future: You're going to die; your legacy is pitiful; your realm will be split between the Persians and the Medes. Daniel's promoted and rewarded, but it doesn't change things. That night Darius the Mede has Belshaz-zar murdered and sits on his throne.   —Rob

Gladiator? (Daniel 6:1-28)

1-5

Daniel's promotion up the ladder from King Darius means he's gained plenty of enemies among the suits of the new government. But he's so squeaky clean that, throw as they might, nothing seems to stick. Until ...

6-9

The suits go to the king and grovel, "Long live King Darius! We've got together — the administrators, the governors, the councillors, the advi-sors — all of us. We've agreed the king should enjoy a special Appreci-ation Month from his people. In fact, we think you should pass a law making it illegal for anyone to contact any god apart from you for the thirty days. Pass the law and put it in writing so some rich guy can't squirm out of it with expensive lawyers. After all, the statute book of the Medes and Persians is binding. Here's a pen ... sir." King Darius likes the idea and puts the law in writing.

10-12

Daniel gets wind of the new law and goes into the attic room of his house and faces the west window towards Jerusalem as usual: his daily routine of talking to God three times a day facing west isn't going to change. 'Course, the suits are spying on Daniel and find him asking God for help. They go back to the king and check with him, "Isn't it the royal decree that anyone caught contacting any other god will be thrown in the cage of the lions?" The king walks right into it: "The law stands. After all, Mede and Persian law is binding," he boasts.

13-15

They spring the trap: "Daniel, the Jewish import, mocks your laws and laughs in your face. He talks with his god three times a day." The king's gutted. He works all day to find a way round the law and get Daniel off the charges. But the lobby group push the fact that no King's Order can be changed.

16

The king knows he's cornered and mutters the order through clenched teeth; Daniel's chucked into the lions' cage. The king shouts through to Daniel, "Here's hoping the God you never stop serving will do something."

17-18

A stone is shunted in front of the cage. The king seals this "door" with his ring and those of his nobility, making it final. Then he mopes off to his palace and spends a sleepless night, refusing any food or escapist entertainment.

19-20

Sun up, the king rushes straight to the cage. As he gets there he shouts, "Daniel, God's tireless worker, has your God been able to keep you alive?"

21-22

Daniel's voice booms back, "Long live the king! Too right!! My God dispatched an angel who held the lions' mouths shut all night. I was innocent in front of you and God – they've not even licked me!"

23

The king's ecstatic! He gives the order to have Daniel sprung from his prison. He comes out with not a scratch on him – the product of relying on God.

24

The king gives a new order and the suits who framed Daniel (plus their families) are replacement lion feed for the day. Before they even hit the deck, you could hear the crunch of tooth against bone.

25-27

Then King Darius sends a memo to all his people, reading, "Live long and prosper! This is my order: the God of Daniel is to get total respect, right across my kingdom. He's alive and always will be; his kingdom won't get usurped: his influence is permanent and total. He liberates people with spectacular effect, like Daniel who he rescued from the ravenous lions."

28

So Daniel's career makes great strides forward during the rest of Darius's time on the throne and also into the reign of Cyrus from Persia.

Daniel's proved he's got the guts and the wisdom to handle big stuff, so God lets him in on some more of his plans for the future. We're on to cosmic scale now: divine struggle of good vs evil, world catastrophe and the new era to come. Apocalypse soon! Daniel's dreams are full of fantastic special effects: lions with eagle's wings and human hearts, four-headed leopards with four wings, ten-horned monsters with iron teeth. All these symbolize different world powers: the fall of Babylon, the rise of the Medes and Persians, the Greeks, the Romans and the permanent kingdom to be run by God's Liberator. All the images, codes and numbers give Daniel a headache trying to work them out — and that's with the angel Gabriel as a tutor!   —Rob

Reign of the Liberator (Daniel 7:13-14)

In my night vision I saw in front of me a man coming down from heaven on a cloud. He walks straight up to the Eternal God, and he's given absolute influence, fame, distinction and total control. Everyone from everywhere celebrates him every way they can. His control is total and permanent. His jurisdiction is never going to suffer a takeover: it's here to stay. End of story!

Basically, God wins.   —Rob

The Minor Prophets / The Dangerous Dozen

Twelve couriers, three sections:

- First group of six – written when Assyria was top dog on the world stage.
- Second group of three – written when the dog was going a bit mangy.
- Last group of three – the dog's dead! The new dog (Persia) doesn't believe in leashes and lets the Jews return home.

Get ready with your scroll keys: we're shifting through history in both directions.

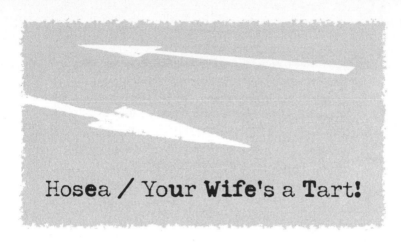

Hosea / Your Wife's a Tart!

Bad time to be a Jew: the northern kingdom, Israel, is being threatened with a takeover bid from a larger company. Hosea gets to announce the winner.   —Rob

Go marry a tart! (Hosea 1:2-3)

When God starts using Hosea as a courier, first thing he says is, "Go find a tart, marry her, have kids with her. Why? 'Cos Israel's a tart — guilty as charged: walking out on our relationship and having lurid affairs with other gods." So he arranges the wedding with Gomer Diblaimson and makes babies with her.

She can't kick her addiction to other men and separates from Hosea.   —Rob

The full picture (Hosea 3:1-5)

1

God says to Hosea, "Go find your wife; tell her you love her and you want her back. Yeah, I know she's having an affair with someone else and she's been totally unfaithful to you. But love her like I love the Jews, even though they go off with other gods and get off on the raisin cakes used at their sacrifices."

2-3

So I cough up the customary bride price (fifteen silver pieces plus 150 kg [330 pounds] of barley) and tell her, "Come on, let's get engaged again. Let's be an item. Don't go out on the town all pushed up and painted up. Don't get off with anyone else – I'll wait for you."

4-5

'Cos the northern Jews will be kingless for a long time. They'll be without all the trappings of their religion and will feel out of touch with God. But then they'll come back, spend time with their God again; they'll look for another king like David. They'll come back to God with their hands shaking out of respect and he'll do them good again.

> Hosea reads out the charges facing the Jews: disloyalty, stubbornness, lying, murder, stealing – pretty much breaking most of Moses' Big Ten. He also gives the verdict – guilty. —Rob

Kids! Who'd 'ave 'em? (Hosea 11:1-5)

1-4

God says, "When Israel was young I loved them as sons! I called them back out from Egyptian slavery. But the louder I called, the further off they crawled. Hidden miles away from me they got into weird religions, polished bizarre statues, sacrificed to non-gods. I taught them to walk, I held their hands as they wobbled, but they've got no clue it was me who was there for them. Did I use ropes or sticks to lead them? No, just love. I took all the heaviness off them; I got down on my knees to feed them."

5

"And now, 'cos they won't turn their lives round to face me, they've got to go back to 'Egypt' – Assyria will take them off and run their lives for them."

> So the charges, the verdict and now the sentence – eviction from Israel to be Assyrian slaves in Nineveh. —Rob

180 Degrees (Hosea 14:1-9)

1-3

Come back, Israel. Come on back to your God. You've slipped up in your own mess. Here's your script; say it like you mean it: say, "Acquit us of all the charges we're facing; make it like we're innocent. Take us back; welcome us with open arms and we'll give you all the credit. We'll face the truth – Assyria's impotent. What can they do for us? Their warhorses won't help. Those stupid idols we chiselled with our own hands? We'll stop calling them 'our gods'. We're fatherless, but we know you love us with a passion."

4

God says, "I'll treat them for their wanderingitus. I'll love them wildly, 'cos my anger's all used up."

God says he'll be the gardener and Israel will flourish there.   –Rob

9

Anyone with any brain, anyone with an ounce of sense, will know this: God's methods are spot on. Those who do the right thing do the God-thing. But the anarchists hit the ground hard as they trip over his Rules.

Joel / Pest Control

Judgement Day's coming. The Jews think they'll get special treatment, but Joel's got bad news. Forget hiding behind your passport – sort it out with God before it's too late ...   —Rob

Day of the locust (Joel 1:1-6)

1-3

God dictates a message to Joel Pethuelson, "Listen up you leaders and you led. Ever seen anything like this? Ever heard your granddad doing his 'in my day' routine to match this? Tell your kids. Get them to tell their kids. And on."

4

It's all gobbled up! Swarms of hungry locusts systematically stripped the fields of anything worth anything. There's nothing left. Nothing!

> Clouds of insects darkening the skies – great image for an invading army.   —Rob

6

A foreign army flattened our border defences. Uncountable troops with invasion orders. Each man psyched up and dangerous as a champion boxer on speed.

> But marauding squadrons of a ruthless world power are a play fight with a puppy compared to God's Judgement Day. It's coming ...   —Rob

Too late? (Joel 2:11-13)

11

God's like an ear-shattering thunder as he strides out in front of his army. His forces are an awesome fighting machine. God's Judgement Day is the ultimate bad-news day, the mother of all endurance challenges. Who's going to get through it alive?

12-13

"There's still time!" says God. "Come back to me with commitment. Prove you're serious; go without food – grieve for what you've done. Let's see some real tears." All the clothes-ripping rituals are just a cliché. He wants to see ripped hearts. Come back; use your return ticket. He's generous. He's passionate about you. He bites his tongue to stop him giving the "Wipe out!" order. Why? 'Cos he's crazy about you: he loves you. He'll call off the troops, he will. Come back!

And when they show they're serious . . .   –Rob

What locusts? (Joel 2:18-32)

18-19

Then God will go easy on his land. He'll pity his people. He'll answer their begging, "Supplies are on the way. I'm sending food, wine, some luxuries, some indigestion tablets (it's rich stuff). No way are you going to be the butt of foreigners' jokes."

God goes on to announce he's going to send the foreign army packing and his people will throw parties again. Plus . . .   –Rob

25-27

"The years wasted by the locusts: you'll get it all back. And some! You'll have cupboards full of top cuisine; you'll be stuffed full. It'll go past its 'best before' date 'cos you just won't be able to eat it all! You'll thank me for getting the shopping in and covering it on his card. You'll know I've worked miracles and you'll never again mope around, head down in humiliation. 'Cos then you'll know I'm around, that I'm your God and no other god comes close. Never again will you feel guilty to be alive."

28-32

"After this I'll dose you up on my Spirit. Your kids will hear from me again – direct. Your OAPs will get vivid dreams straight from heaven. Your young guys will get potent images from my communications department – with subtitles. There won't be a 'No Go Zone' for my Spirit: I'll pour my Spirit out on the widest spectrum of people. There'll be warnings: spectacular miracles in the atmosphere and on the ground, bloodshed, raging fires, toxic fumes. It'll eclipse the sun, turn the moon blood red. And all this is just the warm-up for the horrendous Judgement Day of God. But anyone screaming 'God! Help! Please!' will get a result. Jerusalem will have some hand-picked survivors."

God will pronounce sentence on the other nations who gave his people a hard time.　　　　　　　　　　　　　　　　　　　　　　　　　–Rob

Decision Valley (Joel 3:14-16)

Record-breaking crowds standing shoulder-to-shoulder in Decision Valley. The countdown to God's Judgement Day is down to single figures, and Decision Valley is where it'll all happen. The sun, moon and stars will be scared off by the blast of God's roaring voice. The earth and sky'll shake with the thunder hitting Jerusalem. But God's people will hide in the eye of his storming anger. They'll curl up, foetus-like, and tough it out: they'll make it through alive.

But for people who've shed innocent blood, who've committed violence against God's people – Judgement Day means exactly that.　　　　　　–Rob

Amos / God Hates Your Religion

Scroll back up history. If you get to Elisha, you've gone too far. Scan forward through the blood and gore of King Ahab and Jezebel till you get to King Jeroboam II. God's speaking to Israel through a farmer from Judah. The northern Jews are keeping their options open on the god front — and it seems to be working. They think they're keeping God happy by doing all the religious stuff, and that he hasn't spotted their scams that are ripping off the working classes. Hasn't he?   —Rob

After all I've done! (Amos 2:10-13)

"I drag you out of Egypt, guide you through forty years of nomadic life, give you the deeds of Amorite land, talk direct to you through my couriers. Or am I wrong? Answer me! Did I mumble? Did I make myself scarce? No! You've just not listened. You pollute my select, make them go back on their promises to me; you slap a freedom-of-speech ban on my couriers. So I've no choice but to crush you like a runaway truck, fully loaded."

No one'll escape. They're his picked-out people, so they get disciplined. He warns them through his couriers, but they've no clue on how to be good.   —Rob

Trash the place (Amos 3:11-15)

11-12

So God says, "An enemy army will take out your defences and swarm all over you, looting your homes, lifting your valuables. Some of you will scrape through alive. Just as bits of a sheep survive when a shepherd yanks back a leg or an ear from a lion's mouth, so some of you half-breed Jews from Samaria will get away with the leg of a table, the corner of a blanket, maybe."

13-15

God told me to announce bad news: "When I come down heavy on Israel, I'm going to make sure the religious centres at Bethel are completely trashed. I'm *sick* of it all. I'll demolish their town houses and their holiday homes in the country; their poseur palaces and macho mansions will be rubble." That's what God says.

> All this 'cos the Jews from the northern kingdom, Israel, haven't contacted God for years. They've just gone through the motions of their religion and carried on filling their savings accounts with money ripped off from the poor. God's tried to get through to them by organizing droughts and epidemics, but they've got their heads down, too busy counting the cash to listen.   —Rob

God hates religion (Amos 5:11-24)

11-13

"You step on the poor. You tie them in so they've got to sell to you at rock-bottom prices. Now it's your turn to cough up. See your mansion? You won't be needing your keys. See your vineyards? You won't taste the wine. 'Cos I've got reels of closed-circuit TV footage all marked 'Israel's Corruption'. I know how messed up you are: good people get smacked down; evil people get paid off; poor people get nothing from the courts. If they've got any sense, they don't even protest. What's the point? Too many evil people, with too much to hide."

14-15

"Put *good* words through your search engine, not *evil* ones, and you might live. Hate what's wrong; love what's right; make your courts fair. Then, *maybe,* God'll look with some pity at those of you who survive."

> The Judgement Day of God is coming.   —Rob

21-24

God says, "Can't stand your religion — it turns my stomach. I detest your meetings. Yeah, fine, you bring me your offerings by the book, but I'll throw them back in your smug faces. You bring me your peace offerings, but they mean nothing; so I'll ignore them. Oh, and your songs: just shut up; they're doing my head in! If I hear one more tambourine, I'm going to scream. What I want to hear is the roaring river of justice sweeping through your towns. What I want is for the right things you do to wash away the dry, hard, crusted build-up of evil."

> All this isn't exactly popular: Amos saying they're going after other so-called gods; that they're getting cocky; that the king'll die and the people will be slaves abroad. Not exactly crowd-pleasing material. The king wants to kick him out, back down to Judah. But God's message won't be censored just because it's gory.   —Rob

Spring-cleaning (Amos 9:8-12)

8-10

"I'm watching every evil thought Israel has. It's wipe-out-a-nation time, but I'll leave some survivors," says God. "I'll give the orders and Israel will be shaken like dirty grain in a sieve. Decent people will survive by being thrown over the borders into foreign soil. But the dirt and the stones will be chucked out. Anyone who says, 'What's the problem? Nothing's going to touch us,' will see the sharp end of a foreign knife!"

11-12

"But one day I'll mend David's messed-up country: total reconstruction — it'll be as good as it ever was."

> He'll bring them back and help them make the place like a home again, permanent.   —Rob

Obadiah / Rival's Revenge

Way back when Isaac had the twins Jacob and Esau, it was stated that both family lines would become large nations. Sure enough, Esau's lot, the Edomites, are now a powerful country. Rivalry with Israel has been a running theme, and now that Jerusalem is smashed to pieces, the Edomites are loving it and helping themselves to the pickings. Obadiah forwards this warning from God.　　　–Rob

Full circle (Obadiah 10-15)

10-12

"You were violent with your brother, Jacob. So you're going to be dragged down shamefully – you're going to be terminated. You stand there all distant while foreigners stuff their bags with his family silver, while they play dice for Jerusalem – you're as bad as they are. Don't look down your nose at your brother just 'cos he's in schtuck. Don't buy a round of drinks to celebrate their crashing out. Don't be so cocky when they're so messed up."

Don't kick a dog when it's down. Why? 'Cos ...　　　–Rob

15

"God's Judgement Day is creeping up quietly. What you've dished out, you'll have to stomach yourselves. Everything you've given out will backfire and smack you full in the face."

Obadiah goes into some detailed geography on who's going to get their land once they've been wiped out. Ironically, Jacob's lot, Israel, does pretty well out of it.　–Rob

Jonah / Courier on a Detour

Back up about 200 years: Jonah Amittaison gets instructions from God to go east to Nineveh, capital of Israel's enemy Assyria. He's to warn the city that God's on their case. But Jonah knows his God: if they get the warning, they might sort themselves out, and then God won't destroy them! So he legs it to the western port of Joppa and buys a ticket to Tarshish (Spain). God sends gale-force winds and the boat nearly does its *Titanic* impression. Jonah tells the crew ...   —Rob

It's my fault! (Jonah 1:12)

"Chuck me overboard; then watch the waves flatten out. This storm's down to me."

They do and it goes calm. They're all freaked out. God sends a huge fish to swallow Jonah whole. He's in its stomach for three days. Jonah's pleadings echo around its belly, but he knows God's heard him. Sure enough, on God's cue, the fish throws up onto the beach and Jonah is delivered, but not looking his best — hair bleached in digestive acids and smelling of parfume de fish vomit. God gives him a second chance: Nineveh asap. Same message. This time Jonah goes, gives them God's warning and starts the clock on a forty-day countdown. As he feared, the wake-up call works and they sort themselves out with God, so he cancels his large lightning order. 'Course Jonah's well miffed.   —Rob

I knew it! (Jonah 4:2-4)

Jonah spits out at God, "I knew it! This is exactly what I said back home. Why d'you think I was on turbo drive to get to Tarshish? I know you: you're generous! You're passionate about people. It takes a lot to rile you and you can't help loving people. You just love it when you can call off the dogs. So kill me now, God – I'm better off dead!"

God comes back at him, "Who d'you think you are? What right have you got to be angry?"

> Jonah storms out of Nineveh and fumes for a while, watching the skies, hoping for an electric storm to hit the city. God grows a vine to protect Jonah from sunstroke, and Jonah grudgingly thanks him. In the night God commissions a worm to chew the life out of the vine, Jonah wakes up to find it withered and pathetic. The day's a scorcher and Jonah's getting dizzy with the sun. He's in a mood 'cos the vine's gone and he does his "take me now, God" routine again.   —Rob

Yeah, even them (Jonah 4:9-11)

9

God comes back at Jonah, "What right have you got to be angry about the vine?"

Jonah's not thinking straight: he still wants to die.

10-11

God says, "You took a liking to the vine. But did you water it or plant it? Was it down to you that it grew? No. One day it was here; the next gone. And you're in mourning for it! Well, Nineveh has 120,000 people (plus cattle) who are like little kids, not sure if they're coming or going – they need a dad! Why can't I care for them if I want to?"

> Hard question to someone convinced God's only interested in the Jewish nation. It's tough admitting you're wrong!   —Rob

Micah / Justice's Downside

Scroll down a little from Jonah to Isaiah's era and you'll get Micah announcing doom and gloom for both Israel and Judah. Like in Isaiah's material, there's a balance of future treats after the threats have come true. There are also hints that the Liberator is waiting in the wings ready to start the Final Act of world peace.   —Rob

Sleaze City (Micah 1:3-5)

Watch out! God's coming down from heaven to stomp on every pagan mountain shrine. Mountains will melt under his boots like hot candle wax. Valleys will split down the middle like flood water gushing down a city street. And it's your messing up that's brought it all on. Israel's capital city of corruption is Samaria. Judah's head offices of sleaze are all in Jerusalem.

So warm up your grieving tackle. Get your water levels up for all those tears to come. Your capital cities haven't long left.   —Rob

You cannibals (Micah 3:1-4)

1-3

"Listen up, you politicians, you bureaucrats. You, of all people, should have a handle on justice. But you detest good things, and the more depraved it is, the more you love it. You rip the skin off the backs of my people. Then you take the flesh off their bones. You're like a bunch of cannibals, skinning my people, breaking their bones and boiling them up for your daily meal."

4

"You'll call out to God but he'll stay schtum. He'll play hide-and-seek with you and you won't even get 'warm', 'cos of the evil you've made happen."

> Similar bad news for the fair-weather couriers, who just say what people want to hear, that "every little thing's gonna be all right" – Jerusalem levelled is not "all right"!
>
> –Rob

World peace (Micah 4:1-4)

1

But in the final era everyone will look up to the mountain where God's HQ stands tall. It'll be like a magnet to countless nations – they'll queue for days to get inside.

2-4

They'll lose track of how many nationalities visit. They'll all say the same thing in different languages: "Let's go to God's mountain. Let's go to the HQ of Jacob's God. He'll give us a crash course in how things should be done. He'll coach us to be like him." 'Cos Jerusalem's where it will all happen. That's where God will break the news of his plans. He'll negotiate peace settlements with major players across the world. They'll construct giant factories to convert their weapons into tools. There'll be world peace! No armies, no ministries of defence, no martial arts – no need!

> God'll bring back the survivors of his short, sharp shock and make them secure again.
>
> –Rob

The Liberator's home town (Micah 5:2-5a)

"OK, Bethlehem, I know you've got an inferiority complex. You may be a small noise in the Judah region, but the one who's going to run the whole of Israel will be a Bethlehemite. He's the Ancient One. He's been around a long time already. God will make himself scarce until this boy is born. All my people spread globally will come back because of him. He'll be a guide and a guard to his people, a minder and a mentor, and he'll have unlimited access to all the power of God to do it. He'll resonate greatness. Individuals and nations will be secure, 'cos his charisma and easy authority will have won over the whole world. He'll be their peace."

But for those who won't step in line, God'll wipe them out – his people should know better what God requires.   —Rob

What God wants (Micah 6:8)

Hasn't he shown you what's good? Don't you know what he expects from you? It's very simple: to be fair with people, to give people some slack and to know your place with God.

But they've done none of that. So they're going to get God's discipline. It'll be a rough time, but eventually God will bring them back, like he did when they were trapped in Egypt.   —Rob

Acquitted (Micah 7:18-20)

Who's like you, God? You acquit us, though we're guilty and we know it. We're the survivors, the last of your inheritance. But you're not angry forever: you love it when you can free people who don't deserve it. You'll not be able to suppress your passion for us indefinitely. You'll stamp the life out of our dark side; you'll bag up the evidence against us and chuck it into the sea; you'll be loyal to your people – you'll not treat us as we deserve. You promised all this way back, and you stand by what you say.

Start of the second group of couriers – the old dog Assyria's on her last legs. —Rob

Nahum / Nineveh's Nightmare

Fast-forward about fifty years after Micah and Isaiah have left the scene and Nahum prophesies God's payback on Nineveh, capital city of Assyria, and Judah's number one threat. The Assyrians had ripped into Israel's capital, Samaria, torturing its leaders before executing them and uprooting the whole population. Over a hundred years before, Jonah announced Nineveh's destruction, but they sorted their act out and God called off the catastrophe. But they're *back* to their old, disgusting habits, so . . .

—Rob

Revenge of the Deity (Nahum 1:2-8)

2-3

God takes his rivals out with ruthless violence. When it's payback time for his enemies, they know it! It takes a lot to wind God up, but provoke him too many times and you'll see first hand his full force. No guilty party gets away with it forever.

Not even the mountains can stand straight when he shouts in anger.   —Rob

7-8

God is intrinsically good: a safe house for the anxious, a bodyguard for anyone who'll rely on him. But Nineveh's going to get swept off the map by a tidal wave of an army. God'll chase them till their lights go out.

God'll block all their anti-God plans and free his people from their chains.   —Rob

History (Nahum 1:14-15)

God's given the orders for your fate, Nineveh: "Your family line stops here. No kids will be left alive to carry on your name. I'll smash up your wannabe gods – tacky, makeshift models that they are! I'll dig your grave already, chisel out the words 'Vile Assyrian' on your headstone. So, Judah, look up! On the horizon! A messenger with a beaming smile – good news! Peace! Now you can enjoy your national holidays; you can do what you promised. Assyria won't be hassling you any more – they're history."

And then, direct to the top man . . .   – Rob

Dozy politicians (Nahum 3:18-19)

"King of Assyria, your government ministers are dozy. Your movers and shakers are still in their beds while your people are refugees wandering aimlessly in the hills with no leader. No bandage will stop the gushing blood: it's a fatal injury. And when people watch the news, they'll applaud; they'll whoop and yell. 'Cos they've all felt the sharp edge of your cruelty."

Sure enough, Nineveh's swamped by Babylonian soldiers at the back end of the seventh century BC. The city's ruins are discovered centuries later, covered in desert sand.   – Rob

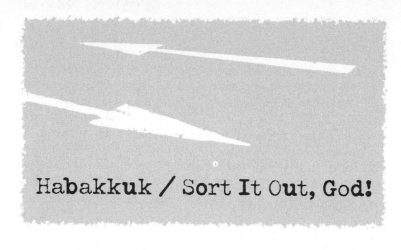

Habakkuk / Sort It Out, God!

Soon after Nahum, the Babylonians are overtaking Assyria on the cruelty stakes. Habakkuk's shaking his fist at God, "How come you let them get away with it?!"

—Rob

Q&A (Habakkuk 1:2-2:20)

2-4

"What have I got to do to get your attention, God? Are you deliberately ignoring me or what? I'm screaming out 'road rage, field rage, house rage everywhere', but you do nothing! Why do I have to watch all this corruption? Why d'you let them get away with it? Everywhere people are so aggressive: vandalism, fights, mindless destruction; it's epidemic. The law's hamstrung – no one gets a fair trial; good people are trapped in a perverted system."

God comes back at him . . .

—Rob

5-6

"Hang in there. Keep up with current affairs. You'll be blown away by the incredible plot line I'm working on. Talk about a twist! I'm backing the ruthless Babylonians. They walk over nation after nation and don't even wipe the blood off their boots."

He goes into detail on their violent track record. Habakkuk risks questioning God again.

—Rob

12-13

"God you're timeless, birthless, endless. You're my God, purity itself, and you're saying you're using *them* to punish us? How can you even look at such people, let alone work with them?! OK, we're bad – but they're worse! Loads worse!"

> God assures him that there's bad news for Babylon too, but only once they've taught Judah a lesson. —Rob

2:4

"The wicked man struts around so sure of himself, but his fantasy life is crippled and bent. Good people will get through life by relying on me," says God.

> Mr Wicked's arrogant, greedy as Death itself. —Rob

6

Bad news round the corner for those who stockpile stolen goods, who live off the profits of extortion: it won't last.

> Those who you owe will come knocking on your door. Tables will turn. The victims will victimize you. —Rob

9

Bad news down the road for those who create an empire from ripping people off.

> You've done a job on so many, lying to them. The walls of your luxury homes will scream! —Rob

12

Bad news with faulty brakes, careering down the road towards those who build a city on bloodshed, who run a place on crime.

> You spike the drinks of neighbours so you can get them playing strip poker. The drinks are mixed up and you lose control. —Rob

19-20

Bad news with no driver at the wheel, hurtling towards those who say to bits of wood and stone, "Live, won't you?" Do inanimate objects give good advice?! OK, so it's been sprayed with gold or silver, but it doesn't breathe; it can't talk – it's dead! But the Awesome God is alive and well in his HQ: the world will shut up and shake in silence.

So Habakkuk says to God . . .   –Rob

Again! Again! (Habakkuk 3:2-19)

2

Awesome God, I know your track record. I'm dumbstruck by what you've done in the past. Please, do it again! Turn up today like you did before. In your rage, don't forget to be gentle with us.

He lists some of God's most famous victories.   –Rob

16-19

When I heard these stories my heart raced, my lower lip twitched, my bones went weak, my knees knocked. But I'll sit tight. I'll wait, cool and calm, for the day this invasion force gets run down by God's anger. Whatever happens, I'll celebrate God, party in my heart 'cos he liberates me. Even if the shelves are bare, even if the cupboards are empty, I'll party, celebrate God. When the projects fail, when the screen goes blank, I'll party, celebrate God. He liberates me. The God who runs the cosmos is what keeps me going. He makes my every step as sure-footed as a deer on the mountains. I can climb because of his energy and protection.

Zephaniah / Judgement Day and Beyond

Scroll back a tad from Habakkuk and you find a distant cousin of a previous Judaean king getting messages on God's hotline. And it is hot! God's anger's burning through Zephaniah, and Judah soon realizes it's not only "pagan foreigners" who get put in line by God. As ever, the only escape clause for Judah is to wake up and turn round to God. Will they do it before Assyria flattens Jerusalem? God says . . .   —Rob

Judgement Day (Zephaniah 1:4-9)

"I'll flex my muscles and Judah and its capital, Jerusalem, will fold. I'll cancel any future for the fertility god, Baal, and no one will remember the pagans who ran his services. I'll wipe the slate clean of the stargazers who run their lives by lumps of rock. I'll wipe the smiles off the two-faced Jews who swear by me and swear by Molech 'just in case'. I'll turn my back on those who turn back from living my way, those who live as if I don't exist. Stand up and shut up before me – Judgement Day is ticking closer. I've sent invites to your enemies to join in the sacrificing of my people. On this day I'll discipline Judah's leading figures and royal family; I'll sort out those who act like pagans; I'll slap down the superstitious who avoid stepping on thresholds and pump the HQs of their wannabe gods full of aggression and mistrust."

More gory detail on the looming catastrophe.   —Rob

Maybe you'll survive (Zephaniah 2:3)

"Any of you guys who know your place and live my way, you who connect with me, look to do the right thing; check you're not getting too cocky; then, maybe, you'll survive my Judgement Day."

> It's not just Judah being straightened out; it's the surrounding nations too. But after the disasters . . .
>
> —Rob

Beyond Judgement Day (Zephaniah 3:16-20)

16-17

"But one day, you'll hear the words, 'Don't panic! No Jewish hands need go limp with fright. The Awesome God's on your side, and he's well strong enough to liberate you. He'll go overboard for you – whoop and yell at full volume, going crazy over you. He loves you – he'll prove it. You'll *know* it and will become calmness itself. He'll show you off to everyone, singing songs about you.'"

18-20

"All those who really miss the religious festivals – I'll bring you together. You won't be the butt of jokes anymore. The people who oppressed you – I'll deal with them. I'll protect the injured, round up the rejects, make sure you enjoy respect and privilege everywhere you were mocked. Then I'll guide your trip home. I'll make sure the whole world admires you, toasting you at their parties as I give you back the success you once enjoyed. This is what God says."

> The next three couriers all come from the same period: the Jews have served their seventy-year punishment in Babylon and many have gone back home. But making ends meet is tough for most of them. God spells out why – they've all got luxurious houses, but no one's bothered with rebuilding his HQ.
>
> —Rob

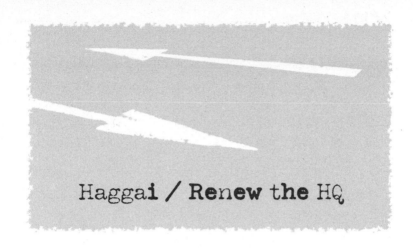

Haggai / Renew the HQ

Priority buildings (Haggai 1:5-9)

5-6

God says, "Think about it. What you doing? You invest loads of energy and get little back to show for it. You fill your faces, but you never seem to fill your bellies. You drink, but your mouths stay dry. You dress, but you still feel the cold. You pick up your paycheck, then stuff it into pockets with holes."

7-9

God says, "Think it through. What's up? Go to the mountains and chop some trees. Build my HQ with the timber. Make it extraordinary again. Make me proud to be seen there. You had high expectations, you were all pumped up, but face it, it didn't amount to a fraction of what you'd imagined, and now you're deflated. Everything you bring home, I flush it straight down the toilet. Why? Because my HQ is still a pile of rubble while you lot are spending all your spare time doing Feng Shui on your own pads."

> Basically, sort it! They get chopping and God promises to fill the place so it's glowing, even more than Solomon's old HQ did. Before the foundations were in place, God sabotaged everything they did. But now they've got their priorities sorted, he's going to make them prosperous. —Rob

Zechariah / Get Shovelling!

Leave the scroll keys alone: Zechariah's doing his thing round the same time as Haggai. This Babylon-born courier gets loads of visions of the Jews getting things together again. Now that they're back in Jerusalem, they need a king from David's family line. He prophesies the coming of the Liberator: no names, no ETA, but a clue as to his "big entrance". Till then Zerubbabel's the guvnor.　　—Rob

Open arms (Zechariah 1:2-6)

2-6a

"God was livid with your granddad's crowd. So tell them, d'you know what the Awesome God says? 'Come back!' he booms. 'Come back to me and I'll connect with you again.' Don't be like your ancestors, the guys who were told by the couriers that the God who says what goes, says this: 'Quit the dark stuff.' But they had selective deafness – whenever I said anything, they looked blank. Where are your grandfathers now? Dead. Did the old couriers live forever? No. But what I said through the couriers came true and swept your granddads off the scene."

6b

"So they swivel round a full 180 degrees and face the music, saying, 'We got what was coming to us. God treated us as we deserved, like he said he would.'"

Loads of vivid images symbolizing the reconstruction of Jerusalem, God's HQ and God's people.　　—Rob

Don't just give up chocolate (Zechariah 7:4-14)

4-7

Then the awesome God comes to me and says, "Ask the people and my reps this: 'When you give things up for religious reasons, d'you really do it for me? When you have your religious feast days, isn't it just an excuse to fill your faces? Isn't this just ditto on what the previous couriers said when you had peace?'"

8-10

God says to me again, "This is what I say, 'Give people a fair deal: give each other some breaks 'cos there's genuine love between you. Don't rip off the disadvantaged, the foreigners or the poor. Don't let negative thoughts about people fester in your souls.'"

11-12

"Did they listen? Did they heck! They gave me the cold shoulder and turned up their headphones to drown me out. They toughened up their consciences till they were hard as tempered steel. The Rules and the couriers' messages were deleted from their memory banks and I was fuming."

13-14

"I contacted them but they wouldn't return my call. So when they needed me, I played the same game," says God. "I made like a hurricane and scattered them across the known world – to live as foreign lowlifes. Their homeland was trashed, totally uninhabitable. They'd turned a paradise into a desert."

> God's jealous for the Jews, so he's going back to Jerusalem and he's brightening up lives there – old and young. His people will return to a great place.   –Rob

Get your hod out (Zechariah 8:9-15)

9-11

"You old guys who remember what the couriers said the day the HQ foundations were checked off as finished: get your hands dirty; harden them up – there's a place needs building! Up till now there were no jobs. Who can run a business when society's disintegrating into gang rule? But from today the survivors get a new deal," says God.

> Promises of better production figures and a turnaround in public opinion about the Jews. —Rob

14-15

God says this: "When your granddads wound me up, I pulled the carpet from under them. But now I'm going to do you good. Don't lose sleep over your future."

> Their side of the bargain: a similar list to before about doing the right thing. —Rob

Unexpected entrance (Zechariah 9:9-10)

"Go crazy! Dance the night away. Your King's making his entrance. The Liberator who does the right thing, who doesn't hype it up or pose – he arrives on a baby donkey! I'll evacuate the armoured vehicles from Jerusalem; the weapons will be melted down. He'll announce 'peace time' to world nations and his worldwide jurisdiction will make sure it happens!"

> God's on his way. ETA soon. Watch this space. He'll look out for the Jews, bring them back and send their enemies packing. Fast-forward to the day when Jews will grieve that they did the Liberator in. But their mess will be written off and the survivors will come through the trauma like refined gold. We're left with God in battle gear, trouncing his people's enemies and having his coronation as King.
> —Rob

Malachi /
Halve Your Double Standards

So they listen to Zechariah and get the HQ built. But hassle and hard work take the edge off the Bright New Future atmosphere, and standards at God's HQ are slipping. His reps are just going through the motions, and the people are losing sight of their intended future. Malachi agrees with Nehemiah's slamming of general attitudes. He's sent to broker a new deal: sort out what you give to God and he'll give you more back, guaranteed! —Rob

God gets the butt-end (Malachi 1:6-8)

God's memo coming through Malachi: "A son shows respect to his dad; a worker holds the door for his boss. So if I'm your father, where's my respect? If I'm your boss, how come you slam the door in my face?" asks God. "You reps are the worst – you misuse my name and wear it out. 'Course you come back all innocent and ask, 'How?' You only sacrifice stuff you don't need. Yeah, and you still ask, 'How?' (either bluffing or stupid). You make a mockery of the whole sacrifice system: I only get the butt-end of the deal – is that right? I only get the damaged goods you'd chuck out anyway – is that right? Try giving this rubbish as a present to your boss. D'you think he'd promote you? D'you think he'd take you out for lunch?"

God's not best pleased with them. He wants them to give of their best, to sacrifice something that costs them. Then he'll know they're serious. But all they do is moan at him 'cos he's all distant. He'll show – but in the form of *fire* to burn off all the dross! —Rob

Ripping off God (Malachi 3:5-10)

5

"I'll stop being distant. I'll turn up as prosecutor with cases full of evidence against witches, sleep-around merchants, liars in contempt of court, fat-cat bosses who rip off their workers, anyone who steps on those at the bottom end of the ladder and all who stop foreigners getting a fair trial – basically, those who give me no respect," says God.

6-10

"I'm solid, stable, and I don't have whims. If I did, you Jews wouldn't still be here! Right the way through you've systematically rubbished my Rules. Come back to me and I'll connect with you again," says the Awesome God. "But you go, 'How do we come back?' and I answer, 'Don't rip me off!' You come back, 'Whoa! How we ripping you off?' And I say, 'In what you give back to me. The agreement was, I give you 100 percent; you give me at least 10 percent back. This is why there's such an overkill of bad news – 'cos you're ripping me off. Bring the full amount to the HQ: don't try and get away with half measures, but make sure there's food in my house. Try me out: see if I don't turn the good-news taps on full and drench you with so much stuff you won't know what to do with it all!'"

> Lots of discussion. Decisions are made and promises written out and signed. The people choose life. —Rob

Dads and lads, mums and misses (Malachi 4:1-6)

1-3

"It's on its way, the big day. The cocky dealers of darkness will be burnt up like a pile of straw in an industrial furnace – ashes. Nothing else," says God. "But you lot who respect me, the sun will rise in the sky and its warm rays will heal your sores and scars. You'll leap around like a puppy let off the leash. Then it'll be role-reversal time: you'll walk all over the evil dealers. Their ashes will get stuck in your boots when I make all this happen," says God.

4

"Keep reminding yourselves of the Contract I made with Moses at Horeb for all of you — the terms and conditions still apply."

5-6

"Before Judgement Day comes, I'll send Elijah the courier to you. He'll renew the bonding between fathers and sons. Fathers will burst with love for their sons, and children will love their fathers. Otherwise, I'd have to come back and unleash more bad news on the place."

Then for about four hundred years, it seems like God loses his voice — or maybe he's just not speaking to them. All they have to go on is what he's already said: there will be a Liberator. But everything's up in the air. Not only who this Liberator is, but also who they're going to need liberating from. Major shifts in world power: delete "Medes and Persians"; paste in "Greek Empire". Alexander the Great is focused on making Greek the first language of the whole known world — handy for any future world religion to spread! The Jews struggle under Greek rule until a twenty-four-year war that wins them a brief eighty-odd years of independence.

But in 63 BC the Roman emperor Pompey marches into Jerusalem and it's back to square one. As ever they don't excel at keeping to God's Contract with the distractions of another culture plastered on every wall. The changing culture gives the Pharisees the excuse to rework the small print of God's Contract and the Jewish nation is feeling pretty picked on. In 47 BC Julius Caesar gives the job of policing the Jews to Herod the Great. He's such a creep, true Jews prefer the name "Herod the Hand-Puppet". Herod knows his impure Esau-derived blood is a major block to popularity, and he tries to win people over by spending huge amounts on rebuilding God's HQ in Jerusalem. Cynics reckon his press office is leaking rumours about him being the Liberator. It doesn't wash, but the Jews are on the lookout. Where's the Liberator? When's he going to show? When?   —Rob

NEW TESTAMENT

New Promise

The Liberator

Matthew / Mark / Luke / John / 4D Biography

One life, four bios from four angles, for a whole range of characters with different personalities, cultures and personality types. Matt writes with a strong Jewish accent for the in-house audience, linking events back to past courier predictions. He paints the central character as a life coach big on doing what God says. Mark's the first of the four to publish, using more of a Roman style, going for the bigger readership with a shorter, pacier account of Jesus, Man of Action. His main source of info is Pete, so he leaves the teaching content to those who were actually there. Dr Luke's also opening things up to non-Jews by writing, more formally, for a Roman official, Theophilus. Big into God's Spirit, he later writes the sequel, "The Early Years". Jonno's view is of a broader type: his big thing is the Liberator being both human and God. He uses a range of your everyday things as poetic images to make these huge concepts more digestible . . .   —Rob

Intro (John 1:1-18)

1-2

Nothing. No light, no time, no substance, no matter – the Voice was there. Before anything moved, mutated or mated, Jesus, God's Voice, was there with God from the kick-off. How come? 'Cos Jesus, "God's Voice", is God. Before anything began, they had always been. Before there was even anywhere to be, they were there.

3-5

Jesus got the name "God's Voice" because he just spoke and stuff started. From nothing to everything, sparked only by the Voice. There's nothing that doesn't have the phrase "made by Jesus" stamped on it somewhere. His words were life itself, and they lit up people's lives – his light could blast its way into the dingiest corner, and yet the people who preferred darkness still missed it.

6-9

So God sends John Baptizer to raise Jesus' profile: to lift up the Light. His job spec doesn't exactly fill an entire page – it just reads, "Help people take it in and take it on". Obviously, John's not the Light: he's just there to build expectation and commentate when the genuine article makes his entrance and starts lighting things up.

10-13

And when he does? Bizarre! No one recognizes him! He speaks them into existence, but they don't recognize him or his voice. He arrives at the front door of his people, and most don't even peek out of the spyhole to check. The few who take the risk realize who he is, open up and knock a meal together. To these guys he starts doling out adoption papers to sign them up as God's children. Conceived by *human* passion? No, by *God's* passion!

14

So God's Voice gets flesh and blood, skin and bone. He spends time with us; we hang around with him, get to know him, see what he's like. And? As magnificent, as superb as you'd expect God's only Son to be . . . and heaps more! God's over-the-top gifts oozing from every pore: everything he does and says rings true.

15-18

Like John Baptizer says, "Yeah, I hit the headlines first, but *he's* the one you should get excited about. He was around well before me." And because he was so stuffed full of good stuff, we've benefited – big time. OK, Moses gave us the Contract, but Jesus the Liberator gave us God's gifts and God's truth – loads better. Who's seen God? No one. But we've seen his only Son, Jesus, and you don't get closer than that.

Arrival

Top angel, Gabriel, picks up his work order for the day. It reads, "Destination: Nazareth. Contact: Mary Davidson. Message: God's Holy Spirit will get you pregnant with his Liberator." Mary can hardly believe it – she's a virgin: how's she to have a baby?! But she hears him out, realizes the privilege and goes for it. She's ecstatic. Joe, her fiancé, isn't! The only sane conclusion: she's been sleeping around. But a second visit from Gabriel persuades Joe to face the flack from the family and look after his love and her miracle child, Jesus. Meanwhile, on the political front ...   – Rob

Delivery suite 38b (Luke 2:1-7)

1-3

He-who-must-be-obeyed, Augustus Caesar, announces the Big Count-up. He wants accurate population stats across the Roman Empire at the time of Quirinius, governor of Syria. Everyone's expected to trek back to their family home town for registration.

4-7

So Joe Davidson sets off on the 129-kilometre (80-mile) trip south from Nazareth, County Galilee, to Bethlehem (aka Davidstown), County Judah. He takes his fiancée, Mary, who's pregnant and showing. They arrive and realize someone else is about to show! Her waters break. Crisis! "No Vacancy" signs in every B&B window. Decision. Joe delivers the baby in a shed full of livestock. Mary wraps strips of cloth round the baby and uses the animals' food trough as a cot. It's a boy!

Around the same time another angel gets his work order: "Destination: hillside near Bethlehem. Contact: sheep security team. Message: the Liberator's arrived – he'll be in a feeding trough. Personnel: whole heavenly army squadron plus choir." Once the guys recover from the shock of the laser-show announcement, they check it out. Sure enough, they find the baby in the makeshift cot. The next days all the pubs echo with Liberator talk.   – Rob

Great-Uncle Simeon (Luke 2:21-35)

Eight days on, the Davidson family sort out the religious and legal side of things at Jerusalem HQ. God's Holy Spirit directs an old guy, Simeon, to be there the same time. He holds the baby and says,   – Rob

29-32

"You're in charge, God. You told me I'd see him, and here I am cuddling the bundle of wonder! Bury me a happy old man: I've seen your Liberator, the eye-opener of outsiders, the pride and joy of Jews. I'm happy. Take me now!"

33-35

The Davidsons are gobsmacked. Simeon's got a PS for Mary: "This baby's going to impact everyone, one way or the other. I'm talking controversial. He'll expose people's true thoughts and for some people that'll be an ugly business . . . It'll be a sword through the soul for you, Mum."

Eastern astrologers (Matthew 2:1-16)

A group of Eastern astrologers turn up at King Herod's palace in Jerusalem, with questions about the birth of the new king. "What new king?" growls Herod. He checks it out with his advisors and they quote the seven-hundred-year-old prophecy of the courier Micah: –Rob

6-8

"OK, Bethlehem, I know you've got an inferiority complex. You may be a small noise in Judah, but the one who's going to run the whole of Israel will be a Bethlehemite."

'Course Herod's worried sick, but he's too sharp to let the astrologers spot it. Instead, he makes all enthusiastic, sending them down to Bethlehem with instructions to report back where he should go to pay his dues to this future king . . .

9-11

They make for Bethlehem. The star they've been tracking from the East stops; they work out the coordinates – right over where the boy is. In danger of embarrassing themselves with excitement, they arrive at the house and see the baby in his mum's arms. They kneel, awestruck by him. Once they recover from the impact, they give their presents: gold, incense and myrrh ("perfume with anaesthetic qualities"– it says on the tin).

12

That night one of them gets a God-dream: "Avoid Herod like he's contagious!" They make a detour on their return trip.

13-16

New dad Joe also gets a God-dream: an angel gets them ahead of the game, spilling the beans on Herod's plan to kill the baby. The message is clear: "Go to Egypt. Stay there till you get the OK." They skip breakfast and go. Just in time: Herod's fuming at being outsmarted by his foreign visitors. Playing back their conversation, the boy could be anything up to two years old by now. So his troops get the order to kill every boy under two. Herod's not keen on competition!

> Once Herod dies, his son Herod replaces him as king (the family's not exactly original on the name front). Joe gets the angelic all-clear and settles the family in Nazareth, County Galilee. Matt shows how all this (Egypt, infanticide, Nazareth) was flagged up by couriers way back when. Then nothing. For thirty years. Except one glimpse of the boy growing up . . .   —Rob

Zitty? (Luke 2:41-50)

41-45

It's the family annual jaunt to Jerusalem for the Flyby National Holiday. Jesus is twelve – it's bar mitzvah time. A whole posse travel down for the party. After the event they make their way back to Nazareth assuming he's with friends up front. After checking, no one's seen him since Jerusalem, and Mary and Joe turn back. After three days of panic-searching and three nights of sleepless fretting . . .

46-48

. . . they track him down to the foyer of God's HQ. He's sitting there with the teaching staff, soaking everything up and asking profound questions. The whole crowd are stunned by his grip on spiritual things and the answers he's coming out with. His parents spot him and break up the seminar. "How could you do this to us?" his mum asks. "Your dad and I have been looking all over, worried sick!"

49-50

"Was I that hard to find?" he says. 'Didn't you work out I'd be getting stuck into my Dad's business affairs?" They have no idea what he's going on about.

Then nothing for another eighteen years. All we get is that he's not a typical teenager – he does what he's told! He grows through puberty into manhood. He's popular with people and with God. Apart from that, nothing.   –Rob

Impact Year 1: Launch

Back to John Baptizer from the Intro. Wild character, living in the Judaean desert, raising expectation of the Liberator's launch. People are catching the mood: sorting themselves out, turning back round to God and outing themselves as God-followers by having John baptize them in front of the crowds. But it's not just cheap symbolism; John insists on lifestyle changes. Problem is, some of them think John's the One. Jesus, now thirty, turns up and John makes it perfectly clear that it's Jesus who's wearing the label "God's Liberator".   –Rob

Dove from above (Mark 1:9-11)

Jesus turns up from Nazareth (Galilee) and gets baptized by John. Jesus is just coming up out of the water; he sees the clouds split and God's Holy Spirit landing on him in the form of a dove. A voice comes booming through heaven's PA system, "You're my Son. I'm crazy about you and well into everything you do."

Jesus has to get into the desert alone and is there for forty days. No food, no home comforts, just Satan needling away at him, offering him the easy life of power and fame on his terms. Jesus swats him off with quotations from the ancient manuals. Heaven's a bit low on angel numbers; most of them seem to be in the desert backing Jesus up.

Meanwhile John's winding up King Herod who's married his brother's wife. The yes-men in the palace don't have the guts to tell him it's illegal. John Baptizer does! So Herod sticks him in jail, indefinitely. Mrs Herod wants him killed, but that's a tad too permanent. Besides, in a weird way, Herod sort of likes listening to the guy.

John's groupies Drew and Pete sign off from the Baptizer, and Jesus takes them on. Next day Phil joins the team. They go with Jesus to a wedding where he pulls off his first supernatural spectacular . . .   –Rob

Cheers! (John 2:1-11)

Jewish weddings are known for their amazing spreads – plenty of "keeping up with the Cohens" going on. So the last thing you want to do is to finish the last glug of wine when you're only halfway through the party – an absolute no-no ...   –Rob

3-4

As the last drop of wine is squeezed from its carafe, Jesus' mum says to him, "Wine's gone!"

Jesus comes back, "Don't get me involved – I'm waiting for a cue and it's still way off yet."

5-6

Mary primes the drinks staff to do what Jesus says – to the word. Camera focus pulls over to six huge stone jars holding about 100 litres (22 gallons) of foot-washing water – each.

7-8

Jesus' voice echoes round them, "Get some water, fill the jars right up." The drinks staff do what he says – to the word. Then Jesus tells them, "Take them to the guy in charge of tasting." They do.

9-10

The boss man does his wine-tasting routine. (He has no clue the liquid came from a water tank instead of a vineyard – only the drinks staff are in on it.) Then he asks for a quick word in the bridegroom's ear: "I've been around; I know the normal routine. The groom has the best wine served up front and brings out the cheap stuff for when they've had too much and their taste buds are a bit shot. But you've turned it all on its head, bringing out the vintage wine *last*. Unheard of!"

11

This was the first of loads of supernatural showings done by Jesus – in pokey ol' Cana, Galilee County! It was a glimpse of his roots, and his team didn't miss the point: they were sold on him.

They set off for Jerusalem to be there for the Flyby Holiday festivities ...   –Rob

Jesus the vandal (John 2:14-17)

Jesus walks into the religious HQ at Jerusalem and thinks he's in a market: animal stench, sale signs with "You'll go coo at our dove deals!" on them, traders shouting, "Spotless sheep here!" For those who can't stretch to the rip-off prices, an aquarium of loan sharks. Jesus takes his time creating a rope whip, then makes like a demented cowboy driving the animals into stampede. He vandalizes every cash kiosk out of business, creates total havoc. He's screaming, "Vamoosh! Get this filth out of here. My Father's place is no shopping mall!" One of his team quietly starts singing David's song "Passion for your place pumps me up"; the rest get the reference.

> But the religious leaders are livid, frantically working out how to eliminate him. Problem is, the people are wowed by the previous weekend's supernatural spectaculars. They know they can't ignore this factor, but Jesus can. He's not relying on such a fickle fan-base.   —Rob

Two birthdays (John 3:1-21)

1-2

But not all the religious leaders are paid-up members of the Tutting Club. One guy, Nicodemus, corners Jesus late one night: "Coach, it's obvious from the miracles that God's backing you up, that he's sent you to teach us stuff about God's world."

3

Jesus comes straight back, "No one in this world gets to see God's world unless he's reconceived, redeveloped, redelivered and then reborn."

4

"Whoa! Hang on! You mean, go back into his mother's womb?" Nicodemus asks.

5-7

Jesus comes back, "Truth is, you can't enjoy God's world unless you celebrate two birthdays, one physical, the other spiritual. Physical people create physical babies. God's Holy Spirit brings spiritual people to life. Close your mouth! Is this 'reborn' info really so shocking?"

But the top religious teacher doesn't get it – and Jesus is just on the ABC's. He goes on to hint at his own execution – "elevated on a cross" for all to see . . .

14-15

"Moses in the desert, remember? Bronze snake up on a pole and the people who looked got healed? Same principle: this person, yours truly, will also be elevated so that everyone who recognizes him will get limitless life."

16-17

"'Cos God's so passionate about the planet that he donates his one and only Son. Whoever invests their life in his Son doesn't die, but gets given this limitless life. D'you think God sends his Son to slam people down? No! He sends his Son to liberate people."

18-21

No one's written off if they're convinced about Jesus. Some go for darkness 'cos they're up to no good and light would blow their cover. But truth-lovers always get drawn toward the light; they're up for God getting the credit for the right lifestyle they're into.

He's the Real Thing (John 4:1-42)

1-9

Jesus picks up that the religious leaders have their spies out and goes back up to Galilee via the region of the Samaritans (long-term second-rate cousins of the true Jews). Around midday Jesus sits down by a well, pooped by the long walk. A local woman comes to get water and Jesus asks her for a drink. She's shocked. One: she's a Samaritan. Two: she's a woman. And he talks to her!

10

Jesus comes back with, "If you had the first clue about the freebies God's got for you; if you had any idea who I am – you'd be asking *me* to get *you* a drink."

She's not catching his drift, so Jesus gets a little less ambiguous . . .   –Rob

13-14

He says, "You drink from this well, you'll be back here tomorrow gasping again. You drink from the water I've got to give and you'll not need anything else. It'll be like a well inside you, springing up and bubbling over with limitless life."

15

She says, "I'll have some of that! It's exhausting traipsing out here daily."

16

He tells her, "Go bring your husband back."

17

"Ah, I've got no husband," she says.

18

"At least you're honest!" he smiles. "Truth is, you've had five and now you're just living with your lover."

> She's blown away by him knowing her life story. She realizes he's some sort of courier from God, so she quizzes him on some Samaritan/Jewish stuff . . .   —Rob

25-26

She says, "When the Liberator comes, he'll sit down and explain it all to us."

Jesus tells her, "I'm the one!"

> The team come back from doing the shopping in town. She goes back to town and gushes about this mind-reader guy she met, that he could be the Liberator. The team just want to eat, but Jesus tells them . . .   —Rob

34

"My food is completing my mission: doing what God's asked me to do."

> The locals interrupt their meal, begging this possible Liberator to stick around awhile so they can suss him out. He gives them two days, after which . . .   —Rob

42

They say to the woman, "Now we haven't just bought into it 'cos of what you told us. We've heard him! He's the real thing! The World Liberator in our backwater town!"

Remote control (John 4:43-53)

43-47

They set off for Nazareth again after the slight delay and arrive back in Cana, where Jesus' popularity rating is sky high from the wine-supply event and all they've seen at the Flyby Festival in Jerusalem. Some upper-class guy's son is on his deathbed and he begs Jesus to come over and do something . . .

48

Jesus moans, "The only thing that'll get you off the fence is something spectacular, isn't it!"

49

"Please come. He'll die if you don't," the guy says again.

50

All Jesus says is "You go. It'll be all right: he'll live."

51-53

He takes him at his word and starts back home. One of his staff meets him halfway and tells him the boy's fine. The guy asks when things picked up. "One o'clock yesterday. The fever just went!" The dad realizes that was exactly the time Jesus told him his son would make it. He's convinced. So's his family!

> Jesus is the main attraction right across Galilee County. He arrives at his home town, Nazareth, stands up in the local HQ and reads from the courier Isaiah . . .   —Rob

History now (Luke 4:18-21)

18-19

"The Holy Spirit of God is coursing through every part of me. He's commissioned me to announce the breaking news – top news for the poor: He's sent me to mend broken hearts, to liberate those slammed up in dark prisons, to announce the news – that this is the era of God going gentle on his people."

20-21

He closes the sacred book, hands it back to the altar boy and takes his seat. They're all gawking at him. He says, "These words have come to life, right here, right now. In 3D."

> They were initially proud of their local-boy-made-good, but now Joe's boy is really pushing it. They're incensed. They take him out of town to throw him over the local cliff, but he just walks straight through them and moves to Capernaum. First Rest Day there he's up front in the town HQ teaching people. This lot love it. He's got something the rest don't have – clout.   –Rob

The exorcist (Mark 1:23-28)

23-24

Bloke in the HQ crowd who's demon possessed starts screaming, "Leave us alone! Don't snuff us out! They call you 'Jesus from Nazareth, but I know who you *really* are – God's Sacred Liberator!"

25-26

Jesus answers him, "Silence! Come out! You're evicted from this poor guy as of now." The bloke convulses, grotesque noises, thrashing limbs, then nothing. The guy's himself again.

27-28

The crowd are stunned. They start whispering, "Who *is* this guy? New ideas backed up with such clout. He tells evil spirits where to go – and they go!" Stories spread like foot-and-mouth disease across the whole of Galilee County.

The religious leaders have a theory: he's possessed. So how come he's messing up his own side? It's not much of a theory!

Then a man with a serious skin condition gets baby-soft skin. Jesus wants the healing kept on the QT. But the guy blabs his mouth off and Jesus is mobbed like a pop star everywhere he goes. He ends up staying in obscure places, but the people still trace him.   −Rob

Double-tough call (Mark 2:1-12)

1-4

One time he's teaching in someone's house and it's packed, inside and out. People are taking it in turns to breathe! Then, above them, a scratching sound, a ripping sound, bits of plaster landing on heads, a gap appearing in the roof. Four guys are ripping through the ceiling! Next thing, they're lowering a disabled guy down on a makeshift hammock. He lands at Jesus' feet . . .

5

Jesus sees they're convinced that they just need to get their mate to him and the guy'll be walking again. So he says to the paralytic, "All you've ever done to mess people up is straightened out and sorted. No blame. You're in the clear."

6-7

Some of the religious law enforcers sit bolt upright, thinking, *What'd he say? He can't wipe a guy's slate clean − that's God's job. Who's he think he is?*

8-12

Jesus reads their minds like they've got cartoon speech bubbles coming out their heads. He says, "Why so cynical? Huh?! Question: which is the tougher call, to tell him, 'Your slate's clean with God,' or to tell him, 'Roll up your hammock and stroll back home'?" Silence. "But to thaw out your cynicism and prove I've got the kudos with God to wipe slates clean down here . . ." He turns to the disabled guy and tells him, "Roll up your hammock and stroll back home." And he does. Everyone sees it and gives the credit to God. Everyone agrees they've *never* seen anything like this.

Outland Revenue (Luke 5:27-31)

27-30

Jesus decides to build a bigger team and signs Matt up. This is controversial, as Matt's a tax collector, aka a Roman lackey. (Generally tax collectors weren't only fund-raising for the enemy; they were also often on the make for their own pension fund.) Matt throws a party at his house to celebrate, but the religious leaders and the law enforcers snipe at Jesus for eating with corrupt money launderers . . .

31

Jesus responds by asking, "Who needs the doctor more: fit people or healthy people? I'm here to get the jaywalkers back on the road to God. Not to have picnics in the middle of the road with those who think they're doing fine."

> They continue to provoke Jesus, but he continues to answer all cryptic. One Rest Day Jesus and the team break some petty subsection of some obscure clause some legalist added to Moses' Rule Book years before. The religious leaders accuse him of breaking their oh-so-important Rest Day Rules. Jesus tells them he's more important than the Rest Day!
>
> Another Rest Day, Jesus spots a guy with a shrivelled hand (probably a plant: front row – bit obvious!). He gets him to stand up and asks the crowd about what's legal: to do good or evil, to help or harm on a Rest Day? Then he heals the guy's hand in full view. The religious leaders are hamstrung – they can't lay into him for helping the bloke, for doing someone some good. So they're back to the drawing board.
> —Rob

The dirty dozen (Luke 6:12-16)

Jesus spends the night on a mountain thrashing out his final twelve with God. Next morning he gets the squad together and commissions the team. In alphabetical order: Bart, Drew, Jamey (Alphason), Jim (Zebson) and his twin, Jonno (Zebson), Judas (Jameson), Judas (Iscariot, who'd later stitch Jesus up), Matt, Pete, Phil, Si and Tom.

> The Liberator's now launched and well out of the harbour. His supernatural sessions and radical views have made him No. 1 celeb from Judaea in the south to Syria in the north.
> —Rob

Impact Year 2: Popularity Peak

Who's laughing? (Matthew 5:1-17)

1-2

Jesus sees how the troupe of groupies is growing, so he goes up the nearest hill and lets them follow. They listen in as he teaches his team:

3-12

"I'll tell you who'll laugh last: the people who don't think too much of themselves, who *know* they're a mess – their ticket to heaven's already in the post (first class).

"Who'll be happy? The people who know about grief, who don't shove the mess behind the sofa, but face it – God himself is going to put his arm round them.

"Who'll be content? The modest, gentle types, who don't go round grabbing – they'll get given the world.

"Who'll be laughing? The people who only want to do the right thing, like it's their food and drink – their 'good news in tray' will be piled high.

"Who'll be laughing? The people who don't hold grudges, who forgive and forget – they'll get treated likewise.

"Who's laughing, deep down, already? The people who aren't polluted with stuff that mugs the heart – they'll get to see God.

"Who's laughing, deep down? The people who stop fights and start friendships, who turn fists into high fives – they'll get known as God's children.

"Who's laughing? The people who get slapped down for doing the right thing – they get given the security code to heaven's gates.

"And you're laughing if people despise you. You're delirious if they pick on you. If they slag you off just because you're on my side – throw a party! Go wild! Paint the town – your bonus in heaven is hitting the humongous mark. Because that's exactly what they did to all the couriers who prophesied my arrival."

13-16

"You guys are the world's natural preservatives. Like salt, you bring out the flavour. But if you go bland on me, what use is that? You might as well be chucked out and go join the wasters at the landfill site. You guys make the world visible. You bring light. You can't camouflage a fireworks display. You don't put floodlights behind a brick wall, so don't pull curtains across the good things that brighten up people's lives. Let them see it. And get God some great reviews for what he's done in your dark corners."

17

"It's rumble-the-rumours time: I'm not here to diss Moses' Big Ten Rules. I'm not here to do a character assassination job on the couriers. I'm not here to finish them off – I'm here to complete them."

> He goes through rule by rule, and it gets radical! Don't murder = Don't hate. Don't go off with someone's wife or husband = Don't even fantasize about it. If someone smacks you one in the face – drop your defences and let him have another go. Don't just be good to those who are your mates – love your rivals; ask God to do them good. Don't just go through the prayers in front of an audience – God's your only audience; impress him. He gives them a structure for when they're talking to God ...
> —Rob

Template for talking to God (Matthew 6:9-13)

God in heaven, you're our Dad.

We respect everything you stand for. We want others to.

Please bring heaven on earth: people living life your way, like the angels do.

Please bring us what we need to keep us going each day.

Please acquit us, as we cancel our grievances and throw them all away.

Please pull us back from the edge of evil, if we're falling or being thrown.

'Cos you're all that matters; you're able to do it and you're to take the credit.

You're on your own.

It's your throne.

Absolutely!

> More instructions on using the hotline to God: don't milk it; do it in secret – God sees. Don't invest in goods with a sell-by date; build up your balance in heaven. Don't let cash boss you around. Don't panic. Don't judge, especially when you're just as guilty. Don't waste sacred things on couch potatoes or airheads . . . –Rob

Keep on (Matthew 7:7–12)

7-8

"Keep on keeping on at God. Keep asking – you'll get it. Keep searching – you'll find it. Keep pushing the doors – you'll get through. If you don't ask, you won't recognize the answer. If you don't search, you won't remember what you're looking for. If you don't push the door, you won't know if it's been opened."

9-12

"Your son asks you for a bread roll; d'you give him a rock? He asks you for fish and chips; d'you give him a venomous snake with a cyanide side salad? So despite your dark side, you can still give good things to your kids. So multiply that by infinity when God's doling out good things to those who ask. Shall I sum it all up? The Rules and all the volumes of the Instruction Manual? It's this: 'Handle other people as you'd like them to handle you – with love.' Simple enough?!"

> Some final warnings: don't follow the crowd – they're probably lost too. Don't follow a guy who sounds good, but doesn't live good. Don't build a life on dodgy foundations – winter storms will wreck the whole thing. Build your life on this teaching and you'll be rock solid. It won't stop the storms, but it'll stop them getting to you.
>   –Rob

One-of-a-kind (Matthew 7:28-29)

Jesus stops speaking and everything's silent. The crowd are gobsmacked! He's so different from their usual religious instructors – he's got . . . what? Well, that word again – *clout*.

What social spectrum? (Luke 7:1-35)

Back home in Capernaum a Roman army officer's got a staff worker at death's door. He doesn't think he's worthy of Jesus coming into his plush pad, but, being a soldier, he understands orders – "Just give the word and it'll happen," he says. Jesus is well impressed and heals the guy for him.

A while after, there's a widow walking at the front of a funeral cortège. It's her only son in the coffin. Jesus knows the formula: no husband + no son = destitution. So he goes up to the coffin and brings the son back to life!

Jesus talks up John Baptizer as "great", even though his profile's dived since being banged up in jail. All the people agree, except the religious leaders (who've not been baptized by John). But then they'll never be happy: John ate virtually nothing, and they called him satanic; Jesus enjoys a good party, and they call him a drunk! Make your mind up, boys!   –Rob

Smelly feet (Luke 7:36-50)

36-38

Jesus gets an invite to a dinner party with one of the religious leaders. Just after the hors d'oeuvres this woman barges in and gives Jesus a deluxe foot-washing service, involving perfume, her tears, her hair and a thousand kisses – the woman's obviously a major fan!

39

The religious leader sees this and thinks, *Some courier! He can't even tell that this masseur is as pure as the filth on his sandals.*

40

Jesus reads his mind and says, "Simon, a story for you . . ."

"Sure," he replies.

41-42

"Two guys, right? Both up to their hairlines in debt. Trouble is, one guy's almost bald – he owes about eighteen months' wages. The other has a full head of hair and only owes about two months' wages. Both have no cash to get close to paying it off, so the creditor cancels both accounts. They now both have a clear credit rating. Which of the two will be more grateful?"

43-47

Simon says, "The bald one, who had the bigger debt written off."

"Right!" says Jesus. He turns to the woman and says to Simon, "I come in, usual animal filth caked between my toes. D'you get me a bowl of water and a towel? She uses her *tears and her hair!* D'you give me one kiss on the cheek? She's not stopped kissing my *feet!* D'you pass face cream or hand cream to me? She wastes good perfume on my feet! How much debt d'you think she's been released from? Exactly. Must be loads! From her response she's obviously been let off a load of dark stuff. But for someone who's done little wrong, we're right down the other end of the spectrum – not that grateful really!"

48

Jesus says to her, "Your mess is cleaned up. You're straightened out and sorted in God's books."

49

The rest of the table are now mouthing to each other, "Who's he think he is? Can he wipe slates clean for God?"

50

Jesus lets the woman go: "Your trust has got you through this. Walk away content."

"Work it out yourself" (Luke 8:1-15)

Jesus goes on the "Heaven on Earth" tour. The road crew include the Team Twelve and a posse of women healed from diseases and demon possession (e.g. Mary Magdalene).

A large crowd of villagers are by the lake. Jesus gets into the boat and starts telling stories . . .   –Rob

5-8

"A farmer's out sowing seeds. Some land on the path — stomped on, only good for the birds' supper. Some seeds land on the stones — grow a bit, but when the sun slams down they wither: haven't got the roots to get decent moisture. Some seeds land over in the brambles — they grow quite well, till the brambles win the civil war and choke the life out of the good crops. Other seeds land on good soil — *they* produce a crop, 3,000 percent, 6,000 percent, even 100,000 percent increase on what was planted."

The crowd look at him as if to say, "And . . . ?" He just says, "If you've got a brain and a heart, work it out!"

9-15

The team quiz Jesus later, "That story: d'you forget the moral, or what?"

"Please! It's a metaphor!" he tells them. "You lot have the inside story. But for *them,* it's all kept in stories and pictures — to chew over . . . if they're hungry! If not, they'll watch but not *see,* they'll listen but not *hear.*" He explains this story to the team: the farmer's spreading out God's message. For some, the evil one nicks it the second it hits the deck. For some, it lands but they've no root, so it doesn't last. For some, it lasts longer, but the hassles of life choke it back. For others, it lands, takes root, grows strong and produces fruit.

He tries them with other pictures of heaven on earth: a lamp on a stand symbolizes hidden things becoming visible. Another story: rich guy, only into getting richer, gets called a fool by God 'cos he's about to die and he's got nothing to take with him. To the team after, Jesus comes off the back of the story by saying, "Make God top priority and he'll sort out your wardrobe and your meals. Check your balance in heaven's bank, not just how much earth currency you've got."

More stories with camouflaged meanings in Matt's bio. Different images used for different audiences: for farmers, heaven on earth is painted as a farm deliberately infested with weeds by an enemy, only to get sorted right at the end. For fishermen, an image of a net full of fish, good and bad, only to be sorted back on shore. For the cooks, an image of tiny bits of yeast lifting the whole loaf into life. For everyone, two similar stories of people selling up everything to scrape the cash together to buy a buried treasure chest / a unique pearl.

Mark joins in with some of these plus new ones: a seed grows – though we don't know how; the smallest seed becomes the biggest bush – mustard. All images of heaven on earth. This is how Jesus connected with the public . . . –Rob

Jesus and the public (Mark 4:33–34)

With loads of stories and images, Jesus teaches them about God's ways. He feeds them as much as they can take in without giving them indigestion. Nothing's explained. He says nothing to them without using an image, picture or symbol of some sort to get through. But when he's "backstage" with his team, he explains everything.

Storming (Mark 4:35–41)

35–38

Evening arrives; Jesus says to the team, "Let's go across to the other side." They leave the crowd and their small flotilla pushes off onto the lake. Gale-force winds whip up the lake so the waves are like something from an ocean disaster movie. Jesus is oblivious to it all – tour fatigue – and is catching up on some sleep down in the hold.

Some of the team go down and shake him, "Boss, you not bothered if we drown, or what?!"

39

He takes his head off the cushion, goes up on deck and lays into the wind and waves, "Whoa! Calm down. That's enough!" The wind holds its breath and the waves sulk like told-off toddlers.

40

He says, "Why so freaked? D'you still not trust me?"

41

Now they're more scared than they were of the wind, asking each other, "Who *is* this guy?! He's even got the elements eating out of his hand!"

Another time Jesus tells people . . .   –Rob

"Carry my cases" (Matthew 11:28-30)

"Burnt out? Running on red? Pull in at my service station and I'll give you a break. Agree to carry my cases; copy me on how to carry them best – listen to my quietly spoken advice, that I'll never shove down your throat, and your soul will think it's on a luxury holiday. 'Cos what I ask you to carry for me is light and streamlined to cause least resistance. It'll be so part of you, you'll hardly notice its weight!"

"Hurry up!" (Mark 5:21-43)

Another time Jesus is on walkabout and a guy called Jairus, a big noise from the local HQ, pushes through the crowd and asks Jesus to come heal his dying daughter. Jesus follows him; the crowd follow Jesus. But one lady is about to delay him. Quick potted history: twelve years ago she started haemorrhaging ("bleeding" to us non-medics), she'd paid thousands to doctors, herbalists, alternative therapists – anyone in the phone book even close to "healer". Nothing works. She's desperate. Famous healer Jesus is walking past; she touches his coat and gets healed. Jesus feels power surging out of him and stops – she's petrified but comes clean with the whole story. Jesus tells her, "Being convinced and doing something about it is what's healed you! You're well now – go enjoy life." Jairus is listening to all this when he gets the news: it's too late – his daughter's dead. But Jesus says, "You convinced? You going to do something about it?" They go to Jairus's house and Jesus goes in and tells the girl to get up. She does! Jesus tells them to keep this quiet.

Jesus realizes there are too many people for one man to help, so he delegates. He sends the team out in pairs. They apply what they've seen and find they can communicate, heal people, tell evil spirits where to go. They come back and debrief.

–Rob

Impact Year 3: Opposition

Has Jesus got a death wish or what? He's winding up the religious strict and particulars like he doesn't want there to be a tomorrow. Doing people good on Rest Days (technically illegal), talking up John Baptizer (politically dangerous), chatting about God like God's his Dad (capital punishment offence). He's set a collision course with trouble, and now he's putting his foot down on the pedal, getting all confrontational with the religious leaders ...

–Rob

Missing the point (John 5:39-40)

Jesus lays into them . . .   —Rob

"You got your degrees in the sacred books, PhD's in books about the sacred books, and you're convinced they'll get you into heaven. But for all the points you score — you miss *the* Point: it's all about me! It's jam-packed with huge stomping clues about *me*. But you can't admit it, 'cos then you'd have to ask *me* for the limitless life you want."

John Baptizer is murdered while in custody. Herod's macabre daughter-in-law wants his head on a plate and so tricks the old man into giving it to her . . . —Rob

Fifteen thousand for supper (Matthew 14:13-21)

13-14

Jesus gets the news about John and it hits him hard. He takes off in a boat, solo, badly needing some space. Fat chance! Crowds don't do "sensitive". Local rumour merchants pick up the latest sightings and chase round the lake telling everyone where he is. Jesus moors up and sees the huge welcome committee. His need for space is blown away by his concern for the state of their souls. He starts healing the sick people they've carried to his "mobile clinic".

15

It's getting dark. The team come up to him and say, "This place is a marathon run from anywhere. The day's almost turning in. Send them off to the nearest village: they'll need to eat."

16-17

Jesus says, "No need. *You* give them something."

"What? With five bread rolls and two fish?" they stutter.

18-21

"Pass the food here," he says. He signals for people to take a seat. He's got hold of the five bread rolls and the two fish; he's looking up, thanking God for them; then he starts handing them round the team, who go off and hand them round the crowd. Everyone gets plenty. Nobody asks for seconds — they're stuffed full! The team keep to the countryside code and collect up the leftovers, filling twelve huge baskets! Reckon there were around 5,000 men there – plus their wives and kids – so you could triple that and you'd not be far off!

Water-walking (Matthew 14:22-33)

22-24

Straight after this, Jesus sends the team back by boat to the west side of the lake. He sticks around to send the people home with the personal touch. Eventually they've all left and he climbs up the mountainside to talk things through with God long into the night. Meantime, the team are well out on the lake and the waves are looking nasty.

25-26

Sometime, three maybe four in the morning, Jesus walks out to them across the waves. Freaked out, they scream, "Ghost!" as one man.

27-28

Before they've time to scream again Jesus shouts, "Whoa! Don't panic! It's me."

"If it's you, Boss," shouts Pete, "give me a go?!"

29-30

"Come on, then," says Jesus.

So Pete swings his leg over the boat and tests out the water – and his foot doesn't go under! The other leg joins it. It takes his weight. Seconds later he's walking across the lake towards Jesus – on the water! He's doing fine till a face full of wind slaps him back to normality. He freezes, loses focus and starts going under, screaming, "Grab me, Jesus!"

31-33

Jesus does and holds Pete there saying, "Chicken! Why'd you bottle it?" Soon as they get back in the boat, the wind stops playing with the waves.

The team can't take their eyes off him. Can't stop coming out with their own variations on "You're the real thing – God's Son! You're him! You are!"

Life bread (John 6:25-71)

25-34

The crowds catch up with Jesus the other side of the lake. But he knows what they're after (probably dessert!). They chat through the desert-bread Moses had on daily delivery from heaven. But he raises the stakes and steers them from physical to spiritual bread. They come on ultra keen, clamouring, "Give us this spiritual bread."

35

Jesus tells them, "I'm the life-giving bread come down direct from heaven. Take a slice of me and you won't need any other food. Plumb your life into me and you won't need anything else to drink."

> Some of them can't stomach this (they can't stop seeing him as the pimply teenager helping his dad in "Davidson Designs"), and now he's talking about coming down from heaven. Even some of his own squad struggle with all this weird cannibalistic stuff and drift off disaffected . . .   —Rob

67

Jesus asks his select team, "You off too, or what?"

68-71

Pete's straight in there with, "Where? You've got limitless life to dole out! You're God's sacred one — we know it."

Jesus is chuffed with his choice — though he knows one of them (Judas Iscariot) is going to do the dirty on him.

> After another three-day teaching marathon Jesus does the bread-and-fish-thing again with around 12,000 faces fed this time from seven bread rolls and a solitary fish.
> No real pattern to Jesus' tour. He just goes with the flow. Sometimes right up in Tyre, sometimes around County Galilee, then maybe back up to Caesarea Philippi. But mostly in the north, for now . . .   —Rob

The real business (Matthew 16:13-27)

One time up near Caesarea he asks his team . . .   —Rob

13

"What's the gossip? What are people saying about me? They worked it out yet?"

14

They answer: "Varies: the shortest odds are on you being a reincarnation of John Baptizer. Elijah gets quite good odds. Jeremiah too. More of a long shot for other couriers."

15

"And you?" asks Jesus. "What d'you reckon?"

16

Pete jumps right in again, "You're the Liberator. God's Son."

17-19

"Pete Jonahson, you'll be glad you said that! You've not picked that up from office gossip or pub chat; you've got that direct from God in heaven. Your name means 'rock'. And this is the rock-solid foundation I'm going to build my new community on. And they're going to batter down the outer gates of hell. I'll tell you the security codes of heaven: if you block something happening down here, heaven will make sure it stays blocked; if you give something the green light down here, heaven will make sure it goes through."

20

Then he changes mood. Gets all stern and tells them not to spill the beans on him being the Liberator.

21

From then on Jesus starts telling them the plot. It involves Jerusalem, councillors, head God-reps and law enforcers. It involves his execution and the greatest comeback of all time – coming back to life two days later.

22

Pete takes him aside, tries to get him thinking more positive: "No way will all this happen to you."

23

Jesus looks straight through him and says, "Satan, you're in my way
and you're messing up my head. You're not into God-stuff, just trivia.
So back off!"

24-27

Then Jesus unloads more heavy-duty news: "You want to go my way?
You've got to jack in all your personal ambitions, psyche up for some
serious pain – then you're in. If you're only into looking after No. 1,
you'll end up being nothing. If you're up for the ultimate sacrifice, then
you'll get limitless life. Think about it: what's the point in taking over
the world if your soul goes out the window in the process? What's the
going price for a soul these days? One day I'll stride out from behind a
thousand hovering angels – huge production values, as only Dad can –
and I'll be handing out rewards for what people have done."

Glimpse of heaven (Matthew 17:1-9)

1-3

Around a week later Jesus takes just Pete, Jim (Zebson) and Jim's
brother John up a mountain. They're looking at him and his aura
changes in front of their eyes – he gets all heavened-up. His face radiates. Supernatural brilliance, like he's wearing some light-generating
face make-up. His clothes are dazzling white – none of these blue-
white gimmicks: this is white-white, again shining like it's plugged
into a generator. As their eyes adjust, they see he's locked in discussion with the big two – Moses (rep of the Rules) and Elijah (rep of all
the couriers).

4

Pete blurts out to Jesus, "Boss, this is awesome! We need a monument!
What if I build three shelters, one each?"

5

God interrupts. Camouflaged – probably for safety reasons (their
safety) – by a sun-saturated cloud, his voice comes out of the centre:
"This is the Son I'm passionate about and so proud of . . . when he
speaks – you listen!"

6-8

By now the three of them are flat out, face down on the ground, quivering. Jesus comes over and touches them: "It's OK. Relax!" he says. They look up and it's just Jesus, on his own, normal again.

9

They're coming back down the mountain and Jesus tells them, "No one gets to hear about this, right? Not till I've come back from the dead."

> This isn't the only time Jesus talks about dying and coming back. It worries the
> team stupid.　　　　　　　　　　　　　　　　　　　　　　　　　　　　　　−Rob

Soft spot for kids (Mark 9:33-42)

33-35a

In their digs in Capernaum, Jesus catches the team after some verbal arm-wrestling about who's the vice-captain of the team; i.e. second behind Jesus. He lays out the full picture . . .

35b

"Whoever wants the top job must go to the bottom of the ladder and give the others a leg up."

36

He picks up their hosts' toddler, puts him on his lap and says, "You make time for one of these and you make time for me; you make time for me and you're making time for my Dad who sent me."

> Then later . . .　　　　　　　　　　　　　　　　　　　　　　　　　　　　　　−Rob

42

"But anyone who pollutes the simple trust of one of these kids, turning them into little cynics before their time − they'll be in more trouble than if their feet were set in concrete and about to 'fall' off the boat of some drugs baron."

> Another time, he tells the team to stop hustling the young kids away − "They're
> what heaven's all about," he tells them. Another time, a story about a farmer being
> a one-man search party for his one directionally-challenged sheep, while the

ninety-nine are safe in the farm – an image of a God who doesn't want the most vulnerable of children discarded like rubbish.   –Rob

Money drags you down (Mark 10:17-31)

17

Jesus is just setting off when a young guy rushes over and bows at his feet. "Good coach," he starts, "this limitless life you go on about. How do I get it?"

18-19

"Why *good* coach? Only God's really good! Anyway, what's it say in Moses' Rule Book? You won't murder. You won't do adultery. You won't thieve. You won't lie about someone. You will respect your parents."

20-21

"I can check all those off since I was a boy!"

Jesus looks at him and surges with love for the guy. "You're missing one thing, though," he says (the guy's ready for some stunning new theology). "Sell up! Everything you own – sell it and donate the money to charity. Not as a tax dodge, just give it. Your bank balance in heaven will be off the top of the graph. Then when you've sorted the finances, come join the posse."

22

The guy's face shifts through the gears, from anticipation down to hollow. He walks off looking suicidal – he's stinking rich.

23

Jesus says to his team, "It's virtually impossible for rich people to live life God's way."

24-25

The team are stunned. Jesus adds, "It's so hard to get into living God's way. How hard is it for a people carrier to squeeze its bodywork through the tiny hole at the blunt end of a needle? That's easier than it is for the rich set to live life God's way."

26

Now they're really stunned! They're whispering to each other, "So what chance anyone getting straightened out then?"

27

Jesus tells them, "No chance! Not humanly speaking. But with God there's every chance. Anything's possible when God's on the case."

28

"*We've* jacked it all in to be with you," says (guess who? Yep . . .) Pete.

29–31

"I'm not kidding," Jesus says. "Everyone who's given up home, family or wealth for me and my way of life, everyone will enjoy a 10,000 percent increase in homes, families and wealth – plus tyranny and torture – in this era. And in the next: limitless life. Those at the top of the ladder will end up the wrong end when I turn the world on its head. Those at the bottom will be laughing from above the clouds."

> Only recently he's talked about getting radical with the things that mess up your chances of heaven. He's convinced that if your hand or foot or eye keep on messing you up, then chop them off / gouge them out. What's a hook, a limp or tunnel vision compared to losing out on heaven? Radical.   —Rob

"How many times!?" (Matthew 18:10–35)

> They've been chatting through the policy on what to do when other squad members lie to you. Pete wants some strict guidelines . . .   —Rob

21

He asks Jesus, "Say someone close does the dirty on me. I know I've got to wipe their slate clean. But what if they keep doing it? Where's the line? Seven times?"

22

Jesus answers, "No, not seven. More in the range of seven times seven, or seventy-seven times, or seventy times seven."

(Whichever manuscript you dig up, it's loads more than a measly seven!)

He moves into story-telling mode again: a servant owes the king thousands, but the guy begs and the king lets him off. This same guy then goes straight round to someone who owes him just a hundred, starts laying into him for the money. But he's spotted and the king gets to hear. "How ungrateful can you get?" asks the king, and throws the guy in jail till he pays up. This is in-house, just the crew there. So Jesus tags on the moral, just in case they missed it: "God's given your filthy slate the complete clean-up service — even the mess you haven't yet done. Least you can do is go easy on people who let you down every now and then."

After the success of sending the team out in pairs, Jesus decides to spread the scheme out to the wider squad. Seventy-two signed-up members go ahead of him, again, in pairs. Call it the warm-up act, call it mentoring, call it throwing them in the deep end, whatever. Jesus knows he's not going to be around much longer. The general direction is south — towards Jerusalem — towards danger.   —Rob

Neighbours (Luke 10:25-37)

25-26

One of the religious law profs tries to catch Jesus out: "What've I got to do to get this limitless life?"

"You're a lawyer. What's the law say?" asks Jesus.

27-28

He rolls off the pat answer: "Love God with everything you've got and love your neighbour as you love yourself."

"Good answer," says Jesus. "Do it and you'll get this limitless life!"

29

But he couldn't resist posing: "But who qualifies as, quote, 'neighbour'?"

30-36

Jesus says, "There's a guy leaving Jerusalem on Jericho Rd, OK? He gets mugged, left in the gutter half-naked and two-thirds dead. One of the God-reps is passing, sees him and crosses the road . . . to avoid him!" (He waits for the gasps to die down.) "Then an HQ worker goes past, sees him and does the same." (Slightly smaller gasps.) "Next up a Samaritan goes past. Sees him and, what d'you reckon? Tell you what — multiple choice: (a) walks on past, (b) goes over and sees if they've left any money so he can steal it, or (c) starts kicking him in to finish off the job. No idea? Well, the answer is . . . (d) cleans his injuries, lifts the guy onto his donkey, walks him to the next country pub, pays for bed and full board, promising to cover the excess if the bill tots up to more." (Major rumble of shocked voices.) "So who's down in the characters list as 'neighbour' then?"

37

The slick lawyer mumbles, "The Sama— . . . uh . . . the guy who looked after him."

"So, go do the same," Jesus says.

> Major debates from religious bigwigs to farm workers. "Who is he?" Opinions range from "dangerous impostor" to "a courier" to "the Liberator himself". The religious suits mostly sign up to the first and send guards to arrest him. But they come back virtually converted! Mission aborted. The religious leaders almost choke on some turbo-charged tutting. They need a different approach . . .   —Rob

"What's he writing?" (John 8:1-11)

> Jesus is busy teaching people when the religious leaders and law enforcers haul in a half-naked woman claiming they just caught her in bed with someone else's husband. Moses' Instruction Manuals say they should chuck stones at her till she's dead meat. What does he think? (You can spot the tripwire from a hundred paces . . .)   —Rob

6b-8

Jesus crouches down and starts writing in the dust with his finger. They keep pushing him for an answer. He stands up, looks straight at them and says, "Whoever has never done anything wrong, let him chuck the opening stone." Then he goes back to what he's writing.

9-10

Silence. Nervous shuffling of feet. People leaving. Footsteps getting quieter as people leave, the older ones first, followed by the young fiery ones. Jesus eventually looks up to see it's only her and him left. "Where've they gone? Your prosecution council seems to have dropped their case!"

11

"Yes, boss!" she says sheepishly.

"Me too. I'm not about to write you off. Go home and sort your life out."

> But it doesn't stop there – more heated discussions. In the end Jesus drives the religious ones wild by saying he was around before Abraham. Now they pick up stones with his name on, but he gets away . . . this time.
> Everything he claims, he backs up. Says he's the light of the world, then proves it by giving sight back to a guy born blind. Says he'll liberate people, just after freeing someone from demon possession. Calls himself a gate, after opening people up to new ideas. Calls himself a sheep-welfare officer who'd die to protect his flock – this one he hasn't backed up . . . but he intends to. Some are convinced. Others think he's a couple of sentences short of a story.   —Rob

"You're like sick bowls!" (Luke 11:37-54)

37-38

But sometimes he gets pretty direct: at a meal with a religious leader he doesn't go through the full religious rigmarole of washing before eating. His host starts tutting . . .

39-41

Jesus lashes at him, "You religious leaders scrub the bowls and cups so they're sparkling on the outside, but on the inside you leave the bacteria of greed and evil to fester and grow. How stupid is that? Did God make the outside and delegate the inside to someone else? No! Sort out your sick, putrid hearts. Give the cash-strapped some of what you're keeping from them and you'll feel a whole lot cleaner."

> "You de-liberators got bad news round the corner . . ."   —Rob

1. You give God his 10 percent commission but blank out justice and love.

2. You love posing around HQ, with your permanent "Reserved" signs on the best seats.

3. You love people nodding to you, opening doors for you, looking up to you.

4. You load people down with guilt and tut when they stumble under it.

5. You cut the ribbon on new tombs of honour for past couriers, but it was exactly your type who killed them.

6. You've got the keys to the doors to knowledge, but you don't use them. Worse, you make sure no one else can either.

53-54

Jesus leaves them seething, desperate to catch him doing something illegal so they can arrest him.

Jesus starts warning the team against them – they're like yeast: tiny particles, but affecting everything. "But don't freeze with fear – they can only kill your bodies. The one you should worry about is the one who can throw you into hell! But God's got hourly updates on how many hairs you've got on your head, so if you say you're with me, I'll persuade his angels to protect you. When they arrest you, don't write your defence ahead of the trial – just wait for God's Holy Spirit to dictate your speech at the time. Make sure you're ready for when I come back."   –Rob

Rest Day (Luke 13:10-17)

Still making his way down to Jerusalem, Jesus is outlining God's ways in a local HQ. Middle of his talk he straightens up a woman bent double for eighteen years. Problem is, it's a Rest Day. The tutters and frowners lock horns again with Jesus. He wins. The audience love it. Public humiliation. More diesel on the open fire.   –Rob

"Me and God: like this ..." (John 10:22-33)

22-24

He arrives in Jerusalem and the Jews ask him the Big Question: "Are you the Liberator?"

25-30

Jesus answers, "I've told you already! But I forget, you're all cynics. The supernatural is natural for me 'cos I'm tapped directly into God's power– it's all the proof I need! You're dubious 'cos you wouldn't recognize God if he were standing in front of you! If you *were* his people, you'd recognize his Voice. My people only need to hear one word and they know it's me. They live my way and I let them in on limitless life. They're not going to curl up and die all bitter and twisted. They're not going to be kidnapped. No one's going to send God a ransom demand. No, Dad's given them to me, and no one arm-wrestles with him and wins. No one's about to rip them out of his strong grip. Me and Dad are like this – one."

31-33

Not for the first time the Jews pick up the nearest rocks and take aim at Jesus' cranium. He says, "I've used Dad's power in all my hundreds of miracles. Which one am I going to be killed for?"

"None of them!" they shout. "You're a heretic! You're flesh and blood, and you make out that you're God – so we'll draw some blood to prove it!"

> The argument goes on. He says, "Look at the proof" – a track record of supernatural events liberating people in their thousands. But they're still baying for his blood. He escapes.
>
> Jesus carries on with his Rest Day policy. He tries to stop the religious head shakers strutting round like peacocks, with a story: Posh guests turning their noses up (even further than normal) at invitations to a big do – so the homeless get invited instead. He talks about doing your sums: working out what life God's way is going to cost you (potentially, everything) and then doing it anyway. He talks about those with a brain and a heart working it all out. The religious hierarchy struggle in at least one dept.
>
> —Rob

Dad of the decade (Luke 15:1-32)

1-3

Jesus is surrounded by a whole range of undesirables. 'Course, the religious leaders and law enforcers spot this and start their "tutting and frowning" routine again. "This chap doesn't only talk to these lowlifes; he actually shares his lunch with them!" they whine. So Jesus says, loud enough for the Tutting Club to hear . . .

> A trilogy of stories about losing things. But the first two, a coin and a sheep, are just warm-ups for the big one . . .   −Rob

11-12

"This factory owner guy has two sons. The kid brother gets it into his skull that he's had enough. He goes to his dad, and as much as wishes the old man dead: "I want my half of the inheritance." The dad almost has a heart attack from the shock, but he sits down, does the sums, sells some shares and hands over half the family assets."

13-16

"The son doesn't even hang around to hear his dad's top ten tips for survival. He legs it. Within weeks he's off to foreign climes, spending the nights filling the glasses of the designer set with his liquid assets. He has such a great time he can't remember any of it the next day. 'Course, the money goes down the toilet. So do the 'friends' when they realize he's broke. So he surfs around and finds a site called www.worstjobs poss.com. He scrolls through the search results and ends up cleaning out the pigsties − not such a great career move, since he still counts himself Jewish."

17-20a

"He's there with his shovel, scratching away, and suddenly a light bulb goes on just above his head: *What am I doing? The worst job in the old man's empire is, like, jet-setter status compared to this. If I had any food in my stomach, I'd be throwing up. I'll hitchhike home. Work on a speech − something like 'You don't have to think of me as family, but please, give me a job.'*"

20b

"After a long hot trip, he turns the corner into his old street. His dad sees him and runs out into the street in his slippers, throws his arms round him, lifts him up and spins him round. And the noise! The whole street hears it. Sooo embarrassing!"

21-24

"The son starts his speech, but the dad cuts in, telling his assistant to arrange the biggest street party ever: 'My son was virtually dead, and he's come back. He was lost and now he's turned up. Let's party!'"

25-27

"Don't you just love a happy ending? Me too. Sorry, not this time! See, there's still the big-brother issue. He's coming home from work, he turns the same corner and thinks he's in a scene from an old musical: dancing, music, tables right up the middle of the street and everyone having a fantastic time. He calls over one of the waiters and asks, 'We just win the lottery, or what?' The employee answers, 'Better than that, sir: your brother's back, and your dad's blown the whole entertainment budget on the party!'"

28-30

"That's the trigger. He loses it. Furious, he walks off, kicking lamp-posts, ranting and swearing. His dad catches up with him but he has to fend off words he'd never heard before from his eldest: 'I've slogged my guts out. Slaving over your accounts. Doing exactly what you told me to do – I've not even taken sick time when I fancied a day down the beach – and did you ever, *ever* throw a party for me and my mates? No! But when this waster comes crawling back, oh yes, he gets the full treatment. Well, thanks for nothing!'"

31-32

"'Son,' his dad says, grabbing him by the shoulders and eyeballing him, 'you're around all the time, and I love it. What's mine is yours. But how could I not throw a party – as far as I knew, your brother was dead! Now he's alive. He could've been anywhere, and now he's here, with us. Come on, join the party.'"

No doubt, the religious leaders, and most of the audience, knew why Jesus told this story. The suits know which part's theirs. More dynamite on the barbecue.

—Rob

Heaven and hell (Luke 16:19-31)

19-21

"Another story: two guys, a beggar and a millionaire. They're technically neighbours, but only because the street beggar's patch is at the gate of the other guy's palace. The street beggar has screaming open sores, the rich guy's had his latest facelift and it still itches a bit. Both die . . ."

22-24

"The beggar gets an angelic cavalcade direct into Abraham's arms. The rich guy ends up in a torture chamber in hell. From the window of his cell he looks up and sees the beggar enjoying Abraham's comforting stories. He shouts up, 'Abraham, give us a break. Send what's-his-name down with some water for me; I'm in agony in these flames!'"

25-26

"Abraham comes back, 'Sorry, but no can do! It's all-change. You had all the breaks in your previous life, and Lazarus here got the rough end of the deal. Now it's vice versa. Anyway, if he *wanted* to come down, he couldn't – it's blocked off.'"

27-29

"'OK,' says the rich guy, 'send, uh . . . what was it? "Lazarus"? Send him back to my five brothers. They've got to know hell's worse than the worst horror story they've heard.' Abraham shouts back down, 'So Moses and the whole list of couriers weren't good enough, huh?'"

30-31

"The rich guy's struggling now: 'But surely, if someone comes back from the dead, they'll be all ears.'"

"Abraham doubts it: 'They were all mouth with Moses, and they added in hand gestures to the couriers – they're not shifting even if someone comes back from the dead!'"

Jesus heals ten guys from SHOD (Skin Hospital Outpatients Department). Only one of them comes back to say thanks – the Samaritan. Jesus probably isn't too surprised!

–Rob

Different audience, different story (Luke 18:1-14)

A story for the team on how talking to God is more like a late-night marathon discussion than a passing chat in a shopping mall, or, in his words – a bent judge eventually weakens and gives a widow justice just 'cos she nags him to distraction.

Then a story for some cocky geezers: two guys talking to God in HQ Jerusalem – a religious leader (aka a "holier than thou" club chairman) and an Outland Revenue official (aka a Roman lackey).

–Rob

11-12

"The religious professional has his best voice on and he's booming out as if God's deaf, 'Ooohhh God!' Checks people are watching; not sure; ups the volume: 'OOOOOOHHHHHH God!!' That's got them. Then, 'I thank thee that I'm not like these lower socio-economic groupings, with their stealing, adultering and general naughtinesses. I'm particularly gratitudinous that I'm not like this dirty Roman lackey person standing disturbingly close to me. Thank you that I go without food at least *twice* a week. Thank you that I give you all of your 10 percent commission. Thank you that I am such an asset to you. You must be so very proud of me. Amen.'"

13

"The Outland Revenue worker stands at the back. He doesn't even feel he can look up, he thinks he's such a sleazeball. He's slapping himself in punishment, murmuring, 'God, I'm so messed up. Please . . . please go easy on me.'"

14

Jesus says, "I'm telling you, it's the second guy who walks out in God's good books. Anyone who sets himself up as something special will crash. Anyone who knows his place, and shows it, will get promotion."

Face the music (Mark 10:32-34)

The Flyby Fest is not far off. Jesus tells the Team ...   —Rob

33-34

"This is how it's going to be," he sighs. "We'll arrive in Jerusalem; I'll be handed over to the HQ Board of Directors. They'll pronounce the death sentence and hand me over to the Romans. I'll be dissed, spat on, smacked about and executed. Two days after, I'll be back, alive."

Even though this is what the old couriers had already said, it flies right over the Team's heads. They just don't get it. Something blocks them from taking it in ...   —Rob

Playing status games to lose (Mark 10:35-45)

Jim and Jonno Zebson really know how to pick their moment – not! They take Jesus aside for a quiet chat. They ask him to put a word in for them to get them the best seats in heaven. But Jesus says, "That's Dad's department." Then ...   —Rob

42-45

Jesus calls a Team talk: "You know how the world works: the movers and shakers tell the lowlifes what to do and when to do it. Our New World cuts right across all that. If you want kudos, you've got to take on the menial jobs that'll help others. If you want to be top dog, you've got to work like a slave for others. If you need a mentor for this – look and learn. I've turned up with a one-track mind: to serve others. Even to hand over my life to buy people back from darkness."

Equal rights? (Matthew 20:1-16)

Another story about heaven on earth: the owner of a wine merchant company hires a group of guys at 9am at the going daily rate. He goes to get more workers at midday, again at 3pm, and then again at 5pm. Come knock-off time he pays all of them the full day's wage. 'Course the guys who'd worked all day start talking about getting their union reps involved. But the owner points out, "Am I ripping you off? I'm paying you what I said I would, aren't I? It's not your business if I want to give my money away. Clear off!" Jesus just rounds off with one of his catch-phrases: "Whoever wants the top job must go to the bottom of the ladder and give the others a bunk up."   —Rob

The ultimate comeback (John 11:1-44)

Laz and his two sisters, Mary and Martha, are great friends of Jesus. Jesus stays with them in Bethany whenever he's down near Jerusalem. He gets the news that Laz is terminally ill, but he hangs around two more days before leaving for Bethany. By the time he shows, Laz has been dead four days. Mary and Martha are livid with Jesus, convinced that he'd have been able to cure him if he'd not been hanging around with people he didn't even know!   –Rob

23-24

Jesus tells Martha, "He'll live again."

Martha moans, "Yeah, after the great Death of Death Day, we'll *all* come back!"

25-26

Jesus says, "I'm the Death of Death. I'm Life with a capital L. Invest all you've got in me and you'll live, and that includes dead people. You put it all on the line for me and you'll never die. Or d'you think I'm talking twaddle?"

27

"No, I'm convinced. Have been for years. You're the Liberator, God's Son, the one the couriers told us was coming. You're the One."

Jesus follows the two sisters to the cave where Laz is buried. They get there and . . .   –Rob

35

Jesus bursts into tears.

A huge crowd is watching him, some touched by his grief, others more cynical, saying, "That's all very well, but why wasn't he here when the guy was still breathing?" Jesus ignores their whisperings and asks for the tombstone to be dislodged from the front of the cave. Martha objects 'cos of the dead-body stench. Jesus insists . . .   –Rob

40

"Didn't I tell you, 'Trust me and you'll see how incredible God is'?"

41-42

A couple of heavies shoulder the tombstone to the side. Jesus looks up and says, "Dad, thanks for listening; thanks for always listening to me. *I* know that, *you* know that, so now prove it to this lot watching."

43-44

Then he projects his voice across the whole audience and into the back of the cave: "Laz! Come on out!" It echoes round the cave and comes out again, "Laz! Come on out!" And again, quieter, "Laz! Come on out!" Before the echoes have died out completely the ex-dead man's walking out! He's wrapped up like an Egyptian mummy, but he's hobbling. Jesus calls the shots. "Unwrap him; let the guy breathe."

The plot thickens (John 11:45-53)

45-47a

So Jesus pulls off the big one in front of a big audience. Loads of them are convinced he's the Liberator. Some of them are so convinced, they think the religious leaders should be in on the great news! They run to tell them. The religious leaders call an emergency meeting . . .

47b-48

"Plan B, anyone?" they ask. "If he goes on like this, he'll have more hits on his website than us; every Jew in the land will be a paid-up member of the Jesus fan club. The Romans will demolish our HQ and move their heavy artillery in. The few concessions they've allowed us will be out the window."

49-50

The Chairman of the Board this year is Caiaphas. He pulls rank, "You've got no idea! Weigh it up – which is better? One guy to be got rid of, or a whole nation to go under?"

51-53

He thinks this is his idea, but it's more profound than that. He's being used as a temporary courier to predict that Jesus is about to die for the

Jewish nation and all the Jews spread across the planet. Sacrificing Jesus will unite Jews everywhere. This is day one of the "kill Jesus" deliberations turning into a concrete plan.

But they know they can't do anything during the Flyby Fest – they don't need a riot. Jesus prepares for the Jerusalem festival by going incognito for a while. He holes up with the Team in a nowhere village called Ephraim near the desert in East Judaea (today's West Bank).   –Rob

Blind Bart (Luke 18:35-43)

35

Still on the way down to Jerusalem, a big crowd from Jericho have come out as a reception party for Jesus and Team. They're shuffling along, shoulder to shoulder. No one spots old Blind Bart the beggar sitting in the gutter with his tatty sign "Blind since birth: You give – I live!"

36-37

Bart hears the excitement and asks no one in particular, "What's up?"

Someone tells him to shut it. Someone else tells him, "Jesus Davidson from Nazareth is paying us a visit."

38-39

So he starts yelling, top of his voice, "Jesus Davidson!! Give me a break, please!" The locals tell him to button it, but he really lets loose: "Jesus Davidson!! Please give me a break!"

40-41

Jesus stops, gets the man brought to him and asks, "You want me to do something for you? What would that be then?"

He answers, "Chief, I'd do anything to see."

42-43

Jesus says, "Go on then! You know I can do it, so I will!" Straight off, the eyes he didn't even have, start working! He follows Jesus round, giving the credit direct to God. The crowds are wowed. God goes up in their thinking several notches.

Payback time (Luke 19:1-10)

1-6

Still passing through Jericho, on the Jerusalem Rd with a crowd jostling around him, Jesus stops under a fig tree, looks up and says to the branches, "Zach! Grandstand view, eh? Good plan!" The crowd look up to see the town's top Roman lackey Zacchaeus perched in the tree. "You want an even better view? Come on down; you've got guests!" Zach climbs down (that's a first!) and stands there in all his shortness. The Team think, *That explains the bird's-eye view.* Zach's chuffed; it's open house . . .

7-8

The crowds start griping about Jesus having a dinner party with the most corrupt guy in town. Zach, though, is a changed man. He puts on his public-speaking voice and makes the announcement: "Sir, to commemorate this occasion, I hereby declare if I've defrauded anyone out of anything – they just have to submit the paperwork and I'll reimburse them to a multiple of four."

9-10

Jesus, in his excitement, says, "Liberation makes house calls! Whatever you lot think, this guy's *also* a distant relative of Abraham. This is why I'm here: to track down the missing persons and reintroduce them to life."

Wasteful? (John 12:1-10)

1-6

Quick time check: Flyby Festival weekend minus six days. Jesus comes back to Bethany to stay with Mary, Martha and Laz (who's still milking lines like "You only live twice" etc.). Mary does a virtual action-replay of the woman about a year back with the perfume and the hair. This time it's the Team who complain about washing Jesus' feet in expensive perfume. Judas Iscariot blabs on, "It's a year's wages and could've been given to the poor" – not that he's bothered about the poor; just that the more money in the kitty, the easier it is to launder – allegedly! Jesus defends her . . .

7-8

"Back off, guys!" he says. "She's spot on. Name me three things perfume's used for: [they get up to two: 'to smell nice, to cover up a nasty
stink and . . .'] to prepare someone for burial! She's kept this perfume
back for a special job. There'll always be poor people needing help; I
won't always be with you. She's done the right thing."

9-10

Crowds are buzzing round more than usual – to see Jesus, but also to
see the freak-show that is Laz. The religious leaders meanwhile are
working on Plan B: How-to-Kill-a-Popular-Public-Figure-and-Get-
Away-with-It.

The Last Week

Jesus gets close to Jerusalem. He sees it in the distance, stops, takes in the view
and tears come. He knows what's going to happen to the place in only a matter of
decades – razed to the ground. And why? Because they reject God's peace deal . . .

–Rob

Big entrance? (Matthew 21:1-11)

1

Jesus and team walk the 5 kilometres (3 miles) from Bethany to
Jerusalem. At the halfway point, Bethphage on Olive Mountain, Jesus
delegates the transport issue to two of the Team . . .

2-3

He asks, "See that village? Walk in and you'll find a donkey and its
baby tied up. Bring both to me. If you get stopped, just say, 'The Boss
needs them' – there'll be no hassle."

4-5

All this slots in nicely with clues the old courier Zechariah gave: "Put
fliers through every door in Jerusalem, posters on every free wall: tell
them, 'Look! Your King's making his entrance. But he doesn't hype it
up or pose: he arrives on a baby donkey!'"

6-9

The two get to the village and it all fits Jesus' description. They bring the donkeys back, use their coats for a saddle and Jesus gets on. He rides up to Jerusalem and the crowds are going crazy, chucking their coats and palm leaves on the road in respect and shouting different slogans: "Free us!", "Liberation Now, Now, Now!", "God do you good, Jesus Davidson!" and "There's only one God in heaven, one God in heaven!"

10-11

He arrives at Jerusalem and the whole city's buzzing, "Who *is* this guy?" The crowds bypass the grapevine and just keep shouting, "It's the courier Jesus, from Nazareth, Galilee!"

The religious leaders don't need to ask: they know.   −Rob

"I know the ending" (John 12:23-33)

23-26

Jesus tells Phil and Drew, "It's time! Time to show my full colours. Truth is, unless a wheat seed hits the ground and goes under, it'll only ever be *one* seed. But if it dies, it'll grow and produce loads of new seeds. Anyone who clings on desperately to their precious life will lose it. But the guys who see through the shallowness of *this* life will get limitless life in the next. You want to be on my team? Then copy me. You'll end up the same place with me. My Dad will dole out the bonuses for those who work with me."

27-29

"Now my heart's shredding itself. What do I say? 'Dad, a million miles from here – press the Transfer button now'? No! The whole point of coming is to be right here, right now. Dad, boost your reputation through me."

Then a voice booms out from above (no reverb, no special FX – no need when you're God), "I've already upped my reputation and I'm not about to stop now." Descriptions varied: some said the voice was as deep as thunder; others guessed it was an angel talking to him.

30-33

Jesus tells the crowd, "The voice-over wasn't laid on for my benefit, but for yours. Judgement Day's ticking closer! Prince Evil's pulling the chains and conducting the noise, but he'll be tied up and booted out. When they put me up on that tatty, wooden structure, I'll be like a magnet attracting people of opposite poles straight to me" (a hint at the type of death he'd face).

He goes back to Bethany for the night. Next day he checks on HQ and does an action replay of the DIY Destruction scene (see p. 268). Turning the tables isn't just vandalism; it's like burning the national flag. He's turning up the heat. The strict and particulars know who's going to get the grilling.   —Rob

"Who's your sponsor?" (Luke 20:1-8)

1-2

One time, he's at HQ helping people understand God-stuff when a posse of bounty hunters dressed up as head God-reps and religious law enforcers turn up. They ask him, "Who's your sponsor? Who's backing you up here?"

3

Jesus steps calmly over their tripwire and answers with a question: "Where did the backing for John Baptizer come from? Was it a spiritual thing or a human thing?"

5-7

They were done! Answer (a) "spiritual", and he'd say, "Why didn't you rate him then?" Answer (b) "human", and the plebs would chuck rocks at them for slagging off their hero-martyr-courier. They mumble, "Not sure."

8

Jesus says, "You've not answered my question; I'll pass on yours."

Friendly welcome (Luke 20:9-19)

Jesus turns back to the people he'd been chatting to and starts a story about an absentee landlord of a wine-growing set-up. He sends a series of staff to collect the rent owed, but each time the workers beat them up and send them packing. After the third comes back, black eyed and limping, the landlord decides to send his son – "Maybe they'll show him more respect." He arrives and the workers think, "He's the heir! We get rid of him and we get the dosh!" So they kill him.   —Rob

19

The religious law enforcers and head God-reps are frantically flicking through the Law Books – they know this last story was aimed at them. They also know there has to be a huge swing in public opinion: right now from tabloid to broadsheet readers – people love him.

"Whose money is this?" (Matthew 22:15-22)

But they've got a new plan: they send a delegation of some of their top debaters with some of King Herod's men to quiz him, "Should Jews pay taxes to Caesar, or not?"   —Rob

18-20

Jesus susses their motives and says, "You two-faced con-artists! Your trick questions aren't exactly subtle. Show me the coin you were thinking of giving to Caesar." They fumble around, pass him a coin. He looks at it and asks, "Who's picture's this on the back?"

21-22

They answer, "Caesar's."

"Well, give Caesar what's his, and God what's *his*."

Silenced, they slope off.

The best rule is love (Matthew 22:34-40)

34-35

A different department take their turn trying to catch him out. Some hypothetical question about some small print in the Rule Books. Jesus proves they don't know the book – not as well as *he* does. The crowds love it. Now it's the turn of the top dogs themselves to ask questions . . .

36

"Of all the 613 rules, which would you say is the most important?"

37-40

Jesus answers straight, "'Love Awesome God with everything you've got – your emotions, your will, your thoughts.' This is the No. 1, top priority, absolute must, the Big One. The No. 2, second absolute must is 'Love people around you as you love yourself.' A thousand column inches of writing by Moses and the couriers boil down to these two rules."

Jesus turns the tables and asks them a question. They can't answer him. From then on they back off from quizzing him in public — he's too sharp.   —Rob

"Not my kind of people" (Matthew 23:1-39)

He's fended off three sly attacks from different groups of religious bigwigs; he's told two stories about farms and feasts, aimed directly at them. Now Jesus goes direct — just in case the team or the public are in any doubt where he stands on the religious powers that be . . .   —Rob

2-4

"They sit where Moses sat — so make sure you listen and you do what they say. But don't do what they *do!* 'Cos they're two-faced: one face spouts great ideas; the other looks for loopholes, sniffs out the vulnerable and barks at them like a rabid dog. They weigh people down with 'shoulds' and 'musts' and 'have tos', but don't risk breaking a precious nail to help them get people standing strong again."

He lays into them for "performing", doing their religion for the applause of the crowd and celebrity ratings. He warns them that those who set themselves up will be brought crashing down, and vice versa. He's on a roll now; he launches into a series of slappings . . .   —Rob

13

"You're looking down the barrel of bad news, you religious leaders and law enforcers. Two-faced actors the lot of you: God opens the door marked 'heaven on earth'; you slam it shut in people's faces. OK, maybe *you're* not interested, but how dare you stop *others!*"

15

"You're riding for a fall, you top brass, you HQ hypocrites! You travel the world on your company card, bring back your trophy converts, then indoctrinate them into doubling your tally of evil."

23-24

"You're washed up, you religious fraudsters, you phoneys, you kidology experts! You give God his 10 percent to five decimal points, but you forget rules exist for fairness, love, loyalty. You blind guide dogs! You use sterilized tweezers to fish out the hair from your soup starter; then you chomp into your mad-cow-diseased steak for the main course!"

25

"You're down the tubes, you ringers for real religion! You're just HQ window dressing!

"Like I said before, you scrub the bowls and cups so they're sparkling on the outside, but on the inside you leave the bacteria of greed and selfishness to fester."

27

"You're up the creek without a paddle you back-stabbing braggers, you garden-path tour guides! You're like marble-paved graves — all suave on the surface. But 6 feet under? Decomposing bodies giving off stench."

29-30

"You're in schtuck, you fakes, you con-men, you gazumpers! You put flowers on the graves of the couriers, but you're just like those that came before you — stamping out anyone that threatens the status quo."

33-36

"You've hell to pay, you snakes, you colony of cobras! You've got a one-way ticket to hell; no stations on the way down. You're the reason God had to send so many couriers — your great-granddads kept lynching them, bumping them off. Your generation is going to take the heat for all the good blood wasted right from the start."

37-39

"Jerusalem! Your track record makes depressing reading: a list of tortured couriers who died in action. So how come I want to cuddle this place, look after you like a mother cat curls round her crop of kittens?! But you won't have it. You're off! Only interested in sharpening your claws. And soon you're trashed, nothing left to recycle. Next time you see me won't be until you've learnt your lines: 'Elevate him who turns up glowing with God's approval.'"

Collection-box techniques (Mark 12:41-44)

41-42

Jesus takes a break, sits down opposite the collection boxes. He watches the loaded wafting their big notes around so everyone can see how much they're giving to God's charity. He doesn't miss the cash-strapped widow who sneaks up and tries to get two measly little coins into the box without them clattering around and giving her away . . .

43-44

Nudging his team, Jesus points her out and says, "Truth is, this woman's put in more than the rest put together! If we're talking percentages, they give a tiny fraction of their vast disposable income – she gives all of it, 100 percent."

Closet fans (John 12:37-50)

By now, most people have seen or heard the reports of the spectacular healings Jesus has pulled off. But still there are plenty of sceptics – obviously the grey suits are mostly anti, but some of the religious elite reckon he's the genuine article. 'Course they can't afford to "come out" – that'd be professional suicide. They get creative with excuses like "I've worked hard to get this job", "Why should my kids suffer for my beliefs?", "Best to change the system from within" etc. On the ball, as ever, Jesus says . . .   – Rob

47-50

"What about those who accept what I'm saying, but can't turn it into a lifestyle choice? Well, I'm not here to interrogate anyone. I've come to liberate people, not pronounce sentence. God'll judge them on the Big Day and I'll just give evidence as I saw it. Everything you heard is direct from God, the content, the style, the whole thing. I know if they do as he says, they'll get limitless life. I'm just telling you what Dad says to pass on."

Alarm bells before the Return (Mark 13:1-33)

1

Jesus and the team are leaving the HQ; one of the team looks up and says, "Awesome architecture!"

2

Jesus replies, "I tell you, all this'll be like a Lego tower with a toddler – flat, not one stone left on another."

3-4

He's sitting on the hill, looking down at HQ, and Pete, Jim, Jonno and Drew have a quiet word: "When? When's all this tower-toppling grief going to happen? Are we going to get to feel the rumblings?"

5-8

"Keep sharp," Jesus says. "You're going to see the headlines, the news-flashes about this guy or the other guy who's making out he's the One, and loads'll sign up, but you lot: switch channels, retune, turn over to the sports page – ignore them. When you see the documentaries on wars, atrocities, grief-stricken cities, I won't be around to say, 'I told you so,' but it'll all come back to you. It has to happen, but don't panic – that's not the end ... the fat lady hasn't even started warming up her voice yet! Countries'll flex their pecs at each other, beat the heaven out of each other; earthquakes are going to rip places apart, from shanty towns to skyscrapers – like I said, Lego bricks."

9-11

"And this is just for starters – just the contractions before the real labour pains kick in. You're the target. You're the ones they're after. They'll come for you. Rush you to the local cop shop and give you a practical workshop in assault – all because they've got reports of you with my badge or bracelet or phrases. But the final curtain can't come down till my story's been told, and I'm talking global. So when they stick you in the dock, don't wobble about what to say to the councillor – my coun-sellor, God's Holy Spirit, will cue you the right words at the right time. Just open your mouth and hear his poetry pour out."

12-13

"Brothers are going to grass each other up. Daughters are going to report their own mothers. Dad's are going to slam up their own sons – on death row. Everyone's going to hate you, because of me. But if you take it on the chin, if you stand there and take what they throw at you – even if it is bricks (and now I'm *not* talking Lego) – you'll be cast in a key role in the ultimate sequel."

14-23

"When people see all this bedlam, all this havoc, they're not going to hang around; they're not going to go back for the family photos – they're going to leg it with a one-way ticket to anywhere. It's going to be misery for pregnant women. Beg God that it won't happen in winter, because this is as bad as it's been, and as bad as it gets. If God didn't step in for the sake of the Selected, if he didn't clap his hands and say, 'Enough already. Hold it right there!' no one would even survive. Don't say I didn't warn you. If you overhear people raving about this liberator or that liberator, with their magic shows, supernatural spectaculars that might even sucker the Selected (if that were possible), don't buy into it. Keep on your toes. I've told you the plot ahead of the game."

24-25

"After all this trauma, as old Isaiah put it: 'The sun'll go pitch black; the moon'll have nothing to reflect; the stars'll go into free fall; the spiritual forces of the cosmos will curl up and quiver.'"

26-27

"All this is my entrance cue. I'm on! I'll surf the clouds. It'll be the ultimate display of power and brilliance. The angels will pick up those I've selected from every grid-reference point on the planet."

28-31

"It's like with a fig tree – locals learn the signs that summer's on its way (tender twigs, leaves etc.). So I've told you the signs to spot; when you see them, you'll know it's close. Truth is, we Jews'll still be around. The planet and the atmosphere will collapse, but the truth of what I'm saying will still stand."

32-33

"The exact timing's kept absolute top secret. The angels have no idea. Even I've not been told. Dad's the only one who knows when. So don't drift off. Keep on the ball."

Trilogy of "On the ball" stories (Matthew 25:1-46)

Images of the apocalypse flying round their heads gives the right backdrop to Jesus' next three stories.   —Rob

Story 1: Great reception

Ten bridesmaids waiting for the groom to arrive. They're all carrying ornamental oil lamps, but only half of them have back-up supplies of oil. The groom takes ages to show and they all nod off. It's midnight by the time he turns up. They all wake up, check their hair, and then check their lamps — all nearly empty. But the smart ones have spare oilcans. They meet the groom and get top table seats at the wedding reception. The stupid ones are flying round town trying to find a garage open. At midnight? Unlikely. They miss the celebrations. Jesus' pay-off line goes ...   —Rob

13

"So keep sharp. You never know the exact timing."

Story 2: Investment Trust

14-18

"Imagine a man, loaded, goes off on a long business trip. He sends a memo round to three of his staff, calling them into his office. They arrive and he tells them, 'I've sold my stake in the business and I need you guys to look after the dosh while I'm away.' He pulls out three briefcases and starts handing them out. The first guy (a real talent) gets a case stuffed with 500 grand's worth of crisp notes; the second guy (good, but nothing stunning) gets 200 grand, and the last guy (steady) gets 'just' 100 grand. Then the boss says, 'I'm off!' and leaves them staring at each other in shock. The first guy goes off to read up on his investment mags; he picks the brains of financial advisors and eventually comes up with a detailed investment portfolio. After a while he's doubled the money and hit the million mark. He's well happy. The second guy also goes off and puts together a strategy. And likewise, doubles his money to 400 grand. The third guy, however, bottles. He thinks, *What if the market crashes? What if there's a run on the banks? What if I buy gold and they discover an enormous gold mine lying 2 feet under every garden in the city, and the gold price plummets?* So he buys a safe, stuffs the money inside and buries it in his back garden."

19-21

"Ages later, the boss comes back and rings round the three: 'I'm back; let's meet, usual place.' The first sits there, looking smug, and says, 'You gave me 500 grand and I've done a bit of wheeling and dealing, ducking and diving, dodging and weaving – all legal of course – and I've doubled your money.' He hands over two briefcases, stuffed full with a cool million. His boss says, 'Well done; done well! You've proved yourself; now you get to manage bigger projects for me. You and me, we've got good times lined up!'"

22-23

"The second guy, also looking pleased with himself, says, 'You gave me 200 grand, and I've doubled your money as well.' Handing the boss the case, he says, 'There's 400 grand in there.' Likewise, his boss is impressed: 'Well done; done well! I've got some good projects for you too. You'll have nothing to worry about from now on.'"

24-25

"The third guy is twitching by now. The boss turns to him and says, 'And?' 'And . . . you gave me only 100 grand,' he mumbles. 'And what did you do with it?' frowns the boss. 'Well, I've heard the rumours, about your middle name being "Ruthless" and how you can't be doing with losers, and I didn't want to risk losing the cash, so . . . I buried it . . . in a safe place . . . in a safe . . . it's all here, not a fiver missing, the whole caboodle.'"

26-27

"The boss is fuming: 'You lily-livered, useless, gutless, spineless excuse for a half-life. You're pathetic. If you knew I was so ruthless, why didn't you get your act together and at least put the money into an interest account – is that really so hard? What's the inflation rate? How much have I lost? Unless you're too lazy to get off your backside and do the sums!'"

28-30

"Then he takes the briefcase and gives it to the first guy, saying, 'You have it, 'cos those who've got loads get given even more; and those who've got zilch, even what they've got'll get given to those with loads. That's how it works! And get this loser out of my sight! Throw him out onto the streets where he belongs. If he gets piles from the pavement, tough.'"

Story 3: Sheep or goat?

31-33

"When I come back and dazzle the planet with the light show and the angel chorus, I'll be on the throne looking out over the total world population and I'll start separating people out: 'sheep' on my right side, 'goats' on the left."

34-36

"I'll say to the 'sheep', 'You're in God's good books: come forward, collect what's been waiting for you since before I made the planets. All this 'cos I feel I owe you – when I was starving, you made me meals. When I was thirsty, you poured me a drink. I was a loner in the corner; you opened out the circle and brought me in. When my clothes weren't up to the job, you went through your cupboards for me. When my health was bad, you nursed me back to strength. I was in my prison cell; you swallowed your pride and made the visiting hours.'"

37-39

"Those who've done the right thing scratch their heads and ask, 'When? When did we make you meals, or pour you a drink, or bring you into the circle, or give you new clothes, or nurse you, or visit you?'"

40

"I'll tell them, 'Truth is, every good thing you've done for the lowest of the low – my brothers, sisters, it's like you did it for me!'"

41-43

"But the 'goats' on the left will get the opposite treatment: 'Get out of my sight. You're in the biggest hole you could imagine, and the hole's on fire, heating up for Satan and his cronies later. 'Cos I was starving and you moaned about you being overweight. I was thirsty; you complained about the cheap wine being served. I was a loner; you laughed at me and told me to get a life. I was freezing cold; you told me to jump up and down. I was ill; you told me to snap out of it. I was locked up; you would've told me I deserved it, but you couldn't even be bothered to make the trip to rub my nose in it!'"

44

"'Whoa! Hang on,' say the 'goats'. 'We wouldn't be like that to *you!* With someone like *you* we'd be thoughtful, sensitive, inclusive, generous, caring. With someone like *you* we'd never make you feel forgotten.'"

45

"I'll say, 'Truth is, the lowest of the low *is* someone like me! So whatever you didn't do for *them,* you didn't do for *me.*'"

46

"They'll get taken away to permanent punishment. Those who did the right thing, they'll enjoy limitless life."

The (Com)Passion

The plot dilemma (Matthew 26:1-5)

Jesus knows it's two days and counting to the Flyby Festival. He also knows he'll be betrayed and executed. Scene change to Caiaphas's place (top God-rep of the year). Secret meeting, only one point on the agenda – how to dispose of Jesus without causing a riot at Festival weekend ... —Rob

The plot solution (Luke 22:3-6)

Then Satan makes his breakthrough. He finally penetrates Jesus' inner Team and gets inside the head of Judas (Iscariot). Judas turns up at Caiaphas's place and they agree to fit him in under "any other business".

When they hear he's offering to hand Jesus over to them, they're fighting back the cartwheels. Judas starts spending the reward in his head, while keeping an eye open for a quiet location, away from the crowd, where he can hand Jesus over.

Bread breaking on the menu (Luke 22:14-20)

14-16

Jesus and the team are sitting round the table for the traditional meal to kick off the Flyby Festival. He makes a speech: "I've lost sleep thinking about this great meal with you guys. It'll be my last meal before the torment starts, my last till God's New World Order really arrives for good."

17-18

He picks up a wine cup, thanks his Father for it and says, "Pass this round, let's all drink from the same cup. It'll be my last till Heaven on Earth is more than just talk."

19

Then he takes a bread loaf, thanks his Father again and rips it into pieces; each of the team gets a chunk. He says, "This is my body. Do this and remember me."

20

They finish the meal and Jesus picks up the cup, deep in thought. He says, "This cup is the New Contract sealed with my blood. Blood that'll hit the ground for you."

> Somehow the table banter evolves into who's Team captain, who's written in ink before the others are built in around them, who's indispensable ...   —Rob

Leadership seminar (John 13:3-15)

3-5

Jesus knows his Dad has delegated everything to him and supplied the resources to make everything possible. He also knows he is on a two-way ticket from heaven and that the return trip is about to leave. So he gets up from the table, takes off his jacket, rolls up his sleeves and puts a towel round his waist. He pours water into a bowl and, one by one, washes the team's dirty, sweaty feet and dries them with the towel.

6-9

Pete's next in line and he can't quite handle it: "Boss, no way you're washing *my* feet, surely?"

Jesus answers, "You can't take it in right now. But one day you'll get it."

"No way!" says Pete. "I'm not having *you* wash *my* feet."

"If I don't, you're not part of it all," says Jesus.

"OK, then wash me head to toe. I'm in – totally!"

When he's finished all twelve (including Judas Iscariot!), he explains . . .

14-15

"If I've washed your stinking feet and I'm your Boss, your mentor, your coach, then you've got to wash each other's feet. As ever, I'm not asking you to do something I wouldn't do. I'm your example – so copy me: get washing!"

Usual suspects? (Luke 22:21-22)

"And the guy who's going to stitch me up and hand me over has his legs under this table! He's here now. What's about to happen to me is written in stone, but for the guy caught with the chisel in his hand? Big trouble." The atmosphere changes, the team start suspecting each other. Fishing for clues as to who's planning the mutiny.

Jesus gives Judas a coded message: "Do it quick," he tells him. Judas leaves. It's dark.
–Rob

All words! (Mark 14:27-31)

Jesus knows the rest of the team aren't going to be exactly supportive. Pete swears he'll stick by him till the end. Jesus knows otherwise . . .
–Rob

30

"Sad truth is," says Jesus to Pete, "by the time the rooster does his next alarm clock impression, you'll have sworn blind that you don't know me. Not once, not twice, but three times!"

31

But Pete's adamant: "I'd rather die than disown you." The others are nodding, punching their fists on the table and looking determined.

Final speeches 1 (John 14:1-31)

1-4

"Don't look so stressed! You rely on God. So rely on *me!* Dad's place has thousands of vacancies. I'm going ahead to get your apartment suites ready, to book you in. Would I lie to you? No, you know it. When it's all sorted I'll come and pick you up. I'll be desperate for you to be with me. You know the route."

5-6

Tom says, "Boss, if we knew where you're going, we might be able to work out the route, but we don't!"

Jesus comes back with, "*I'm* the route, the true route. And I'm the energy to propel you along the right route. I'm the only way you get to meet my Dad."

Phil asks if they can see Jesus' Father.   —Rob

9

Jesus answers, "Phil, how long have I been with you? D'you still not know me? If you've seen me, you've seen my Dad. So how come you say, 'Show us your Father'?"

He gets them thinking about all the supernatural things they've seen – "aren't they proof enough?" But he says they're going to outdo him in the supernatural stakes: if they contact him at his Father's place, he'll make sure whatever they ask gets done.   —Rob

15-16

"If you love me, you'll live as I tell you to live. I'll ask Dad to send you a new Advisor – his Holy Spirit. He'll be contracted to you permanently."

Then more on how the future pans out. It's simple enough (in theory) – they love him, they do as he says, they get to live with him and his Father.   —Rob

25-27

"I've let you in on this while I'm still around. But my replacement Advisor – God's Holy Spirit (who Dad will substitute me with) – is a superb coach: he'll trigger off things I've said and they'll finally spark into life. You're going to get the best leaving present – my serenity. Not the serenity on the adverts that runs out when the packet's empty! My serenity. So take it in and watch your heart rate stabilize. No fear. No panic."

Then to round off this speech . . .   —Rob

30-31

"We've no time left to talk; Prince Evil's stalking me. He couldn't touch me, but people need to know that I love my Dad and do exactly what he tells me. So, come on. Let's shift."

Final speeches 2 (John 15:1-16:8)

The next speech is outside. (Who knows, possibly near a vineyard.) He sets up the image of him as a vine plant, his Father as the pruner and the team as branches. They need to keep contact with him if they're going to produce grapes. If they get lopped off, they'll be part of the next bonfire. But if they hit production targets, it'll prove they're well connected to him.   —Rob

11-17

"I've told you all this to cheer you up. To pump every part of you full of joy. My rule reads, 'Love each other like I've loved you.' There's no love that tops this love, the love where someone gives up his life for his mates. How d'you know if you're my mates? You'll do as I tell you. I don't call you 'staff' or 'employees', 'cos mere workers aren't in on the boss's plans. No, I call you 'mates', 'cos everything Dad's told me, I've told you. I've held nothing back. Been totally open. You might think you opted into the team, but actually I picked you. Why? So you'd be productive and that your produce would last. So ask my Father for what you like, and he'll give it to you if you charge it to my account. Don't forget my rule 'Love each other.'"

18-19

"If the public can't stand you? Hmm, there's a surprise! They hated me first. D'you think you're going to get any different treatment? You're not one of them. That's why they can't cope."

> Jesus adds, "If they stonewall you, they do the same to me and to my Dad. They saw spectacular proof of people's lives being sorted, but still hated me. But the Advisor will back up your evidence with solid proof that'll persuade some. The rest will think they're doing God a favour by kicking you out and trying to finish you off. Don't say I didn't warn you."   —Rob

16:6-8

"Now you're all down in the mouth! But honestly, it's best for you that I go. If I don't go, the Advisor can't come. Once I've gone, I'll send him to you. Once he's here he'll convince people their lives are out of line and need the mess sorted and straightened out.

"When the Advisor comes he'll make it clear what's right and what's not. It's going to be a rough ride. The System will drag you down, but I've beaten the System. So relax. Sample some serenity."

Jesus' one big ask (John 17:1-24)

1-5

Then Jesus looks up: "Dad, it's time! Elevate me, so I'm in a position to elevate you. You gave me the right to hand out limitless life to the team you'd given me. Limitless life is knowing you're the only God and that I'm the Liberator you sent. I've done you credit by fulfilling my part of the arrangement down here. So now, Dad, lift me back up to the status I had before we made the cosmos."

6-7

'The squad you gave me, I've shown them what you're like. They were yours before. You trusted me with them and they've lived life your way . . ."

11

"I'm almost out of here, but they're stuck in this place for a while yet. Dad, you're 100 percent pure. Protect them by your status. Make them united, going for one thing, together – like we do . . ."

15-18

"I'm not asking you to lift them out of the System. But surround them with forces that'll keep the evil one off their case. Like me, they're not card-carrying members of the System. Keep them distinct. Keep them unpolluted by its smog and filth. Keep them straight and true by knowing your instructions and living them out. You sent me on a mission; I've done the same to them: sent them on a mission . . ."

20-21

"But not just them! All the thousands that'll opt back into your way 'cos of what my squad tells them. I've got one big ask – keep them together, united, one huge team living the way you and I relate. But doing it down here. Keep them plugged into us, so it'll be obvious that you sent me . . ."

24

"And one more thing – these new squad members, I want them to see the real me. They missed me this time round, but please, work it so they see me glowing with the love you've had for me since we made their planet."

It's getting late on Thursday evening . . .   –Rob

"Must I . . . ?" (Mark 14:32-36)

32-34

They come to their regular refocus park, Gethsemane. Jesus tells the team, "Take a break here while I go talk with God." He takes Pete, Jim and Jonno with him and starts being sucked down into a black hole of mental torture: "My soul's suffocating . . . all this grief . . . feels like I'm, feels like I'm dying!" He tells them, "Stay here; stay alert for me, yeah?"

35-36

He goes off alone a bit further, but he can't walk: he hits the ground and begs his Father to cancel their plans for the next day. "Daddy," he cries, "with you, everything's possible. But do I have to? Must I drink the whole cup? Can't you find a way round it for me? Please . . . please . . . please! But if there's no other ending . . . no other way . . . then . . . ignore what *I* want . . . carry on with our plan . . . let's do it."

He struggles back for some moral support and finds Pete, Jim and Jonno asleep! (Probably too much food and wine at the Flyby meal earlier.) He urges them to keep contact with God; otherwise, they'll not be up to the job ahead. He goes back and wrestles some more with his Father. Next time he comes back they're snoring away again! Third time, same story. He's going through the ultimate dark night of the soul and they're catnapping like they're on a sunbed in southern Spain. By now it's the early hours of Friday morning – Flyby Festival Weekend – he comes back to Pete, Jim and Jonno and spots Judas sneaking into the park with a posse of men, all looking up for a fight . . .

–Rob

Sealed with a kiss (Matthew 26:47-56)

47-49

Jesus is still talking, when Judas, the team treasurer, shows up with a mob psyched up by the head God-reps. They look very threatening, wielding their bats and knives. The defector has a signal worked out: "Arrest the one I kiss." Judas walks right up to Jesus, says, "Hi, Coach," and kisses him.

50-51

Jesus asks, "Mate, what's all this?"

The braver ones from the mob move forward, get Jesus into a hold and arrest him. Seconds later there's a flash of a knife, some frantic action. Next thing, one of Caiaphas's servants has lost an ear. (Matt's not naming names, or may not have been close enough to see. But Jonno says it was Pete who did the damage, which fits!)

52-54

"Put it away, now!" barks Jesus. "Weapons don't win you battles; they lose you people. Anyway, one word from me and my Father will give the green light to the dozen squadron of angels on action alert. But that would blow what the couriers said would happen, wouldn't it?"

55–56

Then he turns to the mob and says, "Am I head of some military coup, or what?! Why all these bats and knives? Day after day I was there at HQ, coaching people in God's prescribed lifestyle. How come you didn't arrest me there? I'll tell you why: 'cos then it wouldn't have lined up with the couriers' writings."

The team leg it, while they can.

> Jesus is taken off. The guards pass the dark hours of early Friday morning by blind-folding him and playing "guess whose fist" as they use him as a punchbag. They outdo each other with some ugly jibes at Jesus. Still way before breakfast they get the instructions to bring him to Caiaphas's house where they've set up a makeshift court – they need Jesus in the dock asap. They've been trawling the city for witnesses who'd say something incriminating against him. Best they can do is two guys who swear Jesus said, "I can destroy this HQ and reconstruct it in two days." Thing is, he had! But his metaphor had gone right over their heads: he was talking about his body being God's true HQ, and he was going to be destroyed and then reconstructed two days later . . .
>
> —Rob

The big question (Luke 22:67–71)

67

"Look, it's very simple," the religious leaders reason. "If you're the Liberator, just tell us!"

68–69

Jesus comes back, "It's *not* simple. If I tell you I am, you won't believe me! If I ask you what you're really getting at, you won't answer. Not so simple! All I'm saying is this: pretty soon I'll be sat there on my throne next to the Awesome God."

70

They all blurt out, "So you reckon you're God's Son now, do you?"

"You said it!" Jesus answers.

71

"That's it!!" they say, fuming mad. "Cancel the rest of the witnesses. We've heard it from the horse's mouth!"

They all know the law: what he's said has only one verdict – the death penalty. The religious leaders think they're finally on a roll . . .　　　　　–Rob

Jesus' friend? (Matthew 26:69-75)

While all this is going on, Pete's sidled his way into Caiaphas's backyard. The servants are hanging round, putting bets on what'll happen next. Some of them half recognize him as one of Jesus' team. He laughs it off. They keep pushing. He flat denies it again. By the third time it's starting to get a bit lighter; they can see more of his face turning red as he swears blind that he's never met Jesus. Then the rooster does his wake-up call and Pete's face changes from red to white. Jesus' words "you'll have sworn blind that you don't know me" are jumping in his brain like a scratched CD. He runs, hardly seeing where he's going through the tears.

Cross fade scenes to more tears from another close friend (ex). Judas hears they've announced the death sentence and realizes he's made a huge mistake. He tries to give the money back, but they won't take it. He runs off, throws the coins into the HQ and goes and hangs himself . . .　　　　　–Rob

Pilate's signature required (John 18:28-39)

28

Jesus is frog-marched from Caiaphas's place to the palace of the Roman governor, Pilate. Powerful guy – has a big say in who gets the top job for the top reps (Caiaphas got it the previous year), has last word on the HQ and its budget and (this is the big one) has to ratify any death sentence passed by the Jewish religious leaders. So they need him. Tricky situation: they've got to suck up to this guy, but they can't step inside his Roman palace this close to Saturday's Flyby Festival . . .

29-31

So Pilate comes out to them in his dressing gown: "What's the charge this time?"

"He's a criminal!" they assure him. "Otherwise, we wouldn't waste your time."

Pilate sighs, "You've got your laws; won't they do?"

"As you know, sir, we're not allowed to execute!" they answer.

Pilate rolls his eyes and invites Jesus inside . . .   —Rob

33b–34

He asks Jesus, "So, are you the Jewish king or not?"

"Who's briefing you?" Jesus asks. "Or is 'Jewish king' your own phrase?"

35–36

"You calling me a Jew?" Then Pilate backs off: "Look, your people handed you over! What've you been up to?"

Jesus tells him, "My kingdom isn't a geographical area, with counties and borders. If it were, my people would start a war rather than see me turned in so easily. No, my kingdom is totally other."

37

"So you *are* a king then," says Pilate.

"Absolutely, and I was born for this. I'm here to point out what truth is. Anyone who really wants to know will be all ears when I'm speaking."

38–39

"Truth! What's that?!" But Pilate's had enough philosophical debate for this time of the morning.

He goes back out to the Jews . . .

Poor defence (Mark 15:3–5)

3–4

The Jewish top brass are listing off their charges against him. Pilate turns to Jesus and says, "Aren't you going to argue your defence? You just going to let them reel off their charges unopposed?"

5

Jesus stays calm and quiet. Pilate's never seen anything like it.

Pass the buck (Luke 23:4-12)

4-5

Pilate insists, "The guy's innocent!"

They're desperate now: "But he's causing riots, from his old stomping ground, Galilee, down to the capital."

A great idea hits Pilate. The ultimate cop-out strategy. Years of political manoeuvring have trained him well. It was their use of the word "Galilee" – King Herod's patch! Jesus is from there, so this is Herod's problem. Plus (now everything's just falling into his lap) he knows that Herod's here in Jerusalem for the Festival. Perfect! He can sort the mess out. Herod's happy to help: he's been itching to meet Jesus. But Jesus Davidson is exercising his right to remain silent and it's not much of a conversation. The religious leaders are sticking their oar in, stirring up trouble. Herod gives up asking questions and decides to have a laugh. He eggs his soldiers on by dressing Jesus up as a king; they ham-act their grovelling citizens role. When the novelty of this wears off, he passes Jesus (and the buck) back to Pilate, fully dressed in the robe of Herod's black humour. This turned the corner for Roman/Galilean relations. Pilate and Herod were good mates from here on.   —Rob

Nothing doing (Luke 23:13-18)

13-16

Pilate walks out to the Jewish leaders and says, "The case is full of holes. He's done nothing! I've talked with him; Herod's talked with him (or 'to' him). We agree – he's done nothing to get him even close to the death penalty: I'll have my men flog him and let him go."

But the mob don't want this and they're not subtle about letting him know. —Rob

"Execute!" (Matthew 27:15-23)

15-18

The governor has a tradition he calls "The Flyby Amnesty". Every year, at Festival time, he lets one of their prisoners go – anyone they vote for. This year one possible "walker" is a guy, surname Abbasson – a ruthless terrorist, in for murder and politically motivated damage of Roman property. Pilate asks the crowd, "Who's going to get lucky? Abbasson or Davidson?" (He knows why the religious leaders have Jesus on trial –

they're jealous of him. But he wants to know which way the crowd will vote.)

19

Just then, Pilate's wife has a quiet word in his ear: "I've just had a horrific nightmare about this Jesus, the Galilean – he's innocent! Don't touch him with a javelin pole."

20-21

Meanwhile, the religious leaders are hyping up the crowd, canvassing them to vote for "Abbasson" (the usual "he's not a *terrorist;* he's a *freedom fighter*" argument seems to be working). Pilate asks them again and they start up the chant "Abbasson! Abbasson! Abbasson!"

22-23

"OK, I get the message!" Pilate says. "But what about Jesus Davidson, aka 'the Liberator'?"

"Execute him, Roman style!" they scream.

"For what?!" Pilate calls over the bedlam. But most of the crowd don't hear: they're locked into the chant "Execute! Execute! Execute!"

"One word from me ..." (John 19:6b-10)

6b-7

Pilate shouts back, "*You* execute him. I told you: I say he's not guilty!"

The Jewish religious leaders get blunt: "He says he's God – by our law, that's a capital offence!"

8-10

Pilate's getting rattled now. He takes Jesus back inside and asks him, "Where you from?" But Jesus doesn't answer.

Pilate resorts to sarcasm: "Silence is really going to help! That's virtual suicide! Don't you get it? One word from me and you walk free. A different word and you're pinned up to die! Slowly! Painfully!"

"Not my fault" (Matthew 27:24-26)

24-25

Pilate knows he's getting nowhere and that this is threatening to go up a gear into a full-scale riot. So he sends for a bowl of water and makes some big gestures. The noise dies down and he says, "I've tried! My hands are clean. I've got none of his blood on my hands. You want it; you take the weight of it!"

The people yell back, "No problem; we'll have his blood on our hands. Us and our kids."

26

So Pilate gives the signal for Abbasson's cell to be unlocked and for the prisoner to be escorted to the open prison gates and to walk. Pilate arranges for Davidson to be whipped with a lead-tipped whip and then executed, Roman style.

Beatings (Mark 15:16-20)

The Roman soldiers manhandle Jesus through to the Praetorium and call out the whole battalion on shift. They get hold of a purple robe and stick him in it. Someone gets creative and makes a mock crown out of thorn stems. They press it down hard on his head so it's not falling off. Some of them start giving him the verbal: "We salute you, Jewish king!" Others are whacking him across the head with their javelins. Others are getting more vulgar, spitting in his face. Some are down on their knees, maliciously ripping into him with their sarcasm. Eventually they get bored with the game and swap the robe for his old clothes. Then they lead him out to be executed.

> They slam a heavy rough-hewn plank across his shoulders and tie him to it by both wrists. Under guard he carries it through the crowds. He's exhausted, collapsing under the weight. It's taking too long, so the guards press-gang a black guy, Simon, to carry it the rest of the way out to Skull Hill. Some of the women are crying for him. (A brief glimpse of humanity on an ugly morning — a very bad Friday.) —Rob

Jewish king (Mark 15:23-32)

23-24

The execution team offer him a drink — wine mixed with the painkiller myrrh. It tastes disgusting and he turns his head away. A soldier with a large mallet drives heavy wrought-iron nails through Jesus' wrists — they staple him on to the cross bar. Another huge nail through his ankles into the upright stake. They crucify him, literally. They rip his clothes off and gamble for them.

25-30

Time check: Friday 9am. A small makeshift sign is tied above Jesus' head with his crime written out (as a deterrent to would-be revolutionaries). It reads, "The Jewish king". The two thieves each side of him have their crimes written out too — their signs are bigger with smaller fonts. The crowds get stuck into the macabre scene, hurling abuse at Jesus: "Destroy HQ and rebuild it in two days, eh? Bit off schedule, aren't you? Come on down and save yourself!!"

31-32

The head God-reps are stirring it with the law enforcers, giving out as much hate as the rest of them: "How come you free so many, but you can't seem to free yourself? Tell you what, you liberating king of Jews, you come on down — think of the publicity! We're all watching. Come on; do it and we'll believe you." Even the two thieves join in.

> Some of the religious leaders take time off to put in a formal complaint to Pilate about the "Jewish king" sign, but Pilate's not shifting.   —Rob

Fair cop (Luke 23:34-43)

34

Jesus looks up: "Dad! Don't hold what they're doing against them — wipe their slate clean. They've got no idea what's going on here!"

> They carry on spitting out their jibes …   —Rob

39-41

One of the two thieves gets a second wind: "Aren't you supposed to be the Liberator? Get liberating, won't you? *You* need it; *we* need it!"

The other guy calls across, "Would you talk to God like that? Huh? You're getting what you had coming to you; this guy's done nothing wrong. So shut it!"

42-43

This second thief turns to Jesus and says, "Jesus, don't forget me when you get to sit on your throne, eh?"

Jesus answers him, "Truth is, before the day's out, you and me, we'll be in paradise together!"

New relations (John 19:25-27)

Front row of the crowd is Jesus' mum, his Aunt Mary and Mary Magdalene. Jesus spots his mum standing right next to Jonno and says to her, "Lady, this is your new son." He looks straight at Jonno and says, "She's your new mother." From then on Jonno looks after Mary like she's his own blood.

The different biographers are standing in different places; they hear different things.

Dead (Mark 15:33-37)

33-35

Time check: Friday 12 midday. It goes dark, totally dark, for three full hours. At 3pm Jesus draws in all the breath he can and calls out, *Eloi, Eloi, lama, sabachthani?* which means, "My God, my God, why've you abandoned me?"

Some think he's calling for Elijah . . .

37

Then Jesus lets out one last cry and dies.

Rewind: Jonno's viewpoint . . .   —Rob

Dead (John 19:28-30)

Jesus knows the job's finished, and another courier's prophecy is checked off: "I'm gasping; get me a drink?" They dip a sponge into some sour wine, put it on the end of a lopped-off branch and hold it up to his lips. Jesus tastes it; then calls out, "Done! It's done!!" He drops his head and dies.

Back again: Dr. Luke's account . . .   −Rob

Dead (Luke 23:46)

Then Jesus shouts, "Dad, I trust you with my soul!" − his last words. He dies.

Matt's memory of it goes . . .   −Rob

Dead (Matthew 27:50-52)

50

Then Jesus shouts out one more time, and lets his soul exit his body. He dies.

Mission accomplished.   −Rob

51-52

That second, back in the Jerusalem HQ, the thick curtain that marks the no-go point of God's most sacred space gets ripped in two − from top down to the bottom: God's open for business! There's an earthquake, rocks rip apart like the curtain, graves are opened up and the corpses of spiritual people climb up out of them, alive and happening.

Reaction (Luke 23:47-49)

The Roman officer stands there taking all this in and says, "No way this guy was guilty!" The crowd at Skull Hill see it all as well. Their adrenaline dies down and their mood changes. Within minutes they realize what they've just seen, drop into depression and trudge back to their homes. Jesus' mates, including the women who'd come down from Galilee, stand way back, trying to take it all in.

Definitely dead (John 19:31-34)

Tomorrow's no ordinary Saturday; it's Flyby Saturday. The religious leaders can't allow the victims still to be dying on a national holiday. They approach Pilate to order his men to break their legs (to stop them being able to push up and gulp in air, so making sure they die quicker). Pilate gives the word: the soldiers get the order and break the legs of the two thieves. When they come to Jesus, they realize he's already dead – they've seen enough of these to know when a guy's dead, so they don't touch his legs. One of the soldiers lunges a spear into Jesus' side and, sure enough, the blood's already separating and a watery fluid pours out alongside the blood. He's dead, alright.

> Jonno sees the whole thing. He realizes it's to fit the courier writings "he won't have a broken bone in his body" and "they'll look on the one they pierced". –Rob

Buried (Mark 15:42-47)

It's getting towards evening on the Friday. A rich bureaucrat, Joseph Arimatheaton, is a distant fan of Jesus. He goes to Pilate and asks if he can bury the body. Pilate's a bit surprised that Jesus is dead already. He checks with the Roman officer and then gives Joseph permission. Joseph wraps the body in linen strips and places it in his tomb-cave. He has a huge stone shunted across the entrance. Mary, Jesus' mum, and Mary Magdalene are with him watching the burial.

> Jonno heard that Nicodemus – the guy in the "reborn" conversation – was also there. Apparently, he brought the myrrh ointment they used to embalm the body – the same stuff as the astrologers brought on Jesus' birth day.   –Rob

"Guard it!" (Matthew 27:62-66)

The religious leaders' paranoia has got them thinking ahead. They go to Pilate and get him to send some guards to stop Jesus' team from exhuming the body and claiming his "restored in two days" claims have come true. Pilate agrees and guards watch the tomb round the clock.

Irony is, Saturday's supposed to be a sacred celebration, the day Jews remember God freeing them from Egypt. Instead, the team (minus Judas Iscariot) spend the whole day huddled together totally disillusioned, scared stiff, silent. Their depression beyond words. They just wait for the door to be knocked – or knocked through – by the authorities, the beatings that'll follow and, who knows what else?   –Rob

He's back! (Luke 24:1-9)

1-8

Early dawn, Sunday, the women get to the tomb-cave. Their bags are packed with the burial spices – they've not had time Friday night and Saturday was Flyby Day. This is the first chance they've had. They get there and the boulder's been shoved to one side. They go in, but Jesus' body's not there. They're stunned: "What could've happened to it?"

Next thing, two angels are lighting up the whole cave with their dazzling bright clothes. The women hit the deck, petrified. The angels ask, "Why you looking in a grave for someone who's alive and well? D'you think he'd hang around in a tomb? He's out of here. He's back from the dead! Remember what he said up in Galilee? He'd be handed over, executed and then he'd come back after two days. Don't you remember?" Suddenly they do! It all comes back. He told them and they missed it!

9

They get back to the Eleven and the others to tell them.

Matthew tells the same event like this . . .   –Rob

He's back! (Matthew 28:5-10)

5-7

The angel says to the women, "Don't panic! You're looking for Jesus, aren't you? Executed last Friday? Well, he's not here! He's back from the dead, like he said he would be. Look where his body was – empty! So go straight back to the rest of them; tell them he's alive. Tell them he's making his way back up to Galilee. They'll see him up there."

8-10

The women run! Weird combination of scared stupid and ecstatic. They're locked on to their target – to tell the rest of them the news. Then Jesus steps out and says, "Hi!" They stop and land at his feet, flat out in front of him. He tells them, "Don't panic. Go tell the rest of them to head back to Galilee, they'll see me up there."

Mark says Pete tells it this way ...   –Rob

He's back! (Mark 16:6-8)

The angel says, "Don't look so shocked! You're looking for the Nazarene, Jesus, executed Friday just gone? He's not here! He's back from the dead. Look, this is where he was. Now go back to the rest of them, including Pete. Tell them, 'Jesus is going up to Galilee. You'll see him there, like he promised before they killed him.'"

The women leg it from the tomb, shaking and confused, running straight past everyone, 'cos they're too freaked to talk.

After the women come and tell them, Jonno and Pete go see for themselves ...
                                                                         –Rob

He's back! (John 20:3-18)

3-9

Pete and Jonno run to the tomb on pure adrenaline. Jonno gets there first and looks in. He spots the linen cloths lying there, but he's rooted to the ground. Pete catches him up and goes straight in. He spots the linen strips and the head-covering folded neatly on the side. So Jonno follows him in, and he knows it's true – Jesus is back! (But neither of them clicks that the couriers knew this was coming years before.)

10-12

They go back home, but Mary Mag is still outside the tomb, sobbing away. She leans down to look into the cave and sees two angels, in their white garb, sitting where Jesus' body has been: one at the head; the other at the feet.

13-14

They ask her, "Lady, why the tears?"

"They've taken my No. 1 away," she says. "I've no idea where they've put him." She turns round and sees Jesus standing there (not that she recognizes him).

15-16

"Lady," he says. "Why the tears? Who you looking to find?"

She assumes he's the gardener and says, "Mister, if you're the one who's cleared him out and taken him off somewhere else, then tell me. I'll go get him."

Jesus just says, "Mary!"

She knows. "Coach!"

17-18

Jesus backs off: "Don't grab on to me. I've not yet gone up to my Dad. Go for me; tell the guys I'm going back up to my Dad and your Dad, to my God and your God."

Mary Mag tells the rest of the squad, "I've seen Jesus!!!" She garbles out all the things he said to her.

The cover story (Matthew 28:11-15)

While the women are giving the team the good news, the guards are giving the religious leaders the bad news. No probs: the guards are bribed to recite the line "'Jesus' cronies hid in the bushes, waited for us to drop off and then stole the body." They're promised full back-up if Pilate gets to hear about it. They take the money. The story's still doing the rounds in cynic clubs across Israel.   —Rob

Other sightings (Luke 24:13-43)

Two squad members spend time with Jesus on their 11 kilometre (7 mile) walk to Emmaus. They chat through the whole thing with him and it's only right at the end, when he thanks God for the food, that they realize who he is. Before they get a chance to talk more, he disappears. They bomb back to Jerusalem to tell the rest, but the squad are already talking about Pete having seen him. Voices are booming with excitement; then Jesus turns up – silence. "Stay calm!" he says. They freeze; the rest of their bodies close down to give their brains a chance to process what's happening. He shows them the scars on his wrists and ankles, lets them touch him to disprove the "ghost" theory flashing through their minds. Then he asks for food – they give him some fish and he eats it; it's like he's in some zoo with people's eyes locked on to everything he's doing.   —Rob

More sightings (John 20:24-21:17)

24-28

Trouble is, Tom missed it all. He comes back, but Jesus is gone; the guys are high as kites. He's dubious: "No way! I'm not Mr Gullible. I want proof. Finger-through-scar-hole-type proof!" A week later Jesus turns up in the room again (despite bolted doors). This time, Tom *is* there. Jesus goes straight to him and lets him have his finger-through-scar-hole proof. Tom's won over.

29

Jesus tells Tom, "Fine, you're convinced 'cos you've seen me. Even better if people are convinced who've *not* seen me."

The third time Jesus shows up is when the team are back up in Galilee. Seven of the old team are fishing on the lake. Jesus is on the shore, but too far away to make out. He shouts, "Caught anything?" They shout back, "Nothing!" He tells them to put the net out on the starboard side. They do, and the net's so full they can't drag it back in. Pete realizes, "It's the Boss!" and swims to the beach. The rest moor the boat and join them. Jesus has made a fire; they grill some of their catch for breakfast. When they're stuffed full Jesus confronts Pete on the denial thing and the rooster. He's gentle, but asks how much Pete loves him. The answer: totally. Pete's given the job of building up the squad.   —Rob

The job (Matthew 28:16-20)

16-17

All eleven of them are up a mountain in Galilee. Jesus shows again, and tells them . . .

18-20

"God's given me absolute first and last word in heaven and down here on earth. So I'm commissioning you to do a job: Spread out, worldwide, help people commit 100 percent to my way of life. I want them to prove it with the symbolic sign of Baptism – dying to one way of life and waking up to the new way of life. Get them on board and God the Father, God's Holy Spirit and I will underwrite them all. Inspire them with my instructions, coach them to keep living it out. I'm with you 24/7/52 till the end of the era."

Last words (Luke 24:44-49)

Jesus works through the Instruction books, the Poetry and the Couriers with them . . .   —Rob

46-49

"It's all here," he says. "The Liberator will die and then two days later he'll come back – people in Jerusalem and the whole world will turn round 180 degrees and face their God; their slates will be wiped clean. Stay in Jerusalem till I send God's Holy Spirit to you. He'll fill you with the divine power you'll need for all this."

Going up (Luke 24:50-53)

Then Jesus takes them back down to Bethany. He lifts his hands up to the sky; he's coaching them, inspiring them, motivating them, doing them good. He's still in full flow when he starts hovering off the ground, going up gradually back to heaven. They are mind-blown, blown over, overawed, awestruck, struck dumb, dumbfounded, found speechless. Eventually they go back to Jerusalem as instructed. They hardly leave HQ, spending every waking hour finding new ways of talking God up to anyone who'll listen.

Now Jesus is where he said he'd be— sitting there on his throne next to the Awesome God. Now he's taken the rap, now the HQ dividing curtain is torn, now he's beaten death. Now he can start implementing the new world order he talked about. How? By starting with a team of twelve minus one, plus some extras!

–Rob

Just for starters (John 20:30–21:25)

20:30-31

The team saw Jesus do loads more supernatural stuff than's been written out here. Why include these bits? So you'll end up convinced that Jesus is the Liberator, God's Son. Why? So by being convinced you'll get a life!

Then Jonno puts his neck on the line . . .   –Rob

21:24-25

"All this happened. I was there! I know it's the truth and nothing but the truth. As for the whole truth? The world's not big enough to hold all the books it'd take to write down *everything* Jesus did! This'll have to do."

The Jesus
Liberation Movement

Acts of the Apostles / JLM: The Early Years

Title: The Jesus Liberation Movement (JLM) – sequel to *The Liberator* © Dr Luke AD 63. **Lead roles:** Team plus Paul Benson. **Director:** God's Holy Spirit. **Location:** Mediterranean nations. **Contents:** Speeches, journeys, events, prisons. **Plot:** Ripple effect of the JLM from Jerusalem through the Middle East and on to Europe . . .

Dear Theophilus (Acts 1:1-26)

Follow-up letter in the outbox to Theophilus Godfriend. Luke fills him in on Jesus going back up to heaven and what happened next: Not a lot for a while – the squad (about 120) are waiting for God to deliver his Holy Spirit, as Jesus promised. One of them, Matthias, gets promotion up to the first team – to sub for Judas (topped himself). Then . . .   – Rob

Hot (Acts 2:1-47)

1-4

Seven weeks on from the Flyby Festival comes the Jewish Thanksgiving Holiday. Jesus' whole squad's hanging out together. From nowhere, this noise like a wild wind blasts around the room. Freaked, they look at each other: flames are flashing round the room like someone's got them linked into a remote control and they're spreading out, zapping everyone systematically. No one gets even first-degree burns, just filled up with God's Holy Spirit. The supernatural overflow is incredible — they're suddenly fluent in languages they've never even heard of, as handed out by the Holy Spirit.

5-12

Being Thanksgiving, Jerusalem's packed full of religious Jews from all over the known world. They follow the noise and a huge crowd forms, all wide-eyed and open-mouthed, everyone tuning in on some squad member talking their language. Totally gobsmacked, they ask, "They're from Galilee, yeah? The accent gives them away. So how come we all hear them talking in our own language?"

> At least fifteen countries are represented. Pete tells them, "No, we're not drunk: this is what the courier Joel talked about — God marinating people in his Holy Spirit" (go to www.couriershotline.com.ot/pestcontrol). They know the bit, they're gripped, so Pete explains about Jesus being the Liberator . . . —Rob

22-24

"You Jews, listen up: Jesus Davidson from Nazareth got God's rubber-stamp of approval — supernatural proof of God working through him. It's common knowledge. God was ahead of the game, but still he let Jesus get arrested and pulled in. Then you lot team up with some dodgy characters and have him executed by crucifixion. But God had other ideas: he ripped out the claws of death and pulled Jesus back out of its grip. Jesus held by death? Just not possible!"

> He does a review of some of David's song lyrics, explains what they were really getting at — i.e. Jesus coming back from death. He's building up . . . —Rob

32-33

"God gave Jesus a hand up and out of the grave — we saw him with our own eyes! Then God moves Jesus into the top penthouse office, with a never-locked connecting door to his central control room. He gives him full access, top priority, complete authority, total control, ultimate supremacy — Jesus is top dog again. Yes!! He sticks by what he said and pours out God's Holy Spirit — that's what all this is."

> Again he backs it up from David's song lyrics — it's been there all the time: he's not making this up. Still building . . . —Rob

36-37

"So, don't doubt it, this Jesus – who you executed – God's put him back in position, right at the top, the Boss. He's the Liberator."

The crowd are gutted: "We've blown it. What can we do?"

38-39

Since they asked, Pete tells them straight: "Turn right back round to God, a full 180 degrees. Prove your connection with Jesus the Liberator by going public with it and getting baptized, all of you, and your mess will be sorted with God. Plus you'll get his Holy Spirit – free!"

He's at full throttle, but he keeps going. Stern stuff. Three thousand join up. –Rob

42-47

They're totally committed: hang on every word the team teaches, into community big time, never miss the symbolic breaking of bread, spend hours talking with God. All of them are stunned by the supernatural stuff the team trigger off. They live in community, everything under common ownership; they sell their stuff and donate crazy amounts to the poor. Every day they're at God's HQ, doing the breaking of bread in their homes, partying together, doing each other good, celebrating God. And the locals love it! No awkward neighbours hassling over parking rights – they think it's great. God's upping the numbers daily, as people are having their lives sorted.

It's all there (Acts 3:1-19)

Pete heals a disabled guy with direct-line power from Jesus. Crowds form; he lets them have it, explaining the Jesus-Phenomenon from their sacred books ... –Rob

17-19

"You and your top guys didn't have the first clue what was going on, but God told the couriers that the Liberator would go through hell and back, and this is how he made it happen. So turn back round to God – he'll wipe your slate clean and you'll get a new start, care of the Boss."

More proof from old heroes (Moses and Samuel onwards) and the lights come on for around five thousand people – they're well up for it. But God's reps and the

traditionalists AREN'T! They clamp down on the movement by throwing the ring-leaders, Pete and Jonno, in the clink. Next day, the Big Noises swan in and Pete passes on the message direct from God's Holy Spirit: Jesus the Liberator is alive, here and happening. The old school are hamstrung: the JLM's popularity is rocketing, and the ex-disabled guy is standing there as "Exhibit A" to prove their higher connections – all they can do is give Pete and Jonno an ultimatum, "Quit the Jesus-speak or else." Pete and Jonno risk the "else" option and stride back to the rest of the squad and ask God to up the pace even more. God's Holy Spirit obliges with more house-shaking and personal power top ups for the crew. This community thing is no empty talk – people put their money where their mouths are, even to the point of selling their house and letting the team split the proceeds. But one couple try pulling a fast one . . .   –Rob

Don't mess! (Acts 5:1-11)

1-2

Married couple – Ananias and Sapphira – sell some property. They make out they're giving over the full amount to the team for the Community Fund. It's all smiles and handshakes as Ananias hands it over to the top guys. Trouble is, it's all spin – they've actually stashed away a good chunk of it for their own "holiday fund", without coming clean.

3-4

But Pete sniffs something's up and goes straight for it: "Ananias, how come Satan's got straight through to the core of you? How come you can lie to the Holy Spirit without even blinking about the money you've marked 'Ours!' back at home. Before you sold the land, it was all yours, no? Even once the sale was sorted, it was still yours to give away, no? But why the scam? Where did the thought even come from? You've tried to rip God off, not us!"

5

The words register with Ananias. Seconds later he's hit the floor, dead. The story spreads and people get the message: "Don't mess!"

Three hours later his wife, Sapphira, strolls in, clueless about what's happened. –Rob

8

Showing her the money, Pete asks, "Was this the price you and Ananias got for the land you sold?"

"Yes," she says confidently, "that's the price."

9

"How could you even think of pushing the Holy Spirit like this? Look! Timing or what?! The young guys who buried your husband are just back from the cemetery. Now they'll have to do the same trip with your corpse."

10-11

Her death is instantaneous. She collapses right in front of Pete's feet. The makeshift undertaker crew pick her up and bury her next to her partner in crime. Major "let's get serious with God" chats spread through the whole JLM and beyond.

> Despite, or who knows, maybe because of, these people being taken out of the equation, more people get healed, some just by Pete's shadow! More time in jail for the big cheeses – this time they're sprung by an angel. He tells them, "Keep up the good work." They do, and are soon hauled up in front of the so-called God-reps who tell them to shut it! Pete and Co. refuse; the reps are about to rearrange the local rubble via their faces – i.e. stone them – but one old guy, Gamaliel, argues, "Whoa! This Jesus guy's not the first weirdo to collect a fan-base. Don't make martyrs of his cronies; when the main guy dies the movement soon stutters to a halt; same'll happen here . . . unless it is a God-thing." They see the sense and agree, sending the ringleaders off with a darn good beating. But the JLM's booming – even some reps are switching parties. Inevitably the admin's becoming a headache, so the Core Team give jobs to seven guys to sort the practical side of things. Works much better, but the old guard are stirring things . . .   –Rob

Steve RIP (Acts 6:8-8:1)

One of the JLM cream, Steve, really gets up the religious leaders' noses, so they frame him with paid-off witnesses who'll say anything for the right price. Steve's on trial for his life and takes them through a potted history of couriers roadblocked by the men in suits. He pulls no punches . . .   –Rob

7:51-52

"You guys just won't budge, will you? You're history, stuck on 'repeat'! The track's called 'Stick Your Heals In' off the album *Stop the Spirit*. Name me one courier you lot didn't hassle. You snuff out those predicting the Liberator, then you finish off the guy himself!"

> They weren't exactly expecting an apology, but this really winds them up – they're like Dobermans straining on a leash. Steve calls up to God, making out he can see Jesus standing right next to God. They blow a fuse, the leash snaps, and they rush him ...
> —Rob

58-60

They drag him outside the city and start stoning him. They fold their designer jackets and leave a young guy, Saul, to look after them. The rubble's hitting Steve's body; the blood's hitting the floor. He's shouting up to God, "Jesus! On my way up!" He's on his knees calling his last words: "Boss, don't mark this down against them." Then a stone catches him smack on the forehead and he folds, dead.

8:1

Saul's there, watching the whole thing, grinning. This is the turning point. Day one of the JLM facing public backlash. The movement is hounded out of Jerusalem. Saul's got a taste for it now and he moves up to the top league, filling up prison cells across the country and out to Samaria. But the wider the JLM is pushed, the more people get the message. But Saul's not giving in ...

Blinded by the light (Acts 9:1-19)

1-4

Saul's acting like a one-man gang of bounty hunters, spending every drop of adrenaline on liquidating the JLM. At a meeting with the top dog of the top HQ, he gets official authority on signed-and-headed notepaper, addressed to every HQ in Damascus – the letters are straight to the point, something like "Cancel all leave; go over budget on overtime: Saul's Smash-the-JLM Project is top priority. Jails here in Jerusalem are on standby." Saul's almost got to Damascus when this almighty blast of light smacks him full in the face. He hits the deck

sharpish and then hears this voice boom out like something from a stadium gig, "Thank you . . . for nothing, Saul. What's all this aggro? Why
you harassing me like this?"

5-6

Saul stutters, "Sir, who are you?"

"I'm Jesus, who you're abusing!" the voice answers. "Now get off your
knees and go into Damascus where you'll get your next set of instructions."

7-9

Saul's crew are stunned. They hear the voice, but see nothing. Saul drags
himself to his feet and realizes he's blind as a brick. His crew lead him
by the hand into Damascus. He sees nothing, eats nothing, drinks nothing for three days.

10-12

One of the JLM in Damascus, Ananias, has this weird vision where God
tells him to get to Judas's pad on Straight St. "Ask for a guy called Saul
Benson from Tarsus," God tells him. "He'll be praying. He's just had a
vision of a bloke called Ananias sticking his hands on him, giving him
his sight back."

13-14

"Whoa!" says Ananias. "You mean, *the* Saul Benson who's been slapping
your crew around in Jerusalem? The same Saul Benson who's got the
head rep's signature to carry on the arrests here? I'm really not sure . . ."

15-16

But God says to him, "Move! This guy's going to be my special rep. On
top of the stuff he'll do at home, he's earmarked to head up my foreign
campaigns, to have influence with kings. He's also going to get a
glimpse of the hassles ahead as he works for me."

17-19

So Ananias goes. He finds Saul, puts his hands on him and says, "Saul,
Jesus the Liberator, who you heard loud and clear on the way here, sent
me. You're going to get your sight back and you're going to be full of
God's Holy Spirit." Straight off, the cataracts drop off and Saul can see

again. He gets up and Ananias baptizes him. Then they have a great meal together and Saul feels human again.

Saul starts talking for the opposition – big crowd puller, seeing the sworn enemy admit he was wrong. Death threats keep him on the move. Thing is, till now it's a Jew-thing. Membership of the JLM is strictly Israelis only. But this is all about to change. Pete gets direct orders from the top to visit a Roman army officer and sign him in. He baulks a bit, but a God-dream swings it. Pete kicks his racism into touch and non-Jews get in on the new JLM order. God's Holy Spirit shows up just in case Pete pulls out. Pete reports back at a big pow-wow with Jerusalem JLM bosses, who cope with the paradigm-shift pretty well.

Switch focus from Pete to Saul (soon known as Paul) who's had years in the Saudi Arabian Desert to get his thinking straight. Then he's headhunted by Barnabas and goes on three massive tours around the Mediterranean countries as Foreign Rep of the JLM – filling people in on what's happened in Israel and opening out the liberation to all comers. Paul's past life as a trainee religious leader is great prep for hot debates with insiders and outsiders. God doesn't hold back on wisdom supplies and supernatural backup, which makes Paul's work hugely successful. The JLM is soon well established across the Middle East and southern Europe.

Paul gets back to Jerusalem and Jewish purists almost lynch him – they've heard he's pro-foreigner. He's arrested and carted off by Roman soldiers for his own protection. He's at the steps of the barracks when he gets permission to talk to the crowd, who are still screaming obscenities at him. He speaks to them in their own language, tells them about his religious training, his anti-JLM activities, being headhunted by Jesus himself, and his new role as Jesus' Foreign Rep.

Quiet till then, the racists have a knee-jerk reaction and call for his blood. The Roman officer's about to flog him, when Paul shows him his Roman passport – oops! *Can't arrest a Roman,* thinks the officer, who passes the buck to the Jerusalem City Council (Jewish division).

The trial gets aggressive at times, but Paul argues his corner well. Court's adjourned; that night God tells Paul in a dream, "This trial's just a dress rehearsal for the big one . . . in Rome." Early hours, the commander hears through Paul's nephew of a plot to assassinate Paul on the way to court the next day and he transfers the case to Felix in the Roman capital of Palestine, Caesarea.

Felix keeps Paul in prison, holding out for a tidy bribe from him for his freedom. No bribe comes and two years later Felix gets his marching orders from Rome. Festus is the new Roman official and he's keen to appear pro-Jew, so he keeps Paul in prison. Another trial and Paul cites his right to be tried in Rome –

Festus is off the hook. Before Paul's shipped off, King Herod Agrippa (great-grand-son of Herod the Great) wants to hear what all the fuss is about. Paul tells him his life story; Agrippa's gripped.

Paul leaves for Rome, gets halfway across the Adriatic Sea when a storm smashes the boat and they're shipwrecked on Malta. Paul resists the chance to escape and some months later they make it to Rome where Paul's under house arrest before his trial by Jewish leaders. Again he gives it to them straight. Mixed response. Paul's closing statement quotes Isaiah, where he talks about the Jews being deaf to God. He's proved non-Jews have better hearing. Loads storm off. But Paul rents a pad in Rome and has an open-house policy, telling anyone who'll lis-ten about Jesus the Liberator. He's a busy guy, especially if you count in time spent on writing stacks of emails to people he'd met on tour . . .   —Rob

Paul's Work
"Sent Items" Box

Romans / Paul to JLM
Rome Branch

From: paul.benson@teammail.org.nt

To: jlm@rome.org.it

Date: AD 57-ish

Subject: Basic stuff – laying it down for you

Rough guide to Rome: Stonking great public buildings, baths and aqueducts. **Must-see sights:** Ruined city walls (400 yrs old), Nero's Golden House (not open to public), the Roman Forum buildings (world power base), Theatre-land (West End), Circus (south and west). **Must do:** Boat trip on Tiber River.

Jury's decision – Guilty (Romans 1:1–2:11)

1–7

Job spec? Volunteer worker for Jesus. Special brief? Getting people up to speed on Jesus liberation news: this news has been on God's wall planner for ages. God's couriers got a glimpse of it and now, finally, it's on general release. What news? That Jesus the Liberator was both a Davidson *and* God's Son – as proved beyond any reasonable doubt by his Holy Spirit bringing him back to life. Now he's officially Jesus the Liberator, our Boss. I was headhunted into the team and fitted up with all I need to get this news out there, global. With his help everyone gets the invite to take God at his word and live his way, giving the credit straight back to him. You guys are now all well into this. D'you realize? God's passionate about you, he's hand-picked you as crew members, and he and Jesus are up for doling out the good stuff to you, topping it off with major helpings of serenity.

8-13

I thank God, via Jesus the Liberator, for all you guys. 'Cos the way you take God at his word is getting rave reviews, and I'm talking worldwide. God knows, I don't stop begging him to give you good stuff. And I'm itching to come visit – get some quality time, do each other some good. I can't tell you the number of times my Rome trip's been written large on my organizer diary page, yet something always comes up and scuppers the whole thing. But it'll happen. Don't doubt it.

14-15

As you well know, to me it doesn't matter which side of the river you're from, what team you support, what car you drive or what side of the road you drive it on. If you've got a soul, I'll talk long into the night with you. Which is why I'm itching to get to Rome.

16-17

You know it – I'm no bottler. I don't miss a chance to brag about the great news. Why? 'Cos it works. I've seen it time and again. It's life-changing – God straightens people out, gets them sorted and gets them living by taking him at his word. Who cares whether you're Jewish or British or Finnish, when you can be God-ish?

18-20

What winds God up big time is the dark stuff that people get stuck into just to drown out the truth. But the truth about God is built into our programming – it's in our circuits. The evidence smacks you in the face, from the smallest microcosm to the biggest star system – all trade-marked "God". And it doesn't take a genius to work out what God's like from what he's made. No excuses.

21-23

You can't miss it. Unless you're not looking! Which they're not. They've got their eyes closed, their heads down and their souls switched off. And the darkness makes everything scream, "What's the point?!" They think they're so clever. Tell me, what's so clever about swapping God for an idol with four wheels and a metallic finish? Or a great voice and designer stubble?

24-27

So God stands back and watches till their sex drives leave them less than human. They strike the stupidest deal in history: trading in the vault of God's truth for a skip full of lies. They pawn God in for hard-core porn – and have the sores to prove it. They live for the product instead of the producer (who gets the longest, loudest standing ovation in history – absolutely!). Question: What could he do? His hands were tied; he didn't want robots, so what were his options? He had to back off and wince through the window while the orgy went on inside. He had to watch while the disease of body and soul got passed round from man to man, from woman to whatever, like a sick game of pass the parcel bomb.

28-32

And since they'd chucked God out, they had plenty of spare soul-space to stock up with a whole lot of emptiness: stolen van loads of lust; depots full of depravity, bags and boxes bulging with filthy merchandise – all long past their sell-by dates, festering away, and waiting to be stuffed down at some all-night binge. Write out a list of the darkest stuff you can admit possible, and they've been there, seen it, sold the T-shirt: abuse, aggression, hate, malicious gossip, blatant deception, cocky arrogance. They compete to gross each other out with their violence (their parents gave up hope way back). They're so heartless they've got to keep drawing their own blood to check they're still human. And the thing is, they know they're sliding into death, but not only do they keep on waxing the skis – they make heroes out of everyone who joins them on the piste.

2:1-4

There's no wheedling your way out of it – if you slag them off for what they're into, and you're doing the same stuff on the sly, then you're up some side street in a huge truck with nowhere to turn. God's fair and he'll come down on you like a sumo wrestler with attitude. You've got a nerve! Don't you dare flick the vick at God's patience. If he hadn't given you so much slack, you'd have kept on in the same direction and hanged yourselves yonks back.

5-11

But because you stick your heels in and give it all that "I'm not shift-ing" backchat, you're just winding God up big time, and that's a game you're not going to win. The video footage of your attempted coup against God is going up on his big screen. God'll pass sentence, you'll get what's coming to you and you'll know it's a fair cop. Those making a habit of checking off the good things on their to-do list, they're going to get life with no limits. Those who slap an "Out of Order" sign on God's truth and just look after *numero uno* at the expense of everybody else, they're going to get God's angry side. Anyone who swears by the Do-It-Yourself-Satisfaction Manual is going to pay for it, big time – wherever they're from. Anyone who makes good things happen is going to get bags full of credibility, job lots of kudos and such serenity they almost forget what *stress* means. Again, this has nothing to do with your postal address, 'cos God's not racist or sexist or any other "ist" – he deals with people straight and fair.

> He doesn't let it drop: everyone knows the Rules instinctively and breaks them so easily it's scary. Heart sends memo to brain, brain presses the "evil alert" buzzer (we know the noise well), but then we do it anyway – even elitist Jews! They've memorized the Big Ten Rules, but there's still a huge gap between theory and prac-tice. We're all seriously messed up ...
> —Rob

Judge's decision – Acquitted (Romans 3:19-31)

19-20

The Big Ten Rules are there to shut us up, stop us chatting back at God. But who's up to reciting them while looking God in the eye? No one. We all know the ref's decision: we should get the red card and a per-manent ban. So no one's getting the fair-play award, 'cos we've all pushed it way too far. Trouble is, it's only down to the Rules that we know we're in a mess.

21-26

So, question: How do we get in with God? God's couriers and Moses' Rules tell us how. But it can't be by keeping Moses' Big Ten, 'cos none of us can. But hang on, God's made a special appeal that affects every-one the same. The answer is: He uses the Jesus Liberation Ruling, which changes the whole game. Now we *can* live right – by taking Jesus at his word. We're all the same. No one's innocent. We've all messed up and dropped well short of God's target for us. But at no cost to us, he sets us straight and sorted, 'cos he bought us back with the priceless currency of Jesus' blood when he was ceremonially sacrificed. And, no, God's not just wangled it; he's not pulled a fast one, or gone soft on us just to get us off the hook – it's all totally above board. See, Jesus took the rap that we should've got. So God stuck to the Rules, and still got us out of our mess, for those who take Jesus at his word.

27-31

Another question: So who's boasting? Who's mouthing off about being in God's crew? On what grounds? By keeping to the Rules? No chance. But by the new rule of relying on Jesus – yesss! We've done nothing. God's not just the God of the insiders. God's up for all of us to get straight and sorted, "insiders" and "outsiders". So do we white-out the Big Ten, then? Not in a million years! In fact, this new Jesus Ruling proves how crucial they are.

Abe (Romans 4:1-25)

1-3

What about our ancestor, Abraham, who started all this off? Was he down in The Book as "straight and sorted" because of what he'd done? If he was, fine; he's entitled to mouth off. But what does the Instruction Manual say? No, it says he was down in The Book as "straight and sorted" because he took what God said as on the level – nothing to do with him *doing* anything.

4-6

If someone does a day's work, they don't see their wages as a gift, do they? No, they broke sweat for it – so they deserve it. But if someone does nothing except take God at his word, God marks them down as "straight and sorted" even though they've not earned it. David says as much in one of his songs (go to www. peoples-poetry.com.ot/songlyrics, track 32). He talks about a man being happy when God checks the "sorted" box under his name, even though he doesn't deserve it:

7-8

Wanna be the guy whose mess is sorted out, who'll die with no regrets, Who's OK with his past, walks past everyone he knows, goes, "You got nothing on me"? (x 2)Wanna be the guy who sits down with God and knows, "You sorted me" (x 2) –The guy who's no fraud, whose tongue's no double-edged sword,The guy who's free? Want him to be me.

9-12

Question: So did all this happen before or after Abraham lopped bits off himself for religious reasons, hmm? Would it have happened if he kept his foreskin, hmm? Answer: God had Abraham down as "straightened out and sorted" well before his scalpel saw active service. So now Abraham's a father figure to all of us who've been brought up with all that religion stuff, and he's a father figure to all of you who *haven't,* but have sussed what it's all about – taking God at his word.

> Paul fills the Romans in on how Abraham stuck it out, despite the lengthening odds against him having kids when he'd moved into triple figures. God had promised. God could do it. That's the attitude God loves – what he wants from us . . .
>
> –Rob

24-25

We'll be marked down as sorted if we rely on the one who brought our Boss, Jesus, back from the dead. He died to sort our mess. He came back to straighten out our lives.

Clean start (Romans 5:1-11)

1-5

So this is the result – and what a result! Since we've been sorted through taking God at his word and through our links with Jesus, we're not at war with God anymore. It's peacetime, 'cos of Jesus. And 'cos of Jesus we've got a lifelong pass into this free-gift zone. And we're beside ourselves with the prospect of getting to know this Awesome God. Not only that, we're even happy with our hassles 'cos hassles produce grit, grit produces character, character gives us prospects – prospects that don't let us down. 'Cos God has doled out humongous helpings of his love by giving us his Holy Spirit.

6-8

See, right on cue, with precision timing, when we were flailing around totally helpless, Jesus died for the messed up. How often does someone die for someone else? It's not daily news, is it?! Alright, for a really happening guy, maybe some would die. It does happen. But get your head round this: God proved his love to us, 'cos it was when we were totally messed up that Jesus died for us.

9-11

Since Jesus' death got our lives sorted, how much more we will escape God's fury through our connection with his Son! 'Cos if, when we were at war with God, he brought us back close through Jesus' death, how much more, now we *are* back, will we see total life, 'cos Jesus' death-defying life pulses through our veins. It's no wonder we're beside ourselves! We're in with God!

> History-cramming session – one guy, Adam, messed it up for everyone. One guy, Jesus, cleans up for everyone. Nice symmetry.   —Rob

Lifestyle change (Romans 6:1-23)

1-4

What then? Shall we mess up big time so God's free gift looks even more over the top? Wrong, big time wrong! We're dead to all that. If all that mess tries to nudge us, suck us back in, get a reaction: we don't move, 'cos we're dead to it. It doesn't touch us. Have you forgotten what it all meant? That's why we did the baptism thing: to spell it out to people – under the water – in the coffin, dead. And just as Jesus didn't stay dead but got pulled out to the credit of his Father, so we got lifted out as well, out of the water – alive to a new life.

5-7

'Cos if we're linked with him in his death, there's no two ways about it: he'll want to know us now he's alive again. Like I said, the Old Us was killed off, dead and buried, left to rot. We're rid of it, with all its stench. It doesn't click its fingers and we don't jump – not anymore, not now it's dead.

8-10

So the Old Us is dead and the New Us gets to live with Jesus. And we know the Liberator came back to life so he can't die again. Death's no longer the big noise. Jesus died to sort out our mess, once, for all our accounts. But in his new life, he lives facing God and looking him straight in the eye – 'cos he can.

11-14

Likewise, count yourself as dead to the mess, and live your life facing towards God – full on, standing toe to toe. And don't let the mess call the shots, so you're just a puppet, pulled into all sorts of stuff that's part of the Old You – forced to dance to whatever's on the ghetto blaster. Cut the strings. Pull the power. Wake up. Get a life; then offer that new lease of life to God, so he can use it to make good things happen. The mess is not your boss, 'cos you're not answering to the Rules but to God's gifts, delivered with freedom included.

15-18

What then? Shall we create even more mess, just 'cos we don't have to answer to the Rules? No way! Haven't you been listening? If you say to some guy, "Yeah, sure, whatever you say," you're like his yes-man, his slave, aren't you? The choice is, slaves to the mess, product equals death. Or slaves to doing the right thing, product equals life. Thank God: though you were a slave to the mess, you went 110 percent for the teaching you were given. So you've been set free from the mess and you freely signed up to doing the right thing.

19-23

I'm keeping the visual aids simple 'cos you're still a bit slow on the uptake with some of this. You were one of the filth-slaves. So now sign up as one of the volunteer slaves to the pure. And all that – that you're now so ashamed of – what did you get out of it? Apart from death! But now you're free of all that, and you're volunteer slaves to God. You're well set up and I'm not just talking money. I'm talking purity and life with no limits – result! Your old paycheck had nothing but slow death crawling out of it. But God's gift is quality life that lasts and has no sell-by date, 'cos of Jesus our Boss.

Can't stop (Romans 7:7-25)

7-12

So the next question is: Are the Big Ten Written Rules evil? No! We'd never have known what "evil" was unless the Rules had been published and circulated. Rule 10 basically says, "Don't drool over what's not yours", but of course, my dark side takes its cue from this, and what happens? I'm gagging for stuff that's not mine and never should be. At one point I was doing OK, oblivious to the Rules; then my dark side moves into top gear and I die an agonizing death. The very Rules that were published with the tagline "Life's better with boundaries" actually hamstrung me. Evil grabbed its chance with both claws, ripped me off and left me for dead. The Big Ten *are* good for us; they're God's code book for good clean-living.

13

So how come something that's good can mess me around? Evil just does what evil does best – twists good things till they do serious damage.

14-20

The point is, the Big Ten might be good, but *I'm* not. I'm only human – messed-up human at that. I just don't get it! I write out my New Year's resolution and it lasts about a week – max. The stuff I want to *give* up keeps kicking in, and the stuff I want to *start* up just stalls on me. But just 'cos I can't keep to the Rules doesn't mean I slag off the Rules. No, *they're* not the problem: *I* am. Well, not me, but the "old me", my "dark side" with all its mess is still running the show. 'Cos I'm not under any illusions – in the "old me" there's nothing worth keeping. Look, I plan good stuff, but my dark side slams the brakes on. The good I plan gets left undone, and the dark stuff I swear I won't do, happens every time. So in a way, it's not really me who does all this stupid stuff; it's my dark side, the old me, who's doing it.

21-25

And it's not just on a bad day; it's every time. Who said there's no absolutes?! The second I think I'll do something good, my dark side pulls the shutters down and I grope around trying to remember what I planned. Stupid thing is, I think God's Rules are brilliant. I love every word. But something else kicks in at gut level and it doesn't seem to matter what I *think;* the software that's running the show messes me up. What a state! What a saddo! What a loser! Question: Who's going to get me over the border and out of this civil war with myself? Who's going to take over the driving and stop me flying over the cliff? Thank God – the answer is Jesus the Liberator, the Boss – he's going to. Yes! Basically, I want to do the right thing, but the old me stops it every time.

Under new management (Romans 8:1-39)

1-4

HOWEVER (and listen up: this is a huge "however"), no one's about to get written off, sidelined or slammed down – not if they're crew of Jesus the Liberator. 'Cos this connection with Jesus means the Holy Spirit of God unlocks us from the prison we were in, where "mess" was the norm and "Death" was the warden. The Rules were too weak 'cos our dark sides had taken their teeth out. But what the Rules couldn't do – God could! And he did it by sending Jesus, as a normal guy, to be killed in a gruesome sacrificial killing, to take the rap for all the mess we've created. This way, God sorted the dark side in all of us. Not by just turning a blind eye to the Rules – no, this is way better: he sorted it so that we could check all the "yes" boxes on the qualification form for a life run by God's Holy Spirit. Then he rubber-stamped our transfer and marked us "Under New Management".

5-8

Those whose lives are run by their dark sides have their thought lives tuned into whatever they've got the cravings for at the time. The only channel-hopping they do is from one type of filth to another. Those whose lives are run by God's Holy Spirit? Same story, only in reverse – they have their thought lives tuned into what *he's* into. Behind the eyes and between the ears of the wicked lurks nothing but death. But the mind run by the Holy Spirit of God is life to the max with serenity piled on top. The wicked mind has nothing but fists and elbows flying at God; it doesn't show a crumb of respect for God's methods. It can't! People run by their dark sides haven't even got a lottery's chance of making God smile.

9-11

However, you guys aren't run by your dark sides, but by God's Holy Spirit – if his Spirit is in you. And if he's not, then you're not part of the Jesus Liberation Movement. If you're connected with the Liberator (and you are), then your dark side's snuffed it and the real you is alive and kicking, big time. And by the same logic, if the Spirit of God that brought Jesus back from death is living inside you (which he is), then he'll bring you back to life too.

12-14

So come on, guys, it's payback time! Not to the dark side – we don't owe that bloodsucker anything. All it brought us was death. But through the influence of God's Holy Spirit, you get to kill off the crimes of the dark side – you'll have life oozing out of every pore. 'Cos all those lined up in convoy behind God's Holy Spirit, they're God's kids.

15-17

Question: Is what you were given about to riddle you with fear again? "What if this?" "What if that?" Flat "No!" for an answer: what you were given was the certificate of being a son or daughter (depending) and by his Spirit we get to call the totally Awesome God "Dad"! And somehow his Spirit inside us whispers, "It's kosher." And it doesn't take a genius to work out that if we're God's adopted kids, then we're in line for a pretty massive inheritance as God's heirs, sharing it with Jesus. Given that we're part of his struggles, we'll also get to be part of the party.

18-21

I look at today's hassles, and it's hardly worth calling them hassles up against the celebrations being lined up. The whole cosmos is holding its breath, waiting for God's kids to be paraded out in public. The planet's messed up – not by a design fault; but when we messed up, it kicked off the decay DNA in nature. God didn't override it, but decided to delay Liberation Day for the planet till his kids were freed up and ready to celebrate their own escape from pollution and mess.

22-25

So the Earth's like a pregnant woman whose contractions have just started. And we're doing our fair share of groaning as well – we, who got the first edition of the news of God's Spirit, we groan on the inside as we're on the edge of our seats waiting for our new selves to be delivered. Our new anti-decay bodies (together with all the adoption papers) will be brought back up from the grave where they were heading. Isn't that what we hoped for when we got straightened out? And you don't hope for what you've already got, do you? No, we haven't got it yet. But we wait, patient.

26-27

Same way, God's Spirit helps us in our wimpish whinings. We're clueless as to what to ask God for. But even in this, his Spirit steps in for us with sighs and groans way beyond words. And God, who does a full recce of our hearts, knows the mind of his Spirit 100 percent, 'cos he speaks up for us in sync with what God wants.

28-30

We know that whatever happens – God's on the case 24/7. Doing us good, 'cos we love him and we're into what he's into. For God knew ahead of the game which of us had a destiny to gradually become like his Son, so that Jesus would be the big bruv of a whole army of siblings. And the ones he knew had this destiny, he picked out. And the ones he picked out, he set straight. And the ones he set straight, he'll also include on the guest list of the party to come.

31-36

So how d'you respond to all this? If God's on our side, who cares who's on *their* side! If God's planning to do us good, who's about to give his plans the red light? If he didn't hold back on having his only Son killed for us, if he stopped the angels from drawing their swords and stepping in all pumped up for revenge, for us, isn't he going to give us loads of other stuff – the whole package that goes with his Son? Isn't he? And who's about to accuse the ones God's picked out? It's God who set us straight, so who's about to claim we're crooked? Jesus who died, more, who was brought back from death, is at God's side speaking up for us. Who's going to cut us off from Jesus' love? Will hassle manage it? Or pressure? Will us getting victimized cut the tie? Or will starvation do it? Or hypothermia? Or cancer? Or aggro? Or an Uzi 9 mm? Like David's lyrics (track 44), where it goes:

'Cos of you, we're looking death in the face all day long we are.
They gawk at us like we're sheep in an abattoir.

37-39

No, whichever way you look at it, we're winners all ways round, 'cos of our connection with the one who loved us. I'm totally sold on the fact that, at the end of the day, there's nothing that can cut our ties with God's love that Jesus proved. Nothing – not life, nor death; angels nor demons; the now nor the future; nor any of "the powers that be"; not distance nor anything else in the cosmos – zilch, a big fat 0. *Nothing* can cut off God's love supply to us. Nothing. End of story.

> Paul tackles the tricky issue of the Jews still libelling Jesus. "Yeah, and they'll pay for it," Paul says. "And don't even think of whining, 'That's racist!' – God doesn't have to answer to you. Back off! Anyway, they're not out of the frame completely. It's all part of God's long-term plan for getting the news out, global. But the Jews won't always write Jesus off as a nobody. God's ultimate plan for them is still worth waiting for" (which makes Paul's day). Like he said before, "God's not racist – he deals with people straight and fair ..."
>
> —Rob

Whoever (Romans 10:9-13)

How d'you get straight and sorted? How's it work? Like this:

1. Say, nice 'n' loud, with feeling, "Jesus is Boss."

2. Everything inside you has to accept that God brought him back from the dead.

If you do this – that's it, done, sorted. Both are crucial: your heart and soul take it on board; your mouth makes it public – God acquits you, straightens you out. Like the Instruction Manual says, "Anyone relying on God won't be embarrassed." Jew? Non-Jew? Whatever! God is the Boss of bosses and piles up the benefits for whoever comes asking. Anyone who cries out to him will get straightened out and sorted.

> He gets to the end of the theory section and is just blown away by the size of God's brain. It gets him going all poetic ...
>
> —Rob

Sheer scale (Romans 11:33-36)

No way you're gonna measure it – the height, the depth, the scale of all God knows.

No way you'll get ahead of him – what he decides, which way he goes.

Who can understand 0.1 percent of God?

Who's advised him, surprised him – is there anyone God owes?

For it all comes from him; it all goes to him,

All matter orbits round him, all permission goes through him.

He's beyond superb. He outlasts infinite. He's the intimate. The ultimate.

The all-round Awesome God. All credit goes to him, absolutely.

Which is the perfect springboard for applying the theory to real life ...   –Rob

Living it in-house (Romans 12:1-21)

1-2

So I say – and I can't say it strong enough – with all this "God writing off our mess" in mind: give it up for God – your life; give it up. Like A sacrifice, only a live one. Put your body on the butcher's block, your neck in the noose and let God's hands hold the controls. This is what "being spiritual" means; this is "worship" – making God smile. Don't get moulded by what the adverts say you should have / should do / should be. Keep on becoming more and more outstanding – literally, standing out, as your thinking's freshened up, regular. Then you'll know what God wants for you. What his plan is for your life – the plan that can't be criticized.

3-8

'Cos of the ability given me, I tell you guys this – don't get an inflated view of yourself. When you think of yourself, be serious (as much as you can, given the state you're in!) and take God at his word. We've all been made the same – one body, different bits. Each bit has a different job.

Ditto with the JLM: it's like a body; each bit belongs to all the other bits. We've all signed different job contracts. So if your job's speaking out God's mind, do it, as much as you sense God's letting you in on it. If your job's serving people, then serve them. If it's teaching, teach. If it's cheering people on (or up!), break sweat doing it. If it's being generous, go over the top. If it's being a leader, work hard at it. If it's looking after the broke, the wobbly, the wrinkly, do it with a smile.

9-13

Love has to be the genuine article. Hate evil. Get a grip on what's good and don't let go. Love each other like the best of brothers. Rate other people higher than yourself. Don't lose your attack. Go for it. Keep on going for it. Keep smiling when chewing over what's up ahead. Keep going when it all goes pear-shaped. Keep hanging in there when you're talking to God. Don't get tight-fisted with God's people. Ring people up. Have people round. Take people out.

14-16

If someone has a go at you, do them good. Always want the best for them, even if they're out to get you. If someone's got something to celebrate, be the life and soul of the party. If someone's had someone die on them, be there with an arm and a fresh tissue. Get on with each other. Don't get cocky. Mix more, especially with people you'd have thought were below you (in your previous life). Don't act like Mr/Mrs/Miss/Ms Know-It-All.

17-21

You don't have to fight back. If someone does you wrong, rise above it. You don't have to give as good as you get. Do the right thing. If it's down to you, keep the peace. Don't take it into your own hands; leave it in God's — they're bigger. As he says in the Manuals, "It's my job to dole out the punishment." Instead, if your rival looks a bit peckish, buy her a sandwich. If he's spitting feathers, get him a drink. You might even shame him into shifting his attitude. Don't get sucked under by his evil, but drag him back to the surface by doing him good.

<u>Living it: out there (Romans 13:1-14)</u>

1-5

Stay on the right side of the law. 'Cos like it or not, God put the law there in the first place. So if you scream for anarchy, if you trash the system, you're doing it straight at God – bad move! If your car's taxed, insured, you've had nothing to drink, you're not on drugs and you're not burning up the tarmac, then you can pass a cop shop and your pulse won't have to put in overtime. And get your head round this: presidents and prime ministers are put there by God to do you good (whether you voted for them or not). But if you're out of line, then you'll have to keep looking over your shoulder – the law isn't there just to fill up the shelves in a library. So like I say, stay on the right side of the law, not just so you won't get caught, but 'cos you know it's right.

6-10

That's why you don't fiddle your taxes. The government run the place, full-time, for God – they need paying. If you owe it, pay it. Whatever it is – tax, honour, respect. And don't keep debt dragging around your neck, except the debt to love each other. If your love gland is active, you're going to keep the Big Ten Rules, aren't you? If you love the guy next door and want the best for him, you're not about to sleep with his missus, are you? If you genuinely love your boss and want the best for her, you're not about to poison her cappuccino, are you? If you love your mate and want the best for him, you're not about to nick stuff from him, or drool over his new wheels, are you? All the Big Ten Rules boil down to the BIG ONE: "Love the guy next door like you love yourself." Love doesn't hurt people. So love keeps the Rules.

11-14

Love and keep up with current affairs. Wake up – Jesus' big return is closer than when you took all this on board. It's almost sunrise on the New Day; it's almost with us – the dew is settling nicely and I'm your alarm clock. So get rid of the stuff that goes on in the dark – the gropings, the nickings, the knifings, and put on the khakis of the kingdom of light. Better than that, wear Jesus – not just on your sleeve, but all over so they can't miss him. And don't fantasize about how to titillate your dark side.

Tricky debates re religious practices come down to letting God, not us, do the judging. "If someone's got a thing about food or alcohol or festivals, or anything, don't trip them up just 'cos you reckon you're oh-so-liberated. Put yourself out for other people, so the JLM isn't ripped apart by disputes."

Paul tells them he's planning to drop in on his way to Spain; then a whole list of guys he wants to say hi to, warnings about troublemakers and a few PS's ...

–Rob

<u>C</u>heers (Romans 16:19–27)

19–20

The way you do what God says is famous, and I'm well chuffed. But wise up on the good stuff and stay naïve on the evil. And the God of serenity will soon crush Satan with your size tens. Here's to Jesus our Boss pouring out over-the-top gifts on you.

21–23

Timo (my colleague), Lucius, Jason and Sosipater send respect. Tertius, who took this down for me, says hi. My landlord, Gaius, and all the crew, send respect, as does Mayor Erastus – oh, and Quartus ...

25–27

God has the clout to set you up for life like the Good News Project says, in line with the breaking of the best-kept secret ever. So now the truth *is* out there. The couriers have done their job and the limitless God has made it front-page news – so everyone gets the chance to take it in and take it on. So let's give the credit to the all-knowing God; let's send it via our contact up there – Jesus the Liberator. Absolutely!

1 Corinthians / Paul to JLM Corinth Branch

(Email No. 2 – No. 1 got wiped!)

From: paul.benson@teammail.org.nt

To: jlm@corinth.org.gr

Date: AD 54-ish

Subject: Your letter re hassles and questions, and some . . .

Paul's clicking on "reply to author" from across the Aegean Sea in Ephesus (Turkey) to the JLM house-branch set up by Priscilla and Aquilla. He knows them all pretty well – he spent a year and a half working in P&A's tent-making business to fund his JLM work. Most of them are broke; some are rolling in it. They're getting some weird ideas that need sorting before the cliques split the branch. Paul's big into not having the "body" hung, drawn and quartered by disputes.   —Rob

Rough guide to Corinth: Cosmopolitan trading centre on strip of land joining mainland Greece to the Peloponnese (population: 0.25 million free, 0.4 million slave). Mix of Greek and Roman architecture / food / music tastes. **Must-see sights:** Temples, esp. Apollo's – huge! Contact Corinth Tourist Board for dates of foot-race weekends. **Must do:** Recover from retail-fatigue by washing your face in the Peirene Fountain.

Wise up / dumb down (1 Corinthians 1:1-2:5)

Hi's and how-you-doings. Compliments re their spirituality. Enthusiasm for their prospects. Then, straight to the point . . .   —Rob

10-12

Plllleeezze! Everything our Boss, Jesus the Liberator, stands for screams out, "Quit the argy-bargy!" No more cliques. I want you of one mind. One of the guys from Chloe's place dropped the bombshell – that some of you are standing toe-to-toe, slugging it out. I'm getting at all this "Paul's top" / "No, Apollos's the biz" / "Well I'm into Pete" / "They're all pants – the Liberator's No. 1" stuff. It's guff, all of it.

> Basically, "Stop it; don't follow me. I'm just the courier, with a dead-simple message." —Rob

18-19

If you're set on messing your life up, the message of Jesus' execution sounds bananas. But for us lot, having our lives straightened out is a powerful God-thing. Like God says through Isaiah, "I'll change the rules on what's clever and what's dumb: the academics and experts will be stumped for words."

> He bangs away at Greek National Pride with its philosopher heritage. "It's not about elitism, clever theories or IQ scores." —Rob

22-25

Jews are into the supernatural. Greeks are big on philosophy. All I talk about is the execution of the Liberator, which trips up most Jews and makes most Greeks go, "What?!" But if God's picked you, "Jewish" or "Greek" labels don't matter. You're in and the Liberator is God's power and God's wisdom in person. For God's daftest idea (if he could have one) is brilliant next to our best "eureka" moments. In God's weakest moment (if there was one), he'd still arm-wrestle all of us simultaneously and win.

26-31

Think back, when God picked you, you weren't exactly the cream of the crop, the big thinkers – most of you. You weren't the movers and shakers. Hardly the aristocracy of Greece. Fair? But God selected the brainless things of the world to confuse the clever. He wanted those with no influence to embarrass those with clout. The low status, the written off, the non-existent things – he wants these to wipe the smile off the face of the establishment. Why? So no one gets cocky and thinks it's their personal charm that's pulling it off. God's the reason you're connected with Jesus the Liberator, who defines the word *wisdom,* who unpacks what "doing the right thing" means, who buys us a clean slate. So like Jeremiah says, "If you're going to start bragging — brag about the Boss."

2:1-5

Think back further. Remember when I first turned up? I didn't spruce up God's mysterious plans with flashy words and fancy ideas, did I? No, I decided to talk about nothing except Jesus the Liberator and his execution. What was your first impression? What d'you remember about me? Thin, tinny voice? Nervous-looking? Shaking hands? Yup, I wasn't going to bluff you out, or wow you with an adrenaline-charged, intellectually sophisticated, award-winning speech. I turned all that in for the power of God's Holy Spirit — so your new lives wouldn't depend on human cleverness, but on God's power.

Different wisdom (1 Corinthians 2:6-16)

Current thinking's so far off wisdom, it's laughable ...   —Rob

9-10

Like Isaiah says, "No one's seen the shadow of . . . no one's heard an echo of . . . no one's even dreamt of what God's got ready and waiting for those who love him."

But God's Holy Spirit is in on it and has sneaked us a preview of God's deep thoughts!

11-16

Our wisdom comes personal-delivery from God, but if you try reading it without his Spirit's decoder — it's mumbo-jumbo. We've got privileged access to the Liberator's mind — we can download it, use it, apply it. We've got a different wisdom! We can tap into the Liberator's thought processes!

> He has a go at them for being such toddlers, with their Paul vs Apollos fan-club cliques. He explains how it works: different people at different times to do different jobs — Paul plants, Apollos waters, God grows. So sign up for God's fan club. Maybe change the image: from "plant" to "building" — Paul lays the foundations, Apollos is the brickie, but Jesus is the granite it's all built on. Another bullet bit-

ten: some of their sex lives need confronting. He calls for strong leadership, kicking out the pervert with hyperactive hormones. Hopefully, the jolt of giving up his membership will help him get his head straight, and there'll be a happy ending. Then generally . . .   —Rob

Internal JLM discipline
(1 Corinthians 5:11-13)

11

Don't get matey with JLM members whose lives don't match up: who can't control their sex lives, their stomachs, their shopping lists, their vocab, their drinking, their finances. Don't even sit down to a meal with them.

12-13

What non-members get up to is God's business, not mine. But we need some internal standards — it's in Moses' Manual: "If an insider's evil — kick 'em out!"

To sum up: Sort your disputes in-house. Don't let everyone see your dirty washing.   —Rob

God's new HQ - you! (1 Corinthians 6:18-20)

Sort your sex lives. All the rest of your mess doesn't get into your bones like a dodgy sex life does. It eats away at you like nothing else. Haven't you caught on? Your body is God's new HQ. His Holy Spirit lives in you, permanent contract. *You* don't own *you* anymore. God's paid out well over the asking price and he owns the freehold. So if you respect God, then respect yourself — God's your long-term lodger.

Direct answers to their previous email. Top of the list? Sex: including singleness and sexual frustration, marriage, divorce, remarriage, mixed marriages (i.e. member/non-member), virginity. His answer? Basically, don't waste time — focus on God-stuff; the world's almost past its sell-by date. Next on the list? Kosher food: it's no big deal, but it is if it messes up other members — so think of others. Last but not least? His position on the top team — he waives his right to a salary for his work, pays his own way, adapts his style to the context he's working in and keeps his focus. Jewish history sets the background for warnings . . .   —Rob

Tempting? (1 Corinthians 10:12-13)

You're standing there, all confident; then, from nowhere, "Duck!!!" – too late, you're flat on your face. All these dark things that suck you in just prove you're human. God's not gone AWOL. He won't let them turn up the magnetic force of temptation past your personal capacity. You'll be getting drawn in, and he'll make sure there's a door within arm's reach for you to step out of the pressure and keep your integrity. You've just got to use it!

> He moves on to how to run their sessions. And he's not best pleased with the friction and hassle flying round the place. He goes over what the sacred bread-and-wine meal means and promises more detail when he's with them.
>
> He deals with the supernatural stuff God's Spirit is generating through them: "Don't use it to pose, but to do people good." He uses the image of the JLM being a body: different parts, different roles, but one director – God's Spirit. No "foot" should be kicking some "hand" off the park. No, the best way is love . . .   –Rob

Love (1 Corinthians 13:1-8)

1-3

If I get supernatural talent to speak fluent Matabolese, or even Angelese, but I'm rusty on the language of love, then I'm just clattering round like a broken drum kit. If I've got access to next month's news, or philosophy's big questions, if I know more than anyone, if I can shift a mountain range by will-power, but I forget how love fits in, I may as well not exist. If I donate my millions to charity, but my love-account's in the red, if I volunteer to be a martyr, but my love gland's dead, then I'm a waste of space.

4-8

What is love anyway? Not the tripe you've been force-fed! No, love gives people space and time; it does people good. It's not jealous, loud-mouthed or big-headed. It's not vulgar; it doesn't look after No. 1. It's not got a short fuse – it forgives and forgets. Love doesn't smile when dark stuff goes on, but throws a party when the truth gets out. It protects more than a blockbuster hero; it trusts more than a toddler. It's always positive; it always hangs in there. Love doesn't let you down.

The Big Three are (1) taking God at his word, (2) believing in his prospects and (3) being capable of love. But top of the Three is love. Everything else is approaching its sell-by date.

"The supernatural's fine, IF it's on the leash of love. Use it as a whip to create chaos and fear and you're pressing the JLM self-destruct button. Let's have some order; let's chew things over; let's do each other good."

He drums in the core principles: the Liberator died to wipe out our mess; then he came back, alive and kicking. There were witnesses and Paul was one of them. If Jesus didn't come back from death, then pack it in, guys! Without that, it's all just a big game: we're just a club like any other (only sadder). But he did come back to life and blew apart Adam's death-chains that hold us back from limitless life. He's in charge and he'll pick off his enemies until it's only the big one left – death itself. Then he'll kill death! All because he came back to life. Like a seed only grows when it's been buried in the earth, so we'll die and get a new lease of life. We don't know the details yet, we can't draw a diagram, but it'll happen . . .   —Rob

Death's blank cartridge
(1 Corinthians 15:50-58)

50-57

I'm telling you, guys, our physical bodies don't get to heaven. You can't have something that ages, rots and dies living somewhere timeless – it doesn't work. But the secret's out. Some of us won't snuff it, but all of us will get a body-exchange. No coded warning: some angel will get the nod; then a blink later he'll blast his trumpet and the dead will come back alive permanently; we'll rip off our mortal clothes in order to step into our new, designer, immortal bodies. Then the old line "Death's drowned in Victory Ocean" will have come true. Like Hosea said it:

Death, you've lost your edge – how come?
Death, your bullets are blank – how come?

Death's ammunition is our mess – he just packs it into bullets that comply with Moses' Rule Book, and then fires it all back at us. But thank God, our Boss, Jesus the Liberator, has emptied the bullets by clearing up our mess, so the bullets are duds and just ricochet off us. Live or die – we win!

58

So my good mates, don't shift. Don't get blown off the road. Go for it 100 percent – you're working for the Boss and you know it's worth breaking sweat for. It's not a waste of time. Hang in there.

Paul sorts the collection for the Jerusalem branch, tells them his tour schedule. Maybe he'll send Timo to them. Respect from the Turkey branches.   –Rob

Cheers (1 Corinthians 16:22–24)

Not in love with the Boss? Dead men walking, all of them. Come on down, Boss! Jesus Liberator–size generosity to all you guys. Signed off with Liberator Jesus–type love. Absolutely!

2 Corinthians / Paul to JLM Corinth Branch

(Email No. 4 – No. 3 got wiped!)

From: paul.benson@teammail.org.nt

timo.apprentice@jlmephesus.org.nt

To: jlm@corinth.org.gr

Date: AD 55-ish

Subject: You got me all wrong!

> Paul's not Mr Popular with this JLM branch right now. Some dodgy characters are stirring it up: "Said he was coming, but where is he?" Truth is, he'd backed off to give them some space, thinking, *One long visit instead of two short ones gives us more quality time.* It also gives his rivals more ammo. Even accusing him of pocketing the cash supposedly collected for the Jerusalem branch. So he wears his heart on his sleeve, gives proof of his integrity (from his first stay-over) and tells them what to do with the stirrers ...   —Rob

Comfort Able (2 Corinthians 1:2-11)

2

Click on the attached files of freebies and serenity from God and Jesus the Liberator. Now!

3-7

Major credit goes out to God, who's the father of our Boss, Jesus the Liberator, the God who loves you passionately and puts his arm round you, like a dad who understands. He's always there for us when it all goes pear-shaped, 'cos then we qualify to put our arm round someone else who's lost the plot. You're well clued up on the hassles of following Jesus – but as the struggle-stakes go through the roof, so do the stats for "Comfort Received". If we're stressed, it's for you guys – to do you good, to liberate you. And talking you through the action replays of God pulling us out of some hole does you guys *more* good. It proves you can handle more than you thought – it inspires you. We believe in you! We know you guys aren't just going for the easy life, but you've signed up for the full package – the hassles and the hugs that come with being the crew.

8-11

You're like brothers and sisters, so you need to know the score. The West Turkey trip was a total nightmare! Everything hit the fan; our lives flashed before our eyes; we were comparing notes on our funeral services. End product? Well, what d'you do when your battery's flat, your tank's empty, your engine's splurging out gunk and there's still a mountain to drive up? You phone God's personal breakdown service. You know he's the only one who can get you going again, even if you've died (he's done it before!). He got us out of schtuck, and he'll do it again – 'cos you keep on nagging him to. The end product is this: loads of people are well happy 'cos God's response record is top.

> He fills them in on the change of schedule for his stay. Tells them it's time to go easy on the guy they had to come down hard on before – "He knows he messed up, so let's not pile on the guilt, eh?" More on trying to suss God's schedule . . .
>
> –Rob

Living proof (2 Corinthians 2:14-3:3)

14-17

But thanks to God for driving us through the streets in an open-top bus, so everyone can get a glimpse of the trophy. Knowing God is like a gust of fresh mountain air blowing the mugginess off the streets. To God, we're like Parfume de Jesus – we walk into a room and people's heads turn: they get a sense of something different. Not everyone's into it. Some say it stinks like death; others find it invigorating, life-giving. It's a big deal wearing this and we're not doing it for the money! No, we know God sent us and he's listening, and that keeps us straight-talking about the Liberator.

3:1-3

Whoa! Are we blowing our own trumpets again? Are we slipping into this trend of needing letter-headed endorsement letters? No way! If anything, *you're* our endorsement. Your lives are proof of us being straight up, and people read you every day of the week – you ring true. You're like emails from the Liberator, set up and connected by our work. Your "ink" is the Spirit of the live God and you're printed direct onto people's hearts.

> He unpacks this New Contract. It's even more dazzling than the Old Contract. Moses brings the Contract down from the mountain, freshly dictated by God, and his face is glowing. He's got to wear a mask, so as not to blind them ...   —Rob

Beauty (2 Corinthians 3:16-18)

But when we turn our lives back towards the Boss, the mask is taken off. The Boss is the Spirit of God, and wherever God's Spirit is, there's freedom. We've got our masks off and God's brilliance is bouncing off our faces; it's changing us – our features are evolving; we're looking more and more attractive as God's Spirit puts plastic surgeons out of work by the thousands. Only our Boss makes us truly beautiful.

> Paul's job is to get the news on the front pages, but ...   —Rob

Blind (2 Corinthians 4:4-18)

4-6

Society's stand-in god blinds those who don't get it, so they've no chance of seeing the great news just glinting off our faces. They're blind to the dazzling light coming off the Liberator, who's God with skin on. We don't build our own empire; we only talk about Jesus our Boss, the Liberator. We're just his team, trying to help you guys promote Jesus' reputation. God calls out, "Lights!" like he did in the pitch black before space and time, but this time he isn't talking to the blackness of a chaotic cosmos; he's talking to our dark hearts. The lights come on and we're glowing from knowing we've seen God's brilliance in the Liberator's face.

7-11

So we've got this pure light shining out from us. But God's not dense; he doesn't swap us for some hi-tech super lamp. No, he channels his brilliance through our scarred and fragile bodies, so there's no question that the glow's from him, not us. We're battered and bruised, but not smashed. We're frustrated, but not suicidal. Victimized, but not given up on. Battered, but not beaten. It's like we're glimpsing some of Jesus' pain and death, but we're also finding his life pouring out of us, through the cuts and bruises. We're alive but it's like we're facing a daily death sentence, so our hearts can be linked up to his better life, which pumps out through our veins to our feet, hands, head.

> It's still all based on Jesus coming back from the dead, so ...   —Rob

16-18

Therefore we're not giving it up as a bad job even though, on the face of it, we're wasting away. But our spiritual cells are being freshly formed, every day. For these trivial hassles, these mini-problems are building up a limitless level of bonuses in heaven. That's our focus, our target — not what you can see, but the invisible things. If you can see it, it's finite. If you can't, it's infinite.

> More on heaven. God's Spirit being the deposit, guaranteeing our ticket to get there. But before all that, there's a job to be done ...   —Rob

Job done (2 Corinthians 5:14-21)

14-15

The Liberator's passion for us is our driving force. He died in the place of all of us. Why? So we have a new No. 1 to live for: him — the one who died and came back to life for us.

16-21

We don't label people like we used to, with our handy pre-printed tags. We even tried doing this with Jesus, but he blew our definitions apart. Likewise, anyone with this God-link to the Liberator is a brand-new human being; not genetically modified — brand new! The old categories don't work; it's a whole new ballgame. God sees us as stolen property and he's buying us back with the windfall from Jesus' sacrifice. As he gets us back, he commissions us to lengthen the Get-Your-Life-Back queues. He's got designs on the whole world, to wipe out all the messy cases against us that keep us locked up and away from him. And who better to talk about the benefits of freedom than a released prisoner? Yes, us! He does all his marketing through us — no flashy corporate image, no high-impact ads, just us! We're God's new reps. His image, his profile, he puts down to us. So we're begging you, "Let God buy your life back!" God piled our mess on to the only innocent man ever to live. He gave him the death penalty for everything we'd messed up, for us to walk free. For us to use our new God-connection to start doing the right thing.

> Paul's gone through a triathlon of hassles to do his job justice and wants them to know it, so they can respect him, listen and get their lives sorted. He also relocates Titus to Corinth to help them.
> He doesn't want them jumping into bed (literally or metaphorically) with people who aren't into the JLM cause. It won't work. "Don't get polluted."
> He's not backing out on the collection for the Jerusalem JLM Branch — even though he's been accused of embezzling the funds. He's that sure of himself to ask them again to cough up and to go over the top …   —Rob

D'you take Visa? (2 Corinthians 9:6-7)

Don't forget: "No pain, no gain." "You get out what you put in." "Got to speculate to accumulate." Why are they clichés? 'Cos they're true! But don't donate money 'cos you're on some guilt trip or 'cos someone's got your arm behind your back. No, decide on the figure, and then enjoy giving it away. God loves it when you get a real kick out of helping others.

> "Don't let anyone mess around with your head. People are going to twist the basics, and before you know it, you'll be in a cult. Don't let them brag their way into the top seat." Paul could boast too …   —Rob

Qualifications (2 Corinthians 11:21-12:10)

21-29

What they bragging about? (I'm talking like an idiot.) OK, I can play that game: descendants of Abraham, are they? So am I! Oh, and Israelis as well? Me too! Pure Hebrew family? Ditto! And they work for the Liberator, huh? (I can't believe I'm doing this.) I've done more! Worked harder, been locked up more, had more punishment beatings, faced death so often we're on first-name terms! Let's compare scars: five lots of thirty-nine lashes, three lots of rod whackings, one time almost stoned to death, three times shipwrecked – including forty-eight hours in the open sea. I've lived out of a suitcase. My life's been like a block-buster: white-water rivers, gangland muggings, race hate from non-Jews, race hate from Jews, treble jeopardy – in the city, in the country, at sea. Plus, enemy double-agents messing up their own guy. I've worked so hard, lost so many nights' sleep, gone hungry, thirsty, almost died of hypothermia. And, on top of all this – the non-stop mental pressure of all the JLM branches. Who reckons they're weak? I'll tell them about weak. Who reckons they're being sucked down, on the verge of really messing up? Sometimes it feels like I'm burning up.

30

If I'm going to brag, I'll brag about the stuff that shows my weak side.

More adventures moving into supernatural experiences, visions of heaven, but he refuses to brag – it's stupid . . . —Rob

12:7-10

After these incredible visions it'd be easy to get cocky, but to keep my feet on the ground I got this stab wound from Satan – the blade's still in there. It's agony; it does my head in. Three times I'm there begging the Boss to pull it out for me, but he says, "All I've given you is plenty to drown out the pain of a tiny flick knife. Anyway, my energy works best when *your* energy's on zero." So now I love bragging about my lack of energy, my weakness – 'cos then the Liberator's power really kicks in. And it's doing his reputation the world of good, so I'm over the moon about all the things that make me weak: the slurs, the hassles, the victimization, the problems. For when I've no energy of my own, it's bizarre, but that's when I'm at my strongest.

Point made! He qualifies all right, and he's on his way to visit – so get ready. —Rob

Cheers (2 Corinthians 13:11-14)

11

To wrap up, guys: cheers. Set your sights on perfection; take in what I'm asking; get on each other's wavelength, be easy in each other's company – then the God of love and serenity will hang round with you.

12-14

Don't just shake hands; let's have some touch – hugs, kisses (but pure). The crew here say hi. I want all of you full of the generosity of the Boss, Jesus the Liberator, bursting with the love of God, and well connected with his Holy Spirit.

Galatians / Paul to JLM East Turkey Branch

From: paul.benson@teammail.org.nt

To: jlm@galatia.org.tk

Date: AD 51–57-ish

Subject: Moses' Rules, and now?

Rough guide to Galatia: A province of Rome in East Turkey between the Med and the Black Sea. **Must-see sights:** Ankara city. **Must do:** Go boating on the Black Sea.

Paul set up this branch on one of his tours, but now troublemakers are ripping into his ideas on core issues. What have they signed up to? All Moses' old Rules, including the ceremonial lopping of their foreskins! Or is all that just for Jews? Or what? Paul sets them straight ...
—Rob

Losing your roots (Galatians 1:6–7)

I'm stunned! How come you wander off from God so quick? He personally picked you to be on the gift list for all the Liberator's freebies, and now you're into a different package, which is just bad news. It's obvious someone's messed with your heads by twisting the Liberator's news – they've got you addled.

The guys doing the twisting – someone can burn their passport to heaven, Paul rants. He got the New Contract direct from the Liberator when he was on his own for years In the Saudi desert and now it's being polluted, so it's anything but "liberating". But it's not new – they had to thrash out what to do with Moses' old Rule Books in the JLM early days. Paul's had a big shouting match with Pete. Paul's side of the argument goes . . .

–Rob

Face-Off: Pete vs Paul (Galatians 2:11-14)

11-13

Pete shows at Antioch and I stand up to him and give it to him straight – I wasn't about to tiptoe around him; he was so far out of line he'd forgotten where the line was! Before James's lot turned up, ol' Pete was stuffing himself full of non-kosher food like there was no tomorrow. But when tomorrow came and brought James's crew with it, Pete backtracked and went all strict kosher, 'cos he knew the Jews had him under surveillance, and he was scared stiff. Of course, all Pete's Jewish mates followed suit, such a total U-turn, such spin, so two-faced, it even had *Barney* caught up in it!

14

As soon as I'd spotted they were out of line with the good news, I said straight to Pete's face, and loud enough for the whole crowd to hear, "You're a Jew, but you live like you've never even seen inside a Jewish HQ! How come you're trying to turn everyone into a Jew?"

He's not exactly shy! He makes his point loud and clear: the JLM is a totally different animal to Judaism, so let's avoid the cross-breeding. It's not about working your way into God's good books. It is about taking Jesus at his word. That's why he's written us in, big and bold.

–Rob

Clean slates (Galatians 2:20-3:29)

20-21

I've been executed with the Liberator. I'm dead. Well, physically I'm still breathing, but it's his breath filling my lungs. I'm "under new management". My new life's run by God's Son, who loved me so passionately, he actually *died for me.* I'm not going to snub God and throw his free gift back in his face: if I could get a clean slate by keeping the old Rules, then the Liberator went through all that grief for nothing!

3:1-5

You Galatians, you demented or what? Who's hypnotized you? Who's interfering with your brainwaves? You had the full works on how and why Jesus the Liberator died: I gave you the full presentation – live and interactive. So answer me this one thing: Did you get pumped full of God's Spirit by keeping every single Rule in Moses' book? No, you got it by taking God at his word. Are you really so dense that you're going to start off with God's Spirit running the show and then switch to manual and go for it on your own? After all you've gone through, don't jack it all in for nothing. Again, why did God dole out his Spirit? Why did he do supernatural things through you? Was it 'cos you had a perfect record and could check off every Rule as "done and dusted"? No, it was because you took on what you heard.

> He takes them back to Abraham who had his slate wiped clean by taking God at his word. Even then, God had plans to get non-Jews involved. Moses' books are bad news for people who can't check every single Rule as "100 percent kept". So what chance for any of us? This ...   –Rob

13-14

We were about to be written off by the Rules but the Liberator bailed us out and had the Judge drop the charges. How? By swapping places and writing off his own prospects. Like Moses' book says, "Anyone executed and left hanging on a tree is written off. It's total humiliation." He bought us back to make the promise God gave Abraham come true – that people from all nations can now, 'cos of Jesus the Liberator, take God at his word and have God's Spirit guiding their lives.

> Check your history – God made the Contract with Abraham over 400 years before Moses published the Instruction Manual. So God telling Abraham he'd have foreign descendants couldn't have been 'cos he'd kept the Rules – they didn't exist yet. No, Abraham got God's promise only because he took him at his word ...   –Rob

22-25

The Instruction Manual says it time and again – our mess gets us locked up, so the only prospect of freedom is if we take on board what Jesus the Liberator did. Before this option, we were trapped by the Rules, jailed up till Jesus launched his liberation campaign. The years in prison were

designed to prepare us: the Rules played coach and it was all designed
to make us so desperate that when the Liberator shows we're ready to
do what he says. Now we've got something to believe in, we're out of
there; Moses can say, "The Rules – job done!"

26-29

You're all God's kids 'cos you took Jesus the Liberator at his word. The
baptism thing symbolized it and now it's a daily habit – like getting
dressed. You wouldn't dream of not putting on Jesus. It'd be like going
out naked, middle of winter. "God's kids" – that's the only designer
label we need. Chuck away the old ones marked "Jew" or "Turk",
"Worker" or "Boss", "Man" or "Woman" – no use for them. We're all
equal! Jesus the Liberator makes sure of it. So if you're one of the Liberator's crew, you're like a great-great-great . . . grandchild of Abraham
himself, which means you're in on the promise – you're in the will!

No Inheritance Tax (Galatians 4:1-7)

But, I tell you, if the heir's still under age, he's no different from a
worker. He can't get his mitts on the money until his eighteenth (or
twenty-first) birthday. Before that the money's *legally* his, but the grey-
haired trustees stop him from blowing the whole thing on some hi-tech
skateboard, or something more stupid. He's tied up. Same with us:
when we were kids we had to work the way the world works, go with
the flow. But with his trademark perfect timing, God sends his Son on
a mission. He's born as a baby, so he's got to play by the Rules; and if
he does, he can buy freedom for us lot locked up by the Rules – so we
can start enjoying our inheritance as God's grown-up kids. You're God's
next of kin, so God pours the Spirit of his Son into your depths, and
since his Son is on intimate terms with him, he calls God "Daddy". So
you're free, you're a grown child of God and you're up for a stupendous
inheritance (tax free).

> "So don't turn back the clock and act like kids again – trapped by religious rules."
> Paul's like a lady in labour, fighting to give them their freedom . . .   —Rob

Freedom (Galatians 5:1-26)

1

Question: Why did the Liberator free you up? Answer: To make you free. Obvious! So don't put your neck back in the leash and get dragged round the place by the old Rules.

> One of the old Rules was circumcision – ceremonially chopping off the foreskin to symbolize God's Contract. But these days . . .   –Rob

6

This is the time of Jesus the Liberator, and religious rules aren't what counts – not now, no, all that stuff is old currency. The only things that register on God's scoreboard are taking God at his word and loving people.

> Paul's Mr Angry with the guys who are tangling them up.   –Rob

13-15

You were picked out to be free. But it's not a "licence to kill" (or whatever else the Old You fancies doing) – no, it's a freedom to work for other people's benefit 'cos you love them. Want a quick summary of all Moses' Rule Books? "Love other people as you love yourself." If you keep on taking chunks out of each other, there'll be nothing left.

16-18

My advice? Tune into God's Spirit; let him run the show – and your dark side won't get a look in. Your dark side wants what God's Spirit hates, and vice versa. They're at war, and you're the war zone – hardly surprising that you feel the pressure when deciding what to do with all those spiritual missiles overhead. But if you delegate the decision to God's Spirit, you put yourself out of claw's reach of the Rules.

19-21

If your dark side's in charge, this is you: you're a twisted, filthy old letch, with only sex on the brain. You waste hours on the latest craze to have seduced you, sometimes just worthless, sometimes full-on demonic. You're hateful, argumentative, jealous, angry. You're a drunk, a pervert, all "me, me, me". You're an ultra-competitive back-stabber, a stirrer, a divide-and-conquer control freak who dies inside every time someone else makes it. Enough? I told you before, people like this aren't part of God's set-up!

22-26

But if God's Spirit is in charge, then *this* is you: you're loving, alive, vibrant, sparkling. You're calm; you walk into a room and friction walks out. You can handle delays; you're not pushy. You're generous with money, with time, with people. You're good and solid, always ready to help. You don't double-cross people; you don't use your fists in anger; you don't lose your cool – you're in control. You're never in trouble with the police. That's you! You're connected with the Liberator, Jesus, and you've murdered your dark side with its "must have" attitude. Now that we're living with God's Spirit, let's get our heartbeat in rhythm with his. Let's not get cocky, competitive or jealous.

Which means ... (Galatians 6:1-10)

1-5

Guys, if someone gets themselves into a hole, you who are "spiritual" should help them back up (and out) *gently*. But watch it: don't get pulled in yourself. If something's dragging someone down, don't just stand there: get your back into it and fulfil the law of the Liberator. If you think you're really something, think again: you're not. Assess your work, take pride in it, but don't compare results with someone else: just take responsibility for your own actions.

6-10

Don't be tight-fisted with those who coach you in God-things. Don't worry: no one pulls a fast one on God. What you put in, you get out. If you invest your time in dark things, you'll generate mess. If you spend your time on what God's Spirit nudges you towards, you'll generate limitless life. Let's tough it out through the tired times and keep on doing the right thing – if we keep going, we'll see results. Whenever we get the chance, do people good – especially if they're part of God's crew.

Last few tips, then ...

–Rob

Cheers (Galatians 6:18)

May the generosity of our Boss, Jesus the Liberator, soak into your souls, guys. Absolutely!

Ephesians / Paul to JLM West Turkey Branches

From:	paul.benson@jailmail.rome.nt
To:	jlm@ephesus.org.tk
Cc:	jlm@laodicea.org.tk; jlm@hierapolis.org.tk
	(and W. Turkey address book)
Date:	AD 60-ish
Subject:	Getting it all together

Paul spent three years in Ephesus with a regular slot in the Tyrannus lecture hall events diary. He had a big impact on the city and helped get the JLM on its feet. But now his work's got him locked up again, so he sends out a circular to the JLM branches in West Turkey. This time he's not writing 'cos they've messed up, just to give them more to chew on – the widescreen picture of the JLM bringing in God's plan of all creation pulling together again, with the Liberator in the driving seat. Paul reckons the JLM's like a human body, a building, a wife (but not all at once).   –Rob

Rough guide to Ephesus: Huge harbour city on the beautiful Aegean Sea. Fourth biggest urban sprawl in the Roman Empire. **Must-see sights:** HQ of Roman goddess of fertility Diana-the-multi-bosomed-woman (aka Artemis) – one of the Seven Wonders of the Ancient World. The baths, library, paved streets in the centre and (if you can stomach the thought) the secret tunnel from the library to the infamous brothel – rated C for caution. **Must do:** Sit in the back row of the Mount Pion Amphitheatre and imagine Paul arguing his corner in front of 25,000 people – with no mic! (Not that amphitheatres have corners.)

Bonuses (Ephesians 1:3-23)

3-10

Celebrate God, the Father of our Boss, Jesus the Liberator. 'Cos of our connection with the Liberator, God's poured out so much of heaven's good stuff that our belly laughs are fuller, longer, stronger than ever before. Way back, before the cosmos was called to attention out of nothing, God let the Liberator pick us out to be his special people, fully acquitted and loved. What God always wanted, what he craved for was for us to fulfil our destiny – to be adopted into his family through our links with Jesus the Liberator. And he loves his Son so much he just piles on the dazzling freebies and we're left speechless – except for making sure that God gets all the credit for everything we've got. Our Jesus-link sparks off all of God's over-the-top generosity. If it wasn't for his wisdom in knowing how we tick, you'd think he was spoiling us with all these bonuses:

1. We're bought back from the enemy at a price calculated in units of Jesus' blood.

2. Our mess is cleaned up and cancelled.

3. We get the inside story on his plans for the future that he's buzzing about bringing in since Jesus completed his mission. Major talk of timing it all to come under Jesus' jurisdiction, all of it – heaven, earth, the whole caboodle – with the Liberator running things his way.

11-14

4. We were the first to rely on the Liberator and we've been picked out, destined even, by the one who runs the cosmos his way, to be the channel through which people catch on how dazzlingly brilliant God is. He'll use us to get others celebrating him!

And you're in on all this. You were all ears, you took the good news to heart and you were liberated. So there's more:

5. You get God's Holy Spirit based permanently in your deepest places, locked in as a guarantee, a down payment for . . .

6. All the rest of your inheritance that God's still got on account for you until . . .

7. You get the full freedom that God's got on line for his people.

Which is why, since you took the Boss, Jesus, at his word and since you love the rest of the JLM crew, I've not shifted out of non-stop "Thank you, God" mode for you guys. I'm always nudging the God of our Boss, Jesus the Liberator, begging the "dazzling Dad" to dole out the wisdom, to pull the blinds back and let us get to know him better. I'm also working with him that your deep places would wake up to connecting with the fantastic prospects you've been picked out for . . .

- the wealth of inheritance that belongs to the crew

- and the power that's now yours. Influence that goes right off any scale known to man.

You're plugged into the same power that meant Death couldn't stand in God's way when he came to get the Liberator back from the grave. You've got access to the same authority that put the Liberator in the top office in heaven, leap-frogging all the lesser spiritual forces, outgunning all the sirs, lords, presidents, generals etc. of all time (including future hopefuls). You're charged with the same energy that God gave the Liberator to be the ultimate Boss, in charge of all JLM business, which is now his hands and feet and heart on this planet – the exact equivalent of the one who's so huge he fills everything. That's some clout! And it's yours!   –Rob

Alive (Ephesians 2:1-22)

You guys were spiritual corpses, murdered by the mess that ran your lives. You went with the flow; you weren't going God's way, so you let the boss of the spiritual underworld dictate your every move like some Mafia godfather. We all did it: we merged in with the crowd, pumped our bodies with whatever our dark side fancied at the time. We were as brainwashed as the rest of them and wound God up big time. But God loves us so passionately he gave us some slack and let the Liberator resuscitate our spiritual side that had been throttled by our mess. Free, no charge, a gift – God's over-the-top generosity is what's straightened you out, sorted your lives, brought you back to life (like he did with the Liberator), and now we're sitting right next to the Liberator, Jesus, in heaven. Why? So he can brag about our lives, show us off as prime examples of the phenomenal value of his freebies, use us as exhibits A to Z of his generosity to us – just 'cos we're connected with the Liberator, Jesus. What's straightened you out isn't down to you. There's nothing you've done that's sorted your life. No, it's all God's generosity that's done it; you've just taken him at his word and even your ability to do that comes direct and free of charge from him. If it were linked to how you lived, you'd end up shouting your mouth off about how brilliant you are. No, we're God's masterpiece, his *tour de force,* his *pièce de résistance.* The Liberator, Jesus, qualifies us to be made from scratch to make good things happen, things he's planned already for us to get stuck into.

11-13

You're not Jews – you're Turks or Greeks or Arabs, whatever. Before, Jews would've looked down their noses at you "foreigners". Don't forget there was a brick wall between you and the Liberator. You were barricaded from the Jewish passport office. There was fat chance of your getting visas or citizenship papers, and an obese chance (!) of getting in on any of the goodies from the Contract with God. You had no prospects. You didn't know God. But since the Liberator, Jesus, sacrificed his lifeblood, your link with him gets you up close and personal with God.

14-18

The Liberator's negotiated a peace deal. He's changed things so now we're equal and the brick wall's just dust blown about in the street. His death brought a full stop to the old Jewish religious system, with its straitjacket Rules. He didn't just find common ground where Jews and "foreigners" could hold Inclusivity Conferences. No, it's more radical than that – he started a new breed of person, a new nationality, with no ethnic squabbles to spark off a war. He brought them together; he brought them and God together. His execution killed off the racial friction. His shuttle diplomacy between Jews and "foreigners" was based on the offer of an open door to Father God made possible by his Holy Spirit.

19-22

Which means this: we've no use for words like *foreigner* anymore. He's done away with words like *alien, outsider* and *stranger.* We're all fully documented citizens of God's new nation, his family. Or change the graphics – call it a house: me, the team and God's couriers are the foundations; you're the bricks built on top and the Liberator holds the whole structure together. And it's starting to look like the drawings of the Boss's new HQ. And you're part of this! You're being cemented into the building that's going to be home for God's Spirit.

Paul's job (Ephesians 3:8-13)

OK, so maybe I'm the lowest of all the crew. But God was generous with me: he headhunted me for the job of getting through to non-Jews the uncountable value of the Liberator. To break down into bite-size pieces how this enigma works. Creator God had it up his sleeve for centuries, but now the JLM gets to download the full hard drive of his wisdom so that spiritual entities like angels and demons can finally get a grip on it. Right from before day one he had it written in to make this happen through our Boss, Jesus the Liberator. Jesus acts like a security codeword, giving us full access to take him at his word and sit round the same table as God, without getting blown away. Some job I've got, eh? So don't go getting dragged down just 'cos I'm in prison. It's just an occupational hazard. And it's done you good – it's upped your reputation! I'm well chuffed.

Wish list for you (Ephesians 3:14-21)

14-19

So my knees are swollen with all the begging I've been doing for you from the Father/Designer/Creator/Originator. I'm asking him to dig into his incredible wealth and up your supplies of his Spirit's supernatural power flowing direct into your core. You'll need these extra surges if the Liberator's going to settle down and make himself at home in your deep places. I'm asking that you'll plug into the Liberator's love and be able to get your head (and heart) round its dimensions: the size, scale, depth, density, scope, range and texture of this love are beyond quantum physics; they can't be squeezed into some formula – they're impossible to measure. But by trying, you'll expand your capacity and will have more space for God to fill – his love supplies won't run short!

20-21

God's always out-thinking us, out-giving us, blowing our tiny little minds by setting off his supernatural power inside us. We ask him for the max and he doubles it. We imagine the best possible result and he betters it. He's the only name on the credits when the biopic of the JLM and its Founder rolls. Don't care when or where it's shown — he's the only one winning any awards for all he's done.

Live up to it (Ephesians 4:1-7)

1-6

I'm stuck here in prison, doing time for the Boss, and I'm pleading with you, you've been picked out for a Mission Incredible — so live like it. Attitude: not cocky, not aggressive, not pushy, not tetchy, but loving. Target: a united front, peace on every personal border with God's Holy Spirit knowing all instructions are received and understood. One's the only number that counts here — one JLM with one thing to be convinced of, one thing to be baptized into: that there's only one Boss, one God, one Father, one Holy Spirit. And he's above, below, beside, alongside, inside everything. He's everywhere, anywhere, always there.

7

We're one, but we're not the same. The Liberator allocated us different specialities . . .

> Such as couriers, communicators, counsellors, coaches. All with the same brief: to train the crew to work together and do others good. The JLM isn't a gullible baby, but an adult. It's not a dismembered, dysfunctional body, but a fully functional, well-balanced, coordinated lover of people. That's the JLM.   —Rob

Stand out from the crowd (Ephesians 4:17-24)

17-19

So I'm being straight with you, straight from the Boss — stand out from the crowd; don't be like the rest of them drifting through life like nothing matters. They're groping round in the dark. They blocked off God's life source and can't quite suss what it's all about, can't quite click "open" on their deep places, everything just freezes. So "right and wrong" means nothing to them. They do whatever they fancy, have whatever they fancy, abuse *whoever* they fancy. And then some more. Deeper, darker, dirtier 'cos, as the song goes, they "just can't get enough".

20-24

But you stand out. You're different: you were coached in the Liberator lifestyle. You've taken it in; you've taken it on; you're convinced by it – it's about debagging the Old You, your dark side, your "former life", which just twists you up with cravings. Then what? You just stay naked? No, God's Spirit advises you and you get kitted out in the New You, your vibrant side, your "new life" – tailor-made for you. You put it on and start looking more and more like God, unpolluted and doing the right thing.

> This New You doesn't fudge the truth. You might get angry, but you don't mess up; you don't lift things that aren't yours; you work, earn, donate. When you open your mouth, you do people good. You don't infuriate God's Spirit inside you. Detox yourself from the cocktails you've been bingeing on, the "Bitter and Twisted", the "Slap Down", the "Malice Attack". Build your immune system back up with some kindness capsules. Work your heart back into the right place. Give people a break, like the Liberator did for you. —Rob

Imitate God (Ephesians 5:1-14)

1-2

Copy God: imitate him; mimic his mannerisms like kids end up walking and talking like their old man. Love people like the Liberator loved you – jacking in all his prospects, giving it all up, letting it all go up in smoke – for you. And the whiff of it will float up to heaven where God will inhale and be moved to tears.

3-7

Don't let anyone use words like *crude, filthy* or *vulgar* when describing you. Don't talk dirty. Don't talk stupid. Make sure your words meet the moment. Simple things like saying "please" and "thank you". Don't doubt it: no one with a mouth full of filth and heart full of greed has any place in God's plans for heaven installed on earth with the Liberator in charge. Don't let anyone rip you off with flashy banter – it's exactly this type of smart alec that gets God fuming. Don't get involved: keep your distance.

That's old territory: dark and dangerous. Now you've been admitted to God's well-lit cities – act like it. Let the light that's in you shine out so you almost don't need the street lights. Be a conveyor belt delivering good, right and true actions. Do your research – find out what makes God happy, and do it. Don't let your name go down on the acknowledgement lists of anything dodgy. In fact, blow the whistle, 'cos it's disgusting what some of these lowlifes get up to in back rooms. When your kind of light gets shone into these filth holes, people find out what's really going on – which is why the old song says:

Wakey, wakey. Get off your death bed,
And the Liberator will pull back the blinds and pour in the light.

Wise up. Tune into God's plans. Don't get drunk on alcohol – get drunk on God. Sing God-songs. Respect each other. Wives, your No. 1 is your man; husbands, your No. 1 is your woman. Work it like the wife is the JLM and the hubby is the Liberator – both working, loving, being for the other. Kids, respect your parents. Dads, don't wind up your kids, but be their life-coach, getting them ready for their next season. Workers, respect your bosses, like you respect your Boss, Jesus, and not just when you're on the closed-circuit TV – in the blind spots too. Bosses, treat your staff well – you've both got the same Boss in heaven, and he's not interested in who earns the most.
                                                                    –Rob

Battle gear (Ephesians 6:10-24)

Before I sign off, your Boss is strong, so channel that strength. If you still want to be standing when the Devil's emptied both barrels at you, then get your battle armour on. Know your enemy: it's not *people* you're fighting; it's the dark spiritual forces that run the evil Systems from their hellish HQ. So you'll need your battle armour to keep you on your feet. Face the onslaught with your Truth Belt fully stocked, with your Bullet-proof Vest of Right Lifestyle fixed on tight, with your Boots being ready to stomp on injustice and escort peace in. Activate your Personal Protective Force Field, so you'll stay totally convinced of what you're fighting for even when the evil one's scudding you with missiles.

And your headgear's essential, so get your Helmet on, with its breathing apparatus to protect you from chemical warfare, and its radio contact with HQ – absolutely crucial. But this isn't just about defence; it's about hitting the enemy where it hurts. What else but the very best weapon, as used by God's Spirit himself: Words. Not just any words; we're on info overload already. No, *God's* words, from the Sacred Instruction Manual. And keep communication lines with God open 24/7; have his Spirit on the conference-call facility permanently. And keep sharp. No point in having all this equipment and being dopey or drugged up. Keep on at God for the rest of the crew's benefit.

19-20

I could also do with you sending some up for me. Ask God to trigger just the right words and, when I hear them coming out of my mouth, to help me not to bottle and clam up. I may be locked up, but I'm still God's rep.

21-22

God's loyal worker Tychicus is on his way over: he'll fill you in on how I'm doing – to buck you up.

23-24

Serenity to you guys. Shed-loads of love and conviction from our Father God and Boss, Jesus the Liberator. God's generosity to anyone who loves our Boss, Jesus the Liberator, to death.

Philippians / Paul to JLM
Philippi, Greece Branch

From:	paul.benson@jailmail.rome.nt
	timo.apprentice@teammail.nt
To:	jlm@philippiserve.org.gr
Date:	AD 61-ish
Subject:	Cheers for the cash / don't let them get you down – be happy!

First JLM branch in Europe. When they heard Paul was under house arrest with a death sentence hanging over him, they sent him some cash. This is his thank-you letter. While he's at it he fills them in on how he is, tells them to show a united front against outside hassles, to keep their thinking on line with God's and to endorse Timo and Epaph who are on their way over. Keyword: "happy".   –Rob

Rough guide to Philippi: Northern Greece city named after Alexander the Great's dad, Philip. Now Roman and proud of it (road signs in Greek *and* Latin). JLM branch is full of retired Roman military types who were given local land as a pension on hanging up their uniforms. Egnatia Rd runs right through the city centre; go left and you end up in Italy; go right and you hit Turkey. **Must-see sights:** The acropolis (can't miss it – big thing up on hill to north). **Must do:** Relax in the city baths and play "Spot the Italian".

Fully done (Philippians 1:3-11)

3-6

Thank God you're there! Every time you spring to mind, I thank God you're there. While I'm at it, I ask him to do you good. And I love asking 'cos you guys have been fully active partners from first off. And I'm sold on the fact that God's not going to leave you half-finished. No way. What he's doing with you is superb and he's going to have you ready for when the Liberator, Jesus, comes back.

> He misses them and asks God to help them, so …   —Rob

9b-11

Your love will outgrow and overflow as you learn and connect with life. Then you'll know what's right and you'll do it, and your track record will be impeccable when the Liberator has his Big Day. He'll recognize his own trademark, his style, his logo on all you've produced, and everyone will give the credit and congrats to God.

> He sees the positive side of being locked up — other crew members have pulled their finger out (some with dodgy motives, but it's better than nothing). He's grappling with this death sentence on his head …   —Rob

To be or not to be (Philippians 1:20-26)

I'm not planning on being shown up; I'm convinced I've still got the bottle and the Liberator will keep on getting a good press from me, whether I live or whether they kill me. I know what living's all about — the Liberator. And dying's even better! Two possible endings: option one, they let me go — great! I'll get more done down here. If it was *my* call? Not sure. I'm torn. Option two looks fantastic: to leave and be with the Liberator — way better! But option one is better for you lot, so it looks like I'll be around for a while, helping you grow happier and happier in your convictions about the Liberator, Jesus, till you explode like a bottle of bubbly!

> Paul says, "Whatever, just live up to what you stand for, even when they hassle you for it."   —Rob

Who's No. 1? (Philippians 2:1-11)

1-4

Some questions: (Check Yes or No)

- Are there big pay-offs to having this connection with the Liberator? Yes/No
- Does his love get you through the dark times? Yes/No
- Does God's Holy Spirit pull you together? Yes/No
- Are you moved when tragic things happen? Yes/No

If you've checked Yes to all the above, then make my day – love each other! Be united, be one, pull together, sing off the same page. Don't elbow people, step on people, stab people in the back just to get yourself noticed. Put a mirror up to the real you, with no fancy "soul enhancing" lighting FX; then look back at anyone else and reckon they're better than you. Don't just look after No. 1, but also look out for each other.

5-11

Get an attitude – as long as it's the same attitude the Liberator had:

He was God, right through to the marrow,
But he didn't use his clout to put himself about heaven.
He took off all the royal bits, cut up his heavenly credit cards,
Chucked his global contacts list, walked off without his body-
    guards.
He unplugged his airwave connection, left his precious star
    collection,
He said, "I give it up." (x2)
And took up a new role – a role well below him:
He became flesh and blood, skin and bone,
And stepped down from his heavenly throne to his new earth-
    home as a normal guy.
And more – he allowed himself to die;
And more – he allowed himself to be nailed up high and executed
    on a cross.

So God brought him back, celebrated him, elevated him to the top
   spot.
Letters behind his name? He got the lot!
So everyone will show Jesus ultimate respect,
Everyone will stand for inspection all "present and correct",
And every mouth will say, "He's Boss, this Liberator, Jesus –
   Boss."
And God's reputation, his credibility, will soar,
As his enemies weep and his fans roar.

Paul says, "So know your place, and his – and get on with the job. Timo and Epaph
are coming soon to give a hand; I won't be far behind. Again, don't get cocky . . ."
                                     –Rob

Useless! (Philippians 3:4-14)

4-6

If people are into trading personal plus points, then I'd beat them all,
hands down:

- Born by the book – foreskin lopped off after eight days, like the
  Good Book says,

- Born a Jew,

- Born into the Benson tribe.

A pure, full-blooded Israeli. Or, if you're talking about keeping the
Rules . . .

- Come on! I was a religious leader! I had degrees hung on my
  wall, so you couldn't see the wallpaper.

Or, if you're comparing commitment levels . . .

- I'd lynch any JLMer who moved. You ask anyone around back
  then.

As for crossing my legal T's and dotting my pedantic I's – I was Mr
Picky.

7-11

But I've chucked it all out – my privileged background. It's useless since the Liberator showed up. In fact, all I had is less than useless. It's a huge minus if I stick it up against having Jesus the Liberator as my Boss. Now he's around, I've jacked all that in. Compared to being *in* with the Liberator, all that stuff's worth less than a pile of crap. God doesn't bring me in on his business 'cos of my track record, my "achievements", my scorecard on Moses' Rule Book. No, I'm down in the book as straightened out and sorted just 'cos I took the Liberator at his word. I qualify just 'cos God says so. So now I'm only into spending time with the Liberator. I'm desperate to tap into the power that brought him back from death. I'm up for showing "solidarity" with him by going through tough times, getting inside his head by facing death and – I don't know how this works, but – even coming back from the dead. I want the lot. I want to know him. Deep.

12-14

I'm just scratching the surface; I'm miles off where I should be. But I'm working on it, like the Liberator, Jesus, is working on *me*. Guys, I'm not "there", I've not "made it", but I'm focused forwards not backwards. Pushing through the pain barrier to hit the finishing tape and collect the medal God's got up there with my name on it. Since the Liberator, Jesus, entered me into the race, God's been "whooping" me on up the slope towards heaven.

> Paul adds, "Don't live like the majority – belly first. You've got a passport to heaven in your bag and you're just waiting to be picked up."   –Rob

Be happy! (Philippians 4:4-9)

4-7

Celebrate the Boss, 24/7. I'll copy and paste that – this time in bold: **Celebrate the Boss.** Quit the aggression – fists and curses are out; palms and calm voices are in. The Boss is at Heaven Junction, ready to come visit. Don't get stressed about anything – whatever hits you, verbalize it with God; balance your "pleases" and your "thank yous", and God's serenity, which even medics can't work it out, will flood your deep places, saturate your thinking, acting like a minder, 'cos you're in with the Liberator, Jesus.

8-9

To round off, guys: stuff your mouth with truth; pack your head with heroic ideas; occupy your hands with doing the right thing; stack up your deep places with purity; focus your vision on beautiful things; fill your imagination with excellence, dignity, distinction. Copy me. Whatever you picked up from my words or mannerisms – work it into your lifestyle, and the God of serenity will hang around you.

He says "cheers" for the cash, but also ...   –Rob

Happy (Philippians 4:12-13)

I can relate to being totally broke. I can understand being loaded. But wherever I am along the cash spectrum, I'm happy – I've learned the knack. If I'm starving or stuffed full, bedsit-scumming it or penthouse posing – whatever, I'm happy. Now I've got God's energy – direct inject – there's no limits to what I can do.

"But cheers for the gift." And a last "cheers" as he signs off.   –Rob

Cheers (Philippians 4:23)

The generosity of the Boss, Jesus the Liberator, soak into your soul. Absolutely!

Colossians / Paul to JLM
Colossae, Turkey Branch

From: paul.benson@jailmail.rome.nt

                timo.apprentice@teammail.nt

To: jlm@colossaemail.org.nt

                jlm@laodicea.org.tk

Date: AD 60-ish

Subject: Refocus on the Liberator

> Paul hadn't been there, but word was out that they were going off line with a pick 'n' mix of wacky ideas about angels, foodfests, self-help regimes – aka Gnosticism (silent G). Paul's under house arrest with Epaph (JLM Colossae branch founder) so writing's the only option. What to say? Talk up the Liberator . . . –Rob

Rough guide to Colossae: Roman city in Lycus Valley. Bit of a has-been town. **Must-see sights:** Not a lot these days. **Must do:** Take short trip to Laodicea or Hierapolis – more happening.

Paul says, "I've heard good things . . ."   –Rob

Jesus = No. 1 (Colossians 1:9-27)

9-14

So from day one of hearing your story we've been pushing your case with God, asking him to fill you in on his plans via his spiritual wisdom package. Why? So your lifestyle will ring true. So they'll look at you and it'll be obvious you belong to the Boss. So you'll make God happy in every category of life – getting on with good things, getting to know him personally because you're plugged into his power supply, which is dazzling, long lasting, the only high worth having. So you'll be bubbling with joy – and you'll know who to credit: the one who's signed you in for a chunk of inheritance (tax free). So you'll realize that the Son he loves has paid up front (in blood) for you to be dragged over the border from the Dark Nation into his Light Country with your slate wiped clean.

15-20

What's God like? Ah! Problem: can't see him – we're too freaked to focus, the light's burning our eye balls, God's invisible etc. But we know what he's like. How come? We've seen the Liberator, God's equal, who runs creation. So what's *he* like?

- He made it all happen: heaven, earth; physical, spiritual; all the "powers that be" – kings, systems, angels, demons. All made by and for him.

- He's the "how" and the "why" of every question – it all comes down to him.

- He's head of the JLM.

- He's the starting line of life.

- He's the first to cheat on death, the first to tell death where to go.

- He's got the capacity to take in the totality of God without exploding.

- He's the ultimate blood donor – donating his life on the cross so that God could complete the operation and slowly draw everybody, everything, in heaven or down here, back towards him.

- He's the basis of the Peace Treaty between us and God.

21-23

Peace Treaty? Yeah, you were at war with God. Your attitude and your lifestyle declared war. But now, the blood of the Liberator has bailed you out. You can stand in his court and look the Judge in the eye – you're guilty, but it's like you're innocent. No one can scream, "Liar/thief/murderer!" at you from the gallery. The Liberator's already taken your death penalty, so there's no case against you. So don't stop being convinced. Don't lose your grip on the good news; don't jack in your prospects. Yeah, you heard it right: the good news got through to you loud and clear, no interference. It's zinging round the airwaves right now, global. My job's to make sure it keeps on zinging.

And it costs Paul to let people in on the mystery ...   –Rob

27

The mystery is that the Liberator lives in you – he's your prospect of an extraordinary future.

Solid ground (Colossians 2:6-15)

6-7

You've started – so finish. You gave the Liberator, Jesus, the nod as your new Boss, so now build on that foundation and live like you're walking on solid ground, live like you're happy about it!

8-10

Make sure you don't get tangled up in flashy arguments that turn out to be waffle. What's it based on? If the answer's "tradition" or "common sense" then forget it. Like I say, build on the Liberator – his normal-Joe flesh and blood was jam packed full of divine DNA. Plus your link with the Liberator gives you all you need – he *is* in charge of the cosmos, you know!

You're linked with deep symbols, gripping metaphors, powerful images to God's power that brought Jesus back from death.   –Rob

13-15

You were dead to God in your mess and your ruthless dark side, but God brought you back to life with the Liberator. He wiped our mess out, cleaned up our back-story, which had huge backlogs of debts. Our spiritual credit rating was disastrous – the interest payments were strangling the life out of us. But he ripped it off our necks and stapled it to the crossbar Jesus was executed on. With this one act he neutralized the dark spiritual forces, humiliating them publicly with a total thrashing.

So don't get sucked into tatty arguments about what to eat, drink, touch etc. You're above all that now.   –Rob

So ... (Colossians 3:1-17)

1-4

It's obvious! Since the Liberator has yanked you up nearer to heaven, make sure your wish-list is full of heavenly goods – where the Liberator sits in his office with a bird's-eye view of earth. Programme your thinking to focus on what's worth something, not just trashy earth junk. Don't forget – you're dead! You only live via your link with God through the Liberator. He's your life. So when he shows up, you'll get to be part of the party.

5-11

So kill off all those dark habits. Starve out sexual deviance, twistedness. Lop off the groping, grabbing hand. All this is what gets God furious. Yeah, that was the Old You in your "previous life" – but no more. Lose the temper, fight the anger, beat the aggression, pick on the cruelty, embarrass the slander, bad-mouth the foul language. Don't lie. All these "old rags" are ripped off you and you're wearing the New You – renewable every time you get more of a glimpse of the Tailor. And this whole movement of new people has forgotten about racism or elitism or classism – 'cos the Liberator is all that counts, and they know it.

12-14

Instead, God's picked you out to be pure, passionately loved. Clothes are a big statement, so let's see you sporting an image that reflects the New You: compassion suits you, kindness goes with the colours of your soul, humility sets you off nicely, gentleness is so "you", patience is perfect with your complexion. It all fits so well, Tailor-made. Bite your lip when someone crosses a line. Wipe it off the record as *your* slate's been wiped by the Boss. But you're still undressed without the finishing touch – love. Love holds all the stitches together, love makes it all look just right, love transforms an outfit into a statement.

15-17

Let the serenity that comes from the Liberator be the boss of your deep places. If the serenity goes, if you're suddenly at odds with someone – that's your alarm! Be grateful, all the time. Let the wisdom of the Liberator soak into your souls, so it seeps out of every part of you and moves people on, keeps people on track. Let your song lyrics be rich with gratitude and wisdom. Whatever you're up to, thinking or doing, act like a rep of our Boss, Jesus – getting your thanks to God through him.

Family values, work ethics. Put a word in for him with God. Some final hi's and byes.
                                                                        –Rob

Cheers (Colossians 4:18)

Yes, this is my scribble, signing off. Think of me and hear my chains rattling! God's generosity rub off on you.

1 Thessalonians / Paul to JLM Thessalonica Branch

(Email No. 1)

From: paul.benson@corinth.mail.nt

silas@corinth.mail.nt

timo.apprentice@corinth.mail.nt

To: jlm@thessalonica.org.gr

Date: AD 51-ish

Subject: Liberator – the sequel

Probably Paul's first letter (on record). He'd founded the JLM branch here but was forced out sharpish – rioting and reports of him winding up the masses to replace Caesar with Jesus as king. Timo brings the latest news to Paul in Corinth: now the JLMers are getting victimized and need a boost. Paul writes a turbo-charged letter saying, "OK, it's rough now, but future prospects are incredible."   –Rob

Rough guide to Thessalonica: Ninety-five miles west of Philippi on the Egnatia Rd. In the top two trading centres of Roman Greece. Capital of Macedonia. Population around 200,000. **Must-see sights:** The Thermic Gulf harbour – busy or what? **Must do:** Take a trip north (two hundred miles) to the river Danube – boat trip's not cheap, but worth it for the views.

Wish-list (1 Thessalonians 1:2-3)

We're on the line to God all day, thanking him for you guys, asking him to help. You keep coming to the front of our minds – you prove you're convinced by how hard you work, you prove you're packed full of love by your energy, you know our Boss, Jesus the Liberator, gives you prospects 'cos you just keep going.

> He goes through their impressive track record. Mulls over his time with them – the hassles, the sweat, the laughs, the results. He was desperate to come see them, but couldn't, so sent Timo instead. Glowing report comes back – they're hanging in there, toughing it out. Maybe God'll smash some roadblocks out the way for Paul to make it to them in person. Till then . . .   –Rob

Please, Boss . . . (1 Thessalonians 3:12-13)

May the Boss overload love on you so it's busting out of you and on to each other, on to outsiders – like we love you. May he muscle up your deep places, so you'll stand in front of God the Father as pure and innocent when our Boss, Jesus, makes his entrance with his crew.

Please the Boss (1 Thessalonians 4:1-12)

1-2

To round off, guys: we filled you in on how to live to make God smile – and you're doing it! Now we're speaking for our Boss, Jesus, and we're saying the same thing again – live to make God smile, grin, guffaw, then some more. You know what we told you:

3-8

What God wants is for you to keep yourselves out of the pollution:

- Sort your sex lives. Purify. Don't let Herman the hormone run your life. Show your sexuality some respect, some dignity – not like those who've never met God. Don't cheat on another JLMer by going off with his missus. God'll slam down hard on you if you mess up like that – you know it: we told you. Why did God pick you out? To be polluted? No! To stand out as outstanding. If you white out this bit, you're not having a go at *me,* but at God who doles out his Holy Spirit for you.

9-10

- Love the other JLMers. (This'll be quick: God's been tutoring you direct. You're doing it, nationwide.) But it's crucial, guys; do it, and some, and some more.

11-12

- What's your ambition? (Hold it, while you think.) Is it along the lines of (a) have a quiet life, (b) keep your nose out of other people's stuff or (c) do practical work? No? Nothing like that? Well, you're out of line with what we told you then. Aim to hear the locals shout "respect" at you. Aim not to be a drain on anyone's energy.

The sequel (1 Thessalonians 4:13-5:24)

13-18

Guys, we don't want you in the dark about what happens when you die. We don't want you running out of tissues at funerals, like you've got no prospects. We're convinced that Jesus was executed and came back to life. We're just as convinced that God'll also bring those who've made their exit back to life again, if they were linked with Jesus. I've got it direct from the Boss – when he comes back, those who've already died will be first in line to meet up with him. The Boss himself will come on down from heaven: huge voice of a Top Angel, massive blast on God's trumpet and those connected with the Liberator will be up and out of their graves first. Next in line will be those linked with Jesus who are still alive and kicking. They'll float up and join with the ex-dead guys and meet the Boss midair – day one of a million infinities with the Boss. Do each other good by emailing, text-messaging, "Post-it" noting each other about your futures.

5:1-3

Now, guys, we're not going to go into dates and times – you know well enough the Boss's Big Day will come out of nowhere, like a night mugging. They'll be strolling along saying, "Aren't the streets quiet tonight!" when whack, *finito!* It's like a pregnant mum: one minute, cool, relaxed, next minute, screaming as the contractions kick in – no way round it.

4-11

But you guys aren't in the dark. You're not going to get caught out. You know the score – no one's mugging you. You're well connected, lit up, bright, focused. You're day people, not night people. You don't lurk in the corners, scheming, spying, snooping. So don't act like the dazed ones. No, you're alert, sharp, in control. Those who sleep, do it at night. Those who get smashed, do it at night. But we're day people! We're in control; we get dressed up in love and conviction, which act like a bullet-'n'-knife-proof vest. Our prospect of liberation is like the strongest visor and helmet. God didn't pick us out to beat us up, but to sort us, 'cos of our connection with our Boss, Jesus the Liberator. He was executed so that whichever side of our own funeral we're looking from, we get to live with him. Do each other good, work each other's conviction muscles into shape – like you're doing.

12-15

I'm looking for a favour, guys. Show respect for your JLM leaders, even when they have to be heavy on you. Love and respect them – they're working for the Boss. Call a ceasefire on your in-house civil wars. These ones are more than a favour: kick the lazy troublemakers into place; bring the insecure out of themselves; support the vulnerable; give some slack to everyone. Don't get into revenge attacks. Be generous with everyone – JLMers, outsiders, everyone.

16-18

What's God want for you now you're linked with the Liberator, Jesus? This: enjoy life, all of it. Keep contact with God 24/7. Be grateful, whatever.

19-22

God's Holy Spirit is like your pilot light – don't put him out. When a courier gets word from God, don't tut. But don't be a sucker either. Suss it out. Work at it. What's good stays. Sidestep dark stuff.

23-24

May the serene God personally process the pollution out of you till you're purity itself. May all of you – body, mind and soul – be kept outstandingly innocent when our Boss, Jesus the Liberator, shows. The one who picked you out won't drop you in it: he'll make sure this happens.

Final hi's. Make sure you read this publicly at a JLM do.   –Rob

Cheers (1 Thessalonians 5:28)

Wherever you go, the generosity of our Boss, Jesus the Liberator, rub off on you.

2 Thessalonians / Paul to JLM Thessalonica Branch

(Email No. 2)

From: paul.benson@corinth.mail.nt

silas@corinth.mail.nt

timo.apprentice@corinth.mail.nt

To: jlm@thessalonica.org.gr

Date: Six months after email No. 1

Subject: It ain't over till the Big Evil shows

Only six months on. Nothing much has changed – hassles are still fine-tuning the Thessalonians' convictions. Some guy's wafting a printout with Paul's signature forged on it – it's saying the Boss is back and we're already in the sequel. Paul clears up the rumours. Tells them to keep working. —Rob

Doing great (2 Thessalonians 1:3-10)

3-4

Guys, it's only right! We're sending up thanks to God for you all the time – your convictions are getting stronger; your love for the crew's getting deeper. We show off about you to other JLM branches – going on about your stamina, the way you just take God at his word despite all the victimization you're facing.

5-10

Proof (if it was needed) that God's spot-on about you – that you're down in the Book as perfect candidates for God's New World, even though it's costing you now. But God invented "fair": he doesn't just nurse you, and us, through the tough times. No, he also makes sure the cruelty backfires on those dishing it out. When? When the Boss, Jesus, makes his big entrance with blockbuster-scale spectacular sights, huge production values, spectacular pyrotechnics and hordes of fearsome angels on the rampage. It's payback time for everyone who only knows "God" as a swear word and thinks "gospel" is just early soul music. We're talking non-stop "seek out and destroy". We're talking the ultimate lock out – they don't get into where God is; they don't get to see his sheer class, his total control. It's the Big Day when his purified crew really go for it, seeing him like he is, telling it like it is. And you've got tickets – you took on what we told you.

> Paul snuffs out the rumour that the letter doing the rounds, which says Jesus is already back, is from him. "Tripe! I told you, 'The Big Evil' hasn't shown yet, so it's not the End." The dark spiritual forces will build their power base, bring in their man, wow the world with spectacular FX and even more spectacular evil. It'll suck in every sucker who loves evil and it'll wipe them out.   —Rob

Brace yourselves (2 Thessalonians 2:15-17)

So, guys, get a grip and prepare for impact, so you're not knocked flying. Keep our coaching – first hand or by (e)mail – in the front of your minds. Our Boss, Jesus the Liberator, and our Father, God, loved us and went over the top with giving us limitless prospects. Now I'm really into them cheering you on in your deep places, building up your spiritual muscle as prep for good talk and good action.

> He wants them "sending some up" for him too. Steer clear of couch potatoes. If you can, work for your bread and butter.   —Rob

Cheers (2 Thessalonians 3:18)

The generosity of our Boss, Jesus the Liberator, rub off on all of you.

Paul's Private "Sent Items" Box

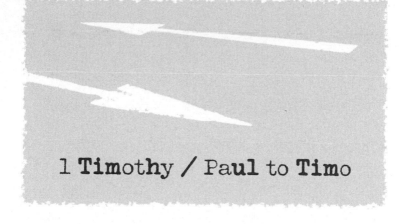

1 Timothy / Paul to Timo

(Email No. 1)

From: paul.benson@teammail.philippi.nt

To: timo.apprentice@ephesus.org.tk

Date: AD 64-ish

Subject: Running the thing

Quick bio: Timo the timid Turk. His mum's Jewish (now a JLMer) and his dad's Greek. A veteran of Paul's Tours Nos. 1–3. On the credits list for six of his other emails. Paul's protégé gets his instructions from his mentor who's off on Tour No. 4 . . .

Even messed-up me! (1 Timothy 1:12-17)

Paul gets out of his Rome jail and sets off on his fourth tour (full circle – Turkey, Greece, Italy, Spain, Crete and back to Turkey). He's delegated Timo to run the Ephesus JLM. Stick it out; keep coaching the best way. Keep them off their petty arguing.   –Rob

12-14

I'm so chuffed that the Liberator, Jesus our Boss, supplies my spiritual muscle and counts me as a loyal worker. Me?! The guy who used his name as a swear word! The guy who used terrorist tactics against his first-generation JLM! But he gave me a break 'cos I had no idea what I was doing. The Boss's over-the-top generosity nearly drowned me – the Liberator, Jesus, stuffed me full of absolute conviction and love.

15-17

Want a reliable statement? Want a motto for life that works? Here: "The Liberator, Jesus, showed on the planet to sort the messed up," me being No. 1 on the "Messed Up" list. Which is exactly why he gave me some slack. If he could handle me – award-winning messer that I was – then everyone starts to think it's possible for them to get in on this limitless life. So total respect and all the credit, full on, for ever, goes out to the constant King, the limitless, imageless only God worth squat. Absolutely!

Good neighbourhood (1 Timothy 2:1-6)

Top priority: lobby God to do people good; but not just shopping lists – thank him for what's already happening. Put your neck on the block for them – break sweat doing it! Include the prime minister / first minister/ president / chancellor / king / whoever – keep on at God for peaceful estates, quiet parks, graffiti artists painting murals with something positive to say. Tell him how much you want to live next door to outstanding, pure, whole people. Good stuff like this makes our liberating God smile. He wants everyone straightened out, sorted and sussed on what it's all about. God never says, "I'd really love to see *him* stay totally messed up"! One God, one negotiator in shuttle diplomacy between God and us – the Liberator, Jesus, gave up his life to buy all humanity back from the enemy. The best news, delivered with perfect timing.

> And Paul's part of God's PA system: he outlines some of God's manifesto – people in touch with God, outlawing aggression, warning women who've got IT against flaunting IT, redefining "sexy". Job description for JLM leaders and administrators. Alarm bells for false coaching. Getting Timo ahead of the game … —Rob

Pump spiritual iron (1 Timothy 4:7-10)

7-8

Don't get suckered by ditties that rhyme, logos that look good, images that sell. Forget all that hype. Get into training to become more like God. You work out in the gym – great, as far as it goes. But training in God's gym goes *all the way*. It qualifies you for this life; it qualifies you for the next life.

9-10

Want another motto that works? "Our prospects are based on the Vibrant God who liberates everyone, especially those convinced by him." Worth working for, no?

> Paul tells Timo not to let them patronize him, just 'cos he's hardly shaving yet: "You've got it, so work at it." Coaching on how to work with different ages/classes/categories/talents – straight down the line, with no sucking up to the power-mongers...
> —Rob

Pounds, dollars, euros etc. (1 Timothy 6:3-21)

3-5

Some won't sign up to our coaching (which is direct from our Boss, Jesus the Liberator) aimed at producing godly people. I've not met them, but let me guess: they're cocky and don't know stuff all. They're heavy into the new, shocking ideas; they love a good verbal about word definitions and original meanings – they get off on winding up the competitive, contentious, nasty, dark, second-guessing side of people, stoking the fire with friction and fiction, rubbing each other up the wrong way till the sparks of frustration fly. They've got no clue what it's all about – they think religion is the route to becoming mega rich. Am I close? Is that them? Thought so.

6-10

Being like God *will* make you rich – but not (necessarily) in money terms. Isn't "rich" not needing anything else? Isn't "rich" being happy with what you've got? Are we born with a bulging wallet of readies? Nope. Has anyone found the exchange rate for swapping cash into heaven-dollars? Nope. But if we've got clothes to cover our skin and food to fill it with – great! The get-rich-quick wheeler-dealers get suckered by the smell of money: it drives them crazy. They chase after this deal, that deal, the other deal, the next deal, the BIG deal. Their office moves up twenty floors, bigger desk, bigger windows, bigger view – it goes to their heads, they're giddy, they push too far and go flying through the plate glass, crashing down to the gutter. Were they pushed? Did they jump? Whatever: they hit the street at terminal velocity. And it all comes back to their love affair with money – this Fatal Attraction, this Cash At All Costs. Download the mental image of a huge "Tree of

Evil", branches dripping with rancid fruit. Dig up the roots, hack them apart and what d'you find? This love affair with money is the sap oozing through the whole thing, feeding it, nourishing it. The fruit's poisoned many people's conviction; they've drifted off, doubled up with gut rot.

11-16

But, Timo, you're God's man, so leg it. Away from money's sweet-talking seduction. Towards doing the right thing. Towards being like God. Taking him at his word. Loving, loyal, lasting. Not loud. Not hard. Not harsh. But fighting the beautiful fight for what you're convinced of, and grabbing your limitless life with both hands. You stuck your neck out, you went public – it's yours. So I'm commissioning you, in front of God the life-giver, in front of the Liberator (who knows about sticking his neck out: ask Pontius Pilate) – live by the Maker's Instructions. Don't bend them or break them till our Boss, Jesus the Liberator, comes back spot on God's cue. The God who runs the show, tells kings where to go, the Boss of bosses, the only limitless leader, living in eye-melting light, the God who no one's ever seen, and no one could see. The God who gets our total respect and all our energy, absolutely.

17-19

Tell the loaded to stop strutting. Tell them money's not gilt-edged: banks crash, pension funds get looted. Money doesn't give you prospects – that's God's dept and he's handing out the goodies just for the fun of it (our fun, his fun). Tell them to do the right thing. To build up stocks and shares in "jobs done for people". To buy the drinks. To sneak off and pay the whole bill. Do all this and they'll get to heaven, check their bank statement and faint at the size of the opening balance. Now we're talking lasting prospects. Now they can get a grip on real life.

20-21

Timo, you've been given big stuff to look after. Guard it with your life. Don't waste your breath on words so shot through with flashy ideas that they can't carry God anymore. You know the poseurs I'm talking about. You know how they've lost it. Don't let that be you. Here's to God's generosity rubbing off on you.

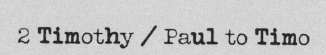

2 Timothy / Paul to Timo

(Last email)

From:	paul.benson@jailmail.rome.nt
To:	timo.apprentice@ephesus.org.tk
Date:	AD 67-ish
Subject:	Last-minute tips – hang in there

Paul's in jail again – not house arrest like before, but chained to cold stone walls, slopping out, death sentence hanging over his head. Time's up. "Got to see Timo one last time, or at least write . . ." —Rob

Keep it hot (2 Timothy 1:1-12)

Paul's missing Timo, who's from good family stock . . . —Rob

6-7

Which is why I'm saying don't let your fire burn out. I put my hands on you to launch your work (it's like it was yesterday) and God's flame was leaping about. But it *wasn't* yesterday – and fires go out if they're not kept up; so keep fanning the flames – keep it hot. 'Cos God doesn't give us a mouse mentality; this isn't a "Wimps for Jesus Club". No, we get spiritual muscle, passionate love for people and strong focus – all direct from God.

So don't bottle out of speaking up for the Boss. Don't go all quiet about yours truly, the prisoner. Show me some solidarity. Go through hassles with me to get the great news out by God's clout. He's straightened us out and sorted us, so now we stand out from the crowd. We're outstanding – and it's not down to us; it's all his planning, his generosity. Our Liberator, Jesus, booked it in our name right back before day one. He delivered the goods when he showed up in person. When he assassinated Death he sorted us, liberated us. He "Jesused" us. Then he escorted limitless life to the front of the stage, down into the crowd, and announced the great news – we get to keep it, take it home. Limitless life, no charge to us! And it's my job to coach people on how it all works, this incredible news. That's why I can handle all this victimization. In a bizarre way I'm proud of it – 'cos I know him, I'm convinced about him: everything I've handed over for him to sort, he'll keep it safe and dry till his Big Day comes round.

> "So keep going!" Paul's feeling deserted by the rest of the crew, but Timo and Onesiphorus have stuck with him ...   —Rob

Work at it (2 Timothy 2:1-7)

So, my boy, use your spiritual muscle on the gifts God's given you since you connected with the Liberator, Jesus. What you've picked up from me, hand on down to solid guys who can coach others. Tough it out with us, like army units in the Liberator's taskforce. Trained combat teams don't get sucked into the daily soap opera of normal life. No, the only thing that counts is the nod of approval from their officer in charge. Or if you're more into sport: the athlete doesn't get the gold if he's taken a short cut. Or agriculture: the farmer who sticks in the hours and pays out in sweat – he's the one who gets to spend the profits. Think about it! The Boss'll turn the lights on for you.

> More on being focused on the things that count – not on stupid brawling, but on doing the right thing, conviction, love, serenity.   —Rob

Them and us (2 Timothy 3:1-17)

1-5

Don't say I didn't warn you: before it all gets wrapped up, there'll be some ugly stuff flying round. People will have multiple love affairs – with themselves, with money. They'll be cocky, arrogant, mouthy. They'll ignore their parents. "Thanks" won't be in their vocab. They'll fit in with the rest of the polluted hate-culture. They'll only bother to talk if it's malicious. They'll only get off their backsides for a good scrap. Good things give them the creeps; they jump ship when it suits them; they do whatever when it suits them and they're so full of themselves they can't take any criticism on board. They'll love the next high more than God. They'll go through the motions of religion, but it'll be unplugged – God's power will be off at the mains. Don't waste your time on them.

> These men take advantage of people, esp. women. But Timo knows Paul's back-catalogue of God-events. Deception will go from worse to worst, but . . .   —Rob

14-17

But you! Keep on track with your training. You're convinced, so carry on, focused. You know where your coaching comes from – you've had the Instruction Manual since you were a toddler, and it's oozing wisdom. It sorts you out when you take the Liberator, Jesus, at his word. It's all straight from God's mouth, totally inspired. It's the only manual you need for coaching, counselling, correcting. If you want to be up and ready for every possible variation on Doing the Right Thing, then the Instruction Manual is the only book for you.

Job done (2 Timothy 4:1-8)

1-5

OK, this is big. (I'm writing this with God and the Liberator, Jesus, looking over my shoulder – who'll give the thumbs up or down to everyone alive or dead when he shows and sets up God's New World.) I tell you this: communicate what God says. I don't care if you feel like it or not, if they're responding or not. Just do it. Correct people if they're out of line, tell them off if they know it, build them up if they don't. Do it 'cos you care, and do it for the long haul. Pretty soon they won't want to know about good life-coaching. No, they'll scan and surf till they find people who'll tell them exactly what they want to hear – then they'll turn up the volume. Truth'll be drowned out by ocean loads of theory, wave after wave of trendy new ideas. But not you! No, keep your head on straight. Tough it out through the hard times; work at your communication; go down the checklist of your job description and make sure it's all being seen to.

6–8

My number's up. I've not got long. My life's leaking away already. Soon they'll unlock me and pour the rest of me out. But I've made a good scrap of it – I've given as good as I got. I've run through the pain barrier; I'm on the last lap and the finishing tape's in sight. I'm still convinced. Right now my head's just full of me and the Boss (the game's fair ref) standing together on the winner's podium. I'm shaking his hand, I'm bowing my head, he's putting the medal round my neck. Then I'm standing there, tears pouring down my face as they play God's New World Anthem. Whoa! The camera's pulling back and it's not just me – the podium's enormous, there's thousands of us, all blown away that it's finally happened . . . he's back.

> Paul wants Timo to visit. Maybe Mark can make it as well. He wants more writing stationary. He's feeling washed up and written off by some, but he leaves God to settle the scores. Says hi to the guys who've stuck by him.　　　–Rob

Cheers (2 Timothy 4:22)

The Boss stick to you like soul-scent, his generosity rub off on you.

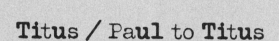

Titus / Paul to Titus

From:	paul.benson@teammail.nt
To:	titus.personal@jlmcrete.org.nt
Date:	AD 64-ish
Subject:	Living it, passing it on
Details:	Paul writes from Tour No. 4 to Titus who's running the Crete JLM. Crete was Sleaze City. Capital of lying down and lying to get away with it.
Quick bio:	Titus was "Foreigner, Exhibit No. 1" when Paul went to Jerusalem to explain how the JLM must export the great news from Israel. He sorted the collection for Jerusalem JLM in Corinth; delivered email No. 2 to Corinth; worked with Paul in Ephesus and Crete, where he stayed to hold the fort. Feisty, well organized, loyal. Rumours are, he's Dr Luke's bruv.

Admin advice on leader's qualifications, esp. since local Cretan lifestyle is dodgy ...
                                                                              −Rob

Pure (Titus 1:12-16)

Even a local-boy courier admits it:

> Q: How d'you know when a Cretan's lying?
> A: His lips move.

> Q: What's the difference between a Cretan and a couch potato?
> A: A couch potato has his eyes peeled.

> Q: What d'you call five hundred Cretans at the bottom of the
>   Mediterranean?
> A: A good start!

A bit cruel, but his routine's spot on. So lay into them for it! Their conviction's got to ring true. They've got to wipe the memory of all the Jewish old wives' tales and weird coaching ideas of those who've thrown out God's Manual. If you're pure, you see the pure in everything. If your conviction's been polluted, then everything's innuendo and smut. They've got three-track minds: filth, filth and more filth. They've had their conscience removed – it's in a jar on the shelf, curled up and comatosed. They spout off about how they and God are "this close". But their lifestyle gives them away – they've never even met him.

> Coaching notes for different ages, sexes, social status, all aimed at being a good advert for the Liberator. But they're not left on their own to grit their teeth and try harder ...   –Rob

How to say no (Titus 2:11-14)

The over-the-top generosity of God that straightens us out and sorts us is fully open to the public. It's this generosity that coaches us to say no to anti-God stuff and dark urges. Into the vacuum come focused lives, standing up for God-things despite current trends, lives with great prospects – the extravagant entrance of our fantastic God, our Liberator, Jesus. He gave up all his rights and became the ultimate virgin sacrifice to buy us back from the enemy's evil and to refine us into a movement he could call his own, a people who cross the road to do good.

> Filling in the details on what "doing good" looks like ...   –Rob

Spot the difference (Titus 3:3-9)

3-8

Classic before-and-after portraits:

- Before God's passion and generosity got through, this is how we looked (and were): stupid, rebellious, duped. Remote-controlled robots with Herman the hormone at the controls, smashing us round the fairground of life. There was a bitterness in our look, our mouths were twisted up by other people's success, our eyes projected pure hate to attack those who hated us.

- After God's passion and generosity got through, things changed: now there's a liberation about us, a release. We look rescued, freed. We look relieved, 'cos it wasn't a lifestyle change on our part that did it. It was God giving us a break. He signed us into his Spiritual Beauty Parlour, gave us the full works: washed us right through, so it's like we're reconceived, redeveloped, redelivered, reborn. Our Liberator, Jesus, massaged lashings of his Holy Spirit into us, all over us. And the end result is astonishing. Purified by his generosity, we walk out like princes and princesses – with the look of someone with serious wealth behind them who knows they're living life with no limits.

Some change, eh? You better believe it! It's about knowing what to underline, what to print up big and bold. Those who've committed to God must dedicate their lives to doing good things. Things that sparkle with excellence. Things that are worth something to everyone.

9

As opposed to finicky, hair-splitting, waste-of-space debates about disputes and family trees and indulgent waffle about this or that sub-clause in the Rules Manual. These are worth nothing to anyone. Winning points in these arguments is futility itself.

What to do with the debate-junkies. Some strategy and personnel changes. –Rob

Cheers (Titus 3:15)

All the crew here say hi to all you guys who love us 'cos we're JLMing. God's generosity rub off on you all.

Philemon /
Paul to Philemon

From:	paul.benson@jailmail.rome.nt
	timo.apprentice@teammail.nt
To:	philemon.trading@jlmhouse.colossae.com
Date:	AD 60-ish
Subject:	People change
Details:	Back six years to Paul's house arrest in Rome. Paul sends this letter as an attached file with his main letter to the JLM at Colossae.
Quick bio:	Philemon was part of the Colossae JLM. A slave owner (most middle classes were) who'd had a slave thieve from him and leg it. His name? Onesimus.
Quick bio:	Onesimus met Paul while on the run from the law. Life changed and he's now willing to turn round and come back "home". Problem is, Philemon, by law, could have the guy killed. Paul wants Philemon to take him back as a JLMer . . .

Matey intro. Memories of good times together . . .   —Rob

Things change (Philemon 8-22)

8-11

So with the Liberator's backing I could bite the bullet, pull rank on you and force your arm. But I'm not going to. No, this old man, this prisoner for the Liberator, Jesus, is just asking you to tune into love . . . for Onesimus. He's like a son to me now, a regular at visiting hours. He was a waste of space to you, but now he's a Godsend to me and you.

12-16

So I'm sending him – this is like mailing my heart back "home". My choice? No, I'd love him to stay as "your rep" while I'm stuck in here. But I need you to have a say in giving the guy the thumbs up. Maybe you lost him short term, to get him back permanent. Not as a worker: better than that – a new brother! My fav. Soon your fav.

17-20

So if we're working for the same thing, then take him in like he's me. Whatever he owes you, charge it to my account. This is my signature – I'll pay what's owed (I won't mention that you owe me your soul . . . oh, I did!). Do me good, eh? Do something refreshing. Give my deep places a boost. I know you will. You'll probably go over the top and make him a partner or something . . .

22

Sort the bedding in your spare room. I'm planning a trip your way.

Hi's from the crew in Rome.   –Rob

Cheers (Philemon 25)

The generosity of the Boss, Jesus the Liberator, soak into your soul.

Thirteen letters written on the road or in prison over ten/eleven years. Probably loads more lost through time. Rumours are that the Rome dungeon was Paul's last-known address and he was executed on the Ostian Way, Rome, in AD 68.   –Rob

Other Email Writers

Hebrews /
Jewish System Changes

From: (Printout torn off at top and lost – some tag it as Paul's or Barney's or Apollos's. We'll never be sure.)

To: (Lost – must be to guys who know the Jewish system)

Date: (Lost – but before AD 70: God's HQ bulldozed in 70 and no mention of rubble)

Subject: Jesus is up to it

Details: The anonymous book. The sender doesn't sign off – but the address book of mainly Jewish recipients obviously recognized his writing style / catch phrases / content / theme.

Quick bio: Impossible.

Couriers pass baton to Jesus (Hebrews 1:1-4)

Your history books show God getting through to our great-granddads via the couriers. Different styles, different eras, but always by courier. But lately he's contacting us direct through his Son – who owns everything, who made everything. The Son is more than just the spitting image of God: he is the "cell for cell", identical species – God's character to a T. The whole cosmos knows Jesus is the ultimate "he-who-must-be-obeyed". After he'd stepped in and taken the rap for our mess, he took up office right next to the King of heaven.

He's top, way beyond angels – they're mere nobodies by comparison. Whoa, there *is* no comparison!

Access all areas (Hebrews 2:8-18)

8-9

God gave him full freedom to open every Top Security file plus the clout to tell everyone where to go, when, how and not to have to explain why. There's no file in heaven's computer that'll give the dreaded "Access Denied" when Jesus taps in his password. Till now we've not seen him click on every "Apply" button, but we've seen him leapfrog the angels and rise back to the top from "ordinary bloke" to "King of Sheer Class", from "nobody" to "Respected Across the Cosmos". Why? 'Cos he went through death so God's generosity could kick in and he could mark it that he'd gone through it for everyone.

> Now those Jesus pulled through he calls "brothers/sisters".   –Rob

14-18

He connected with them by being totally human, so when he died he'd wipe out the one pulling Death's strings – the Devil – and liberate those strung up by panic attacks about death. This wasn't for the angels (they don't die!), but for Abraham's family tree. This is why he had to be flesh and blood, skin and bone. If he wasn't fully human, how could he relate to his "brothers/sisters"? How could he put his arm round them and say, "I know"? How could he represent them in God's courtroom? On top of that, he had to be human for his virgin sacrifice to work, for it to shift the mess that stopped God from being able to hug us. He went through hell when he was being teased, enticed, threatened. So when our dark side sucks us in, he's got the right to say something and he's got the sense to know what's worth saying!

> Jesus is a bigger noise than Moses. Quoting David's song lyrics (go to www
> .peoples-poetry.com.ot/songlyrics, track 95) re God's frustration with Moses' grip-
> ing Jews. "Don't copy them or you'll die in the 'desert' as well." The old "Battery
> Recharge Day" still stands – God wants us to rest, spend time with him . . . –Rob

God's Instruction Manual (Hebrews 4:12-16)

12-13

'Cos God's Instruction Manual is vivid, vibrant, action packed with spiritual muscle; it penetrates deeper than a Kalashnikov bullet – it gets

between body and soul, gets right into your joints, your bone marrow. It works out who's behind all your fronts. Nothing in the cosmos can hide from God. It all comes up on his monitor screens. Everything is digitally recorded, zoomed in on, watched and remembered by God's photographic memory. And we've got to stand there and explain it all in front of him! There'll be no bluffing.

14-16

Good job then we've got good representation! We've got a fantastic Chief Rep – Jesus, God's Son, already up there working on our case. So let's get a firm grip on our conviction; let's make sure it's not just talk. Our Rep isn't distant and cold; he doesn't sit there tutting at our pathetic mess-ups. No, he's been through it all. Been "that close" to everything we've gone through. He's like us: same drives, same needs. Only difference is, it didn't sucker him. He felt the pressure and walked away unpolluted. So now it's on for us to walk up to God's Throne of Generosity and come away fully acquitted and full of God's gifts for the next time the temperature's rising.

> The Jewish system defined the job of chief rep as the middleman between God and people. He ran the sacrifices that put temporary cover on our mess ... –Rob

Jesus' learning curve (Hebrews 5:7-10)

When Jesus was down here he begged God not to let him die. Buckets of tears, sky-piercing screams. And God heard 'cos Jesus didn't make demands: he respected God enough just to ask. He was God's Son, but he still had to learn to do the right thing through sheer blood, sweat and tears. And he did! Thousand percent. Which meant liberation with no limits for everyone living his way. So God signed him in as Chief Rep, like Melchizedek was way back – both Chief Rep and King!

> Paul/Barney/Apollos/whoever (the writer) is narked that he still has to coach the readers/listeners on the basics – the breast milk instead of solid steaks. "Grow up!" he tells them. "God'll keep his side of the New Contract; you work on yours." This New Contract with the Jews leaves the Old Contract redundant and rusty. The old HQ had all the sacrificial trappings, memorabilia, traditions. Now all that killing of goats and bulls is just a trailer to what Jesus did when he became the sacrifice.
> Compared to goats' blood ...   –Rob

Jesus' blood: better than goats' blood
(Hebrews 9:14-28)

14

How many million times better is the Liberator's blood for detoxifying the attitudes that drag us down to death? He offered his unpolluted life, his innocence, for the limitless Spirit to present before God. No goat throats to cut. Now he's made it possible for us to get through to the Vibrant God and work with him.

15

That's why the Liberator's the one to set up the New Contract. That those picked out can get their paws on the promised limitless windfall. He's paid the ransom demand, which was his life, and he's liberated them from the mess they'd got into with the Old Contract.

> Blood's the thing. Both Old and New Contracts work on blood getting spilt. In the Old – goats, calves etc. In the New – Jesus' blood. No blood? No wiping the slate clean. The other difference is that Jesus needed to die only once . . . —Rob

27-28

People die only once; then they face God in his courtroom. The Liberator was sacrificed once to wipe the mess off a trillion slates. He'll show up a second time, not to take our mess away, but to move into the final phase of liberation for those looking out for him.

Clean start (Hebrews 10:15-25)

> The old System only held off the pollution for a while. But the New Contract is a permanent job . . . —Rob

15-18

God's Holy Spirit tells us, "God says this is my side of the New Contract: I'll plant my principles in their deep places, tattoo my ideas into their thinking." And more, "I'll wipe the mess off their slates permanently. I'll lose the hard drive that holds the charges and evidence against them. I'll forgive and forget." And when there's nothing to clean up, why d'you need another sacrifice? You don't – it's done and dusted.

19-25

So, guys, Jesus' body and blood gives us the "all clear" to go through the barrier into God's private place by this vibrant new way. And, on top, we've got a fantastic Chief Rep. So let's make the most of it! Let's spend time up close and personal with God. Let's cut the banter and get serious about our convictions. Let's clean up our crevices so our actions and thinking don't stink the place out. Let's not shift from the prospects up ahead – he said it; he'll make it happen. Let's think through the best way to get each other into gear – loving people and doing the right thing. Let's meet up, regular, not skiving off like some slackers. Let's motivate each other, especially as Jesus' Big Day isn't far off. Come on! Let's.

> But if his people kick sand in Jesus' face, then God'll try us, find us guilty and deal with it. Scary! In the early days you took the victimization on the chin. Police confiscated JLM property, stuck you in jail, but you took it. Get that back. That defiance. That spunk. 'Cos . . .   —Rob

Taking God at his word (Hebrews 10:37-11:40)

37-39

Pretty soon old Habakkuk's line will ring true:

> The one you're waiting for *will* come: to hang around would be absurd.
> The people down in my book as clean are the ones who take me at my word.
> If they bottle and go on the retreat – I'll be so down, my disappointment complete.

Hey! Are we bottlers? Do we freeze? Do we curl up and die? No! We take God at his word that we're sorted. And we are.

11:1-3

What's "taking God at his word" mean? Let me fill you in. It's being dead sure of our prospects. It's being sold on something we've no evidence for, convinced when there's no proof. And it's what the old heroes had truckloads of . . .

"How do we KNOW God made this place? We take God at his word. That was the difference between Cain and Abel: Abel did; Cain didn't. Enoch did too – and God was so chuffed, he let him sidestep death and go straight up to heaven! You can't make God smile if you're not dead sure what he says is on the level.   –Rob

7

Taking God at his word is what got Noah off his backside. The weather forecast came through, but there was no proof, no evidence. But pure respect got him building the boat to protect his family. He was dead sure, convinced, and that was the difference. The world went under and he ended up with a clean slate, because he took God's severe-storm warning seriously.

8–9

Same for Abraham. He got his travel instructions to go stake his claim for land. He upped and went, even though he had no map, no directions, no anything. But he was sold on what God had said, so he pitched his tent in the land he'd been promised. He lived with Isaac and Jacob as nomads, just 'cos they'd had God's word and were convinced he was serious.

Same with God's promise about them having a baby. Abraham and Sarah were well past it, but God said there'd be kids, and the old man got his boy, his "nation in the making". All these guys died still gripping their heavenly visa, and God was so proud he was up the scaffolding finishing off their new pads in his place. God pushed Abraham's trust even further by asking him to sacrifice his boy. Total confusion. But Abraham had the knife ready . . . even though it made no sense . . . till the angel called time out and did a body swap: Isaac for a long-horned ram. Abraham had no clue what was going on; he just hung on to what God had said. The others, Isaac, Jacob, Joseph, were chips off the old block. All of them took God at his word . . .   –Rob

23–26

Same thing made Moses' mum invent the Moses Basket. His parents knew he wasn't just any old baby and weren't freaked about Pharaoh's infanticide ruling. Same thing made the grown-up Moses disown his adopted parents and "come out" as a Jew rather than pose with the Egyptian jet set. He weighed up the long-term pay-off of chucking the high life and slumming it with the Liberator for a while.

Later all the Jews had to take God at his word when the Red Sea split down the middle. The path looked dry, but they still had to step on it.   –Rob

32-38

Time's too short to talk about Gideon, Barak, Samson, Jephthah, David, Samuel, all the couriers. Taking God at his word was the key to a new nation, to justice, to collecting on the promises of God. Acting blind on what he'd said made lions shut their mouths, made blazing ovens more like saunas, made knives go off target, made wimps into black belts, made beaten troops attack and win. Women got their husbands/sons back from the dead. Others were tortured, but they wouldn't crack even when the release deal was there to sign. No, they were sold on having an incredible next life, so they stuck it out. Some took public humiliation on the chin, knowing sick jokes about them were doing the circuit. Others took punishment beatings. Some were locked up, lynched. Others were hanged, drawn and quartered – even sliced up. They were homeless, vagrants, victimized, abused. But they were too good for this world. They were outsiders, loners, living in shop doorways, under bridges, in sewers.

39-40

All these guys were given medals for taking God at his word. But they only got what God said was due to them *after* they died. See, God has exciting plans for our lives, which means we could all stand up on the medal rostrum together, them and us – but only once we've finished our race.

Good coaching (Hebrews 12:1-29)

1-3

Since all these old-timers are now looking down from their stadium seats, shouting our names like we're their heroes, let's kick off the stuff that's tripping us up, let's untie the mess that weighs us down and let's run! Let's channel our stamina reserves and run the race we've been entered for. Let's focus our minds on Jesus, who made us, who coached us: he's there at the finishing line. He went through the hell of execution; he stomached total humiliation so he could take his place in the top office of heaven. While you're running, lock your mind on to him and the pain barriers he pushed through, the blockades put up by messed-up men that he had to dive through. Lock on to him and fatigue won't touch you, you'll have that deep inner belief, and you'll keep going.

> "How bad's it been? Have you drawn blood yet?" —Rob

7-11

Treat these hassles like a good workout. God's just being a dad. Every son knows how dads try and knock off our rough edges. If he doesn't bother (and they all do), then maybe you're not his! We've all had human dads who've stood up to us and we've respected them for it later. So times that by a hundred to show how we've got to take in what our spiritual Father says. Our dads did their best to knock us into shape, and God coaches us so we might stand out like he's outstanding. I'm not saying you'll enjoy it! It'll probably be a rough ride. But it'll build your fitness, and later you'll see the good things that you couldn't have done without it. You'll sense the satisfaction it brings.

> Lifestyle instructions: aim for an obituary along the lines of "Serene . . . outstanding . . . pure". Reminders that God's still awesome, old stories about Moses losing it at the sight of God. So get in line . . . —Rob

28-29

We're signing up for God's Permanent New World package. So let's show some gratitude. Let's work for him out of respect for who he is. Like Moses said, "Our God is a raging forest fire."

> Final tips on lifestyle — love, hospitality, prison visits, decent marriages, simple living, respect for leaders, straight coaching, asking God to support others. —Rob

Cheers (Hebrews 13:25)

God's generosity rub off on all you guys.

James / James to JLM-Jews

From:	james.davidson@jlm.jerusalem.nt
To:	jlm-jews@global.org
Date:	Before AD 50 (probably)
Subject:	Actions shout; words whisper
Details:	A circular memo from the (technically, half-) brother of Jesus. One of the earliest letters to make it into the final compilation.
Quick bio:	First off, James was dubious about Jesus' antics, but he was won over and Paul talks of him as one of the pillars of the church. Now James is Mr Practical (no surprise, being from a carpentry family). He's heard too many people spout off about their convictions and not back them up with lifestyle proof.
Writing style:	Vivid with loads of everyday visual aids to bring his point to life (where'd he get that approach from then?!).

Hassles (James 1:2-8)

A hundred types of hassle? Then change your attitude: think of them as an exhilarating roller-coaster ride. Enjoy it. What?! See, hassles build stamina and stamina stays the distance. End product: you're the genuine article, finished and polished, batteries included. So enjoy the hassles! If your wisdom account's in the red, just ask God. He's over the top in the generosity dept. There's no huge checklist of qualifications – he just doles it out. The only condition is that the request is put in with confidence, expecting results. Hardened cynics are like plastic bags, full of air, out of control, blown about the street. They get a big fat zero from God. Their two-faced, doublespeak schemes make them stable as a two-legged chair.

> Status games – all change! Money doesn't make God's World go round. When the dark side sucks us in, don't blame God. It's only good stuff from his direction …
>
> –Rob

Just do it! (James 1:19-27)

19-21

Guys, you taking notes? Get this down: How many ears you got? Two. How many mouths? One. Two to one's about the right ratio. Listen twice as much as you talk. And put an extension on that short fuse of yours, 'cos losing your cool doesn't help you live right as God wants. So kick out the evil that oozes out of every wall. Get a handle on your status and let God build his lifestyle into you and sort you out, body and soul.

22-25

Just reading the coaching manual doesn't get you to peak fitness. Get off your backside and do it! Anyone just watching the training video from the luxury of his own sofa is like someone who looks at himself in the mirror, walks off and forgets what he looks like. But those who use God's Contract as a mirror, who look into it, keep looking into it and find freedom in it – if they take on what they see and turn it into lifestyle, then they'll be well happy.

26-27

So you think you're religious, do you? Well, if you can't control your mouth, then you're in denial and your religion's a waste of time. Religion that means something with Father God is this: looking out for the homeless, empowering those in the poverty trap and keeping yourself from getting polluted by the System.

> Don't get suckered by rich people – they're no more important than Ordinary Joe. All the "isms" – classism, racism, sexism etc. – are out, not just 'cos it's PC, but 'cos you "love the next guy like he's you".
>
> –Rob

Prove it (James 2:14-19)

14-17

What's the point, guys, if someone spouts off about his religion but his lifestyle just doesn't add up? Is this religion going to straighten his life out? Is it going to sort him? Picture the scene: this tramp comes in, coat in shreds, looking like he needs a square meal or ten; someone says to him, "All the best, good luck, here's to you finding a warm bed and a four-course meal." What use is that?! Ditto with your religion – unless you're putting ideas into action, it's a waste of space.

18-19

'Course, some smart alec spouts, "I'm into religion; you're into social action." You show off your religion like a badge, and I'll prove my religion by doing something about it. Having a set of views about God and religion doesn't change a thing. OK, so you reckon there's one God. Big deal! So do the demons, and it freaks them thinking about it.

> Back to Abraham: the original Mr Practical. Not just "all religious talk", but gritty, gutsy actions, which cost him.
> —Rob

Watch your lip (James 3:1-12)

1-2

Guys, don't push yourself forward to be a life coach, 'cos there's a different set of rules applied to those who've told others where to go / what to do / how to be . . . much tougher. We all mess up in loads of ways. But if you never open your mouth and put your foot in it, then you're perfect. If you can control your mouth, then you've got it all figured out.

3-6

How d'you control a racehorse? With a bridle. Where's the bridle bit go? In the horse's mouth. Pull it left and the whole animal moves left. Right and she moves right. How d'you steer a ship? Tons of metal, massive waves and all you need is a (relatively) small rudder and the ship ends up where the captain steers it. Even the biggest mouth is only small compared to the rest of the body, but it's got big ideas about itself. It takes only one match to burn a thousand trees, and your mouth seems to be a bit of an arsonist. This pyromaniac part of your body is up for burning more than your fingers. It's a lighter fuelled by hell's own white spirit, bent on total destruction.

7-8

Been to a zoo lately, or an aquarium, or a circus? Seen animals trained to jump through hoops, balance beach balls, clap hands, deliver punch-lines? We can train most animals to do something, but can we train our own mouth? Not a chance. It's evil waiting to happen. It's a poison pouch, lethal.

9-12

Our mouths sing worship songs to our Boss, our Father; then, over coffee, the same mouth slags off someone who's made with God's character built in. One minute: holyspeak. Next minute: a filth fountain. All with the same mouth?! Guys, we're out of line. Spa sources don't produce pure mineral water one minute and then putrid gunk the next. You can't get drinking water out of a sewer. It may all be on the same shelf, but apples and pears come off different trees!

> James goes on, "The product of the enemy's farming techniques are basically rotten, whatever the packaging may say. But heaven's output is pure, organic, wholesome, nutritious, healthy.
>
> "You scrap among yourselves 'cos you're at war with yourself. Give God your Wants List; he'll suss if they're for you or for spreading around. Choose who you're mates with – God or the System. Put out the welcome signs for God; lay barbed wire against the Devil and he'll slither off. Don't slam down on other JLMers. Don't assume you've got tomorrow to play with – scribble into your day planner, every page, 'if God gives the go-ahead'. You fat cats have got hell to pay: God's heard your trade union rep's complaints about wages back payments owing. But you were too busy selecting the shade of your new Merc to spot families going down the toilet. Don't look for a spring harvest – wait for the Boss's arrival like a farmer waits for his crop to ripen in autumn. In the meantime it'll be rough, but if Job could stick it out, so can you. Keep your word. Ask God for things. Admit your mistakes to each other. God listens to people with integrity – check out Elijah and the weather forecast episode: God responds!"
>
> —Rob

PS (James 5:19-20)

Guys, if someone jaywalks off from God's way and someone else escorts them back – they're cheating death, they're wiping out miles of mess.

1 Peter /
Pete's Circular No. 1

(Email No. 1)

From: pete.fishman@babylon.akarome.nt
silas.ghostwriter@babylon.akarome.nt

To: jlm.pontus@turkey.org
jlm.galatia@turkey.org
jlm.cappadocia@turkey.org
jlm.asia@turkey.org
jlm.bithynia@turkey.org

Date: Early AD 60s

Subject: Hang in there; it's all part of the prep

Quick bio: Pete is the local boy made good, the working class hero, an inspirational figure – starting life as a fisherman and ending up as one of the main men in the JLM. So his motivational writings are just the medicine in these times of hassle . . .

"JLM-bating" is the latest social fad. The crew are struggling to face up to it all.
                    –Rob

Stand out (1 Peter 1:3-25)

3-9

All credit goes to God, Father of our Boss, Jesus the Liberator. He's given us incredible amounts of slack by taking on the role of midwife and drawing us out into new horizons of life. And all because Jesus the Liberator defied death by coming back alive after execution. Now we've got access to some serious funding that's not going to crash, go belly up or get lifted, 'cos it's stored in heaven and it's got your name on it. You take God at his word when he says he's got his bodyguards on alert for you till the Big Day when liberation gets let off the leash. No wonder it gets you going. OK, so right now it's tough and you might be pushed to the limit, but it's all part of the prep to get your spiritual muscles (better than gold medals or slabs) at peak fitness for the new era. Then you won't just scrape through Qualification, but you'll peak just at the right time and Jesus the Liberator will turn up and get the credit, attention, respect he deserves. You've no clue what he actually looks like, but you love him. You've not shaken his hand, but you're convinced, and the buzz is better than any other high. You're already getting the pay-off of your religion – liberation for the soul.

10-12

The couriers picked up the clues on the freebies flowing your way with this liberation. They spent hours chewing it over, trying to work out the timetable, the setting. They knew the Liberator's Spirit was downloading all this about the Liberator going through the darkest night of any soul and then out the other side into wild celebratory laps of honour. They also sensed it wasn't for them but for you they were wrestling with it all. They knew they were setting up the coaches who'd lay it all out for you and God's Holy Spirit from heaven to make the connections. Even angels don't get access to these files!

13-16

So get your head straight and shift into action mode; get your discipline together, focus on your prospects of the gifts you'll get when Jesus the Liberator is fully profiled. Like kids who do what they're told, don't just go along with the dark urges that used to run things when you didn't know better. The one who picked you stands out as Pure, right through. So you are to stand out from the crowd in everything you get into. Like it says, "Stand out as outstanding, like I do" (go to www.instruction-manual.com.ot/God-repsordersofservice).

17-21

Given that the Father you talk to assesses everyone's track record without any bias, let your lifestyle down here prove it: let your respect for God make you live like you don't quite belong. You were brought down from the shelf of your pointless existence and bought back, but the deal wasn't made in cheap currency like gold or silver. No, the priceless blood of the Liberator is what bought your escape papers. You got out of the waste-of-space-place you'd inherited from your old man and his old man before him. The Liberator was the Perfect Virgin Sacrifice, selected before the world got off the drawing board, but profiled only recently for you. He's your link with God who brought him back from the dead and elevated him so now you can really say that all your conviction, all your prospects, are wrapped up in God.

22-25

Now you've got your act cleaned up by taking in and taking on the truth, you can love the rest of the crew. So go for it. Love them, full on. You've been reconceived, redeveloped, redelivered, reborn, but this time not just by human sperm breaking through human egg (with all its built-in obsolescence). No, this time you're born with God's DNA surging through your body. Like Isaiah says (go to www.couriershotline.com.ot/nopainnogain):

> People are like blades of grass.
> Their best years, like the short flowering season, don't last –
>   they're gone.
> Grass gets mown down, flowers droop and drop off,
> But the Boss's message stands strong and long.

You know this; you got it loud and clear.

Delete the dark stuff (1 Peter 2:1-12)

1-3

So . . . click "delete" on the software that makes you mean-minded, fork-tongued, two-faced, green-eyed and foul-mouthed. Be like babies, crying out, desperate for spiritual breast milk – it's the only way to grow in your liberation, now you've sampled God's appetizer.

4-8

Come up close and personal with him, the living stone — which the builders chucked into the dump, but God lifted out saying, "Priceless!" Now you too are like living bricks being cemented into place in the spiritual skyscraper God's constructing. You're being picked out as God's reps standing in the middle and making sacrifices God welcomes, 'cos you're connected with Jesus the Liberator. Like Isaiah put it:

> Look, here's the foundation stone. Fixed in Jerusalem's rock.
> Priceless and select this foundation stone.
> People who rely on him, who comply with him,
> You won't be able to mock.

You're into this, so this stone is priceless. But it's gone over most people's heads:

> The stone the builders chucked in the skip
> Has become the crucial foundation stone.
> For them it's
> A boulder for falling over.
> A rock that blocks their road.

They go flying 'cos they won't take the coaching on board — that's their fate.

9-10

But not you guys. No, no, no. You are the select, royalty in the role of God's reps to the people, an outstanding nation of ambassadors for God. You live and breathe to profile and celebrate the one who picked you up out of your dark grovellings and stood you in his brilliant light. One time you had no national identity; now you've got the full complement of work visas and passports of God's Nation. Once you only had what you deserved; now God's giving you breaks you'd never have expected.

11-12

So my great mates, I'm begging you — you're foreigners down here, outsiders, so have the guts to say no to all the messed-up urges that snipe away at your soul. Let your lifestyle be like a magnet for the locals. Let them charge you, try and sue you, but in court the jury will see a rare thing — a prosecution lawyer lost for words. And the papers'll write the headlines: "God turns up to take the credit".

Anarchy isn't the way; respect is. Work hard, even if your boss is a hard-nosed money-grabber. God sees your integrity. Jesus is your template... —Rob

Jesus' "steel jaw" (1 Peter 2:21-25)

This is your job spec: take Jesus' example when he took it on the chin for you. Again, Isaiah's covered it:

> He was totally in the clear. No blood on his hands.
> No hint of half a truth in his mouth.

When they slammed into him with libel and defamation of character, he didn't chat back. When they laid into him with their boots and bats, he didn't mark their card. No, he relaxed into knowing that the Judge will call the shots in the end. So he took on our mess till it looked like it was his, and he went to his execution like a dead man walking. Why? So we might be separated from our mess like a dead man from life. *And* that we might live to do the right thing. The punishment beating that left him half-human made us whole and fully human. You were like lost boys, wandering off mindlessly. Now you're back and your Security Officer, your minder, your mentor is looking out for your souls.

Family advice esp. for wives of non-JLMers. Beauty tips beyond the skin deep for the women. Instructions on respect for the wives. Don't all sing the same melody, but make sure your version harmonizes. Don't play tennis with the hand grenades of evil; defuse them and chuck something good back. And if they still try and blow you off the scene, you're still OK 'cos the Liberator's ultimately in charge. —Rob

Final countdown (1 Peter 4:1-11)

1-6

So given that the Liberator went through physical agony, take on the same attitude — 'cos the guy that's gone through the pain barrier has had it with the mess that spawns pain. Result? People don't live down here just for the kicks they can get out of it, but for what God wants to make happen. Enough time's been wasted already in those trendy, raunchy, dirty, drunken orgies where they worship the worthless. They look at you sideways, slag you off, when you don't dive into the deep end of shallow sex. But they'll have to stand in heaven's courtroom and give their report to the Judge of the living and dead. Which is why the good news had to be profiled even to those who've since died. OK, so they're dead – everyone has to go sometime – but they're still in line for the life God's Spirit has set up for them.

7-11

The Final Showdown is ticking closer. So get your heads straight and focus so you can spend quality time talking with God. Top priority: love each other, full on. 'Cos love makes up for mountains of mess. Cook meals, buy drinks, put people up without scoring points. What's your talent? Channel it to help others, doling out God's bonuses for the long haul and not just a weekend whim. If your talent's your mouth, make sure it's God's vocab tripping out. If your talent's more practical, plug into God's stamina supplies. The aim is for God to get celebrated through whatever Jesus the Liberator gets done through you. He'll take all the credit and clout, always, absolutely.

> The hassles are all part of the prep – connecting with the Liberator. It'll be worth it. Hang in there. You people who run the JLMs, don't do it for the cash or 'cos you have to. Do it to do others good. You young guys, show some respect to the seniors. Focus. Keep on your toes. Stare out Satan and watch him skulk off into the shadows. Show solidarity with other JLMers who are toughing it out too . . .
>
> –Rob

Spiritual muscle (1 Peter 5:10-11)

And the God of total generosity, who picked you out for limitless party-time through your link with the Liberator (once you've gone through some rough stuff) – he'll build your spiritual muscle back up, make you solid, strong and sound. Give him total clout, always and longer, absolutely.

Pete and Silas signing off.   –Rob

Cheers (1 Peter 5:14)

When you meet up, show you love each other with a kiss. Serenity to all of you linked with the Liberator.

2 Peter /
Pete's Circular No. 2

(Email No. 2)

From: pete.fishman@rome.nt

To: jlm.pontus@turkey.org
             jlm.galatia@turkey.org
             jlm.cappadocia@turkey.org
             jlm.asia@turkey.org
             jlm.bithynia@turkey.org

Date: (Printing unclear: could be AD 65–68
             or AD 105–108)

Subject: How long till the sequel starts? Which life coach to
             go with?

Life before "J Day". How to handle dodgy life coaches in JLM groups.   —Rob

All you need (2 Peter 1:2-9)

2–4

Here's to you being saturated with God's generosity and serenity by getting to know God and Jesus our Boss intimately. We've got all we need. It's all there. God's set everything up. 'Cos we're well in with the one who picked us out, God's power, brilliance and goodness are on tap for us to live life his way. His direct-inject connection pumps in his promises and we get to opt out of the polluted System of dark cravings and get involved with divinity.

5-9

Which is why you should be busting a gut to top up your conviction with good living, then add some sense, then pile on some discipline, mix in some stamina, some godliness, some comradeship and cover the whole thing with lashings of love. If you've got these ingredients in catering-pack sizes, then you won't be a waste of space. No, with this recipe your connection with our Boss, Jesus the Liberator, *will* make a difference. If you skimp on the portions, or miss some of them out completely, then you're blind as a bat with the memory of a goldfish – how can you go blank on how your previous mess got cleaned up?

> Pete's getting on, but he reminds them he was an eyewitness of Jesus Davidson. Warnings about dodgy life coaches, but they'll get what's coming to them and it won't be pretty...   –Rob

God's angry side (2 Peter 2:4-22)

4-10

If God didn't turn a blind eye when the angels messed up but blasted them over heaven's balcony into hell's cells to wait for Judgement Day, if he didn't pretend not to notice when Noah's world was screwed up but flash-flooded them off the face of the planet (except the good-living Noah Lamechson and Co.), if he "nuked" the cities of Sodom and Gomorrah down to dust bowls of ash and cinder, as a huge signpost to what the pay-off is from anti-God activity (except the good-living Lot Haranson who puked up at the warped sex going on around him), if God did all this – then he's well up on how to throw a lifeline to people living his way who're swimming upstream against the flood waters of filth. He also knows how to incarcerate those stirring up the dirt, giving them hard labour even before their final showing on Judgement Day – especially the puppets dragged through the mud by the sick thinking of their dark side that flicks the vick at any authority.

> Pete heaps more bile against these people who mess up innocent lives, ending with...   –Rob

21-22

It would've been way better for them if they'd never even heard of living God's way rather than taking it on, then tossing the Sacred Manuals out the window. Like the old sayings go, "You can't stop a dog from eating its own sick." Or "An hour polishing the pig, a minute later she's back rolling in the mud."

Judgement Day (2 Peter 3:3-13)

3-7

First up, know this: at about "quarter to twelve" on the countdown to Judgement Day, you won't be able to move for cynics. These sceptics just go with their own dark urges. They'll go, "When's this Big Day, then? When's his Big Come Back he promised? What's the ETA? It's been yonks now and everything's just like it was from the start." But they make a point of blanking out the clout of God when he talks: he gave the order and the cosmos came out of the prime element – water; he gave the order and the same water wiped the sick grin off the face of the planet. Same voice, same order, same clout has labelled our very own universe "Reserved for roasting with the anti-God geeks on Judgement Day".

8-9

What you've lost track of is this, my mates: to our Boss a day or a thousand years, thousand years or a day – no difference. This Big Come Back he promised: he's not slacking or forgetful or behind schedule. No, he's stretching it out to give you some space. His jackpot result would be that no one gets taken out and everyone turns their lives back round to him.

10

But God's Big Day will creep up on you like a top computer hacker. You'll have no idea he's lurking in the long grass of cyberspace; then, from nowhere, he'll click his mouse and it's too late: when God says "Go!" the cosmos will roar past into a black hole, imploding on itself, leaving nothing, not even a vacuum. The atoms will be BBQ'd beyond existence. The planet will be judged and sentenced to fry.

11-13

Since everything's going to be atomized and then the atoms are going to be split, sliced, ground and scattered, whose side d'you fancy being on then?! What lifestyle you going to take on? One that stands out as godly when you're on your toes waiting for his Big Day to come, the Day of flames burning up the stars, the Day of the elements melting in the heat? But part two of the promise was that there'd be a brand-new cosmos, a brand-new planet to look forward to, where doing the right thing is the way everything works.

> This isn't news to you. But don't get sidelined by fast-talking, law-ignoring types. No, prove God's generosity, get to know him better, give him the credit.   —Rob

Cheers (2 Peter 3:18)

May our Boss, Jesus the Liberator, take all the credit now and into the future, for ever. Absolutely!

1 John /
Jonno's Turkish Circular

(Email No. 1)

From:	jonno.zebson@jlm-love/light.nt
To:	jlm.local@turkey.org
Date:	AD 85–100 (just after his bio of the Liberator)
Subject:	Love matters and matter matters
Quick bio:	Jonno was Jesus Davidson's first cousin, ex-fisherman and one of the inner circle of the team. He wrote one of the four authorized bios of the Liberator and Revelation (wait for it!). He runs the local JLM, but some guys have the idea Jesus wasn't 100 percent human (too good to be true) and set up their own separatist cult – "The Anti-Earth Group" – who reckoned the physical world was evil and had no chance of getting cleaned up. Jonno writes to put them straight – you cut Jesus, you got blood; you beat him, he bruised. He was the real thing, right through to the smallest cell. Jonno knows – he was there!

Clean slates (1 John 1:1-10)

1-4

I've seen the Real Thing. He was around from way back before history heard the starting gun. I was there! I heard him, clocked my eyes on him, hugged him. This is what I say about "God's Voice": he showed up out of the blue (literally); some of us saw him and we'd swear in court that he's the genuine article. This limitless life God has the rights to, which we've cottoned on to, we broadcast it, publish it, log it, launch it into cyber space. But you can't separate it from our story, our auto-biography; it got to us – we tell it this way, so you connect with us, like we've connected with the Father and with his Son, Jesus the Liberator. So writing this, sharing our stories, is the ultimate buzz.

5-7

He gave us so much to pass on to you: God is pure, multispectral Light. He doesn't do Darkness. If we brag about our links with him but our lifestyle stinks of dark, dank and dodgy, then we're lying through our toothy grins. But if God's projecting his light through our lives, like he did with the Liberator, then we can really connect with each other since the blood of his Son, Jesus, cleans up our mess.

8-10

If we make out we've got no mess to clean up, we're deluding ourselves and living in denial. But if we face up to it, admit to God that we've messed up, then he sticks by us and sticks by his Rules, wipes our slate clean and refines us. If we bluff that we're in the clear, we're making God out to be a liar and just proving that we've not heard a word he's said.

Council for the defence (1 John 2:1-11)

1-2

My precious children, I'm tapping all this in so you won't mess up. But if you do, we've got an advocate/sponsor/mate who's putting in good words for us with the Father – Jesus the Liberator, the Sorted One. He's the sacrifice that created the interface between us and God and wiped out our mess that got in the way. And not just our own personal mess-mound, but the Everest of global mess.

3-6

Proof positive of whether we've connected with him is if we do what he told us. The guy who goes, "Jesus? Yeah me and him are, like, really close," but doesn't live like Jesus laid down, he's just full of guff. He's had an integrity-bypass operation and he's only just coming round from the anaesthetic. But the guy whose lifestyle matches Jesus' guidelines, he really does love God. You looking for proof of our connection with him? This is it: our lifestyle's got to match up with the lifestyle Jesus had.

7-8

My mates, this isn't some new instruction I've just come up with. No, this is the well-established, tested, time-honoured instruction you heard first up, from the start. It just sounds new since he's changed the paradigm – since the night's been chased out of the corners by the new day creeping over the rooftops.

9-11

Anyone spouting off about living in the light, but then would drop his own brother given the chance, is still in the dark. Living in the light means loving your brother. Living in the light means you don't trip up. If you can't stand your brother you're still in the dark, groping around like a blind man, feeling your way through places you've never seen.

Systematic? (1 John 2:15-17)

Don't get off on your infatuation with the Global System. Don't get off on anything to do with the System. If you're into the System, then how can you be into the Father? It just doesn't add up. For the System stinks of the cravings of messed-up people leering and bragging about everything they've had and done. No way any of that stuff is generated by God's Set-Up. No, that smacks of Global Filth Incorporated through and through. But the whole System's got a built-in design flaw; it's bankrupt, it'll go under. But the guy who lives within God's Set-Up will have life with no limits.

> The countdown to the Big Day is on – we're in the eleventh hour. The Anti-Liberator is in the wings, lines learnt, warmed up and waiting for his cue. So don't get sidelined. Keep online to God so you don't get shown up when the evil one shows.   —Rob

God's kids (1 John 3:1-24)

1-3

How good is this then? God's poured out his love on us like a power shower by calling us his kids!!! And we are! Which explains why the System doesn't recognize our ID – it missed *him* when he came, so why should it recognize *us?* Mates, we're God's kids! We haven't sussed all the pay-offs from this yet, but when he shows we know we'll be redesigned as spitting images of him – 'cos we'll see him as he really is now. And if you've got these prospects, then it cleans up your lifestyle in line with his.

4-6

Every time you mess up, you break the Contract. Definition of "Mess" = Contract Broken. But you're well up on the fact that he showed to get rid of our mess. He had no mess. No one connected with him keeps on messing up. Anyone who does, obviously hasn't met him.

7-10

Precious children, don't let anyone tie you up and tow you off. Anyone who does the right thing is sorted in God's books, like Jesus is. Anyone who keeps on messing up is one of the Devil's cronies, 'cos the Devil's been messing up from day one. Which is why God's Son made his entrance – to send the bulldozers in on his dark empire. Anyone born into God's New Family won't carry on messing up like before, 'cos God's DNA stays in them, so how can they keep messing up? *God's* their Father! The foolproof test in the paternity dispute – take swabs of lifestyle and the one that shows no evidence of someone doing the right thing, they can't be God's kid. Not possible. Same goes for anyone who hates his brother.

11

Which gets us back full circle to where you came in – love each other!

Quick history lesson on Cain's first-degree murder of his brother Abel.   –Rob

16-20

So how do we know what "love" is? We've seen the walking definition – Jesus the Liberator handed in his life-rights for us. Likewise, we should be handing in our lives for our brothers/sisters. Picture this: some rich guy knows his brother's bankrupt, but snuggles up in his top-of-the-range waterbed and loses no sleep over it. How can God's love be pulsing through his veins? It can't. Precious children, let's not just give lip service to love; let's DO something about it. Showing integrity and proving that we're living true. Let's spend time with God with a clean conscience and no guilt lurking in our deep places, 'cos God's deeper than our deepest place: he knows it all.

> Guilt-free and in contact with God – great place to be!   –Rob

24

How do we know he's living through us? We know from his Holy Spirit he invested in us.

> Don't buy it when con-men couriers swear blind they've taken the word *gullible* out of the dictionary. Spotting them's easy: just ask, "Is Jesus the Liberator from God?" Anything other than an "absolutely" – just walk away.   –Rob

Love? Prove it (1 John 4:7-21)

7-12

My mates, let's love each other, 'cos love is God-territory. Everyone who loves is in God's family and knows him personally. Anyone scoring minus points in the love league obviously doesn't have a clue about who God is, 'cos God *is* love. So how did God prove his love to us? He commissioned his one and only, his Son, to enter time and space to open up the option of us getting reconnected with him and getting real life. Love? What it's not: our weedy, warm, squidgy, fluffy feelings towards God. No, love is his world-shifting passion for us that gave him no choice but to send his Son as a virgin sacrifice to lose the mess that blocked any chance of getting us and God together again. My mates, if God loves us that much, we should love each other, eh? Who's set eyes on God? No one. But if we love each other, then God's around, finalizing all his dreams for us – which all revolve around perfect love.

13-16a

We know we're connected with him and him with us 'cos he's invested his Holy Spirit in us. And we've got first-hand evidence of the Father sending his Son to liberate the world. Whoever signs up to the fact that Jesus is God's Son – they've got God living out of them. (Or is it, they're living out of God? Both!) So we're sold on God's love for us.

16b-18

That's God: Love. Scroll through the whole CD-ROM, press Ctrl + H, replace "God" with the word "Love", and it still reads well, makes total sense. So anyone with strong love must be linked with God and God must be living through them. This is how we create perfect love so we can see Judgement Day in the diary and not panic, 'cos down here we're like God. Love is a million miles from fear. Perfect love sends fear flying, 'cos fear's about getting what's coming to you, about punishment beatings. The scared haven't the first clue about perfect love.

19-21

How come we love? 'Cos he started it. He loved us first. Anyone going, "I love God, but I can't stand my brother" – he's full of guff. Anyone who hates his brother, who he can see and touch, can't love God, who he's never seen and couldn't handle. It's in his Instruction Manual – if you love God, you've got to love your brother as well.

God's Son – convinced? (1 John 5:1-15)

1-5

Anyone convinced that Jesus is the Liberator – they're in God's family. Anyone who loves the Father loves his Son. So how do we know we love God's family? By loving God and living life by his instructions. And what do I mean, "loving God"? Matching our lifestyle with his Maker's Instructions. And his Manual isn't major hassle: anyone in God's family has the Global System licked. What is it that comes through for us when we take on the System? Our total conviction. Who kicks sand in the face of the System? Only the guys who are convinced that Jesus is God's Son.

6-12

Jesus the Liberator – two lasting images: soaking wet at his baptism, caked in blood at his execution. But he didn't stop short at the water. No, he went through with the water *and* the blood. And God's Spirit backs it up with all *his* integrity. Three pieces of evidence: the water, the blood and the account of God's Spirit – and they all add up to the same thing. In court we listen to the witness, but what if God stood in the dock? We'd be all ears, especially talking about his own Son. That's a reliable witness by any standards! Anyone convinced about God's Son has this testimony ringing round their deep places. Anyone not convinced about God's statement on his Son is accusing God of lying under oath. His statement was this: "I'm giving you limitless life if you get connected with my Son." If you're in with the Son, you've got a life. If you've broken ties with the Son of God, barred all his calls, deleted all his contact numbers – you've got no life.

13-15

Why do I write all this? To convince you of the reputation of God's Son so you'll be sure of your limitless life. All this means we've confidence in spending time with God, and if we lobby him for something that fits with his manifesto, he's all ears. And if he hears us – whatever we've put in for – he'll make it happen.

> Put in good words for your brothers with God. The evil one runs the Global System, but God's got his minders on full alert for us. God's Son gives us sense. –Rob

Cheers (1 John 5:21)

Precious children, don't get high on anything but God.

2 John /
Jonno to a Local JLM

(Email No. 2)

From: jonno.zebson@jlm-lovelight.nt

To: dearlady+kids@jlm.org.tk

Date: AD 85–100

Subject: Love and life-coach sponsorship

> More from Jonno on love – the perfect partner for truth (which, on its own, often hurts). This time to a "dear lady" – knowing Jonno, it's probably poetic talk for a local JLM.
> — Rob

Love (2 John 4-6)

I'm delirious at the bulletins coming back to me about your kids' lifestyle of integrity, as laid down by the Father. So now, dear lady, I'm not slipping in some trendy new instruction – it's the same one from kick-off: "Let's love each other." And "love" is? – that we live in line with God's Instruction Manual. It's not changed from day one: the direction is lovewards.

> Warnings about shysters and the Anti-Liberator – don't get suckered out of your bonus in heaven; keep on keeping on ...
> — Rob

See you soon (2 John 12-13)

There's loads more, but why write it when I'm planning a trip your way and we can chat face to face. Much more fun! The JLMers here say hi.

3 John / Jonno to Gaius

(Email No. 3)

From: jonno.zebson@jlm-lovelight.nt

To: gaius.hostmaster@jlm.org.tk

Date: AD 85–100

Subject: Re Diotrephes

Jonno's chuffed with Gaius and how he's backing up guys going off to work for God. Fighting talk re Diotrephes, who's been slagging Jonno off behind his back, accusing him of letting the local JLM fund salary packages while Jonno's guys were working with them – not Paul's approach. But this was how Jesus said it should work, so who d'you follow? Jonno tries to help Gaius sort it out . . .   –Rob

Imitations (3 John 11-14)

11-12

My mate, don't imitate evil. Imitate good. Whoever doles out good is clearly one of God's lot. Whoever works in wholesale evil obviously has never seen God. Demetrius – what a star! Integrity! Everyone says so, us included, and we've got integrity too.

13-14

Loads more to say, but let's do it face to face, eh? Serenity to you. The crew here say hi. Say hi to the guys there – on first-name terms.

Jude / Jude's Circular

From:	jude.davidson@palestine.jlm.nt
To:	jlm.crew@global.org
Date:	AD 65–80
Subject:	Re "anything goes" life coaches

Jesus' brother Jude gets his letter included in the New Testament (it's not what you know, but who!). His big point is, "You've got to fight for it." These "anything goes" life coaches have sidled their way in, and they reckon God's generosity means they can get away with polluted lifestyles and cocky libelling of angels. Sharp reminder that God got his people out of Egypt, but the slackers died in the desert. Same unhappy ending for the angel mutineers. Same story for Sodom and Gomorrah – hellfire, stuck on permanent . . .   —Rob

Open sores (Jude 12-23)

12-13

These guys are open, infected sores at the dinner table when you re-enact your sacred love meals – they elbow their way to the food and scoff themselves stupid with no second thought of being a good example. They look like clouds that might bring refreshing rain, when actually they're smog spreading in the wind. They look like fruit trees but they're bare and hacked down at the roots – dead times two. They're waves that leave their polluted gunk on your white-sand beach, dislodged stars getting sucked into a black hole.

14-16

Only seven generations down from Adam, old Enoch saw all this coming: "I can see the Boss coming down with ten thousand of his pure angels pumped up and passing sentence on everyone, including the anti-Godites with their fist-in-the-face-of-God lifestyles and their back-chat-to-God attitudes."

They're moaners, picky whiners, doing whatever they like, mouthing off about their projects and buttering up anyone they reckon they can use.

17-19

But, my mates, what did the inner team of our Boss, Jesus the Liberator, predict? Remember? They told you, "The last hour before 'midnight' will be Cynicism City, packed with people doing their own, anti-God, thing."

These guys will drive a wedge between you. They just go with the gut and don't listen to God's Spirit.

20-21

But you guys build up your spiritual muscle in your purest conviction and talk to God via your Holy Spirit link-up. Keep online with God's love as you anticipate the Boss giving you some slack and delivering his limitless life.

22-23

Go easy on the guys with genuine questions; pull others back from the fire: sort them out; let others off the hook; but don't get polluted or caught up yourself.

Perfect ending (Jude 24-25)

Now to him who's not just able to keep you from tripping up. More, he'll intro you to his dazzling heavenly home as perfect and perfectly happy. To him, the one and only God our Liberator, give all the credit, all the class, all the clout, all the kudos, and send it via Jesus the Liberator, our Boss, from way before time first ticked, our Boss right through every moment and our Boss well after time clocks off. Our Boss. Absolutely!

Revelation /
Apocalypse Soon

From: jesus.liberator@future.heaven
                via jonno.zebson@patmos.prison.gr

To: jlm@ephesus.org.tk
               jlm@smyrna.org.tk
               jlm@pergamum.org.tk
               jlm@thyatira.org.tk
               jlm@sardis.org.tk
               jlm@philadelphia.org.tk
               jlm@@laodicea.org.tk

Date: AD 95?

Subject: How it all ends (and starts)

The Turkey JLMs are being victimized. The new cult makes out Caesar (Domitian) is a god, which is tricky if Jesus is the only one! Tough call: the conqueror vs the Liberator. Go for an away win and you could be losing more than your shirt. Jonno's already been carted off from Ephesus to a penal colony on Patmos (first-century Alcatraz) where God lets him in on some of his upcoming schedule for wrapping things up. God puts the whole process through a vision adapter so as not to over-load Jonno's brain and so Roman authorities won't ban the letter – it's all in code: pictures, high-tech special FX, animation and computer-generated images combine to make the ultimate sci-fi blockbuster (working title, "Wrap it up", Cert. 18), released on the Web for everyone to view and review. Most reckon it's pretty post-modern – fragmented, cryptic, little or no explanation. Some hit the site once, don't get it and never come back. Others hit it once, bookmark it, get hooked and end up doing a PhD so they can tell people what's going to happen and when. Halfway between the two would work best, not ignoring it or being obsessed by it. Basically, hassles build for the JLM, Jesus comes back, evil gets dumped, God wins. But before the website, some short memos . . .   —Rob

Prologue

The A to Z of time (Revelation 1:5-8)

5-7

All the credit, all the clout – give it up, full on, for ever to the one who loves us and liberates us from our mess by donating his blood and making us immigrants into his New Nation of God's reps to work for God the Father. Absolutely!

Look up! Is it a bird? Is it a plane? Is it a computer game gone 3D?

No it's HIM, surfing the clouds, full orbit so everyone gets to see,

Even the ones who cut him deep,

Everyone's gutted 'cos of him.

Bring him on! Absolutely!

8

God the Boss says, "I'm the A and the Z (the 'Start' and the 'Finish'). I exist. Always have. Always will. No limits. Absolute power."

Channels open (Revelation 1:9-20)

9-11

Me, Jonno, your brother, part of the "picked-on-posse", one of the Jesus' New Nation toughing it out in the Mean Time – I'm banged up in Patmos prison 'cos I won't shut up about Jesus. I'll tell you what happened: it's Rest Day and God's Spirit has whisked me off Somewhere Else. A voice behind me blasts out like a jazz trumpet; it's saying, "Get your notebook, write out what you see, forward it to the seven Turkey JLMs from me – Ephesus, Smyrna, Pergamum, Thyatira, Sardis, Philadelphia and Laodicea."

12-16

I turn round to see who's talking. There's seven halogen floodlights, solid gold. Right in the middle is the Liberator dressed like a head rep with a gold belt round his torso. His face and hair are brilliant white, his eyes are on fire, his feet are glowing bronze like they're still in the smelter, his voice is like a wild white-water river. His right hand's holding seven stars and his words are like a samurai sword – razor sharp both sides. Looking into his face is like looking up at the sun . . . from the equator . . . at midday.

17-18

I'm down on the floor, lying there like I'm dead. His hand's on my shoulder, his voice sets my spine tingling: "Don't panic. I'm the Originator and the Finisher. The Vibrant One. Dead once; now alive, permanent. I've changed the password Death was using; I've got the entrance code to hell's waiting room."

19-20

"Steady your writing hand and get down what you're seeing. It's the plot line for the future. Some clues: the seven stars I'm holding = the angels on duty at Turkey's seven JLMs; the seven lampstands = the seven JLMs. Tell them . . ."

Seven Memos

Turn round (Revelation 2:1-7)

From: Star.Holder@future.co.hv

To: angel@jlm.ephesus.org.tk

Date: AD 95?

Subject: The lost love buzz

> "You're gutsy, you've taken hassles on the chin, you've shown the dodgy life coaches the door, but . . ."   —Rob

4-5

"I've got this minus on your card: your love's faded from its first passion. You've crashed down from the top. Turn things round and do the good things you used to do when your love was fresh. Otherwise, I'll close your JLM branch down. At least we're in tune on one thing – the Nicolaitians are horrific."

7

Signs off provocatively – "If you've got a brain and a heart, work it out! What's the Spirit saying to the JLMs?" and "Those that tough it out get to eat off the tree of life in God's paradise!"

Hassles ahead (Revelation 2:8-11)

From:	A-Z/DeathDefyer@future.co.hv
To:	angel@jlm.smyrna.org.tk
Date:	AD 95?
Subject:	Loaded "losers"

"You're poor, you're picked on, but you're rich ..."   –Rob

10

"Don't panic with what's up ahead. I'll be up front: the Devil will push you to the limit by locking some of you up – ten days of torture. Hang in there, even if your life's flashing before your eyes; I'll give you the life crown with your name on it."

11

"If you've got a brain and a heart, work it out! What's the Spirit saying to the JLMs? Those that tough it out won't even get a sniff of the second death."

Comfort eating (Revelation 2:12-17)

From: Doublesided.Sword@future.co.hv

To: angel@jlm.pergamum.org.tk

Date: AD 95?

Subject: Proper ingredients

The samurai sword tongue says ...   –Rob

13

"I know my geography. You live smack bang in Satan Territory. But you stick it out. You stay loyal to me and all I stand for. Even when they martyred my loyal witness – Antipas – you stayed on course in Satansville, Evil County."

"But there is this: you're still using 'Balaam and Barak's Recipe Books' for your appetites (sexual and physical). Don't!"   –Rob

17

"If you've got a brain and a heart, work it out! What's the Spirit saying to the JLMs? Those that tough it out get some of the hidden heaven bread plus a white stone with a secret name chiselled into it."

Sexually transmitted diseases (Revelation 2:18-29)

From: Godson.Fire-Eyes/Bronze-Feet@future.co.hv

To: angel@jlm.thyatira.org.tk

Date: AD 95?

Subject: Seduction, Jezebel style

"Top marks for action, love, loyalty and stamina but ..."   –Rob

20

"You put up with 'Jezebel', who reckons she's a courier. But her coaching is dragging my workers off into perversions of the mind, body and belly."

Jezebel's had her chances to quit her sex games, so now she'll suffer with her partners (and the babies). Why? So the JLMs will catch on that God's Son delves into deep places, knows his way round the subconscious. You'll get the pay-off (good or bad) for what you get up to.   —Rob

20

"If you've got a brain and a heart, work it out! What's the Spirit saying to the JLMs?"

Near-death experience (Revelation 3:1-6)

From: 7angels.7stars@future.co.hv

To: angel@jlm.sardis.org.tk

Date: AD 95?

Subject: Wakey, wakey!

1-3

To the angel working at Sardis, write, "I'm up to speed on your actions ... Your image is great, a 'happening place', but behind the hype you're dead in the water. Wakey, wakey! Work with the bits that aren't frost-bitten and falling off. Your actions are missing the mark in God's eyes. Think back to what you took on before — take it in and turn round. If you don't come round, I'll break in like a burglar and you won't know what hit you!"

But some haven't messed up and are still down in the Book as sorted.   —Rob

6

"If you've got a brain and a heart, work it out! What's the Spirit saying to the JLMs?"

Hang in there (Revelation 3:7-13)

From: David.Keyholder@future.co.hv

To: angel@jlm.philadelphia.org.tk

Date: AD 95?

Subject: Survivors

"I'm on your case — you're struggling, but the stamina's impressive ..."
    —Rob

10

"Since you've gone with my instructions to hang in there, I'll be your minder come the global crunch time. It's soon, and it'll push everyone way past their limits."

11-12

"My ETA's not long off now. Hold on; don't let anyone loot your vandalized storeroom and make off with your crown. You pull through the tough times and I'll make you a major player in God's new HQ – he'll never abandon it again. I'll tattoo God's logo on you, I'll create some stunning skin artwork of the New City of God coming down from heaven, and I'll finish it off with signing my new name into you."

13

"If you've got a brain and a heart, work it out! What's the Spirit saying to the JLMs?"

Let me in (Revelation 3:15-22)

From: Creation.Boss@future.co.hv

To: angel@jlm.laodicea.org.tk

Date: AD 95?

Subject: Lukewarm water

15-18

"I've memorized your case file: you're not one thing or the other, not really frosty, not burning up with passion – you're tepid, like lukewarm lager. Urgh! Shift one way or the other – ice cold and refreshing or a hot mulled wine to warm up your insides. Anything but tepid. Every time I try and taste you, I throw up. You make out you're rolling in it, you don't need a thing. Fact is, you're in a sad state, washed up, broke, blind and exposed. My advice? Invest in gold I've refined in fire; then you'll be rich. Buy some of my exclusive designer wear, so you're not arrested for indecent exposure. Buy my ointment: it'll clear up your cataracts."

19-20

"I only pull you up and back into line 'cos I love you. So get serious. Turn your life back round to God. I'm waiting here outside your front door. I'm pressing the buzzer. If you hear my voice on your intercom and press the 'Enter' button, I'll come in with a full-on takeaway and we'll have a great meal together and put our world to rights."

21-22

"Those that tough it out get to sit on my throne with me. Just as I toughed it out and got to sit on my Father's throne. If you've got a brain and a heart, work it out! What's the Spirit saying to the JLMs?"

Plus some motivational talk to hurdle the hassles and finish the race. —Rob

Virtual Reality Headset

Jesus fits Jonno with a virtual reality headset — with running commentary, subtitles, visuals — all designed to give him a privileged access pass into heaven and how things are going to be wrapped up. Bizarre images of thrones, flaming torches, crystal clear lakes calm as glass while thunder and lightning crash around. A lion, an ox, a man, an eagle, each with six wings and covered with eyes, and they're all gushing non-stop about God being No. 1. Twenty-four senior figures with crowns off and down in front of God's throne saying . . . —Rob

So worth it (Revelation 4:11)

Our Boss, our God, you're worth everything.

Which is why we bring

All the credit, all the respect, all the credibility we can source.

You're so worth it. Of course.

You made everything happen. It all started 'cos you said so.

Nothing would exist without you, you know.

The headset focuses Jonno on the big scriptbook in God's right hand, locked with seven ornamental padlocks. Pull back to hear an XXXL angel calling for volunteers for anyone capable of breaking the padlocks open . . . No one comes forward.

What's in the book? Someone try! What's the plot? Jonno's nearly filling his visor with tears 'cos no one's up to the job. One of the seniors says, "Jesus has won through: he'll snap the padlocks".

—Rob

Innocent power (Revelation 5:6-10)

Then there's this Innocent One, ripped apart (like a sacrifice from a Flyby Fest in Moses' time) standing centre stage by the throne; the four creatures and the seniors are close by. Image zooms in; the Innocent One's got seven horns (subtitle comes up on screen: "symbolic of power") and seven eyes (subtitle: "God's spirits on earth duty"). He takes the scriptbook from God's hand; the four creatures and the twenty-four seniors hit the deck holding harps and bowls full of JLM earth-to-heaven requests. They improvise a new song:

> You're qualified to take the scriptbook
> And to crack open its locks.
> 'Cos you were hated, annihilated, assassinated,
> And your blood's the buying power, which you donated
> To buy people, whatever their state,
> To buy them back for God.
> To make them welcome immigrants: a New Nation of reps who
>   know his worth.
> Who run things his way on earth.

Jonno gropes for the volume control, but can't turn down the deafening sound of a million angels taking over with "He's worth it, whatever you give him — it can't be too much." Backing vocals from everything alive on planet Earth, close-up mics pick up the creatures and the seniors adding their vocals — head buzzing with the scale and passion of it all!

Then the Innocent One opens the first padlock — flash image of a tyrant riding on a white horse, "invasion" in his manic eyes. Second padlock clicks open — war images up on screen. Third padlock — raging famine. Fourth padlock — death for a quarter of the earth's population. Fifth — gripping pictures of martyred souls screaming for justice from God. Sixth — mass evacuations from the cities to the country bunkers 'cos God's on the loose and the Innocent One is seething mad. Just one padlock to rip open before the scriptbook is readable. But, to build the suspense, four angels hold back God's angry hurricanes while another sprays the foreheads of 144,000 Jews who stay loyal to God through the Mean Time. Then the other survivors, all wearing white . . .

—Rob

Survivors (Revelation 7:10-17)

10-12

They're crying out:

> Liberation is a God-thing.
> He and the Innocent One are in charge.

The angels, the creatures, the seniors all hit the deck again and say:

> Absolutely! Give it up for God. Everything! Celebrate his brilliance. Sing.
> He's wise. We're grateful. We respect him totally: his clout, his muscle. Completely.
> Give everything up to God — always, forever. Absolutely!

13

One of the seniors asks me, "Who are these guys in white? Where they from?"

14-17

I come back at him, "You don't know?"

He tells me, "They're the survivors from the Mean Time. All in white 'cos they've washed in the blood of the Innocent One. So . . .

> "They're in God's HQ, 24/7, and God'll protect them:
> In heaven? Hunger? Old hat. Thirst? A memory.
> Sunstroke? Skin cancer? Not a chance; it's pain free.
> 'Cos the Innocent One at the centre of power is their minder, their mentor;
> He'll lead them to the life-springs. He'll welcome. They'll enter.
> God's own hand and handkerchief will drip with their tears."

Then the Innocent One rips open the seventh padlock and . . . silence . . . total silence . . . for half an hour. All of heaven is dumbstruck as the scriptbook falls open.

Then seven angels are given seven trumpets. An eighth has more earth-to-heaven requests, which he mixes with fire — more thunder and lightning and earthquakes rip up planet Earth. The angels blow their trumpets in turn and it's tricky to tell if it's old footage of Moses' plagues or newly recorded material. Whatever, the trumpet blasts make a third of vegetation die, a third of sea life drowns in blood, a third of rivers get polluted, a third of the stars/daylight/nightlight gets snuffed out, people not branded as God's are attacked by plagues of mutant locusts and hospitalized for five months, suicidal with the toe-curling agony, then four fearsome angels are let off the leash to kill a third of the world's population (though the two-thirds left still don't turn their lives round to God). Again, suspense builds, the seventh angel stands with his doom trumpet almost to his mouth, but someone's pressed "Pause" . . .

Over the top of the freeze-frame seventh angel comes another XXXL angel who raises the stakes by saying, "Once the seventh trumpet hits the note, no more delay – God's plans get made public." Same angel recommissions Jonno as a courier and plays the footage of two other powerful couriers. Jonno watches the video scan forward through three-and-a-half years as these two couriers oppose the System; public antagonism builds till the "beast from hell" takes them out and leaves their corpses to rot in the street. Then he sees God bring them back to life. The enemies of God's couriers freak out as they see them rising up on an invisible conveyor belt direct to heaven while earthquakes flatten a tenth of the city, killing 7,000. Survivors start taking God a bit more seriously!

The image fades and Jonno's faced with the seventh angel again, the pause symbol goes and he blasts his trumpet; voices shout, "Earth has become our Boss's territory and the Liberator will run things from here on in." The twenty-four seniors say . . .   —Rob

Judgement Day (Revelation 11:17-18)

We're grateful and overflowing. We know it's you we're owing, God.

Awesome Boss, history shaper night and day.

You've channelled your infinite power supply

And you're running things your way.

The fist-shakers, bellyachers across the world

Are about to know *you're* angry too.

Time's ticked away and it's Judgement Day for the dead,

And reward-ceremony time for your couriers,

Your crew, big and small, who respected you, stayed true.

It's time to destroy those who destroy the planet.

More thunder and lightning, earthquakes and hailstorms act as atmos for the cosmic showdown: Jonno sees a woman about to give birth, cameras pull back to show a seething red dragon wound up and ready to tear the baby apart at birth. She has a boy (subtitles flash: "the Liberator, strong ruler"), but he's flown straight up to heaven before the dragon can pounce; the woman's protected too. Scene shift up to heaven where the dragon and his demons are fighting tooth and claw with Chief Angel Michael and his angel troops. Michael's squadron wins through and the dragon (subtitle: "Devil/Satan") is thrown down to earth to lick his wounds. Bad news for planet Earth: he's furious and he knows his days are numbered. He goes after the woman, but Mother Earth is enlisted to protect her. This winds the dragon up even more: he's on the beach fuming (literally) and about to "unleash horror" on anyone connected with Jesus and living God's way.

Then the dragon's two generals turn up and the dragon gives both full access to his arsenal and network of contacts: First beast — a mutant sea creature, ten horns, seven heads — all crowned with God-libelling filth. (Jonno's thinking, *It's Rome!*) Second beast — arrives from inland and becomes Head of Beast Propaganda, using supernatural forces and violent threats to wow the public with the power of the first beast. He signs people up to the cult of evil and chaos by tattooing his number, 666, on people's foreheads or right hands. No number, no sale. No sale, no food. Jonno does the sums in his head and realizes the letters of "Caesar Nero" (in his first language, Aramaic, if A=1, B=2, etc.) add up to 666. Freaky! The two generals run the show for the dragon for three-and-a-half years — Jonno watches as the JLM crew become target practice and prison fodder.

Everything goes fragmented, Jonno taps the headset to check it's not got a loose connection, images come and go and Jonno's struggling to keep up. First image: the Innocent One on Zion Mountain with 144,000 outstandingly pure ones with "God's own" tattooed on their foreheads, singing an exclusive new release with wild rivers, thunder and harps big in the mix. Second image: three angels swooping low, shouting out urgent voicemails . . .   —Rob

Urgent angels (Revelation 14:7-10)

7

The first angel booms, "Respect God! Give him all the credit! It's Judgement Day minus zero. Wake up to how much he's worth — he made it all, the heavens, the earth, the sea, the rivers, all of it."

8

The second angel announces, "Babylon, Rome, the System – bankrupt and bailing out. The System that pumped the planet with the heroine of filth – it's over, finished!"

9-10

The third angel then shouts, "Everyone with the beast's tattoo is in line for a blast of God's anger; it'll be torture – burning sulphur style – while angels and the Innocent One have to watch!"

But the JLM crew, especially those who get martyred, will have the last laugh. The third image Jonno sees is the Liberator collecting in all the loyal JLM crew before an angel flies out of heaven's HQ with genocide on his work order. He's armed with the firepower of God's anger. Gruesome images of people crushed in winepresses and the blood pouring out of the machinery like wine and flooding the place for almost 200 miles.

Before Jonno throws up, the image on his virtual reality headset changes again: the crew who'd won through their battles with the beast are singing a remix of Moses' all-time classic "The Great Escape". Seven more angels with the last blasts of God's anger get the green light and pour out their dishes of plagues. First, an epidemic of skin boils. Second, oceans turn to blood and all sea life dies. Third, rivers do the same. The fourth dish is emptied on the sun: it's like fuel on flame and the instant global warming fries people (though no one turns back to God). Fifth, the beast's stolen territory goes pitch black – no sun, no electricity, no fire (but still no one turns around to God). Sixth, the Euphrates River dries up, demons produce spectacular black magic, which winds up the world powers who build up their troops at Armageddon for the big showdown. Last, earthquakes way off the Richter scale flatten major cities, sink islands, wipe mountains off the map. Six-stone hailstones pummel down on the debris (still no attitude shift – people still shaking their fists at God as they die).

Then Jonno sees a still image, like a portrait of a high-class prostitute lounging across the beast from the sea (seven heads, ten horns). Top-quality clothes, uninsurable jewellery and a wine glass full of the filth of her seedy lifestyle. Zoom in on the words tattooed on her forehead: "Somehow the whore of the central city of the Global System: the cancer of the people, the pollution of the world". Jonno almost falls backwards when he sees she's drunk out of her skull on the blood of the JLM dead.

The angel gives Jonno some clues: the beast she's riding (thought to be dead) will come back and run a power block of ten countries who'll go to war with the Innocent One and lose. Then the beast will turn on her, rape her, rip her apart and burn the body parts. Jonno gets a preview of an angel celebrating her death, taunting her memory. Another voice calls out, "It's on; it'll happen – she'll suffer, big time!" Her customers, the world leaders, weep at her memorial service. Business people top themselves at the global market crash brought on by the collapse in trade – taking just one hour! Aircraft pilots will switch to automatic pilot to gawk at the great whore of a city on fire. Another angel picks up a rock the size of a dumpster and hurls it into the sea (subtitle flashes up: "same speed as the city will dive").

Again Jonno's ears take a pounding as all heaven shout, "YES!!!" and celebrate the death of the prostitute, and the prospects of justice and joy for the bride of the Innocent One – the Jesus Liberation Movement – now the evil System's dead. Jonno says ...   –Rob

The Liberator @ Armageddon
(Revelation 19:11-21)

11-16

Then I see heaven open, a white horse, a rider called "Loyalty and Integrity". He sees things as they are and goes to war when it's right. His eyes are on fire, his head's full of crowns. He has a secret name only *he* knows. He's wearing an all-in-one robe, bloodstained from before. His public name is "God's Voice". Heaven's full battalion is at his shoulder, all in pure white linen, riding white horses. His words are like a samurai sword that swipes out whole countries. As the old song lyric goes, "Like an iron rod he'll rule straight and true." His footsteps stomp with the anger of the Awesome God. The logo on his clothes and thigh says:

The King that kings answer to.
The Boss that bosses bow before.

It's showdown time and an angel whistles the birds in so they're ready to pick at the bodies of God's enemies once they're dead.   –Rob

19-21

The beast shows. The world leaders are with him, armies psyched and weapons loaded. They're up for full-out war against the horse rider and his troops. They fight. The beast is caught. His head of propaganda, who pulled off the black magic that hyped the masses into queuing for their 666 tattoos, he's caught too. They're thrown alive and screaming into the lake of burning sulphur. The rest of the armies are hacked apart by the sword of the rider on the horse. The birds get their feast.

The snake gets fried (Revelation 20:1-14)

1-3

Another angel swoops down from heaven. He's got a key with a tag marked "the Abyss"; he's also got the mother of all chains. The angel grabs the dragon – aka the old snake, the Devil, Satan – and wraps him tight in the chain, locks the padlocks and sets the timer for a thousand years. Then he hurls Satan down into the Abyss and locks up after him. No more worming his way into the mindset of the nations, not for a thousand years. And after that he'll be free for only a short time.

4-6

Then more thrones, authorized judges on them. I'm seeing the souls of those martyred 'cos they wouldn't say anything bad about Jesus or his Lifestyle Manual. They'd not fitted in with the System of the beast; they'd refused his logo on their foreheads. They'd come back to life and the Liberator appointed them to help him run things for the whole millennium. (A caption flashes at the bottom of the visor, "The rest of the dead will come back to life after the millennium".) This is the first batch of dead brought back. Pure contentment is the package for this first lot. The final death of the soul holds no worries for them; they'll represent God and the Liberator and will help him run things for a whole millennium.

7-10

Fast forward through the millennium: I see Satan let out of his solitary confinement. Straight up he's off manipulating all the heads of state – every single one – into declaring war on God's new System. They pass the resolution and the assembled soldiers are like the grains of sand in a million sandpits. They pour across the planet to encircle God's people in his favourite city. But God's having none of it: he blasts fire down on the troops and atomizes them. The Devil, who put them up to it, gets thrown into the lake of burning sulphur to join his cronies the beast and his minister of propaganda. The sulphur doesn't run out and neither will their agony – ever!

The millennium's done, so the rest of the dead come back to life . . .   –Rob

11-14

Another new scene: a huge white throne. The one sitting on it is too much, too awesome. The earth and the sky can't handle his aura; the place resonates with power. They try to leave, but there's nowhere to hide. As the scene pulls back I see the dead, all of them, famous, infamous, "somebodies", "nobodies", "the movers", "the shakers", "the moved", "the shaken" – they're spread out before God's throne. The files are opened. The file marked "Life" is opened and the dead are judged by what the records show they've done. The sea coughs up its dead, Death hands the keys over to the waiting rooms of hell – they're all there and they're all being judged by what they've done. Then Death itself and hell's entrance foyer get thrown into the lake of fire, and they die the second death – the death of the soul. Anyone whose name isn't found in the Life Files gets thrown into the lake of fire with them.

Everything new (Revelation 21:1-21)

1-4

Then! Everything changes. New. All of it brand new. All heaven, all earth – new. Nothing of the old heaven or the old earth left. Gone: all of it including the oceans. Whoa! This pure, perfect city – the new Jerusalem – is floating down out of heaven direct from God. It's like a bride, perfectly turned out for her loving groom. A loud shout, coming from the throne, "From now on, God's living down there with them. They'll be his kind of people; God'll hang out with them and be God to them. He'll collect all the tears they've ever cried, he'll cancel death, there'll be no grieving, no crying, no pain – all that was in the previous System, and that's history."

5

God on his throne speaks: "Watch me! Watch me make everything new." Then he says, "Take dictation, this is worth getting down word for word."

6-8

Then he says to me, "Done. Dusted. Complete. Finished. I'm the A and I'm the Z. I'm there at the Start. I'm still here at the End. Anyone gasping of thirst, I'll supply pure water from the spring that gushes with life. No charge. Those who toughed it out and got over the enemy's hurdles will get to enjoy all this —I'll be their God; they'll be my kids. But the weak-minded cowards, the sceptics, the vulgar, the murderers, the sexually perverted, the witches, anyone who puts anything higher up their priority list than me, anyone who deceives people — they'll all be bundled straight into the fiery lake of burning sulphur for the second death, the death of their soul."

> One of the seven last "dish angels" shows me the bride of the Innocent One. I'm getting close-up views of the new Jerusalem (a metaphor for God's people) coming down from God, shining with God's dazzling brilliance. It's tough getting the scale of it all against the sky, so the angel measures it for me. What?! Close to two million square miles in area, its walls are 61 metres (200 feet) thick, 2,253 km (1,400 miles) high and made of opaque quartz. The rest of the city is solid gold. Even the twelve foundations (under the ground) are studded with jewels. Each of the twelve gates is sculpted from a single pearl ...   —Rob

THE City (Revelation 21:22-27)

But no HQ building? 'Course not. No need — the Boss, the Awesome God and the Innocent One are the HQ. No sun either. No moon. No need — God's presence radiates light and it shines through the Innocent One as a lamp. The New Nations get about by this light supply; the New World Leaders will display their class under this brightness. No locks on the City gates, no need — no night muggings to be protected from. The best the nations have will be imported to the New City. But nothing messed up, damaged or dodgy. No one outrageous. No one manipulative. Only those down in the Life Files of the Innocent One.

Back to Eden Garden (Revelation 22:1-21)

1-5

Next up the angel downloads footage of a river, clear as crystal glass, flowing from God's throne down the middle of the City's high street. It's the water of life and it's flowing past the tree of life, coming to fruit every month through the year, different crop each time. But it's not just the fruit; the leaves are picked to heal whole nations. Curses are cancelled. God's throne's there, the Lamb's throne's there and his people will work for him. They chat face-to-face; his logo's on their foreheads. No such thing as night; no need for electricity or sunlight; the Boss projects permanent floodlight power. There's no threat to them running things his way permanently.

6

The angel lifts my earphones and says, "This is totally reliable stuff. The Boss, the God of the couriers, sent his angels to get you up to speed on the future schedule."

7

"On your toes. I'm on my way. Soon! I'll tell you who'll be laughing last – the guys who act on what this letter says is pending."

8-9

Me, Jonno Zebson, I'm the eyewitness of all this. When the credits roll and "The End / The Start" scroll up the screen, I take off my headset and hit the floor, blown away by the angel who'd walked me through the whole thing. But he says, "Whoa! Get up. I'm just a worker like you and the other couriers and crew. Do all that to God not me!"

10-11

The angel tells me, "When you've published this, don't stick it on the shelf – it's all too close to forget it. The mess-makers will keep doing their thing, the vulgar will carry on turning stomachs and those who do the right thing – they'll keep on too; so will those standing out with integrity."

12-13

"Stay sharp: I'm just round the corner. I've got tanker loads of bonuses to dole out according to who's done what. I'm the A and the Z, the First and the Last, the Starter and the Finisher."

14-15

"Who's still laughing right at the end? Those who scrub their clothes clean and get the thumbs up to pick at will from the tree of life and stroll through the gates into the City. They leave the scum outside to network with the witches, the sexual predators, the killers, those who put anything ahead of God and all those who get a kick out of polishing their deception."

16

"Me, Jesus, I've commissioned my angel to fix you up with this account for the JLMs to read. I'm pure Davidson, right through. I'm the brightest star in the cosmos."

17

God's Spirit and the bride say this: "Come on!" Let the guys who are listening join in, "Come on!" You thirsty? Then come on! You up for this? Then dive in, head first – it's the water of life, and it's free!

18-19

Warning! Anyone who reads/sees/hears the warnings in this letter better not copy and paste any of their own ideas in. If they do, God'll add the plagues to their life story. Anyone who deletes anything they don't like from this letter, God'll delete them from the list for access to the tree of life and citizenship in the Pure City.

20

The one who makes these statements says, "Yes, I'm on my way. My ETA's not far off!" Absolutely! Make it quick, Jesus the Boss!

21

Here's to Jesus the Boss pouring out his generosity on God's people. Absolutely!

Rob's Story

Rob's journal:

• March 2000: Commissioned to write *the word on the street*; week later the doctor tells Sandra and me, "Your bladder cancer's back"; stop touring my shows due to illness; told to try for a baby before treatment; months of treatment; severe pain.

• May 2000: Start writing the *word on the street* when well enough; tackle the book of Job first; needing the toilet every quarter of an hour – time to think! – up to 30 times a night with my raw bladder; two years of sleep deprivation; Sandra expecting baby Lukas; more treatment; worse pain; more writing *the word on the street* – my lifeline to sanity.

• January 2001: Lukas born; Sandra becomes a sort of "single mum"; develop TB in bladder from multiple treatments; pain terrible; depressed; hermit in own home; *the word on the street* writing doing me good.

• September 2001: Complete first draft of *the word on the street*; working on Revelation the week of September 11th; operation to remove bladder; great prospect of freedom from pain; find cancerous tumour and lymph nodes during operation; told max. of a year to live; recover from op; pray like crazy.

• November 2001: Fly to Mexico clinic for alternative treatment; Bill and Rachel Taylor-Beales with us; wheel-chaired through airports; cancer spread into bones; pain levels impossible; fly to healing conference in Toronto church; half-hour pain relief; fly home; OD'ing on morphine; no relief; rushed into Cardiff hospital; chemo; radiotherapy; drop to under 7 stone (100 lbs) weight; v. weak; needing help to wash; people making "last" visits; family and friends sticking close.

Why me?

But why me? Not her?
Why me? Not them?

It's not 'cos I memorized the whole book of Job. Or wore an anointed prayer shawl or a special hospital robe. It's not 'cos we cried "Mercy!!" a million times. It's not 'cos I wrote a hundred prayers with rhymes. It's not 'cos my wife deserves me, puts the sign "reserved" on me. It's not 'cos my son needs me; Twin Tower workers were parents too. It's not 'cos we've hung on; it's just that God pulled us through.

So is it "because I'm worth it"? Well, I am; I'm worth everything to God. But so was Jacqueline du Pre; so was Eva Cassidy.

So why? And when? Was it already planned right back then? Or did God shuffle and shift? And watch all our prayers lift up past his eyes. And did he hear our cries? And did they all add up to Abraham- or Moses-size? When they dared to do diplomacy with God? Did we, together, negotiate with God?

We'll never see the subplots, the alternative scenes, until we get to heaven, read the script, and work out what it means. There's no recipe for what God gives free; there's no ace to play for grace.

It's not that I toughed it out with cameras up my nether regions,

© October 2002 by Rob Lacey (use with author acknowledged)

• December 2001: Doctors don't think I'll see Lukas's 1st birthday – mid-Janurary; more chemo; depression; faith; hope; poems; despair; prayer; sick and tired; pain receding; more chemo; home for Christmas; sleeping downstairs; talk of hospices.

• February 2002: Bit stronger, but no appetite; steroids; weight gain; more chemo; start editing first draft of *the word on the street;* being creative is sooooo good for me.

• May 2002: Angry red patch appears on lower back; pre-Christmas pain levels; doctors "99% sure" it's cancer again; doctors write me off for second time; assign me to pain control team; more tests taken. Result: No cancer in bones! Phones busy; "God's been busy."

• August 2002: tests for tumour/lymph nodes. Result: No cancer in lymph nodes! Miracle; celebration; confusion; only God knows.

• October 2002: walking better; swimming some; rewriting *the word on the street* as energy allows.

• December 2002: stark contrast; walking pretty well for a dead man, swimming even better – a mile in half an hour; complete *word on the street* final edit; very grateful.

• March 2003: *the word on the street* published in UK, perform 75-minute solo show; able to be a dad at last; Lukas realizes, "Papa no more ouch!"

• September 2003: 25,000 copies of *the word on the street* sold in UK; touring the show of the book to over 10,000 people; still trying to get our heads round it; can't.

• March 2004: *the word on the street* voted Christian Book of the Year in UK! Going global; double my weight from 2 years ago; v. grateful – Psalm 30-size grateful (look it up!).

tubes pushed through my back,
needles in my failing veins,
platinum pumped through every
track. It's none of that. It's not
that I kept a certain attitude
when interviewed. I'm no more
clued than you.

I could've been a saint and still
got stoned, could've interceded
for the lion with my name on it,
been compliant with my giant. I
could've driven into Jerusalem on
a clapped-out Robin Reliant, and
still, it might have been that I
would die. And we might have
no idea why.

Would that have been God's will?
Or is God's plan never to fill an
empty grave? Or does he save
each one of us? So how come
some still die? And why this?
Why that? And with answers so
shy, what's the point in asking
why?

So I won't try to work it out. I
won't sweat to work it through.
For now, Rob, just face it, God's
mercy is focused down on you.

So leave your questions lying
there; you might pick them up
again. Leave your lopsided, left
heavy, rational, rigorous brain.
Just give God his fame. The
always different, ever the same.

Lift up your voice and yell . . .
Thank Emmanuel, thank God
with us. I'm well.

Right now: Halle-blinkin'-lujah!

Psalm 23:4

I crawl through the alley of the shadow of cancer;
I know you know the answer.
And the battle won't rattle me.
You're around, and I've found
There's something about your empathy
Your symphony of sympathy
That comforts me.
You're with me.
You comfort me.

Psalm 30:11

You turned my tears to cheers,
My moping, through coping and on into dancing.
You made me take off my funeral gear,
And suddenly vibrant colours appear.